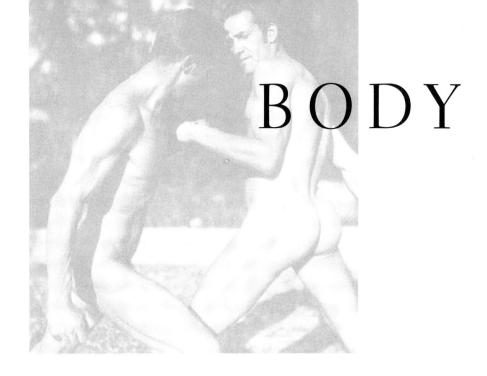

BODY

PAJ BOOKS

Bonnie Marranca

& Gautam Dasgupta

Series Editors

ASCENDANT

Modernism

and the

Physical

Imperative

Harold B. Segel

THE JOHNS HOPKINS UNIVERSITY PRESS *Baltimore & London*

1998

The Johns Hopkins University Press
2715 North Charles Street
Baltimore, Maryland 21218-4363
The Johns Hopkins Press Ltd., London

Title page illustration is from a photograph of gymnastic exercises at the College of Physical Education, 1926. Courtesy Ullstein (Berlin).

Library of Congress Cataloging-in-Publication Data will be found at the end of this book.
A catalog record for this book is available from the British Library.

ISBN 0-8018-5821-6

For Bonnie and Gautam, in appreciation of all they've done for the performing arts

I want to have a word with the despisers of the body. Not that I want them to learn and teach anew, but only to say goodbye to their own bodies—and thus become silent.

"Body am I, and soul"—so speaks the child. And why should one not speak like children?

But he who is awakened and knowing says: body am I entirely, and nothing else; and soul is only a word for something about the body. . . .

There is more reason in your body than in your best wisdom.

NIETZSCHE, "On the Despisers of the Body,"
Thus Spoke Zarathustra

Hatred of the *word* goes hand in hand with hatred of the intellect, for the *word* is, of course, its sign. Language is one of the things to be broken up—a stammer, a hiatus, an ellipsis, a syncope, a hiccup, is installed in the midst of the verb, and the mind attacked through its instrument. A great deal of very good work has been done in that direction.

WYNDHAM LEWIS, *The Art of Being Ruled*

Contents

BODY ASCENDANT

ONE

Introduction

The extraordinary modernist preoccupation with physicality developed, I believe, in the context of widespread disenchantment with intellectual culture in the late nineteenth and early twentieth centuries. Newly regarded as suspect and negatively related to a materialistic and deterministic world view, rationalism was contested in philosophy as much as the conscious was challenged in the arts and psychology. Intuition and spontaneity were the catchwords of the day. The campaign against tradition was dynamic and aggressive, and it sought to subordinate the virtues of the mind to those of the body. Passivity yielded to activism, the rational to the irrational, the conscious to the unconscious.

A culture of the mind presupposed the primacy of the word, but the modernist transvaluation of values, to borrow Nietzsche's term, seriously questioned the epistemological authority of language. The thinkers of the day hammered away at the pedestal on which language had long majestically stood. They thought that the body, too, was language and, hence, semantically worthy. Where words were thought to fail, silence was strength; from Nietzsche to Wittgenstein in philosophy, from Maeterlinck to the new enthusiasts of pantomime in the theater, silence was truly golden. For all its apparent concern, even obsession, with words, modernism was the great age of silence. Unpainted space on canvas, as in traditional Japanese painting, was no longer seen as empty or neutral but was appreciated for its potential for complex symbolism and evocative power. Pauses in Chekhovian dialogue—the ellipses translators often stumble over—are laden with meaning. Maeterlinck touted the superiority of silence over speech in the drama as the gateway to cosmic mystery. Chekhov, like Hofmannsthal and later

Wittgenstein, acknowledged the inability of words to communicate every-thing the human being is capable of feeling or incapable of knowing.

The dethroning of language had wide ramifications for the verbal arts. In the drama, gesture and silence were given equal billing with dialogue. Plays were written by Maeterlinck, Chekhov, Hofmannsthal, Schnitzler, Stein, and others in which the inadequacy of language to convey depths of emotion and spiritual states, or the banality to which language easily lent itself, became dramatic content. The spectacular cultivation of pantomime as a serious literary and theatrical genre at the turn of the century should not be understood only as a reflection of the interest of "high" culture in "low" culture, the interest, that is, of major artists in the entertainments of the folk and fairground. This would be like wearing blinders, occluding the nexus between pantomime, the retreat from and subversion of speech in drama, and the broad-based modernist assault on language in general.

Some of the boldest sallies against the traditional and habitual in lan-guage were launched by poets. No period in poetry can compete with modernism's fervor to remake poetic language. Poets experimented with not only the structures of verse but the very language of verse. The fash-ionable primitivism of the age, which we know so well from painting, also affected their attitudes toward the word. Long-established rules of syn-tax were likened to the constraints of bourgeois society and overthrown. The Italian Futurists, with Filippo Tommaso Marinetti leading the charge, waged war on syntax in order to liberate the word from the fetters that bound it. Allowed thus to move freely, words were to come together in new, unexpected combinations, enhancing their expressive power and at the same time revealing strata of meaning previously enmeshed in coils of convention. The liberation of society from the tyranny of the past, from the mind-set of the bourgeois, had its literary corollary—liberated words, *parole in libertà* (words in freedom), as Marinetti termed it. The Futurists thumbed their noses at rules of punctuation as well. If syntax were to be condemned, why not the comma, the period, and those other antiquated syntactic symbols? And did not adjectives blunt the force of nouns? They, too, could go as well. And what about verbal forms other than the infini-tive? Also expendable. The celebrants of physicality and, concomitantly, masculinity waged a gender war as well. The weakness of the rational com-pared to the irrational, the weakness of the mind compared to the body, the weakness of the traditional compared to the revolutionary, was "feminine." By stripping literary language of the ornamentation of syntax, by ridding it of the flab of adjectives and other emasculating parts of speech, language could be made virile, the right tool in the right hands.

For the true primitivists among the poetic reformers, the primordial vigor of the word had to be newly excavated. Since words are after all combinations of sounds, why not cleanse them of patinas of meaning acquired with time and custom and attempt through sound to restore the authentic relations between sound and sense? At a time when mature artists opened themselves to the world of the child and sought to see the world through the eyes of the child, thereby recapturing its lost wonder, the language play of children took on new meaning. By deliberately "playing" with language, inventing words, valorizing what others might regard as nonsense, could not the poet retrieve the long-lost magic of sound? Could not a new poetry whose "meaning" derives from new combinations of sounds strike responsive psychic chords in auditor and reader alike? Experiments with sounds surpassed the Futurist revolt against syntax and made bedfellows of such writers as Christian Morgenstern, Wassily Kandinsky, the Russians Velimir Khlebnikov and Aleksei Kruchonykh—the inventors of *zaum*, or "transrational," poetry—and Hugo Ball, whose recitation of his own "sound poems" at the Cabaret Voltaire, the birthplace of dada, drained him to such an extent that he could never repeat the performance.

At least from Mallarmé on, the revolution in poetic language acquired also a visual dimension that poetry had not had since the "shape" or "figure" poems of the age of the Baroque. How the lines of the poem, or individual words, were arranged on the page could have a bearing on the reader's response. More was involved than the stanzaic structure of the poem or its auditory character. By manipulating the distribution of words and lines on the page, the poet could operate semantically with space the way the artist might use the unpainted areas of the canvas. Variety of print styles within the same work could also affect the tonalities of the poem. So, too, could the invention of a new typeface, as in the case of the German poet Stefan George, who tried to match print to his own handwriting and deliberately broke with conventions of German capitalization. Also affecting reader response could be the printing of handwritten texts of poems, as with the Russian poet Kruchonykh.

The modernist dismantling of the traditional and conventional, the glorification of the sensual and intuitive at the expense of the rational and verbal, also had broad social and political ramifications. A maligned intellectual culture was offset by a new emphasis on the education and training of the body. Even though in some instances the physical culture movement that swept across Europe and America in the late nineteenth and early twentieth centuries had begun to develop earlier, in the second or even first half of the nineteenth century, it reached its apogee and maximum impact in the early twentieth century. The new emphasis on the organized physical training of youth transformed traditional school curricula. Physical education of young women was seriously undertaken for the first time. So a writer as attuned as Frank Wedekind to the changes taking place in society in his own time and place would not be out of character when he wrote a work as seemingly atypical for him as *Minne-Haha or On the Physical Education of Young Girls*. The training of the body within the framework of a new concern for health and even dress conducive to a vigorous life routine was all the rage at the turn of the century. A liberal attitude toward women often expressed itself as support for greater comfort and casualness in feminine attire.

Seen from the perspective of what I believe we can fairly characterize as modernist physicality, such internationally celebrated paragons of manly physique and virility as Bernarr Macfadden and Eugen Sandow were hardly isolated phenomena. Nor were they merely preening, muscle-flexing figures in a landscape. They founded popular magazines and journals devoted to physical well-being and training; they lectured the world over; they established institutes and even planned communities where their ideas and programs could be studied and practiced. The bohemian poet-laureate of fin-de-siècle Vienna, Peter Altenberg, has long been regarded as idiosyncratic for his views, and prescriptions, on diet, sleep, and healthful dress, especially for women, views dismissed as all part of the Altenberg legend. But Altenberg belongs to the same period as the Sandows and Macfaddens. His concern may have been greater for the inner as opposed to the outer man, but his obsession with nourishment and the care of the body was forged in the same crucible of modernist physicality.

Sandow, Macfadden, Altenberg, and others like them were colorful characters who caught the public imagination and fueled many a rumor mill. Regarded as freaks or showmen by their detractors, as inspirational gurus by their admirers, their impact on society was limited. Because Altenberg was in some ways unique, a master of small forms when they were beginning to enjoy critical approbation, as a writer he has, if anything, grown in stature. Yet his prescriptions on diet and health are taken seriously by few and are considered the jottings of a well-intentioned crank. Sandow and Macfadden, like the later strongman Charles Atlas, are barely remembered except by historians of bodybuilding.

No less symptomatic of modernist physicality, and of far greater impact both socially and politically, were the physical culture and gymnastics organizations collectively representing a great international movement that reached the zenith of its popularity and influence in the period 1890–

1936. The institutionalization of physical culture was inevitable, certainly once the compatibility of its aims with nationalist objectives and military preparedness were discerned. Although hardly a country lacked a national physical culture and gymnastics movement, the most prestigious and organizationally impressive were the Boy Scouts, founded in England in 1908 by a Boer War hero, which created the standard against which all others were measured; the German Turnverein, whose origins in the early nineteenth century cannot be separated from the intense German nationalism aroused by the wars against Napoleon; and the Czech Sokol association, which as a national organization devoted to fostering Czech cultural and political ideals — including the preservation of the Czech language — was at the height of its prestige at the turn of the century. Like the German Turnverein, the Sokol traveled with the hundreds of thousands of immigrants who came to the United States in the late nineteenth century and sank deep roots in American society. The Sokol movement, moreover, spread throughout the Slavic lands and gave rise to similar (and similarly) named organizations among the Slovaks, Yugoslavs, Poles, and Bulgarians.

Even the Boy Scouts — which in their American setting we tend to view positively and benignly, as if looking at a Norman Rockwell portrait of Americana — shared the spirit of nationalism and military preparedness with which the great Continental European gymnastic organizations were imbued. Created in times of conflict and growing national self-realization, the gymnastics movement incorporated into the disciplined communal training of the body a keen sense of national purpose and paramilitary alertness. For the English, paramount was the preservation of empire; for the Germans, it was readiness for war that would never again expose the nation to the humiliation suffered at the hands of the French in the Napoleonic campaigns; among the Czechs and other Slavs, it was resistance to Germanization or Russification and the ultimate goal of national independence.

Accompanying the development of gymnastics organizations and the new physical culture was an emphasis on sport unparalleled in history. Modernism truly became the great age of sport. Public interest and enthusiasm in it had never been as high, nor was it gender limited. As might be expected, popular culture embraced the world of sport and the athlete with astonishing exuberance. But high culture was not to be found wanting. Artists delighted in the new subject matter and responded appropriately. Boxing, wrestling, soccer, cycling, and field and track became as familiar on canvas and in print as on billboards.

The popularity of sport drew prestige from another source. Modernist anti-intellectualism favored action over contemplation and the passive culture of the word. Sensing a certain insufficiency in being a man of letters, the writer now strove to become a man of action as well. Experience was what mattered most; that was how the world was to be learned, not through intellectualization and language. In the days of Theodore Roosevelt, nothing defined the virile male more than outdoor adventure and the hunt. Blood sport was hardly new at the time, but as Roosevelt's engrossing writings on it attest, it had achieved a new level of literary respectability. War was another route to manhood, as Kipling taught us, and as Roosevelt's Rough Riders' adventure suggests, it was, in a way, another sport.

No better opportunity was provided the man of letters to reinvent himself as a man of action than World War I. The much anticipated outbreak of war was the summons to high adventure, and while many members of the literary community chose to wage combat far from the lines in safe government positions, there were others who welcomed it with unrestrained passion. From men of letters they became men of action—in some instances genuine heroes—and made their own experiences the raw material of creativity. D'Annunzio, the Symbolist, and Marinetti, the Futurist, found common cause in the participation in and celebration of war. The Russian poet, Nikolai Gumilyov, covered himself with glory in battle and rhapsodized on the theme of combat in the controlled precision of the rest of his Acmeist poetry. Ernst Jünger, one of the commanding figures of twentieth-century German literature, began his literary career in the 1920s with gripping accounts of trench warfare and hand-to-hand combat in World War I. Like Jünger a few years before him, Ernest Hemingway rode to fame as a writer on the strength of his novel A Farewell to Arms, based on his own experiences as an ambulance driver on the Italian front. This work, together with The Sun Also Rises, about the American expatriate community of Paris after World War I, established him as the greatest prose writer of his generation. The French novelist and playwright, Henry de Montherlant, also saw service in the "great war" and drew on his own frontline combat for his first novel, Le Songe (The Dream, 1922), which like Jünger's In Stahlgewittern (In Storms of Steel, 1920) and Hemingway's A Farewell to Arms (1929), catapulted him to fame.

The virile masculine appeal of blood sport drew such luminaries as Hemingway and Montherlant, glamorizing another dimension of sport. When no longer in combat, the man of letters saw in the killing of animals further reaffirmation of masculinity. As Hemingway has demonstrated in A Farewell to Arms (1926) and in Death in the Afternoon (1932), an eminently knowledgeable treatise on the subject by one of its greatest aficionados, the mystique of bullfighting was irresistible. Montherlant's tauromania was every bit as fervid as Hemingway's, as the novel long esteemed as his best, *Les Bestiaires* (translated into English as *The Matador* or *The Bullfighters*) makes abundantly clear, and Montherlant went Hemingway one better by actually fighting bulls himself and, on one occasion, getting gored.

Hemingway remained loyal to blood sport throughout his career. Once he discovered big-game hunting, like Theodore Roosevelt, he pursued it with a passion and made it and Africa his newest literary venue. The evidence is impressive: stories such as "The Short Happy Life of Francis Macomber," "The Snows of Kilimanjaro," and his superbly evocative account of an East African safari in 1933, *Green Hills of Africa* (1935). Hemingway's ability to transform sport into literary art remained with him to the end. His most popular work, and the one for which he was awarded the Pulitzer Prize in 1953 and the Nobel Prize for Literature in 1954, was the almost mythic story of deep-sea fishing, *The Old Man and the Sea* (1951). Although Montherlant shared Hemingway's love of bullfighting, he seemed to prefer tamer sports such as soccer and track to big-game hunting. Montherlant was actually one of the most exquisite writers on sports of the twentieth century. The descriptions of runners and running in *The Dream* stand out vividly. Montherlant also made room in his world of athletics for women. The more disciplined their bodies through training and competition, the greater their appeal to him, and his descriptions of female athletes, like the gifted runner Dominique Soubrier in *The Dream*, border on the ecstatic. *Les Olympiques* (*The Olympics*), a praise of sport published two years after *The Dream* in 1924, further extolled the contribution of women to athletics.

Worship of the body, which in Montherlant at times combines the clinical and aesthetic, lends itself to facile exploitation by racist supremacy theories. This is the dark side of modernist physicality. With the Germans in the Nazi era, the cult of the physical merged with an ideology of racial superiority that transformed the German male into the modern equivalent of the classical Greek hero. How this could feed the fires of anti-Jewishness, for example, is easy to appreciate. As the archetypical bourgeois *intelligent*, the coffeehouse *literatus*, whose cultural traditions and mores have historically favored mind over body, the Jew was an object of contempt for his putative antiphysicality, hence his weakness of body. The Jew came to be viewed in physical terms as the very opposite of the German. The physically disciplined, hard body of the German was contrasted with the weak, misshapen body of the Jew. Resentful, envious of German physical and racial superiority, the Jew conspired to weaken and ultimately destroy the German by corrupting him culturally and physically. Through prominence in the suspect worlds of art and intellect, the Jew waged war against Germanness on one front, while on another he sought to weaken his enemy by moral corruption and physical pollution. Sex with German women would undermine racial superiority; prostitution and venereal disease were held to be the principal weapons in the Jew's campaign to poison German blood. The widespread acceptance of such views in Hitler's Germany now staggers the imagination.

Belief in the primacy of the body contributed as well to a rejection of the "passivity" and "femininity" of Christianity as well as Judaism, hence the intolerance for both religions, indeed for religion in general, in the extremist totalitarian societies of the twentieth century. Strength of body in combination with strength of will could not be shackled by the restraints of bourgeois society or by the unnatural inhibitions imposed by religious beliefs on which this society bases its moral and ethical standards. For the physical-cultist authoritarian state, whether on the Right or the Left, war against Judeo-Christian morality was inevitable. If Christianity was despised for its constraints on the "natural man" who is at the same time "physical man," Judaism was all the more despicable as the source from which Christianity flowed. The war against the Jews, in its own terrible way, was logical from the viewpoint of Nazi ideology. The Jew was regarded as the racial and physical antithesis of the German, the antithesis of everything subsumed by the modernist cult of the physical. Fearing German superiority, the Jew, it was believed, set out to destroy the German through a systematic contamination of German culture and blood. The Jew, therefore, had to be destroyed before he succeeded in destroying the German. The Holocaust, in its way, can be understood as the last stage, the extreme fulfillment, of the modernist obsession with physicality.

The vast subject of this book does not lend itself to easy systematization. Causality and sequentiality are difficult and at times impossible to establish except with respect to the totalitarian uses of the cult of physicality, for which we have an established chronology. It would be convenient to suppose that philosophical inquiry and discourse preceded developments in the arts; but there is no evidence that this truly occurred despite the responsiveness of artists to philosophical thought. In the case of a few of the gymnastics organizations I deal with, notably the German and the Czech, their origins and ideologies antedate modernism. This does not mean, however, that modernism did not play a role in their further development or that they did not in turn contribute to the shaping of the modernist movements in their respective cultures It is generally acknowledged that the German

Turnverein and Czech Sokol organizations reached their peak in terms of numbers and public support in the late nineteenth and early twentieth centuries. Therefore, it would be amiss not to attribute the broad appeal of the gymnastics movement, at least in part, to modernism and its embrace of the physical.

Rather than propose some pattern or patterns of evolution for the phenomena I address in this book, I have chosen instead to build each chapter around a specific topic or set of topics without particular regard for chronology. I begin with developments in the performing arts—theater and dance—because of the striking way the modernist physical imperative asserted itself in this area. My point of departure is turn-of-the-century pantomime, the most obvious indication of the extreme rejection of the spoken word in a period in which language and speech were besieged along a broad front intellectually and artistically. Since the retreat from speech, as I choose to call it, was taking place in the theater more or less at the same time serious artists began experimenting with pantomime, I follow the more striking developments in pantomime (beginning with Max Reinhardt's great spectacle, *The Miracle*) with examples of the enhanced semantic weighting of gesture and silence at the expense of dialogue in plays by a few leading dramatists of the modernist period. Here I begin with Maeterlinck and conclude with Gertrude Stein, who used a unique form of dialogue to undermine conventional theatrical speech.

The emergence of modern dance was one of the most stunning artistic achievements of modernism. Much has been written on it. In the third chapter, I briefly review the careers of the most celebrated exponents of modern dance, American (Fuller, Duncan, St. Denis) and European (Wigman), then move on to the less familiar subject of the impact of dance on drama and prose fiction in the modernist period. This is by way of demonstrating the enormous impact of dance as liberating rhythmic movement elsewhere in the world of contemporary art. The weight of the chapter falls mostly on the ways dance was appropriated by drama, and the emergence of dance as a new literary theme in fiction. The writers considered range from Henrik Ibsen to Alfred Döblin.

The fourth chapter profiles major twentieth-century writers who most exemplify the man of letters as man of action. Although most of them are well known, the bringing together of such figures as D'Annunzio, Marinetti, Gumilyov, Jünger, Hemingway, Montherlant, and Saint-Exupéry argues the case for the importance of war and sport to the personal self-realization and self-fulfillment of the writer. Since it is war, sport, and solitary physical challenge that define the essence of masculinity in the fiction of these writers, the strong gender orientation is undeniable. With few exceptions, this is a world of men, of male camaraderie, and of aggressive virility, with no entry for the most part to women or, if allowed, only at the cost of marginalization. Whatever their private feelings toward women, these writers tend to shun them in their fiction or to use them as foils to the male figures on whom their greatest interest is concentrated. When involved in war or writing about it, D'Annunzio, Marinetti, and Gumilyov at least temporarily suspend enhancement of their formidable reputations as lovers and womanizers. In the case of Marinetti, the violence and aggressiveness of futurism so shape his vision of woman that the female is little more than an object of rapine conquest. Perceived as the embodiment of romantic love and tenderness, women pose the greatest threat to the martial single-mindedness of the Futurist male, hence she should be treated accordingly. How obsessively single-minded the commitment to the experience of war could be is nowhere better exemplified than in the early works of Ernst Jünger, whose battlefield landscape excludes women, even from memories. Almost mystically exulting in the extraordinary challenges of solitary aviation, Saint-Exupéry inhabits a realm of total male exclusivity. And therein lies much of its appeal, conceivably its greatest appeal. Although a wartime romance figures prominently in Hemingway's *A Farewell to Arms*, everything is viewed through the eyes of the male protagonist-narrator, and the war is a vivid presence throughout, nowhere more so than in the memorable description of the battle of Caporetto. Montherlant's enthusiasm for women in sports is tempered, however, by a curiously misogynistic contempt for the unmuscular rounded contours of the female form. The more the woman's body resembles that of the male, however, the greater Montherlant's admiration, and thus, his embrace of the female athlete.

As if sensing the appropriateness of a style compatible with their exultation in war and high adventure, the writer as man of action cultivated a verbal virility. Languid expansiveness, descriptiveness, lyricism, and psychological analysis become things of the past, their place taken by taughtness, precision, detachment. Hemingway's fiction has long been admired for a prose often characterized as "masculine" in its lean, spare quality. The militaristic aggressiveness of Marinetti's futurism is expressed in a style he called "words in freedom," as if, once liberated of syntax and other niceties such as rules of punctuation, words would fill the air like so much exploding shrapnel. Reacting against the lyrical and metaphysical excesses of symbolism, the Russian Acmeists cultivated concreteness and restraint. The sobriety of their poetry seemed tailor-made for Gumilyov's writing about the war, and his prose, as in "Notes of a Cavalryman," follows the same pattern. Although undercut by a fondness for philosophizing that the Russian Acmeists would have disdained, the matter-of-factness and understatedness of Saint-Exupéry's adventures in the air and on the desert belie the enormity of the hazards he faced and the almost oppressive demands on his nerves that they made. Of course, not every writer who courted the exhilaration of war and sport sought to devise an idiom and style compatible with such pursuits. D'Annunzio's Symbolist floridness was shaped long before the little poet transformed himself into the comandante of Fiume, and Montherlant seemed singularly unconcerned about a certain disparity between his lyricism and discursiveness on one hand and his Nietzscheanism and admiration of the virile and bellicose ancient Romans on the other.

Chapter five considers three important aspects of modernist physicality. The first is the place of philosophy (represented mainly by Nietzsche, Mauthner, Bergson, and in a limited way, Wittgenstein) in the transition from an intellectual and verbal culture to one distinguished by antirationalism, anti-intellectualism, the primacy of spontaneity and intuition, the repudiation of the epistemological value of language, and the celebration of the physical, which was perceived as direct experience of the phenomenal world. The "language skepticism" that formed a paradigm for modernist German-language philosophy is paralleled, I believe, by the revolutionary experimentation in literary language characteristic of such modernist artists as Mallarmé, Kandinsky, Marinetti, the Russians Khlebnikov and Kruchonykh, and Hugo Ball of dada fame. This is the second topic examined in this chapter. Against the background of philosophical antirationalism, language skepticism, and the primitivism of avant-gardist language experimentation, I next examine the rise and apogee in the modernist period of the physical culture movement. My primary focus here, as indicated earlier, is on such mass movements as the Boy Scouts, the German Turnverein, and the Czech Sokol associations.

Had the modernist physical imperative realized itself only in a cult of the body, the emergence of modern pantomime and dance, and philosophical and literary antitraditionalism, this study would have a happier ending. Unfortunately, it did not. Modernist biblical revisionism and the anti-Christian and anti-Jewish writings of a philosopher such as Nietzsche and his literary admirers are easily reconciled with the new emphasis on action, the primacy of the body, and the rejection of bourgeois values, including the moral and ethical beliefs of Judaism and Christianity. Nietzschean and similar thought engendered an elitism that differentiated between the superior individual, whose superiority was manifest in the willingness to spurn Judaeo-Christian morality, and the institution of the church, now perceived as another frangible pillar of the bourgeois system. Once the unnatural constraints of the traditional moral and ethical belief system were tossed aside, they were logically substituted by a worship of manly virtues and unlimited creative energy to be unleashed by the intuitive and irrational. D. H. Lawrence's admiration for paganity, coupled with his disdain for both Christianity and Judaism, is unequivocally expressed in *Apocalypse* (1931) and *Etruscan Places* (1932). Wyndham Lewis's related admiration for what he terms "fascismo," as well as his embarrassing enthusiasm for Adolf Hitler, flow from the same sources. But this is not to suggest anything judgmental. My purpose here is not to pass judgment, but rather to provide as large a framework as possible into which to set and to make sense of the ideas of these writers.

The modernist preoccupation with physicality, in its broad ramifications from the aesthetic to the philosophical, led inevitably, I believe, to the chillingly perverse writings of Adolf Hitler and of the better educated, more prolific, and in some ways intellectually more deadly ideologue, Alfred Rosenberg. German state terror against the Jews was indeed a part of the campaign against the churches and organized religion in general. But, as I have suggested earlier, the Jews were identified as a race incorporating attributes and traits diametrically opposed to those of the archetypical Germanic hero. Corrupted by very different values, the Jew could survive and flourish only at the expense of the German, hence the absolute, irrevocable need for the German to crush a mortal enemy. Anti-Jewish propaganda became an integral part of Nazi physical education, which sought to redress what was now considered a misplaced emphasis on the intellect in traditional German education by thrusting bodily self-perfection to the fore. Just as young Germans were taught the ideals of racial purity, national community, and physical strength, they were also instructed in the telltale signs of Jewish physical imperfection, the easier thereby to recognize the enemy. The modernist indictment of Christianity and Judaism and, finally, the grotesque misappropriation by the Nazis of the entire modernist cult of the physical form, in essence, the subjects of the last two chapters.

In setting forth the nature and scope of this book, I trust that I have at least suggested what it is not. Lest there be any ambiguity on the matter, let me be more direct. Since at least the 1970s, serious scholarly interest has directed attention to the nexus between modernism and fascism. If not necessarily the pioneer of such studies, new ground was broken by Frederic Jameson's 1979 study of Wyndham Lewis as a Fascist, *Fables of Aggression: Wyndham Lewis, the Modernist as Fascist*. In *Reactionary Modernism: Technology, Culture, and Politics in Weimar and the Third Reich* (1984), Jeffrey

Hart explored with great skill the reactionary dimension of modernism in the context of post–World War I Germany. Eva Hesse, in her German analysis, *Die Achse Avantgarde–Faschismus* (*The Avantgarde–Fascism Axis*, 1991), used the careers of two of the most controversial literary artists of the twentieth century, Filippo Tommaso Marinetti and Ezra Pound, to delineate the dimensions of the avant-garde–fascism axis. Reinhard Brenneke, another German scholar, pursued a similar approach in *Militanter Modernismus* (*Militant Modernism*, 1992), a comparative study of the early work of Ernst Jünger. Needless to say, my mention of four particularly commendable studies in this area by no means exhausts the literature on the subject.

The present book necessarily but largely inferentially broaches the matter of the easy accommodation by modernism of extremist politics. It may also suggest ways in which modernism could well have shaped attitudes common to the extremist political movements of the early twentieth century. But tracing the network of connections between modernism and fascism—or communism—is not my purpose here. As I hope I have made abundantly clear, I deal above all with various expressions of what I perceive to be a modernist physical imperative, one that coheres in large measure as a repudiation of intellectual culture and the complex of phenomena, from the cultural to the social, usually attributed to that culture.

Modernist Pantomime

and the Retreat from Speech

in the Drama

Mien, mimesis, gesture, and pantomime, can together express every one of the feelings and emotions more graphically and forcibly than words can do.

G. STANLEY HALL, President of Clark University,
Professor of Psychology and Pedagogy,
Educational Problems (1911)

From here at the end of the twentieth century, how do we explain the enthusiasm for nonverbal theater at the end of the nineteenth? As essential, and beguiling, as words may be to us, the lure of the language of the human body reaches so far back in time that a fair claim can be made for the antecedence of a type of performance that was uncompromised by speech. The new popularity at the turn of the century of pantomime, and the interest among serious artists in developing what had come to be regarded as essentially fairground entertainment into an independent art form, defy simplistic explanation. The modernist affection for folk culture sheds some light. Long associated with mass entertainment, pantomime would indeed have had an appeal to those artists who sought a kind of regenerative inspiration from what they perceived to be a lower level of creative endeavor.[1] There was also the appeal of the challenge to bring new life to a largely moribund tradition. Perhaps of greater importance was the disenchantment felt by many educated people, particularly in central Europe, who had come to believe that their society had for too long placed too great a value on words. Intellectual (and, in some instances, political) depreciation of verbal culture became a sign of the times. Writers and philosophers alike sought to revitalize language, to restore to it a lost vigor, through relentless questioning of meaning, usage, and convention. And while all this was in progress, a parallel shift of emphasis from the spoken word to the physical gesture, from speech to body, was occurring demonstrably and logically. This shows up in many ways in the period extending from the 1890s to the ascendancy of political totalitarianism in continental Europe in the 1920s and 1930s. While we shall have the opportunity in the course of this book to examine the various manifestations of the new cult of the physical in the modernist period, I can think of no better point of departure than the extraordinary cultivation of pantomime, which in terms of artistic accomplishment, reached previously unknown heights in its very long history.

Max Reinhardt's Miracle

Rather than begin with a review of the development of pantomime as an art form in the last decade of the nineteenth century, I will set conventional chronology aside to consider the apogee of the early modernist enthusiasm for silent drama, the celebrated productions of the pantomime spectacular, *The Miracle*, by the great Austrian director Max Reinhardt, first at the Olympia Hall in London in 1911 and then at the Century Theatre in New York in 1924.

The Miracle was a religious epic. It tells the story of a nun who falls from grace by allowing herself to be wooed and won by a knight. As soon as the nun leaves her convent, her place is taken by the Madonna, who descends from the pedestal on which her statue has been standing. Finding the holy statue missing, the other nuns panic and threaten the person they believe to be the nun for permitting the statue to be stolen. But the miraculous nature of the event soon manifests itself, and the nuns change from accusing their sister to rejoicing in their belief that she has become the chosen agent of a higher power. The action then shifts to the adventures of the errant nun, who undergoes a series of calamities, beginning with the death of her lover at the hands of the Robber Count and ending in the birth of a son and her penitential return at Christmas to her former convent. As the nun returns, the Madonna sheds her habit and becomes again a statue. The nun finds her garb where the Madonna left it and, realizing this is a miracle, puts it on. Recalling her son, whom she has left lying on the pavement, she shows him to the Madonna and confesses her sins. The child is no longer alive, but the Madonna momentarily comes to life again and raises the child, who begins to glow, symbolizing his ascent to heaven. When the other nuns and their abbess appear and see the statue back in its proper place, they regard the errant nun as the savior of the miraculous statue. The nun is cheered by all and the statue of the Madonna is taken down from its pedestal to be shown to the populace. As the nun falls at the feet of the Madonna, all sing the "Salve Regina," joined by a chorus of angels on high. The great pantomime ends as the statue is raised and "stars appear through the roof of the church, above the altar and audience. They begin to float downward like flashes of illuminated snow." [2]

The Miracle was written by Karl Vollmoeller, who collaborated with Reinhardt on other productions both before and after it. Vollmoeller had taken the idea from Maurice Maeterlinck's play *Sister Beatrice* (1892). A giant of European literature at the time (and barely read today), Maeterlinck was one of the principal architects of Symbolist theater with such plays as *Pelleas and Melisande* (1892) and *The Death of Tintagiles* (1894). Set in thirteenth-century France, *Sister Beatrice* exemplifies one of the dominant trends in turn-of-the-century European dramatic writing—the neomystery play, "neo" by virtue of the fact that the mystery play had been the principle genre of medieval drama. As its name suggests, the miracle play celebrated the miracles of the Christian faith.

The supernatural proclivities of the Symbolist artist created a fertile field for revival of the mystery genre, whose cultivation from the 1880s to the 1920s rivaled that of pantomime. So great was the zeal for mystery plays that they also furnished the subjects for many of the shadow shows that were much in fashion in the little theaters and cabarets of turn-of-the-century Europe (like mystery plays and pantomime, the shadow show was a very old form of entertainment that took on new life with the advent of modernism).

With an enormous playing area—four times the floor size of the Albert Hall, a roof that rose a hundred feet, and a seating capacity of eight thousand—the sheer size of the London Olympia worked to Reinhardt's advantage. The theater was transformed into a vast cathedral and the audience arranged in such a way as to become the congregation. How apt this was can be appreciated by considering the Symbolist approach to theater as a temple in which spectator and performer were to be united in performances of shared spiritual experience. In the hands of the architect Hermann Derburg, the Olympia's rebirth as a twelfth-century Gothic cathedral was achieved by such effects as six-foot-high gold lamps, a towering gold canopy over the Madonna, and stained glass windows, including a circular one fifty feet in diameter, larger than the original in Cologne and three times the size of the rose window in Notre Dame.[3] The west doors, through which a dazzling ecclesiastical procession entered shortly after the beginning of the pantomime, were seventy feet high and a hundred feet wide, again three times the size of those of the great Cologne cathedral. Since the spectacle incorporated multiple settings, indoors and outdoors, the means had to be found to effect such changes as seamlessly as possible. As Norman Bel Geddes, the designer for the no-less-spectacular American production, wrote in his account of it, the cathedral "must plausibly become—right before the eyes of the audience and without so much as a blackout—a primeval forest, a banquet hall, a wedding chapel, a setting for a black mass, a great throne room for the coronation of an empress, a public square, a stable interior, a roadway through a wintry forest, and, finally, a cathedral again."[4]

In his description of the interior design of the cathedral and the costumes worn by the actors, Ernst Stern, Reinhardt's stage set and costume designer, emphasized their fantastic, antirealistic nature. The pointed arches of the interior of the structure were "decorated with masses of tracery soaring upwards. Improbable and fantastically involved arabesques curled into flowers, leaves and fruit which, on closer examination, proved to be grotesquely distorted masks." And although the costumes were made of authentic materials, with the robes of the Madonna sprayed with concrete to look more obviously like stone, Stern did not consider them to be realistic:

> The costumes were as fantastic as the architecture, like something out of a feverish dream. The actresses wore enormously high steeple hats. The actors wore massive headgear from which stiff folds of cloth shot out like flames. And the leg-of-mutton sleeves were fantastic, more like balloons, whilst the trains of the women were tremendously long and ornate. To add to the fantasy there was a vast amount of scalloping which hung down magnificently rounded, pointed, jagged, from every seam. And on their feet these men and women, dressed like Harlequins and parakeets, wore boots and shoes with excessively long pointed toes.
>
> And then in contrast to this overdressing was the revelation described in the text of bosom, belly, leg and thigh. The fashion was devilish, grotesque and mocking, recklessly extravagant and exaggerated. It grinned, so to speak; it mocked; it stuck out its tongue at the prudish. And the colours were dazzling. The scallops and hangings twisted and twisted in the dance of life like the flames of hell.[5]

The huge success of the world premiere in London on December 23, 1911, to which music by the composer Engelbert Humperdinck contributed greatly, encouraged Reinhardt to schedule guest tours of the pantomime in major European cities. All told, seventeen such productions of *The Miracle* took place.[6] An American tour was planned for December 9, 1914, but had to be postponed because of the outbreak of World War I. The project was never abandoned, however, and the American premiere finally took place on January 15, 1924, at the Century Theatre in New York City. Reinhardt repeated his stage concept of thirteen year earlier, and it was every bit as colossal as the original.

Much of the credit for its phenomenal success belongs to the splendid designs by Norman Bel Geddes, a legendary figure in the history of the American theater. Reinhardt had seen Bel Geddes's work in 1922 at an exhibition of his designs at the Municipal Museum in Amsterdam, Holland. He was tremendously impressed with Bel Geddes's talent, particularly his work on a production of Dante's *The Divine Comedy*. With Kenneth Macgowan acting as intermediary, Reinhardt sought out Bel Geddes on a subsequent trip to America in April 1923, engaged him for *The Miracle*, and invited him to his sumptuous Schloss Leopoldskron near Salzburg for detailed work on the great project.[7]

The rest is history, engagingly described in Bel Geddes's autobiography, appropriately titled *Miracle in the Evening*. The New York production of *The Miracle* was like nothing before it in the American theater. As if by magic, the frumpy Century Theatre was transformed from a horizontal stage with three balconies into a tall Gothic cathedral, twenty columns of which were a hundred feet high and six feet wide. In order for the audience to feel that they were in a real church, the setting was brought into the auditorium, with the stage floor extended out to join the sloping floor of the seating area. The whole theater thus became the stage. The enormous challenge Bel Geddes faced in working with the available space of the Century Theatre can be appreciated when one considers that for the original production at the Olympia in London, as well as for its other productions before the one in New York, *The Miracle* had been staged in arenas similar to but, in fact, larger than Madison Square Garden. The Century Theatre was just that, a theater, with a regular proscenium. Justifiably proud of his achievement, Bel Geddes recalled: "The Miracle was not only the largest theatrical production ever staged, but it introduced new operational techniques of economic importance, which pointed the way to future theatrical and motion-picture developments" (293). So successful was the production in every respect, so tumultuous its reception, that New York drama critics vied with each other to capture the unique appeal of a three-hour drama in which not a word was spoken. George Jean Nathan's effusive praise was typical:

The combined talents of Max Reinhardt, Norman Bel Geddes and Morris Gest [the producer] have brought to the American theatre the most vividly impressive and thunderously beautiful spiritual spectacle, not that it has ever known, but more than that, it has ever dreamt of. Beyond question the greatest production, in taste, in beauty, in effectiveness and in wealth or rich and perfect detail, that has thus far been chronicled in the history of American theatrical art. All the elements that go into the life blood of drama are here assembled into a series of aesthetic and emotional climaxes that are humbling in their force and loveliness.[8]

The Miracle ran for three hundred performances in New York, and closed on November 8, 1924. Over the next three years, it toured other American cities from the Atlantic to the Pacific with no diminution of excitement. Its last performance anywhere took place, appropriately, in London—in 1932.

While certainly the most famous pantomime he ever staged, *The Miracle* was by no means Reinhardt's sole excursion into nonverbal drama. *The Miracle* had, in fact, been preceded in 1910 by one of his most popular early productions, *Sûmurûn*, a dance pantomime—Reinhardt's first—in the then fashionable Eastern style. It was based on an episode in the *Tales of the Arabian Nights*, by the German writer, Friedrich Freksa; the music, one of the production's most engaging ingredients, was composed by Friedrich Hollaender.

Sûmurûn premiered on April 22, 1910, in a modest production at the Kammerspiele of the Deutsches Theater in Berlin, whose direction Reinhardt had assumed in 1905. The work began with a spoken prologue (the only part of the production with words) by the celebrated Viennese actor Alexander Moissi. Moissi played the role of a handsome rug merchant, Nur-al-Din. Squatting cross-legged in front of his shop, he announced to the audience that he was in love with Sûmurûn, the beautiful young wife of the old sheik. The pantomime that followed was an enactment of Nur-al-Din's dream in which he fancies himself romantically united with the object of his affection within the walls of the sheik's harem. In a subplot within the dream, the sheik and his son both conspire to wrest a beautiful dancing girl (a role made famous by Leopoldine Konstantin) from a neighbor of Nur-al-Din's in the bazaar, a hunchbacked showman who has a troupe of performers. In despair over the loss of the dancer, whom he loves, the hunchback tries to take his own life by poison but fails. In a series of twists and turns, the hunchback and Nur-al-Din are smuggled into the sheik's palace in the same huge basket. Finding the sheik and the dancer asleep in bed together, the hunchback plots their murder. But before he can act, the sheik's son enters and awakens the dancer, who agrees to run away with him. When the sheik also awakens, he surmises the situation and plunges a dagger into his son. However, before he dies the son leads the sheik to his harem in order to reveal to him the lovemaking between Sûmurûn and Nur-al-Din. A fierce fight ensues between the sheik and Nur-al-Din, and as the old but strong sheik is about to kill his wife's lover, the hunchback appears and exacts his revenge by stabbing the sheik to death. The way is now clear for the lovers Nur-al-Din and Sûmurûn to unite without fear.

Much of the appeal of the original production of *Sûmurûn* lay in the contrast between its almost austere background and the stunning Middle Eastern costumes and sets by Ernst Stern, one of Reinhardt's most talented and favorite designers.[9] The success of the pantomime thus assured, Reinhardt took the work next to Vienna. Here it caught the eye of Sir Oswald Stoll, who booked it for six weeks for the London Coliseum in January 1911. Audiences were ecstatic over it.[10] The London *Times* of February 20, 1911, extolled the production: "The like of this marvel has surely never been seen in London before! It presents harmonies of colours that are now suave and tender and now all ablaze and dazzling—the quiet hues of an old Persian rug and the glitter of gems; it has purity of outline and grace of movement."[11]

A year later, on January 16, it opened in New York City at the Casino Theatre. It was revived in London at the Savoy Theatre in the winter of 1912 and the spring of 1913 and was mounted in late May 1912 at the Théâtre du Vaudeville in Paris. The first work by Reinhardt to be staged in the United States, *Sumurûn* caught the imagination of critic and public alike. Recalling the New York production nearly a dozen years later, the American poet and artist Marsden Hartley wrote of the impact it made at the time:

> It seems a long, long time since we saw that charming first presentation of *Sûmurûn* by the Reinhardt company at the Casino Theatre in New York, Until then we were ignorant of that kind of simplicity, that kind of directness, that kind of theatrical relativity. And that idea of having the actors come up formally or informally out of the audience, so interesting then, had never been presented before in America. It was all new, agreeable, delightful, and illusory in the best theatrical sense.[12]

Pantomime as a Literary Genre: Wedekind, Hofmannsthal, Schnitzler, Einstein, Kuzmin, Kandinsky

The great interest in pantomime in the late nineteenth and early twentieth centuries led not only to its revival as popular entertainment and its transformation into mass spectacle. Major modernist writers also cultivated it as a literary genre, among them Frank Wedekind and Carl Einstein in Germany, Hugo von Hofmannsthal and Arthur Schnitzler in Austria, the Russian poet and dramatist Mikhail Kuzmin, and the Russian painter Wassily Kandinsky.

Wedekind. The *enfant terrible* of fin-de-siècle German drama, as he is often called, Wedekind epitomizes the efforts of contemporary dramatists to open the drama to subjects regarded as socially indecorous or downright immoral. Needless to say, the subject surrounded by the most taboos was sex, and Wedekind made those taboos his prime target. A talented writer with a keen sense of theater, of which he also had a practical knowledge, Wedekind based his fame as a dramatist on plays dealing forthrightly with such sensitive topics as adolescent sexuality and the power of lust. A true product of his age in this regard, Wedekind was particularly drawn to the subject of female sexuality and explored its dynamics in several works.

A less known facet of Wedekind's career was his interest in pantomime. What stimulated his interest was not just the literary climate's accommodation of the nonverbal, but his own attitude toward the erotic. Real passion, lust, could express itself, he believed, only in physical terms; spoken speech blunted its force. Although the nexus between physicality and passion can be found in a few of his plays, it was principally through pantomime that Wedekind sought to bring together his ideas on human sexuality in the wordless idiom of the body.

Wedekind wrote altogether four pantomimes in the 1890s, which he later called *Tanzpantomimen* (dance pantomimes). They include *Die Flöhe oder der Schmerzenstanz* (*The Flea, or The Dance of Pain*, 1892, first published in 1897); *Der Mückenprinz* (*The Prince of Gnats*, probably written in 1893, first published in 1897); *Bethel* (probably also dating from 1893, published posthumously in 1921); and the best of the group, *Die Kaiserin von Neufundland* (*The Empress of Newfoundland*, written most likely between 1892 and 1894 and published for the first time in 1897). Although *Bethel* is the only one of the pantomimes to be directly related to a circus milieu—Wedekind characterized it as a *"Zirkusgroteske"* (circus grotesque)—this small but interesting body of work also arose in conjunction with Wedekind's enthusiasm for the circus, based on his experiences in Paris and London in the 1890s.[13]

The great circuses of the time included pantomimes among their entertainments and thus contributed to the revival of the form then taking place in Europe. There are those who assume that Wedekind, who was almost always in financial need, wrote his pantomimes primarily in order to cash in on their current popularity. While he was certainly not too proud for this—witness, for example, his writing for and performance in cabarets in Munich and elsewhere—to view his pantomimes wholly or mostly in terms of an exercise for financial gain would be to lift them out of the sphere of contemporary experimentation with nonverbal drama where they properly belong. The popular culture aspect of pantomime must certainly be reckoned a factor in Wedekind's determination to contribute to the genre. Like other artists of his time, Wedekind was alert to the artistic potential of "lower" literary and other forms and showed no reluctance to draw on them when it suited his purpose. Wedekind's work with pantomime was also the more noteworthy for the lack of an antecedent German tradition. Pantomime drama written by serious artists such as Wedekind himself never had much of a following in Germany, and apart from Heinrich Heine's fitful experiments with the genre in the nineteenth century, Wedekind had no predecessors to follow.

The first of Wedekind's pantomimes, *The Flea, or The Dance of Pain,* is the story of a queen (Maria Leczinska), modeled after Maria Leszczyńska (the Polish wife of Louis XV of France), who loses her daughter (Adelaide) to a mysterious beggar woman and eventually recovers the girl in the form of a huge flea. The daughter is magically restored to her mother after the queen has learned to accept the presence of a flea on her person and to love it despite its animal nature.

The "dance of pain" in the subtitle refers to seven trained fleas in a traveling circus that refuse to perform, preferring to escape into the skirts of the queen's ladies-in-waiting. After a night of itching and scratching, the ladies dance a Dionysian dance of joy that carries Wedekind's unmistakable sexual undertones and at the same time demonstrates his affinity for dance as a kindred form of wordless performance. The queen sleeps through all the commotion, but awakes to find a huge flea between her legs, too. When the director of the flea circus (the beggar woman in disguise) demands the return of her star performer, the queen refuses, instead drawing the creature to her bosom and smothering it with kisses. This is sometimes interpreted as an acceptance of animality on the part of the queen, after which, so the reasoning goes, she will again be able to enjoy sexual fulfillment, symbolized by her daughter's restoration to her. Inspired by an entertainment of a "lower order" (the circus), Wedekind used his pantomimes to convey the idea that a similar willingness to open up to "lower" orders of experience, that is, to the instincts of the "lower" social order, holds out to bourgeois and aristocrat alike the promise of erotic regeneration.

Bethel is at once the most ambitious and grotesque of Wedekind's pantomimes. Discovered among his papers, it was published for the first time posthumously. Featuring a huge cast of humans and animals that would surely challenge any director's imagination and resources, the work moves between two worlds, America and Europe. Wedekind had a definite attraction for America, which is reflected in *Bethel*. Though he never visited the United States, Wedekind was long intrigued by the country. His father, a medical doctor, had emigrated there in 1849, his mother in 1856; they were married in San Francisco in 1862, but returned to Germany permanently in 1864, the year Frank Wedekind was born in Hanover. Although they eventually resettled in Germany, they had acquired American citizenship, and their attachment to America was evident in the American names they gave their sons: one was named Donald and the other, Benjamin Franklin, usually shortened to Frank.

The America of *Bethel* is filled with cowboys and Sioux Indians, boxers, trotting horse racers, shady handlers, and spirited Midwestern young women. The title of the pantomime comes from the name of a trotter owned by a Nebraskan farm family named Kneebs. In the hands of the jockey Gary Jeykel, Bethel has made a lot of money for its owners. At a certain point, the horse handler and "capitalist" Heffner wants to enter Bethel in races in Europe. But Bethel, for reasons that remain unclear in the work, must remain in America. The trotter, moreover, has certain physical marks that make him easy to identify. Heffner gets around the problem by disguising the telltale signs and racing Bethel as "Nellie Kneebs."

A similar counterfeiting is worked on Leona, the Kneebs' daughter and Jeykel's wife. An uninhibited young woman who loves to dance, especially the can-can, Leona goes off to Europe in search of fame and fortune, unfettered by her marriage. In other works by Wedekind, a parallel is drawn between an animal representing the freedom of nature and a young woman embodying this freedom, including its sexual implications. In *Bethel*, Leona is the human counterpart of Bethel: spirited, animal-like in her spontaneous behavior, unbridled. In order to strengthen the parallels between Bethel and Leona, Wedekind equips Leona with distinguishing birthmarks that must also be concealed for the European trip.

The trip proves a disaster. Bethel and the Kneebs are ridiculed, and Leona, her marriage to Jeykel kept secret, is paired off with a Prince Galliera, who becomes insanely possessive of her and fires a revolver at anyone who pays her the slightest attention. When suspicion arises concerning the identities of both Bethel and Leona, a "team" of European specialists is sent to America to establish the truth. While in America, the Europeans are besieged by cowboys and Indians, gigantic mosquitoes, hyenas, wolves, and other animals, but can at least witness a July Fourth celebration in Nebraska featuring, among others, the Statue of Liberty, George Washington, Abraham Lincoln, the boxers Corbett and Fitzsimmons, and the American "serpentine" dancer, Loïe Fuller. For sheer exuberance and imaginative energy, the July Fourth celebration is the high point of the pantomime.

The shifting landscape between America and Europe and the parallel disguising of Bethel and Leona are intended to draw a contrast between America, the New World—brash and spirited, unbound by traditions—and Europe, the Old World—stuffy, pretentious, hypocritical. This is the same brief against contemporary European society and culture filed by Wedekind in other works, but in this case, it is strengthened by the implicit contrast with America as the New World.

When the truth about Bethel and Leona is finally revealed, the Americans are taken into custody and a trial is held. In its slapstick humor, the trial rivals the July Fourth celebration for comedy. Most of the humor is generated by the antics of *der stumme Augustus* (Stupid Augustus), the classic clown of the German circus. The trial rapidly dissolves into a circus sideshow. The Americans are found innocent, and the pantomime ends with Leona climbing on the judges' bench to dance a boisterous can-can, with everyone else on stage joining in.

From Wedekind's point of view, Europe, set in its ways, bourgeois in its outlook, pretentious in its manners, was badly in need of rejuvenation. It needed, in a sense, what America could offer, and that is what *Bethel* is meant to convey. But before Europe could accept the gift of rejuvenation from America it had to distinguish the real from the false, as represented by Bethel and Leona. The only one of Wedekind's pantomimes to be set in a circus milieu, *Bethel* uses the circus as the common meeting ground of the New World and the Old. Within the context of the circus, the New breaks down the unnatural reserve and pretensions of the Old, and at the end they come together in a release of inhibitions symbolized by the brash and boisterous can-can.

The Empress of Newfoundland, clearly the most impressive of Wedekind's pantomimes, is a tale of wild and ultimately fatal erotic passion, one of the dramatist's favorite themes. Wedekind probably wrote the pantomime during the time he was in Paris and London in the mid-1890s. Years later he dated it specifically to January 1897, but the evidence still favors the Paris-London period. Whatever its original date of composition, the work was printed for the first time by Albert Langen in 1897 in *Die Fürstin Rusalka* collection. *The Empress of Newfoundland* was performed for the first time anywhere in the famous Munich cabaret Die Elf Scharfrichter (The Eleven Executioners) on March 12, 1902. Its success was extraordinary. The "house" composer, Richard Weinhöppel, himself one of the "eleven executioners," composed the music for the ballet-pantomime out of a mixture of Wagnerian motifs and well-known dances and marches. Wedekind, who performed for a while at the cabaret mostly as a chansonnier, announced the individual scenes in the style of the old German Moritat, or street singer, tradition, on which Bertolt Brecht also drew in a few of his works. The pantomime was staged subsequently, again with considerable success, at the Überbrettl cabaret in Berlin in 1903; at the Münchner Kammerspiele in 1923, where it was performed thirty times with the well-known actress Blandine Ebinger in the lead role; at the Vienna Raimundtheater in 1924; and at the Leipzig Stadttheater in 1929.[14]

The plot of *The Empress of Newfoundland* revolves around the disastrous relationship between the empress, Filissa XXII, and a weightlifter.[15] Seemingly mentally deranged, owing to unfulfilled sexual needs, the slender, graceful, and fragile empress is confined to her bed, where she lies tormented by incessant pains and sinister visions. Dr. Didi Zeudus, the court physician, is brought in to examine her. In the first of several comic scenes in the pantomime, Professor Zeudus follows up his examination with a prescription for the empress that measures three yards long and one yard wide and contains a single word in large letters repeated twenty times: MARRY. When the empress scornfully rejects the advice, Zeudus draws up a new one: it contains the life-size picture of a white skeleton on a black background complete with hourglass and scythe. Reluctantly, Filissa accepts his first prescription and rewards him appropriately.

Hoping thus to alleviate a torment caused, as Wedekind would have us understand, by the absence of physical love, the empress agrees to receive a series of suitors. These are all comic characters. The first is the romantic poet, Heinrich Tarquinius Pustekohl, who reads from a manuscript he has brought with him, then kneels down before the empress and declares his love for her. When this produces more laughter, he draws a dagger and rests the tip of it on his heart, suggesting that if the empress spurns him he will commit suicide. When the empress encourages him to do just that, he leaves the chamber, an expression of deep despair on his face and the dagger clenched in his fallen hand. The next suitor is Napoleon, who enacts boisterous battle scenes for the empress's benefit—and to the consternation of everyone at court. When he, too, is spurned by the empress, he takes out a pair of pistols and holds them to his temples, but he is enraged by the empress's encouragement to kill himself. He aims the pistols at her but is restrained by two policemen, who usher him from the hall. Amid much fanfare, a third suitor appears, Alva Edison. The famous inventor rides in in a two-seater motorcar accompanied by a Negro on whose body he makes various calculations intended to show the empress that he is worth $2 million. But when he notices that Filissa has fallen asleep during his calculations, Edison performs a magic trick that causes his companion to vanish. His place is taken by a large gold nugget that Edison offers to the empress in return for her love. But Filissa has again fallen asleep, and the inventor beats a noisy retreat in his automobile.

The fourth suitor is the weightlifter Eugen Holthoff, whom Wedekind is believed to have based on a real weightlifter of the same name he had met in Paris in the winter of 1892–93. The figure could just as well have been inspired by the famous German-born strongman and weightlifter, Eugen Sandow, whom Wedekind might have seen in London. In *The Empress of Newfoundland*, Holthoff is an imposing figure: "A man of Herculean proportions in a round, stiff, brown felt hat, high, white, lace-up boots, flesh-colored tricot, light brown, checkered jacket, blue waistcoat, white dickey, red tie, his hair meticulously pomaded and parted. Enters the hall and elegantly divests himself of his outer clothes by tossing them to the Representatives of the People standing nearest him."[16]

Holthoff begins to lift weights. In surely one of the funniest scenes of the pantomime, when the weightlifter finishes with his first set, he takes a handkerchief from one of the ladies-in-waiting, mops the sweat from his brow, neck, arms, and underarms, wrings out the handkerchief, making a puddle on the floor, then tosses the handkerchief back to the lady-in-waiting.

But Holthoff so impresses Filissa that she is drawn from her throne as if magnetized. Her response to him encapsulates the message of the pantomime—the empress, a woman of latent passion, cannot be satisfied by art (represented by the poet Pustekohl), power (Napoleon), or money (Edison), but only by a "real" man of sheer physicality such as Holthoff. But as usual in Wedekind, passion carries a heavy price, as we shall soon see.

After Holthoff's next feat, lifting the weights with only one hand, Filissa can no longer control herself. She leaves her throne, removes all her jewelry, and drapes it over Holthoff. She then places her ornate, jewel-encrusted gold crown on his head. Now half-naked, she folds herself into his arms and invites him to occupy her place on the throne. Settling at his feet and beholding him adoringly, she orchestrates a show of support for the weightlifter by her entire court.

In the next act, the empress begs Holthoff to demonstrate his strength again for her. He obliges by lifting a weight with a 200-pound ball at each end and is rewarded with bags of money. In his next show of strength, Holthoff repeats his performance with 300-pound weights. When Professor Zeudus tries to warn Filissa of where all this is leading by unfolding before her the Death Prescription, he is physically removed from the premises. Prodded with yet more money and Filissa's loving encouragement, Holthoff performs next with the 400-pound weights but balks when the empress points, supplicatingly, to the 2000-kilo weights. Filissa, however, overcomes his resistance with ardent kisses and glasses of champagne. Try as he may, however, Holthoff can't lift the weights. Angry and frustrated, Filissa keeps on prodding him to perform the feat, all the while encouraging him with more money extracted from her subjects at sword point. Even the suicide before her of a lovelorn Pustekohl fails to move her. Once Pustekohl's corpse has been carried out, Holthoff rises to the challenge and with a mighty effort succeeds in slowly lifting the 2000-kilo weights. Overcome with passion, Filissa falls into a state of convulsive ecstasy. Preventing a straining Holthoff from lowering his great burden to the ground, Filissa dances wildly around the weightlifter, who can merely follow her performance in utter bewilderment. Only when Filissa swirls around the chamber away from him in her ever more demonic dance is Holthoff at last able to set the weights on the ground. The longer the empress dances, the madder she becomes. Snatching a sword from the hand of Count Lea-Giba, her prime minister and lord treasurer, she lunges at everyone in sight and fatally stabs her page, Raoul. With Holthoff's help, Filissa is finally restrained and straitjacketed. On Professor Zeudus's order, a cage is brought in and the mad empress is forced inside it. Holthoff in the meantime fills a sack with the gold and jewels he had been given, along with the precious stones from the empress's crown, and exits.

The third and last act of the pantomime is set in a sleazy dance hall. Now handsomely attired and flinging money around with abandon, Holthoff is in his element. Women fight over him and are rewarded for their favors with pieces of the empress's jewelry. To the shrill clashing of cymbals from the orchestra, Filissa makes an appearance in a "broad white garment which reaches her feet with very wide half-sleeves, belted with a rope around her waist, sandals on her feet, her hair untidy and tousled, her features twisted and pinched, her hollow eyes staring about her with a vacant, yet feverish look" (374). Once she finds Holthoff, Filissa commences a dance of seduction, but he repulses her. When she catches sight of a meter-long bar with 50-pound weights at the ends, she rolls it to the center of the stage and, fondling and caressing Holthoff, indicates that she wants him to pick it up. Although anxious to leave, Holthoff is taunted into lifting the weights by Filissa and the others. As he struggles unsuccessfully to perform the feat, Filissa notices that the other women are wearing pieces of jewelry she had given to Holthoff, and she begins to yank them away. After being persuaded to stop, Filissa approaches Holthoff and gestures that she wants him to hit her on the temple with one of the balls of the weight. Convinced that Filissa is now mad, bystanders in the dance hall urge Holthoff to put her out of her misery. He begins to lift the weight but drops it on one of his feet before he can bash in Filissa's head. As Holthoff hops about the dance floor in pain, Filissa tries to choke herself with the diamond necklace but fails. In mad despair, she then parts her disheveled hair into two strands, tightens them around her throat, and strangles herself, her forehead pressed to the floor. "She expires," Wedekind writes at the end, "with violent convulsions, her mouth open" (378).

Wedekind's exploration of the tangled web of eros and physicality was not limited to his plays and pantomimes. He seems also to have been attracted to contemporary ideas on physical education, particularly the physical education of girls. The more he reflected on the subject, the more he became convinced that through physical education young women would develop a healthier attitude toward their bodies and a more natural awareness of their own sexuality. He addresses these issues in a curious work of prose entitled *Mine-Haha oder Über die körperliche Erziehung der jungen Mädchen* (*Mine-Haha, or On the Physical Education of Young Girls*). The work is all the more interesting for the fact that it incorporates Wedekind's pantomime *The Prince of Gnats*.

Mine-Haha was presented as the introduction to a projected novel to be called *Hidalla oder Das Leben einer Schneiderin* (*Hidalla, or The Life of a Seamstress*). Both it and the introduction were to form in turn part of a major work on a new sexual culture to which the title "Die grosse Liebe" ("The Great Love") is usually assigned.[17] Before looking at *The Prince of Gnats* as a pantomime, let us first consider the work in which it originally appeared, *Mine-Haha, or On the Physical Education of Young Girls*.

Wedekind worked on a first version of *Mine-Haha* from July to October 1895, but this has not been preserved. A second version was published in 1901 in the journal *Die Insel* under the title "Mine-Haha oder Über die körperliche Erziehung der jungen Mädchen." It presents chapters I through III. In book form, in Albert Langen's *Langens Kleine Bibliothek* (Volume 55), which was published in Munich in 1903, the work also bears the subtitle "Aus Helene Engels schriftlichem Nachlass herausgegeben von Frank Wedekind" ("From Helene Engel's Literary Legacy, Published by Frank Wedekind").[18] Wedekind maintained the fictional claim that *Mine-*

Haha was an authentic manuscript given to him by one Helene Engel, a retired schoolteacher and neighbor of his, shortly before she committed suicide by jumping from a fourth-story window at the age of eighty-four. According to Wedekind, all he did was edit the manuscript for publication.

As to the name "Mine-Haha," Wedekind explains at the end of the work that it is of American Indian origin and means "Laughing Water." It is in fact the name of the child of nature in Henry Wordsworth Longfellow's poem *The Song of Hiawatha* (1855). It was also the name of an old Zurich girlfriend of Wedekind's who represented to him a bodily and rhythmic ideal. Wedekind was so fond of the name that he called himself Cornelius Minehaha for his Ibsen readings in 1895–96.

Mine-Haha, as narrated by Helene Engel, comprises her recollections of the years she spent as a very young girl in a communal institution devoted to physical culture together with other young girls and boys. Apparently taken away from their parents at an early age, the children are kept in prisonlike conditions where their education is limited to the development of physical beauty and the mastery of the body. Dance, and music, are major components of the "curriculum." Intellectual culture has no place in it. At first the boys and girls train together, but from the age of about seven the sexes are separated. From that point on the narrative concerns itself only with the training of the girls. Order and discipline are strict and a hierarchal structure is observed. The girls are all grouped according to age and are under the leadership of eighteen-year-olds. The atmosphere of the institution is cold and sterile: dress is uniform; conversation, even at meals, kept to a minimum. The girls are denied any worldly knowledge, including sexual, are forbidden ever to get into bed with one another, and are prevented from developing any lasting friendships. So strict is the rule forbidding girls to share the same bed that anyone who violates it is never permitted to leave the institution. Since the emphasis is exclusively on the perfection of form, most of the narrative is taken up with Helene Engel's descriptions of the training she and the other girls were subjected to and the physical appearance of this or that girl. The sternness of the regimen, which did not exclude corporal punishment, was applied even to walking:

> All of us had to gather up our skirts and hold them tight with our hands on our hips. Then the march began, so slowly that between steps you could run once around the whole house. At the same time [Gertrude] had her switch constantly on our toes, behind our knees, or at our calves, in case one of us wanted to lower her foot too fast. Lora, the smallest of us girls, who happened to be an exceptionally pretty child, was on the point of crying. At least thick tears had already

begun rolling down her cheeks. But Gertrude threw her such a weird look, that from that moment on she pulled herself together more than all the others. . . . With our other exercises Gertrude saw to it above all that we held our hips as taut as possible as we walked. The moment one of us relaxed her hips or even went over on an ankle, she got a good rap with the switch on her backside.[19]

At a certain stage in their development, the most attractive and talented girls are chosen to perform in a theater located on the grounds of the institution. The productions are run for the benefit of adults and in this way bring in income to the institution. The work the narrator is asked to perform in is a pantomime called *The Prince of Gnats* by an author named "Ademar," whom she says she had the chance to meet twenty-one years later and from whom she received encouragement and support in her career. It is in this way that Wedekind has woven his pantomime into the narrative of *Mine-Haha*.

The isolation and worldly ignorance in which the girls are brought up extends to their participation in the theatricals. The auditorium is illuminated in such a way that they cannot make out faces in the audience. They also have little understanding of the works in which they perform and so cannot fathom the sometimes boisterous reactions of the spectators. *The Prince of Gnats* is an example of this. The pantomime is laced with lust and brutality, but the girls acting in it show little awareness of its contents.

The work begins with the erotic mating dance of two gnats, Aretusa (the female) and Tutos (the male). As elsewhere in Wedekind's pantomimes, insects simultaneously represent nature and the naturalness of sexual behavior. The love scene between the two gnats is rudely interrupted when the arrogant and wicked Prince Leonor enters carrying a butterfly net. Coming across Aretusa and Tutos, he pursues them until, with the help of peasants, he succeeds in imprisoning Tutos in a cage and then, before his eyes, impales Aretusa to death. He then seizes a peasant girl and rapes her under cover of his cloak while the other peasant girls join hands and dance in a ring around them. The prince then dismisses the lot of them, and when the magician Hüchi-Bümbüm and his daughter, Ada, come along, he woos and then marries her. But the prince soon grows tired of Ada and imprisons her in the golden cage in which Tutos has been held captive after he frees the gnat. To taunt Ada, he takes a lady of the court to bed with him in full view of the cage. While they are asleep, Tutos stings the woman. When Leonor awakens and tries to kiss her, she repulses him and pretends, by means of a pillow tucked inside her dress, that her belly is swollen. Leonor dismisses her and then replaces her with the peasant girl he forced to make love to him previously. At an appropriate moment, Tutos stings Leonor who winds up with a real swollen belly. Tutos, however, is captured again and imprisoned in the cage. When the doctor Leonor summons to deflate his belly fails to help him, he cuts off his head. Leonor then drags his wife, Ada, to bed and orders his court chamberlain to make love to her. When her father, the magician, appears, Leonor has him imprisoned in the cage holding Tutos and to humiliate him hurls Ada to the floor, has her pinned down, and orders members of his court and peasants to step on her as they walk over her. But before harm can befall his daughter, the magician frees himself from the cage and unleashes a swarm of gnats who sting Leonor to death. Tutos is then magically transformed into a human being, a prince of gnats truly worthy of the title, and is given in marriage to Ada. The pantomime ends on a happy note, and the narrator mentions that the work was performed two hundred times.

As unsuspecting as the girls are of the nature of the pantomime they perform, so do they fail to understand the nature of the physical and emotional changes they undergo as they reach puberty. As the narrator recalls, "I suddenly became so heavy in the waist and legs, and my breasts swelled. I loathed myself. I kept getting in my way. I was no longer sure of any movement. When I undressed, I felt myself and filled with rage, unable to comprehend that this was the way I was supposed to be. I would have liked nothing better than to take this thick flesh and throw it into a corner" (130–31). Puberty marked the end of her stay in the institution. With other girls who underwent the same changes, the narrator recalls that she was taken off by car under cover of darkness and deposited at a train station from which she was to begin her journey into the world from which she had for so long been separated and about which she knew so little.

As Elizabeth Boa argues, Wedekind's *Mine-Haha* presents more dystopian than utopian features.[20] It evokes a nightmarish totalitarian world of rigid control enforced by the children themselves. Corporal punishment is employed as a means of enforcement, and in the theater episodes, specifically in the treatment of women in *The Prince of Gnats*, there is evident sadomasochism. The girls have little or no understanding of what they perform. Self-awareness, as Elizabeth Boa comments, is reduced to bodily awareness, and the sole discernible goal of the girls' training is physical education as an aesthetic ideal—the body transformed into endless beautiful forms. But without any cultivation of the mind, the body for all its perfection becomes a trap much like the cage in *The Prince of Gnats*.

Mine-Haha can also be read as a grotesque satire of the way girls were actually brought up in Wedekind's Germany. Denied intellectual stimulus, their main concern became their appearance and their physical perfection. Unable to read, they remained in their female bodily world, an imaginary world lacking any temporal extension. When they finally made their way into adult life, it was as trained animals, the horror Lulu complains of in her marriage to Schwarz in Wedekind's most famous play, *Erdgeist* (*Earth Spirit*, 1895).

Hofmannsthal. Hugo von Hofmannsthal's interest in pantomime, like his interest in dance, is best viewed in the context of his disenchantment with language and the growing appeal to him of nonverbal expression. As he declared once in a letter to his fellow dramatist, Anton Wildgans, "how can he who speaks still act, since speech already implies cognition, and thus abrogates action."[21] The point of departure for any discussion of Hofmannsthal's loss of faith in language, however temporary, is usually his essay *Der Brief* (*The Letter*), which he wrote in 1901 and which is widely known in English under the title *The Letter of Lord Chandos*. I will refer to it here as *The Letter*.

In the guise of a Renaissance nobleman (Lord Chandos) addressing a letter to Francis Bacon, Hofmannsthal describes his own critical experience at the time:

> My case, in short, is this: I have lost completely the ability to think or to speak of anything coherently. At first I became gradually incapable of discussing a loftier or more general subject and to have on my lips those words of which everyone, fluently and without hesitation, is wont to avail himself. I experienced an ineffable discomfort at the mere utterance of the words *spirit*, *soul*, or *body*. I found it emotionally impossible to express an opinion on the affairs of the Court, the events in Parliament, or whatever you wish. And this was not out of considerations of one sort or another, for you know how thoughtless my candor can be, but because the abstract terms that the tongue cannot help but employ in order to express a judgment, crumbled in my mouth like mouldy fungi.[22]

Previously Hofmannsthal had conceived "the whole of existence as one great unit: the spiritual and physical worlds seemed to form no contrast . . . and in all of Nature I felt myself" (10–11). But now, in his crisis, his world seemed to disintegrate and to lose its sense of wholeness, of unity: "For me everything disintegrated into parts, those parts again into parts, and nothing let itself be encompassed any more by a single idea. Single words floated all around me; they congealed into eyes that stared at me and into which I was forced to stare back. Whirlpools were they, looking down into which made me dizzy, and whose incessant spinning led into the void" (14).

His alternatives are flight from the world, introversion, the way of mysticism, silence, or the attempt to apprehend and express the phenomenal world in terms of action. For Hofmannsthal the problem was both personal and artistic—to find the road that leads out of pre-existential isolation to the social and the active, to a life of commitment and participation. Hence he broke deliberately with the mode of his early work in poetry and the lyric theater. That he was about to move into uncharted territory is manifest in the closing remarks of *The Letter*:

> You were so kind as to express your dissatisfaction that no book written by me reaches you any more, "to compensate for the loss of my company." At that moment I felt, with a certainty not entirely bereft of a feeling of sorrow, that neither in the coming year nor in the following nor in all the years of this my life shall I write a book, in English or in Latin: and this for a reason the embarrassing oddness of which I leave to your infinite mental superiority to find a place for in the realm of spiritual and physical phenomena spread out harmoniously before your knowing eye: namely, because the language I might be granted not only to write in but also to think in would be neither Latin nor English, neither Italian nor Spanish, but a language of which I know not even a single word, a language in which inanimate things speak to me and in which perhaps one day in the grave I will have to answer for myself to an unknown judge. (140–41)

Hofmannsthal's reservations about language indeed antedated the composition of *The Letter* by a few years, as we can see from his review in 1895 of a book by Eugen Guglia on the celebrated Viennese actor, Friedrich Mitterwurzer. As for the inadequacies of language, Hofmannsthal wrote:

> People are tired of listening to talk. They feel a deep disgust with words. For words have placed themselves before things. Hearsay has swallowed the world.
>
> The infinitely complex lies of the age, the heavy lies of tradition, the lies of the authorities, the lies of individuals, the lies of science and learning, all of them sit on our miserable life like myriads of deadly flies. We are in the grip of a horrible process whereby thought is utterly stifled by concepts. Hardly anyone now is capable of accounting for what he understands and what he does not understand, of saying what he feels and what he does not feel. This has awakened a love for all those arts that are executed without speech: music, dance, and all the skills of acrobats and jugglers.[23]

Akin to these last is the clown Firlanu, who plays such an important, though unobtrusive, part in Hofmannsthal's much later and highly regarded comedy, *Der Schwierige* (*The Difficult Man*), which he began in

1917, published serially in a newspaper in 1920 and, after revisions, in book form in 1921.

True to the sentiments expressed in *The Letter*, Hofmannsthal had actually begun experimenting with nonverbal theater either before or about the time that he began writing *The Letter*. Two works of a balletic nature date from 1900–1901. The first was *Der Triumph der Zeit* (*The Triumph of Time*), a ballet scenario in three acts for which he had hoped that Richard Strauss would compose the music. Because of other commitments, Strauss, however, had to decline. The music was written instead by Alexander von Zemlinsky, an Austrian conductor and composer, and Arnold Schönberg's teacher. But Gustav Mahler's dislike of the text negated the possibility of a production of the ballet at the Vienna Hofoper (Court Opera) of which Mahler was then director.

Der Schüler (*The Pupil*) followed on the heels of *The Triumph of Time* in 1901. Not quite a third of the length of his first ballet, *The Pupil* was originally published in the Berlin journal *Neue Deutsche Rundschau*. The first book printing, in 1902, was in a limited edition of 2300 copies; but Hofmannsthal was dissatisfied with the work and did not want it released. The publisher, S. Fischer of Berlin, complied with his wish.

Hofmannsthal's subsequent writing of pantomime owed much to the stimulus of his friendship with the prominent Viennese dancer, Grete Wiesenthal. This relationship, as well as that between Hofmannsthal and the famed American dancer, Ruth St. Denis, is discussed at greater length in chapter 3. But insofar as it bears on Hofmannsthal's experiments with nonverbal drama, some preliminary information about it is appropriate here.

Grete Wiesenthal, singly and in concert with her two sisters, Elsa and Berta, revolutionized dance in Vienna in the early twentieth century by liberating especially the waltz from its formal tradition. Her first big role was that of Fenella in Daniel Auber's opera, *The Mute Girl from Portici*, which Gustav Mahler gave her in a show of support. After leaving the Court Opera, where she had been studying, in favor of independent choreography, Grete and her sisters overnight became the darlings of Vienna's artistic elite when they performed at the new Cabaret Fledermaus on January 14, 1908, and at the historic Kunstschau later that year. Admired above all for her splendid feeling for music and her uncanny ability to synchronize movement with dance, Grete Wiesenthal also projected the image of the new woman, unfettered from the social constraints of the past, free to express her individuality through the idiom of her body.

Of the artists who toasted her, none seemed deeper in his admiration than Hofmannsthal. Their mutual interest in pantomime seemed to parallel and then converge. Grete and her sisters had already performed (on June 7 and 8, 1907) in the pantomime *Die Tänzerin und die Marionette* (*The Dancer and the Marionette*), based on a work by the German writer Max Mell, and she was interested in the form. Hofmannsthal's friendship with the dancer grew into collaboration, the fruit of which was two pantomimes written expressly with Grete Wiesenthal in mind: *Amor und Psyche* (*Amor and Psyche*) and *Das fremde Mädchen* (*The Strange Girl*). Both works premiered in Berlin's Theater in der Königgrätzer Strasse in September 1911. They were published that same year by S. Fischer under the title *Grete Wiesenthal in "Amor und Psyche" und "Das fremde Mädchen": Szenen von Hugo von Hofmannsthal* (*Grete Wiesenthal in "Amor and Psyche" and "The Strange Girl": Scenes by Hugo von Hofmannsthal*). *The Strange Girl* was made into a film in Stockholm in May 1913 and had its premiere in the Berlin Cinés-Theater in September that year.[24]

The work was tailor-made for Grete Wiesenthal. The lead role is that of a mysterious girl; seemingly a frail beggar, she can dance entrancingly. Against her will, the girl is used by a gang of unsavory characters to lure a well-to-do young man to a squalid part of town where he is robbed, beaten, bound hand and foot, and dumped in a corner. Abandoned by the others, the girl manages to crawl to the young man and untie and revive him. But the exertion costs her her life. At the end, she lies dead in the middle of the street, the young man dazed, uncomprehending, leaning against a nearby wall.[25] *The Strange Girl* is noteworthy for its realistic setting and for exploring the dangerous fascination a criminal underworld comes to exert on a person of wealth, a theme that had preoccupied Hofmannsthal ever since his first story of 1895, *Das Märchen der 672. Nacht* (*The Tale of the 672nd Night*).

Besides her collaboration with Hofmannsthal, Grete Wiesenthal also found the opportunity to express her personal views of nonverbal performance on two separate occasions. On October 27, 1910, she delivered a lecture on dance and pantomime at the Hugo Weller Gallery in Vienna. Recalling her early entry into the world of ballet, Wiesenthal spoke also of her growing disenchantment with what she felt to be the expressive limitations of the ballet form. When she and her sisters were at last able to study piano, she realized that the movements she had come to master in ballet were executed without connection to the music. "For example," she writes, "in Coppelia, I had to adapt our eternally unchanged *pas* to Delibes' delicate and delightful music. It was just a matter of staying in time and not leaving the line, as if we were supposed to be representing a company of soldiers marching past. Nobody knew a thing about the merging of music and movement." [26]

The growing awareness of the formal restrictions of ballet awakened in her a desire to probe a different type of dance, a *wahrhaften Tanz* (true dance) that lay beyond the confines of the ballet. But there were difficulties along the way. As she experimented with new dance movements intended to be "the free expression of my feelings," she perceived—although it was natural enough—that there was something "exaggeratedly chaste" and "almost inhibited" about them in contrast to the ballet dances; with the latter, it was mainly a matter of "the purely technical training of her leg movements which then sometimes bordered almost on the unaesthetic" (38). As a result of her prior experience dancing ballet, she did not immediately grasp that she kept holding her body rigid, that her legs were not being used in any serious countermovement, and that only her arms were moving freely. This free movement of her arms had thus become the sole expression of her emotional response to the music, and was, moreover, shaped by, or tied to, the particular piece of music being played. Her first opportunity to characterize (*charakterieseren*), or interpret, came with her performance of Manon. The role, with its asymmetry, whetted her appetite for more interpretive dancing, for more contrastive movement on stage. The Italian tarantella offered her an ideal vehicle for shedding her inhibitions.

Whereas she had been previously constricted by ballet steps, Wiesenthal also began to realize that by gearing her dance movements to existing music she was imposing on herself fetters of a different kind. As new ideas for dances came to mind—inspired, for example, by things she observed in nature around her that had not yet been set to music—she understood that she had to devise a music of her own. In one instance, she chose the wind and its rhythms as a theme for an original dance composition. Yet even though this afforded her the possibility of the most varied movements and moods, she experienced a new sense of limitation: "Everything, after all was *only rhythm* and movement. All my movements were symbols" (39). For the greatest interpretive possibilities, for "the most understandable drama," she had to return to the realm of people. Thus began her entry into pantomime. Approaching Max Reinhardt with an idea for a composition of her own, she soon found herself performing in *Sûmurûn*, in her words "the first modern pantomime in higher style to be brought on stage" (39).

Now won over by the possibilities of this "new art form," Wiesenthal echoes Hofmannsthal's ideas on silence: "It is now well known that the most wondrous and strongest effects of theater pieces—I may mention, for example, Hofmannsthal's *Electra*—are achieved by mute scenes. I am thinking of the scene in which Clytemnestra is murdered, during which Electra silently strides across the stage like an animal in its cage, or her horrible dance of ecstasy at the end" (40).

In view of the antiquity of pantomime, Wiesenthal raises the question of what then distinguishes what she refers to as the new pantomime: "The new pantomime differs from the old in that it makes itself understandable *not* through a language of signs—as used, for example, by deaf mutes. Instead, the action must make clear all the large mass movements of the individual figures—their lying or sitting, standing or walking—narrated by the action" (40). In closing her lecture, she declares that dance is the highest expression of the new pantomime. That is because it seeks its expression in the formal beauty of movement unhindered by the "ridiculousness" of a language of mutes.

Wiesenthal's shorter article, "Pantomime," was published in a Dresden newspaper in 1911 the day before a guest appearance in the Zentraltheater, where she would also perform in Hofmannsthal's two pantomimes, *Amor and Psyche* and *The Strange Girl*. Dealing primarily with the latter work, the article further attests to the gratifying collaboration on pantomime between Wiesenthal and Hofmannsthal. The dancer extols Hofmannsthal's "great love of dance and deep sense of rhythm that created in him the finest feeling for the construction of wordless drama." [27] In her performance of both works, Wiesenthal expressed the hope that she would be able to show "the victory of rhythm as the essence of modern pantomime (44)."

Hofmannsthal's next work in pantomime after *Amor and Psyche* and *The Strange Girl* was *Josephslegende* (*The Legend of Joseph*). It was written in 1912 in collaboration with Count Harry Kessler, a debonair aristocrat, patron of the arts, diplomat, publisher, and longtime friend of Hofmannsthal's; Richard Strauss provided the music. The pantomime was created expressly for Diaghilev's Ballets Russes and was performed by this troupe for the first time at the Paris Opera on May 14, 1914. Its German premiere was held at the Staatsoper in Berlin on February 4, 1921.

One of Hofmannsthal's most ambitious undertakings in the genre of pantomime, *The Legend of Joseph* had the right blend of the exotic, opulent, voluptuous, and transcendent to make it a splendid vehicle for the talents of the Ballets Russes. Composed of fourteen scenes, with choreography by Count Kessler, the pantomime contrasts the two worlds represented by the figures of Joseph, the young shepherd, and the wife of the pharaoh Potiphar (she is identified in the pantomime only as "Potiphar's Wife"). Transformed into a deity-like figure, Joseph embodies an innocence and purity beyond the possession of Potiphar's wife, whose wealth and power mask an inner emptiness and yearning. Magnetically drawn to Joseph, the pharaoh's wife is determined to overcome his resistance to her. The parallel with the relationship between Salome and John the Baptist in Oscar Wilde's *Salomé* is striking. But Joseph is not the stern, austere figure that John the Baptist is in Wilde's conception. He is a fresh young spirit who combines present and future and whose agile dancing is meant to embody the life force. When Potiphar's wife realizes that she cannot revitalize her own lifeless spirit through Joseph, she orders him taken prisoner and fettered. But before he can be led away to an uncertain fate, a guardian angel descends to free him. Unable to follow them, the pharaoh's wife ends her unbearable frustration by strangling herself with the strand of pearls she wears round her neck.

Like Wedekind, Hofmannsthal thought of his major pantomimes as *Tanzpantomimen*—a rhythmically elevated form of dance-intensive pantomime reflecting the symbiotic relationship between pantomime and dance in the modernist period. In *The Legend of Joseph*, Joseph's childlike innocence and freshness is, in fact, defined through dance. Because he dances, Joseph lives. Movement, in other words, is the life force, the *élan vital*, to borrow Bergson's term. Until she witnesses Joseph's first dance, the pharaoh's wife is "cold" and "dead." She suffers the worst of all maladies from the point of view of the modernist creators of nonverbal theater, "*sie bewegt sich nicht*" ("she does not move"). However, observing Joseph, Potiphar's wife begins to feel herself truly coming alive; possessing Joseph physically is equivalent to embracing life itself. But so weighted is Potiphar's wife by the things of this earth, Joseph must remain beyond her reach, and she is thus condemned to death.

Although Joseph is the focus of the pantomime's dance element, he is not the sole dancer in the work. Of the fourteen small acts into which the pantomime is divided, four are followed by anywhere from two to four multiple dance numbers, each indicated in the original as *Tanzfigur* (dance figure). And where these dance numbers or dance scenes appear, they take up significantly more playing time than the mimed scene they follow. The variety and precision of movement and gesture demanded by Hofmannsthal can be seen, to take a single example, in Joseph's four-part dance expressive of his discovery of God:

FIRST DANCE FIGURE

Expresses the *innocence* and *naivete* of Joseph, the young shepherd. His movements present the way in which the devout youth appears before the countenance of his god and shows him, one after the other, that all his limbs—head, chest, hands, feet—are clean. He appears to say to God: "Lord, behold: my body and my heart are innocent before Thee." His movements are slow and somewhat hesitant, like those of a child who is full of misgivings, devout, and on the shy side.

SECOND DANCE FIGURE (INTERMEDIATE FIGURE)
Joseph executes *four leaps in the direction of the four winds* in a sense demarcating thereby the space in which the next dance figure is to be played.

THIRD DANCE FIGURE
Expresses the *search and struggle for God*, as well as individual moments of doubt. This figure consists in the main of high leaps . . . as if Joseph were trying to leap into the sky. But there is something heavy and earthbound about his leaps, and he falls down once or twice, like someone who missed his goal. The character of the rhythm is heavy and irregular, but not in the least hysterical or sickly. Joseph's search for God is that of a healthy, normal, childlike disposition.

From time to time, Joseph's playmates, the boys with musical instruments, dance along with him at the beginning of this figure.

FOURTH DANCE FIGURE
Joseph has found God; his movements are now a glorification of God. They differ from those of the preceding figures in their lightness. Joseph leaps now with "light feet." He seems to fly. Without exerting himself, he makes high, buoyant leaps, which express the most subtle joy. He seems to be the embodiment of divine laughter. (107–8)

Hofmannsthal wrote what appear to be preliminary sketches for two other dance works in 1912; both were discovered among his papers after his death and published posthumously. These include *Till Eugenspiegel*, first published in 1979, and *Taugenichts* (*Good-For-Nothing*), which first appeared in 1971. The latter represents the scenario for a ballet in two acts and was conceived as a present for Grete Wiesenthal, who expanded it for the composer Erich Korngold. For whatever reason, the ballet was never staged. This was not the case with *The Bee*. Based on Chinese motifs, this scenario in thirteen scenes was written expressly as the foundation for a ballet textbook to be illustrated by Grete Wiesenthal. It was published by the Drei-Masken-Verlag of Berlin in 1916. With music by Clemens von Franckenstein, *The Bee* was first performed in Darmstadt in November 1916 under the direction of Grete Wiesenthal.[28]

Chronologically, the Darmstadt premiere of *The Bee* was preceded by the first performance of *Die grüne Flöte* (*The Green Flute*), which is widely recognized as one of Hofmannsthal's most successful and appealing dance pantomimes. Based on music by Mozart and adapted by Einar Nilson, the work was staged by Reinhardt, together with Hofmannsthal's one-act *Die Lästigen* (*The Bores*), an adaptation from Molière, at the Deutsches Theater in Berlin on April 26, 1916. It was first published in Vienna in 1923. Based on Chinese motifs, like *The Bee*, the work takes place in the fairy-tale land of U, where Fay-Yen, a princess, has been imprisoned by the witch Ho and her sorcerer brother Wu. Responding to the sounds of a flute playing in the distance, the princess manages to escape. She comes across Prince Sing-Ling, the player of the jade flute, on the other side of a river, and they fall in love at first sight. But before they can reach each other, Fay-Yen is recaptured by the witch, who regains her powers when the flute stops playing. Guided by the friendly goddess of the river, Sing-Ling makes his way to U in search of Fay-Yen and engages in a ferocious battle with Wu and Ho. In the course of the battle, the sorcerer changes into a dragon and is about to vanquish the prince when the goddess of the river returns the flute to him. As soon as Sing-Ling begins to play, the dragon takes flight. The continued playing of the flute causes the sorcerer-dragon to go up in flames, and when his sister, the witch, finds his remains, she falls dead of horror. In the meantime, however, Fay-Yen, and other princes and princesses who had been taken captive by Wu and Ho, have been transformed into butterflies. Sing-Ling's playing of the flute returns them to their human forms, but Fay-Yen does not appear among them. When the prince sees her lifeless on a rock, he again plays the flute. Fay-Yen slowly awakens and she and the prince fall into each other's arms. The ballet-pantomime ends with all joining in a round dance celebrating the power of music, which Virtue and Goodness have led to victory over wicked adversity.

Recalling the appeal of Chinese art in the Rococo period (the late eighteenth-century fashion of so-called chinoiserie), Heinz Herald mentions in *Reinhardt und seine Bühne,* which he co-edited with the stage designer Ernst Stern in 1920, that in his designs for the pantomime Stern sought to recreate that China of Rococo fantasy.[29] The basic colors of his designs were black and gold, with other shades introduced only by the light. The goal of the design, as of the production itself, was the integration of all components through the severely limited but effective two-color pattern. Even the river in the fourth scene appears to descend from black hills yet has shimmering waves of gold. The actors seemed to be a part of the decorative scheme and, at the same time, in Heinz Herald's words, its rhythmic reinforcement. When the music played, it was as if they were being called to life from out of the walls.

In undertaking a production such as *The Green Flute* in 1916, Reinhardt sought to move beyond his earlier work with pantomime toward a more dance-intensive form of wordless drama akin to ballet. The successes of the Ballets Russes would also not have been lost on him. Reinhardt, in fact, drafted plans to form his own dance troupe made up of talented actors who were skilled at pantomime and specially engaged dancers such as Lillebil Christensen, a young Norwegian (she was sixteen years old at the time) whom Reinhardt met during guest appearances with the Deutsches Theater in Christiania (as Oslo was then known).[30] But these plans, together with Oskar Kaufmann's design for Reinhardt's own ballet theater, never came to fruition. Nevertheless, Reinhardt's great enthusiasm for pantomime encouraged the establishment of a society of "Mimes of the German Theater" in 1922 and, not long afterward, the International Association of Mimes, which toured with mimes who had studied with Reinhardt and Ernst Matray.

Virtually all the texts of ballet-pantomimes written by Hofmannsthal after *The Green Flute* became known after his death. *Die Schäferinnen* (*The Shepherdesses*, first published in 1971) was a one-page scenario for a ballet intended for inclusion in a translation by Count Wolf Baudissin of Molière's *Countess of Escarbagnas*, which Hofmannsthal had revised. The ballet was actually first staged together with Molière's *The Imaginary Invalid* in a production at the Kammerspiele of the Deutsches Theater in Berlin on March 16, 1916. *Prima Ballerina: Ein Tag aus dem Leben einer Tänzerin* (*Prima Ballerina: A Day in the Life of a Dancer*) was adapted by Einar Nilson, with music by Jacques Offenbach, and first published in Vienna in 1923 without Hofmannsthal's name; the first printing of the short work with Hofmannsthal listed as author came in 1954. *Divertissement*, a ballet scenario inspired in part by Schumann's *Carnival* and featuring fantasy sequences based on *Robinson Crusoe* and Schiller's *The Robbers*, was first published in 1945. *Die Ruinen von Athen* (*The Ruins of Athens*), designated *Ein Festspiel mit Tänzen und Chören* (*A Festival Performance with Dances and Choruses*), was mostly a dance work that incorporated some spoken and sung passages and featured a ballet of "Greek dances," whose music composer Richard Strauss based on Beethoven's ballet, *Die Geschöpfe des Prometheus*; the work was performed for the first time at the Vienna Opera on September 20, 1924, and was published that year as well. And last was *Achilles auf Skyros* (*Achilles on Skyros*, 1925), a ballet in one act and five scenes, the idea for which came to Hofmannsthal on April 20, 1914, on his return from Dürnstein with Max Reinhardt and Grete Wiesenthal. He picked it up again in 1918 and finally wrote the piece in 1925, the year in which it was first published. It was first performed in Stuttgart in March 1926.[31]

As we can see from the date of *Achilles on Skyros*, Hofmannsthal's interest in pantomime, dance, and ballet lasted well into the 1920s and was cultivated in a period in which he wrote such well-known dramatic works as *Der Schwierige* (*The Difficult Man*, 1919), *Das Grosse Salzburger Welttheater* (*The Great Salzburg Theater of the World*, 1922), and *Der Turm* (*The Tower*, 1924, 1926). Indeed, no better evidence exists of the enduring appeal of pantomime to Hofmannsthal than his writing of three pantomimes specifically for *The Great Salzburg Theater of the World*. The first, the short "Axt-Pantomime" ("Axe-Pantomime," 1923), was meant to resemble, as Hofmannsthal says, a "filmlike succession of images" that flash before the beggar's mind's eye from the time he raises the axe with which he intends killing the farmer and others he blames for his misery to the time he lowers his hand, without harming anyone. The second pantomime, "Christianus der Wirt" ("Christianus the Innkeeper," 1927), was originally intended as the middle piece of *The Great Salzburg Theater of the World*, but was subsequently set aside as an independent dramatic work. The longest of the pantomimes, "Gott allein kennt die Herzen" ("God Alone Knows the Heart," 1927–28) was written expressly to be performed on a Reinhardt tour of the United States.

The seriousness of Hofmannsthal's involvement in pantomime is also reflected in his essay "Über die Pantomime" ("On Pantomime," 1911), which he wrote at the height of his collaboration with Grete Wiesenthal. Despite its brevity (under four pages), the essay has been aptly described as the "most comprehensive and illuminating of all his writings on the actor and the dancer, not least because it subsumes both figures and reduces both arts to their common element of gesture."[32] With Lucian's ancient essay on dance as his point of departure, Hofmannsthal begins with the distinction between dance and pantomime. Whereas a performative, pantomimic element cannot be denied even the most primitive forms of dance, pantomime would, conversely, be unthinkable unless permeated with the rhythmic and "purely dancelike" ("*rein Tanzmässige*"). "Absent this," he declared, "we would then find ourselves in a play in which the performers would be using their hands instead of their tongues in an absurd manner, hence in a stupid and arbitrary world in which perseverance becomes oppressive."[33] But Hofmannsthal extols that form of expression that can "combine a rhythmic repetition of movements into a frame of mind, an attitude," one that can express, more concisely and meaningfully than speech permits, a relationship toward those around us," and one that can "shed light on something that is too big, too general, and too near to be captured in words." This form of expression, he went on to say, was common to "simple, heroic times, and especially to the primeval order." He saw it emerging again in his own time, "art offering us one of its ancient forms for a new revitalization" (502).

As examples of how even the simplest action can be elevated to the level of ritual, Hofmannsthal cites performances by Ruth St. Denis; the legendary Nijinsky; the Japanese actress Sada Yacco, who performed throughout Europe at the turn of the century; and the Sarah Bernhardt of *Camille*, who "from the austerity of the actions of a 'lady of the camelias' entered, as it were, the austerity of the actual stage, and the substance no longer of the well-worn theater piece, but of a humanly eternal situation, became condensed for us into moments of a truly tragic dance" (504). Stressing that the language of gesture is no more deficient in its resources than the language of speech, Hofmannsthal declares that in its own sphere "art is as inexhaustible with respect to its means of communications as nature":

> No inclination of the head, no raising of a leg, no bending of an arm is like another; here is art, and like nature it is infinite in infinite ways. A pure gesture is like a pure thought from which the momentarily clever, the restrictedly individualistic, the grotesquely characteristic are stripped. In pure thought, personality emerges by virtue of its nobility and strength, though in a way not immediately perceptible to all. Similarly, in pure gestures the true personality comes to light, and the apparent renunciation of individuality is compensated for beyond all measure. We see a human body moving in rhythmic flow in response to infinite modulations, directed along designated paths by an inner genius. It is a person like us, who moves before us, but freer than we are ever capable of moving, and yet the purity and freedom of his gestures express exactly what we want to express, when we, inhibited and clumsy, discharge our inner fullness. But is it only the freedom of the body that gladdens us so? Does not the soul reveal itself here in a special manner? (505)

Extravagant in his regard for the expressive potential of the human body and the language of gesture, Hofmannsthal now argues for the superior evocative power of the body compared to spoken speech and music:

> Words evoke a keener sympathy, but it is at the same time figurative, intellectualized, and generalized. Music, on the other hand, evokes a fiercer sympathy, but it is vague, longingly extravagant. But the sympathy summoned by gestures is clearly all-embracing, contemporary, gratifying. The language of the word is

seemingly individual, but actually generic, while the language of the body is seemingly general, but actually highly personal. Moreover, the body does not speak to the body, but the human whole speaks to the whole. (505)

Schnitzler. Around the time that Hofmannsthal's interest in pantomime was at or nearing its peak, other German writers were also contributing to the ever expanding repertoire in the genre. Among them was Arthur Schnitzler. He wrote two pantomimes, both inspired by the new interest in the Italian commedia dell'arte and the figure of Pierrot at the turn of the century.

Schnitzler's first pantomime, *Der Schleier der Pierrette* (*The Veil of Pierrette*), was begun, at least in the form of an early sketch, in 1895. But Schnitzler set the work aside for several years, instead incorporating the motif of a woman's veil left behind at her lover's place in his five-act play *Der Schleier der Beatrice* (*Beatrice's Veil*). The original *Veil of Pierrette* still on his mind, Schnitzler returned to it in 1908 and finally completed it in the form of a libretto for a ballet with music by Ernst von Dohnányi. The play was published in 1910 and premiered on January 22 that same year at the Royal Opera House in Dresden. Although overshadowed by Schnitzler's major dramatic works, *The Veil of Pierrette* achieved a certain international renown when it was adapted by the great Russian stage director, Vsevolod Meyerhold, for the opening program of the Dom intermedii (House of Interludes), which he founded in St. Petersburg in 1910 as a small show-case for his experimental productions including pantomimes and commedia dell'arte–inspired productions of one sort or another. We shall return to *The Veil of Pierrette* and Meyerhold's adaptation of it in a moment.

Schnitzler's other pantomime, *Die Verwandlung des Pierrots* (*The Transformation of Pierrot*), was written in 1908, the year in which the dramatist returned to complete *The Veil of Pierrette*. The work was never published separately nor is there a record of any performance. Let us look more closely now at Schnitzler's two pantomimes, as they are among the more interesting specimens of the genre in the early twentieth century and often overlooked in studies of Schnitzler's plays.

Set in Vienna at the beginning of the nineteenth century, *The Veil of Pierrette* tells the story of Pierrette's cruel deception of Pierrot and the terrible vengeance enacted on her by her bridegroom, Arlecchino.[34] Distraught over Pierrette's apparent abandonment of him, Pierrot cannot be cheered by friends who try to raise his spirits. They have brought with them a fat piano player (*ein dicker Klavierspieler*) whom they order to play as they form couples and dance around the forlorn, withdrawn Pierrot. Their dance, a waltz, introduces the first musical motif of the pantomime. Unable to change his mood, Pierrot's friends leave and he is soon visited by Pierrette attired in a wedding gown and with a veil over her head and shoulders. She has a vial of poison with her and seeks to convince her former lover to enter into a suicide pact with her. Pierrot at first resists and wants her to abandon the idea of suicide; this proves to no avail. He downs the poison in a glass of wine, but notices that Pierrette barely brings her own glass to her lips. Pierrot accuses her of cowardice, but when she raises the glass a second time, he scornfully knocks it from her hands. Pierrette flees in horror and reappears in the next act at the banquet hall where her own wedding to Arlecchino is to take place. The festivities set the stage for the second music and dance motif, this time the dancing of a quadrille. Unable to join in the dance because Pierrette is nowhere to be seen, Arlecchino explodes in a fit of anger and smashes everything around him, including the musicians' instruments. The violence of the scene foreshadows the grim finale to the pantomime.

When Pierrette reappears as mysteriously as she disappeared, Arlecchino demands that she dance with him. The musicians at first balk at playing because of their damaged instruments, but Arlecchino insists and they launch into a fast polka that assumes a grotesque quality because of the weird sound of the music. This mad dance, as it were, serves as a fitting prelude to the appearance of Pierrot's ghost, whom only Pierrette can see. When the music stops and Arlecchino notices that Pierrette's veil is missing, he demands to know what became of it. Pierrot then appears at the rear of the banquet hall holding the veil in his hand. Pierrette races toward him, Arlecchino in hot pursuit.

The third and last act returns the action to Pierrot's room where the pantomime began. Arlecchino and Pierrette come upon the body of the dead Pierrot, Pierrette's veil nearby. Arlecchino at first believes him drunk and begins to berate him. When he discovers that his "rival" is dead, he props Pierrot's body up on a sofa, sits at a table facing the corpse, pours two glasses of wine, and drinks to Pierrot's health. Played out in the wan, flickering light of dying candles, the scene becomes nightmarish. After getting Pierrette to drink the other glass of wine, Arlecchino leaves the room, locking Pierrette in behind him. Alone with the corpse of her former lover, Pierrette quickly descends into madness, first frenziedly trying to escape the room, then dancing around Pierrot in ever wider arcs until she collapses, dead, at his feet. When other members of the wedding party gaily enter the now broken door to the room in the morning, they discover the two corpses and recoil in horror.

Schnitzler's darker approach to pantomime brings him closer to the Wedekind of *The Empress of Newfoundland* than to Hofmannsthal. Meyerhold, who regarded the grotesque as the art most appropriate to the early twentieth century, seized on this aspect of *The Veil of Pierrette* in his own production—retitled *Columbine's Scarf*—at the House of Interludes. But the Russian director sought to accentuate the grotesque element of the pantomime, to infuse it even more with the spirit of E. T. A. Hoffmann. He accomplished this by abandoning the three acts of the original in favor of fourteen short, fast-moving scenes meant to convey the ever more frenzied, "mad" pace of the action, and by transforming the figure of the fat piano player into that of a hideous, huge-headed conductor leading a group of four musicians who can only be described as weird. The scene in which the quadrille is danced at the banquet hall is also rendered more grotesque as strange characters whirl about the dance floor to the music of the strange band, being conducted by a bandmaster perched on a high stool above them. When the bodies of Pierrot and Pierrette are discovered at the end of the play, the bandmaster races through the auditorium in terror as if bearing some personal responsibility for the tragedy. In Meyerhold's *Columbine's Scarf*, it is also Pierrot, distraught over Columbine's impending marriage to Harlequin, who proposes the suicide pact.[35]

In both *The Veil of Pierrette* and the temperamentally different *The Transformation of Pierrot*, Schnitzler departed from the usual convention of pantomime by including lines of spoken dialogue. However, the first time this occurs, he introduces a footnote to the effect that even though his characters sometimes speak in his text, what they say will be expressed only pantomimically in performance.

The Transformation of Pierrot consists of a prelude followed by six acts and is thus longer than *The Veil of Pierrette*. The Pierrot of *The Transformation* is a performer in a small troupe of entertainers in Vienna's Prater amusement park. Schnitzler had used a similar setting in his "marionette play" *Zum grossen Wurstl* (*The Great Puppet Show*), which was written in 1901–4. Fancying himself a ladies' man, Pierrot flirts with a young woman, Katharina, whose house he passes one day. Katharina is portrayed as a dreamer surrounded by bourgeois mundaneness, including her intended, Eduard. Although she feigns disinterest in Pierrot's flirtation, he is persistent and slips into her bedroom one night for a romantic tryst unbeknownst either to her parents or to her fiancé.

When Katharina and Pierrot meet again, he is performing at the Prater. Confused as to his identity—the first of several "transformations" by Pierrot—she does not immediately recognize him as the Pierrot of her romantic meeting. As Katharina, Eduard, and her parents make their way to other amusements at the Prater, Pierrot follows them unseen. Sneaking inside the different booths they visit, one way or another he manages to assume the identity of the different proprietors, becoming in turn a swing attendant, a photographer, a fortune teller, and a target drummer figure in a shooting gallery. With each new transformation, Katharina becomes more disturbed, unable to tell the real Pierrot from the transformed actor, unable, in essence, to distinguish illusion from reality. When she fires at the drummer in the shooting gallery and hits the target, Pierrot's face suddenly appears where the drummer's had been. Believing she has killed Pierrot, Katharina runs away distraught. But he catches up with her and tries to convince her that because she loves him, he is ever in her thoughts and so she imagines that she sees him everywhere. Just as Katharina is on the verge of believing him, other members of Pierrot's troupe, including his fiancée, Anna, the theater director's daughter who also plays Columbine in the play-within-the-play, rush in and denounce him for deserting them. When the other characters Pierrot pretended to be show up as well, his game is up. As merry music is heard coming from the Prater, Pierrot quickly regains his composure and invites everyone to join him in celebrating his engagement to Anna. Resigned now to the reality of her own situation, Katharina tells Eduard that she is again his bride. As the two groups move off in different directions at play's end, Katharina and Pierrot exchange bittersweet glances knowing they will never see each other again.

The blurring of the boundaries between illusion and reality, which Schnitzler portrays in *The Transformation of Pierrot*, preoccupied many turn-of-the-century artists. Schnitzler himself had already dealt with the theme as early as 1899 in *Der grüne Kakadu* (*The Green Cockatoo*), arguably the best of his one-act plays, and a few years after that in *The Great Puppet Show*. The intriguing possibility also exists that *The Transformation of Pierrot* was the inspiration for *Samoe glavnoe* (*The Chief Thing*, 1919), the best-known play by the Russian dramatist, director, and theorist of theater, Nikolai Evreinov. Like Schnitzler, whose work was translated into Russian by Meyerhold, among others, Evreinov was similarly attracted to commedia dell'arte and wrote a few Harlequinades, of which the widely known *Vesyolaya smert* (*A Merry Death*, 1908) is clearly the best. Evreinov's interest in the Harlequinade coincided with Schnitzler's, so that it is quite likely that the Russian, stimulated as well by Meyerhold's version of *The Veil of Pierrette*, subsequently followed the Austrian's career and found in *The Transformation of Pierrot* the inspiration for *The Chief Thing*. The only play by Evreinov ever to be staged commercially in the United States (by the Theatre Guild of New York in 1926), *The Chief Thing* is not a short pantomime, like Schnitzler's *The Transformation of Pierrot*, but a full-length dramatic work that serves as a major vehicle for Evreinov's ideas on the transformation of life through theater. The character analogous to Schnitzler's Pierrot is the mysterious Paraclete, who appears in several disguises, including that of a fortune-teller and Harlequin.[36]

Carl Einstein. The year (1910) that saw the completion and first performance of Schnitzler's *The Veil of Pierrette* brought yet another German-language contribution to early twentieth-century pantomime in the form of Carl Einstein's *Nuronihar.* Since *this* Einstein does not enjoy immediate name recognition, a few words about him are in order.

Born in the Rhineland into a Jewish family in 1885, Einstein eventually earned his reputation as a provocative, left-wing, vehemently antibourgeois art critic and theorist whose literary contributions were mainly essays published in journals with which he himself was associated.[37] These included, among others, *Der blutige Ernst* (*Bloody Ernest*), a satirical-political journal edited by Einstein and the artist Georg Grosz; *Die Pleite* (*The Flop*); *Der Querschnitt* (*The Cross-Section*); and *Das Kunstblatt* (*The Journal of Art*). Einstein's play *Die schlimme Botschaft* (*The Bad News*, 1921) got him into trouble for alleged blasphemy, resulting in the confiscation of all copies of the work and a fine. In 1928, two years after his book on twentieth-century art, *Die Kunst des 20. Jahrhunderts* (*The Art of the Twentieth Century*), appeared, Einstein settled in Paris. It was here in 1929 that he founded the journal *Documents, Doctrines, Archéologie, Beaux Arts* together with Georges Bataille, the art dealer Georges Wildenstein, and Georges Henri Rivière and also became advisory editor to the journal *Transition*, with which James Joyce collaborated. Among the avant-garde authors *Transition* published were August Stramm, Gertrude Stein, and Samuel Beckett. Einstein's study on the painter Georges Braque (*Georges Braque*) appeared in 1934; two years later, Einstein went off to Spain to participate in the Spanish Civil War as a member of one of the International Brigades. After Franco's victory, Einstein returned to Paris, where the outbreak of World War II and the German invasion of France resulted in his arrest and eventual transfer to an internment camp in Bordeaux. Although he might have had a chance to escape to Spain over the Pyrenees, following the example of other Jewish refugees, Einstein's participation in the Spanish Civil War on the side of the Loyalists negated that possibility. In despair, he committed suicide in 1940.

Like other writers whose fascination with pantomime was inspired by a particular dancer or dancers and who saw in pantomime a new vehicle for dance, Einstein's muse was the Paris-born Polish dancer Stasia Napier-kowsa. Although she began her career as a classical ballet dancer, Napierkowska's considerable popularity was achieved both as a solo interpreter of a variety of exotic and romantic roles and as a lead dancer in several revues. It was in the latter capacity, for example, that she appeared at New York's Palace Theater on March 24, 1913, where she was billed as "La Napierkowska, pantomimist and Dancer."[38]

Einstein's sole pantomime, *Nuronihar* (1913), was dedicated to Napierkowska. It was preceded by a public homage, more a paean, in the form of a letter, "Brief an die Tänzerin Napierkowska" ("Letter to the Dancer Napierkowska"), which was published in the journal *Der Gegenwart* (*The Present Age*) in 1911 after Einstein had seen Napierkowska perform in a pantomime accompanied by Russian music. Einstein's characteristic provocativeness is plainly in evidence in the opening sentence: "Perhaps nothing detracts from the word so much as dance."[39] In the amplification of his remark, he dwells more on the unique properties of dance as exemplified by the art of Napierkowska than on pantomime as such. Expressing his appreciation of the autonomous language of the body, Einstein emphasizes its freedom from superfluity and sentimentality, yet its power to summon responses that are indescribable:

> Gestures, decided by the wisdom of your body, the knowledge of your limbs. Lines that flatter space, curves that whirl unforgettably for nights on end in the empty theater. To you everything is the uniform movement of total form. We remembered the entire body, not partial qualities. . . .
>
> We recalled the women dancers of Sakkarah, and Greek vases, whose unalterable themes took on new meanings. We recognized your will toward the classical, toward tradition, not that of Pavlova, the remnants of a morbidly lingering rococo, but rather a self-acquired tradition. . . . Only your body writhed before our eyes; everything that could remind us of the sentimental or the spiritual—invisible, dark emotions—was extinguished. Plato must have loved the clear rightness of this dance. We forget everything dark; what remains is the indestructible fabric of your curves. . . .
>
> You endowed us with joy so that we understood—how rare—why people can regard themselves as beautiful, perhaps reminding themselves of a mythical dancer. Yet you gave no beauty that is only observed if it uses sentimentality for support. We enjoyed a passion that is utterly unspiritual. . . .
>
> Your dance is total reason and objectivity. You offer no examples of trained feet—man and space remain unmoved—nor of the banality of flirting fingers. You never forget the unity of your entire body. . . .
>
> We are not experiencing here the dilettante ideology of a "pure" art. You ignore the drama since your body must disdain enhancement through liter-

ary contents . . . Your ascendance is barely endurable, but not literary. It is a logical consequence of gestures, and together with you, when you collapse on stage, something mythical is destroyed that remains unforgettable in our sluggish blood. . . . I have no idea at all how we can continue to be happy after seeing so much beauty. In the future we will be even more scornful; you drew us into something great that makes us shudder before the gesture of the bourgeois even more than previously. For never before did we see so clearly that art is only a kind of beauty. (57–59)

Nuronihar, Einstein's sole pantomime, has an opulent Eastern setting in the style of Reinhardt's *Sûmurûn*. It is based on the novel *Vathek: An Arabian Tale* (1786) by the English writer William Beckford. Nuronihar is a dancer in the realm of the mighty caliph, Vathek. As portrayed by Einstein, she is "a girl who from the start commands the ways of the female sex without ever having developed them; . . she is too preoccupied with herself, and especially her body, to be really interested in another person." Nuronihar, in sum, can express herself only through her body, physically, in dance, and this she does superbly: "Every impression, and whatever she sees, is transformed into rhythmic movement" (174). In a preamble to the pantomime, Einstein makes it clear that the central element in the work is dance, that dance alone, in fact, constitutes the drama and determines everything else. The sets, lighting, and costumes—which are described in sumptuous detail—are there just to "serve, orient, and illuminate the composition of the dance movements" (175). From beginning to end, Nuronihar's dancing dominates the pantomime; each of its three scenes is built around a different dance motif and reduces everything else to relative insignificance.

In the first scene, Nuronihar's dance before Vathek is seductive, even lascivious, intended to establish her power over him. Taking a stand on expressive dance versus classical ballet, Einstein sarcastically contrasts Nuronihar's dancing with that of a ballet troupe who perform first for the caliph: "the classical ballet troupe dances in, attired in sky-blue, pink, and sea-green gauze tutus. They execute a dance of sylphs as classical as it is imbecilic. It presents a dragon-fly hunt, followed by the usual homage to the queen, with palm fronds, and so on. This tender and sweet thing teems with precise toe drills, pirouettes, and the like" (176). However, in the dancing of Nuronihar and others who dance with her, including Vathek himself, their entire bodies come alive with rhythm. Their movements have nothing to do with realistic gestures: "There are no movements of arms and legs, there is no mimicry, only a rhythmic excitation of the entire person. Nuronihar's dance rhythmicizes everything" (174).

In the second scene, the huge figure of the giaour appears. He holds a crystal ball that has the power to draw people to it like the stars. So obsessed does Nuronihar become with the desire to embrace it, she is transformed from a young girl into a "terribly demanding woman." Fixated on the great jewel, she now performs a dance of craving as passionate as the dance of seduction in the first scene. The third and last scene of the pantomime is set in a great cathedral with an underground vault containing the jewel; entrance to it is guarded by the giaour. When the caliph tries to break free of Nuronihar's spell, she removes her clothes as she dances, not coquettishly, but rather as if captivated by her own body. Again succumbing to her spell, the caliph remains. The closer Nuronihar dances to him, the more erotically suggestive the dance becomes. It also turns murderous when Vathek tries to prevent the dancer from going after the giaour's jewel. As Vathek's back is turned, Nuronihar pulls his sword from its scabbard and stabs him with it. He collapses, dead, in the gaiour's arms and both fall to the ground, thereby leaving the entrance to the vault unguarded. Accompanied by increasingly wilder and strange music, Nuronihar leaps over a circle of fire in order to reach the jewel; but the fire envelops her, and she burns in it, "crackling, amid ecstatically agonizing dances" (183).

There is no evidence that *Nuronihar* was ever performed despite the fact the Einstein once offered it to Jacques Rouché, the director of the Paris Opera.[40] Had it been, the exciting dancing written chiefly for Stasia Napierkowska, its sumptuous sets and costumes, and its hypnotically effective play of light and dark in the last scene might well have established it as a rival to Reinhardt's *Sûmurûn*.

Kuzmin. Since pantomime is universally understood to be nonverbal drama, one would imagine that nothing else could be said on that point. And even though Schnitzler introduced dialogue in his pantomimes, as we have seen, he did indicate that the lines were not to be spoken during an actual performance. A different and somewhat curious approach to the matter of the wordlessness of pantomime was taken by the Russian writer, Mikhail Kuzmin.

A gifted, multifaceted poet, prose writer, and musician, Kuzmin's dramatic writing was an integral part of his active participation in Russian cabaret and experimental theater in the early twentieth century. Virtually all his plays are short and intended for performance in the intimate surroundings of such artistically noteworthy St. Petersburg cabarets as Brodyachaya sobaka (The Stray Dog) and Prival komediantov (The Comics' Halt) or in small theaters on the order of Meyerhold's House of Interludes or the Liteyny. A talented musician who collaborated with Meyerhold on several productions, Kuzmin had a natural affinity for dance and interspersed dance, song, and dialogue in several small-scale dramatic works obviously best suited for presentation in the spatially more limited confines of cabaret and experimental theater. These included *Gollandka Liza* (*Liza from Holland*, written in 1910, published 1911), a one-act pastoral with dancing and singing; *Fenominalnaya Amerikanka* (*The Phenomenal American Girl*, written in 1911), a one-act vaudeville with dancing and singing; *Feya, fagot i mashinist* (*Fairy, Bassoon, and Machinist*, written in 1915), another one-act vaudeville with dancing and singing; and *Tantsmeyster s Kherestrita* (*The Dancing Master of London*, written in 1917, first staged in the Comics' Halt on November 2, 1918), also a one-act vaudeville with dancing and singing.

Kuzmin was intent on cultivating all the "small" theatrical forms then in vogue among cabaretists and devotees of intimate theater. And so, apart from one-act plays and vaudevilles, he wrote puppet shows for both adults and children and pantomimes. Like a number of his contemporaries (Vladimir Mayakovsky, among them), Kuzmin was also keenly attracted to the new medium of cinema. Before assessing his contribution to pantomime, we should first consider his views on the genre as expressed in his article "O pantomime, kinematografe i razgovornykh pesakh" ("On Pantomime, Cinematography, and Plays with Dialogue," 1914).

Kuzmin mentions at the outset that the article arose from his recent enthusiasm for pantomime—in which, by the way, the Russians, like the Germans, have no real tradition—and his serious thoughts about cinematography rather than about moviemaking as such. Since only silent films existed at the time, the link between pantomime and cinematography, as the "silent" genres, and spoken drama was logical. Although he understood that pantomime by definition was a play without dialogue Kuzmin was unwilling entirely to repudiate the word and so sought a way to create pantomime without totally surrendering the element of spoken speech in it:

> As a person who loves literature and poetry and is himself involved with them, I cannot and am unable to reject the word and exchange it for some sort of pretty and attractive spectacle. Of course, the theater is a conventional entity. If in opera we can present singing personages, then why cannot we imagine silent heroes? But the fact of the matter is that in the operatic performance the obscuring (but not absence) and conventionality of speech are compensated in part by the music which intensifies the psychological experiences of the dramatis personae. The same can be said about ballet, in which the simple plot is illustrated by dances and music. In other words, musical and choreographical art

are united with verbal art, depriving the latter, of course, of a certain part of its effective strength but adding their own charm hence in certain circumstances even strengthening the general impression. . . . Perhaps purely conversational, literary plays may seem boring and old-fashioned to us, but it strikes me that this is more the result of the insufficiency among our artists of purely verbal technique, of their inability to attract, delight, terrify, and amuse an audience with brisk, living, diverse speech. . . . The absence of words in pantomime or the ballet . . . demonstrates only the unwillingness or inability to find adequately expressive and brisk words that would not retard the tempo of the action. It seems to me that the task of dramatic writers should be the harmonious union and reconciliation of these two elements so that a play that corresponded to the demands of verbal art would at the same time have a pantomimic plan. In one and the same work there would be, so to say, two outlines, precisely coinciding with one another; each scene, and all the scenes in their entirety, giving the artist the full possibility of demonstrating his verbal talent, would present the same harmonious plan as well for the director-balletmaster. This does not mean that the words will illustrate the pantomime, or the other way around, but that both elements will be necessary. In this way, the literary part of the drama would be deprived of those verbal longueurs (even if of first-class value) that are not beyond the skill of our performers, while the pantomimic spectacle would be deprived of its busyness and would instead acquire a logical and aesthetic sense, precisely corresponding to the intentions of the author.[41]

Of Kuzmin's three pantomimic works, the first, *Vybor nevesty* (*The Choice of a Bride*), was written in 1906 and so antedates the ideas expressed in "On Pantomime, Cinematography, and Plays with Dialogue." Subtitled a "mimetic ballet" and only two pages long, *The Choice of a Bride* was first staged in 1910 at a concert in St. Petersburg by M. A. Vedrinskaya. It was performed a second time in 1913 at the Liteyny Theater, the most highly regarded of the privately owned, intimate theaters for which early twentieth-century St. Petersburg was justifiably renowned. With the Eastern setting so popular among pantomimists at the time, *The Choice of a Bride* is built around the motif of dance in which Kuzmin was then greatly interested. Pipet, a girl, loves Mirliton but does not dance well enough to win his heart. His servant, Kadeli, berates him for this, but Mirliton explains that he swore to honor his father's dying request that he marry only an outstanding dancer. Even the dancing of Gülnara, the sultan's daughter, and her Turkish companions fail to please him.

Kadeli decides to cure Mirliton of his "madness." He dresses in women' clothes, dons a mask, has Mirliton summoned, and then dances before him in a way that leaves his master excited to the point where he gets down on his knees and declares his love for the dancer. When Kadeli reveals his true identity, Mirliton falls into a faint. Regaining his senses, he realizes the error of his ways, renounces his oath to his father, and offers his heart to Pipet, who, he declares none too romantically, is "a bad dancer, but nevertheless a girl."[42] As if to show him up, Pipet then dances a splendid waltz, which takes Mirliton pleasantly by surprise. Gülnara, who has been admiring Kadeli all along, immediately beckons him to her and the ballet ends on this generally satisfying note.

Although preceding by several years his article "On Pantomime, Cinematography, and Plays with Dialogue," *The Choice of a Bride* adumbrates Kuzmin's later views on the compatibility of dialogue and pantomime. The thin little work is nothing more than a pretext for dance. The small amount of dialogue is clearly outweighed by the dance scenes, first that of Pipet, followed by those of Gülnara and the Turkish girls, then Kadeli's in disguise, and finally Pipet's waltz at the end. The pantomimic element of the ballet is further strengthened by the mimed action preceding or accompanying the dance scenes, so that, in the aggregate, the few lines of dialogue in the work neither detract from nor compromise the overwhelmingly nonverbal nature of the work. To be sure, the sparse dialogue is could be dispensed with, the same ideas conveyed as well in mime. But there is one exception—Mirliton's oath to respect his father's wish that he marry an outstanding dancer. Since Kuzmin chose to build the story around this oath, he then had to verbalize it as there would have been virtually no way he could have accommodated it by mimed action.

Kuzmin's enthusiasm for dance need not have been the sole or even principal rationale for a mostly pantomimic trifle like *The Choice of a Bride*. An avowed homosexual, which hurt his literary reputation especially during the Soviet period in Russia, Kuzmin was not averse to manifesting his sexual preference in his writing. The cross-dressing of Kadeli and the romantic-erotic effect his dancing has on Mirliton, unlike that of the women who dance for him, is unequivocal evidence of this. But whatever the roots of *The Choice of a Bride*, the "mimetic ballet" exemplifies Kuzmin's untraditional approach to pantomime a few years before he wrote his article on the genre. This lack of reverence for the long history of pantomime may be understood, in part, by the absence of a tradition in Russia with which Kuzmin could identify.

Kuzmin's next pantomime, *Dukhov den v Toledo* (*All Souls' Day in Toledo*), was written around the same time as his article on pantomime and appears to have been designed as an exemplification of the views advanced in the article. The work was staged—only once—on March 23, 1915, by the Moscow Kamerny Theater under the direction of Aleksandr Tairov. The pantomime also seems to have been commissioned by Tairov so that the season in which it was performed would be represented by at least one pantomime, given the contemporary interest in nonverbal drama. As Tairov himself declared:

> Not wishing to be left that year (1914) without a work in pantomime, we found ourselves in a very difficult position in view of the fact that *all the literature on pantomime belongs to German authors and composers* [italics mine] . . . . We then turned to Russian authors, and M. A. Kuzmin showed an interest in our proposal and wrote the pantomime *All Souls' Day in Toledo. This work is the first effort by a Russian writer in the sphere of pantomime* [italics mine].[43]

The one performance of *All Souls' Day in Toledo* did not, however, work out to the satisfaction of author or director. Divided into three acts and three scenes and longer by a few pages than *The Choice of a Bride*, *All Souls' Day in Toledo* has a Spanish setting and the familiar ingredients of a work about Spain by a non-Spanish writer: hot-blooded Spaniards ready to plunge a dagger into someone over a real or presumed insult to one's honor; the haughty, flirtatious Spanish woman; intense jealousy and rivalry over a man between two women, culminating in the suicide of one; the revenge murder of the other woman; and a fervent Catholic religious procession. The women in question are Rosalia and Maria; Maria is Fernando's fiancée, who eventually kills herself over her intended's romantic interest in the flirtatious Rosalia. At the end, a remorseful Rosalia, holding herself responsible for Maria's suicide, embraces a huge nearby cross, then rushes over to the bishop heading the religious procession on the road to Toledo to beg forgiveness. But immediately thereafter, Juan, who has made no secret of his affection for Maria and his contempt for Fernando's flirtation with Rosalia, steals up to her and kills her.

The trite plot is a secondary consideration in evaluating Kuzmin's success or lack of success in implementing his ideas on pantomime. Although there is mimed action in *All Souls' Day in Toledo*—most notably Rosalia's seductive dancing for Fernando's benefit and public dancing and an outdoor marionette show in the vicinity of Toledo—the pantomime as a whole has much more dialogue than any other pantomimic work by Kuzmin. The dialogue, however, consists of very short sentences, so that the work can to a great extent be imagined without it. As in *The Choice of a Bride*, dance is the most important component of the mimed aspect of the play. The Punch-and-Judy-type marionette show, in which Pierrot kills

Harlequin because of Colombine's flirtation with him—the meaning of which Juan applies to the relationship between Maria, Rosalia, and Fernando—is not quite the same since it lasts a shorter period of time than the dance scenes. In fairness to Kuzmin's ideas about pantomime and his obvious desire to retain the presence of the spoken word, it should be said that while the pantomime might succeed without any speech, the dialogue, essentially unobtrusive in its briskness and brevity, as Kuzmin desired, complements the mimed action by obviating the necessity for the additional action necessary to convey the same sense. What Kuzmin was striving for was sufficient dialogue to eliminate the gestural "busyness" (or fussiness) he decries in his article on pantomime. Since his goal was a modern (and modernist) interpretation of pantomime, only minimally beholden to the long tradition of the genre, he saw nothing offensive about preserving just enough dialogue to avoid excessive gesturing and too little dialogue without the essential pantomimic nature of the work being called into question.

Unfortunately, Tairov's production proved a disappointment to him. Having equipped Tairov with the literary outline of the play, in the form of the dialogue, it was Kuzmin's understanding that the renowned director would work out all the mimed action along the lines of Kuzmin's stage directions. Apparently things did not turn out that way, and despite a favorable reception by the audience, critics dismissed the work as flawed. They complained about the inadequacy and inappropriateness of the music—the chief complaint from all the critics—the banality of the subject matter, the unrealized operatic quality of the piece, and the apparent diminution of the spoken element of the play to its detriment since it was felt that the action was insufficient to carry the play as a whole.[44]

Despite the setback with his Spanish pantomime, Kuzmin was willing to take another stab at the genre and in 1916 wrote his last pantomime, *Vlublyonny dyavol* (*The Devil in Love*). Five scenes long and just a little shorter than *All Souls' Day in Toledo*, the work is based on a novel of the same name by the French writer Jacques Cazotte (1719–92). The novel was published in 1772; the serialization of a Russian translation of it in the journal *Severnye zapiski* (*Northern Notes*) in 1915 presumably provided the inspiration for Kuzmin's pantomime. Whether his experience with *All Souls' Day in Toledo* had anything to do with it or not—and the fact that he based the pantomime on a French novel would also appear to be of no importance in this regard—Kuzmin did something of an about-face in *The Devil in Love* by drastically reducing the dialogic component relative to mimed action.

Amid a setting of Italian ruins, a young man named Alvar conjures up the devil in the form of a woman named Biondetta, who appears first as the head of a camel. Dressed as a page, Biondetta is ready to do his every bidding. When he loses heavily in a Venetian gambling casino, she produces bag after bag of gold until he finally wins. When he accuses her of being a demon, she avers that she is only his loving servant. Other strange events follow, until at last a mournful, weeping Biondetta coaxes Alvar into declaring his love for her as well. But as they kiss and exchange vows of love, Biondetta's face becomes more passionate and terrifying, and she admits that it is Beelzebub who loves Alvar. Shortly thereafter, an enormous camel descends between them from above. As Alvar makes the sign of the cross in sweeping gestures, "Biondetta" flies away like a cloud.

After his frustrating experience with the staging of *All Souls' Day in Toledo*, and possibly convinced that he was never going to make the case for his own view of pantomime, Kuzmin turned to a more conventional type of pantomime in *The Devil in Love*. He was still unwilling to entirely abandon dialogue but reduced it in this work to some two dozen lines of just a few words each. Mimed action definitely predominates, but the pantomime is arguably Kuzmin's least interesting and attracts attention mostly for its undertones of homoerotic love, as in *The Choice of a Bride*, and its Venetian setting. This was not the first time that Kuzmin used a Venetian carnival background. One of his best dramatic works, *Venetsiasnkie bezumtsy* (*The Venetian Madcaps*, 1912), is set in eighteenth-century Venice, "the Venice of Goldoni, Gozzi, and Longhi."[45] Divided into two acts and featuring prose and verse, as well as singing and dancing, the work represents Kuzmin's most effective use of the masks of the Italian commedia dell'arte. But the Venetian carnival setting itself serves as a mask concealing homosexual love, female seduction, and murder. A pantomime is also called for in the play, but remains largely unrealized, further demonstrating Kuzmin's essential discomfort with pantomime in its pure form. A splendid writer, with a great feeling for language, Kuzmin, his strong interest in dance and his musical abilities notwithstanding, could never wholeheartedly embrace nonverbal drama. And so in *The Venetian Madcaps*, his verbally richest play, the pantomime that is supposed to be performed with the key figures wearing the traditional masks of the commedia dell'arte never actually takes place.

Kandinsky. Although usually studied independently of the new rise of pantomime at the turn of the century, the Russian painter Wassily Kandinsky's experimental stage composition, *Der gelbe Klang* (*The Yellow Sound*), may be thought of as a species of wordless drama related to pantomime. Inspired, as others before him—Maeterlinck, for example—to break out of the confines of traditional drama by shifting the theatrical axis from external to internal experience, Kandinsky wrote *The Yellow Sound* as an exemplification of his views. He expressed these in a preface of sorts to *The Yellow Sound* under the title "Über Bühnenkomposition" ("On Stage Composition"). Taking issue with the concentration of the nineteenth century on material phenomena and the material aspect of phenomena, Kandinsky dismissed the drama of the preceding century as

> in general a more or less refined and profound narration of events of a more or less personal character. It is usually a description of external life, where the spiritual life of man is involved only insofar as it has to do with his external life.
>
> *The cosmic element is completely lacking. The external event, and the external unity of the action comprise the form of drama today.*[46]

Opera and ballet are dismissed for basically similar reasons:

> Apart from the fact that Wagner remained entirely in the old tradition of the external, despite his efforts to create a text (movement), he still neglected the third element, which, in isolated instances, is used today in a still more primitive form—color, and connected with it, pictorial form (decoration).
>
> *The external event, the external connection between its individual parts and the two means employed (drama and music), is the form of opera today.*
>
> Ballet is a drama with all the characteristics already described and the same content. Only here, the seriousness of drama loses even more than in opera. In opera, in addition to love, other themes occur: religious, political, and social conditions become the ground upon which enthusiasm, despair, honor, hatred, and other similar feelings grow. Ballet contents itself with love in the form of a childish fairy-tale. Apart from music, individual and group movements are made use of as well. Everything remains in a naive form of external unity. It even happens in practice that individual dances are included or omitted at will. The "whole" is so problematic that such transactions remain completely unnoticed.
>
> *External action, the external connection between its individual parts and the three means employed today (drama, music, and dance) is the form of ballet today.* (55)

Viewing the question from the standpoint of the internal, however, Kandinsky finds that the external appearance of each element vanishes and that its inner value takes on its "full sound," sound in the sense in which Kandinsky uses it here connoting resonance or affective power. Once the inner sound is used, the external action can become incidental and even dangerous insofar as it obscures our view. External unity is thus shown to be a weakness rather than a strength in that it unnecessarily limits or weakens

the inner effect. Applying his ideas to practical stage composition, Kandinsky declares that it is possible to take only the inner sound of an element
as one's means and that action (which he refers to as the "external proce-
dure") can be dispensed with, which in turn causes the external connection
between the parts to collapse of its own accord. The more one comes to
appreciate the necessity of the inner unity, the greater the awareness of the
external lack of unity. Concluding his analysis of the inherent weaknesses
of traditional stage composition as attributable to its externality, its preoccupation with "action" and those means that advance action, Kandinsky
offers in *The Yellow Sound* a short work designed to serve as an example of
new creative directions.[47]

The composition is divided into an introduction and six scenes of different length. Although a few voices are heard speaking several understandable words in the introduction and in scene two, the work has virtually no
dialogue. The texts of the introduction and the six scenes just describe the
setting and the action, such as it is, in the manner of traditional pantomime.
In view of the importance of color to Kandinsky, much of the composition
is taken up with the interplay of various colors, which often change to the
tempo of the music, and with dark and light scenic effects. Human figures
appear from the second scene on in *The Yellow Sound*; they are seen in large
numbers, are assigned almost no speech, and vie for attention with huge
bright yellow giants with indistinct faces who dominate much of the action
through the rest of the work and sing, or intone, meaningless words. A number of people wearing "long, garish, shapeless garments" in different colors
also enter in scene two holding large white flowers that resemble the flower
on the hill in the background. These people are the only figures in the work
who speak actual words. In various voices, they recite the following lines:

> The flowers cover all, cover all, cover all.
> Close your eyes! Close your eyes!
> We look. We look.
> Cover conception with innocence.
> Open your eyes! Open your eyes!
> Gone. Gone. (276)

After their joint recitation, which is spoken very distinctly ("as if in ecstasy," Kandinsky notes), the people repeat the same words individually,
one after the other—alto, bass, and soprano voices. As they do, different
colors dominate the stage coordinated with the pattern of the singing. Attention then shifts to a mass of tiny figures crossing the hill from right to
left, indistinct and having an indeterminate grayish color. When the people

already on the stage see this endless line of figures, they act terrified, throw away the flowers they are carrying, and run together toward the front of the stage. It suddenly turns dark.

The giants reappear in the short third scene and barely move throughout it. Attention centers mostly on the brightly colored rays that fall from all sides, meet in the center, and become intermingled. The colors then vanish almost as soon as they have appeared. After a short period in which the stage is sunk in darkness, a dull yellow light comes up and intensifies until the whole stage is a bright lemon yellow. The music in the background moves contrariwise to the light; the more intense the light suffusing the stage, the darker and deeper the music. As this occurs, no objects are visible on stage; light dominates everything. When the brightest level of light is reached, the music dissolves and the giants again become distinguishable. They seem bigger. After a long pause, a shrill tenor voice is heard from offstage. It is "filled with fear," shouting "entirely indistinguishable" words very quickly; only the letter *a* can be made out. Kandinsky at this point illustrates the type of "word" in which the frequency of *a* might be met: "Kalasimunafakola."

Discernible individual human figures appear in scene four. As a very fat man garbed all in black watches, a small child pulls the rope of a brass bell on a Chagallesque crooked building resembling a "very simple chapel." When the man yells, "Silence!" the child drops the rope, and the stage becomes dark.

The fifth scene is the longest in *The Yellow Sound*. From the point of view of action, it is also the most interesting, albeit difficult to summarize in a few words. Attention alternates between giants making odd gestures and a mass of people clad in tights of different colors, the hair on their heads corresponding to their attire and their actions resembling those of marionettes. They are joined by gray, black, white, and different-colored people. The various groups execute a variety of unrelated movements. When they finally take up different seated positions on the stage, the music undergoes frequent changes of tempo, during some of which one of the white figures executes a kind of dance that sometimes corresponds with the music. All the other figures on stage gradually begin staring at him until the dance ends abruptly and the dancer sits down, "stretches out one arm as if in ceremonious preparation and, slowly bending this arm at the elbow, brings it toward his head" (281). The giants, who now become visible, stand motionless and erect, but are heard whispering. As individual colors resound from the orchestra, red light travels across the stage, and the giants begin to tremble in alternation with the passage of light. Before long, movement is noticeable at different ends of the stage. Various people move in and out of groups that constantly split up and then reform. Gradually everything takes on an arhythmic movement. Confusion reigns in the orchestra. As various lights crisscross the stage, a general dance strikes up. The movement of people on stage is frenzied; there is much running, jumping, and falling. Some who do not join in the dance "make rapid movements with their arms alone, others only with their legs, or behinds. Some combine all these movements. Sometimes, whole groups make one and the same movement" (282). At the moment of greatest confusion, the stage darkens and only the giants remain visible, appearing to be slowly swallowed up by the darkness.

The sixth scene, which contains less than a dozen lines and which Kandinsky in a stage direction indicates must follow as quickly as possible after the preceding scene, consists essentially of a single action. One of the bright yellow giants appears in the middle of the stage. He slowly lifts both arms parallel with his body, palms downward, and in doing so, grows upward. At the moment he reaches the full height of the stage, his figure resembles a cross and the stage becomes suddenly dark. The music is expressive, resembling the action on stage. At this point, *The Yellow Sound* ends.

Permeated with elements of ritual and, at the end, Christian imagery, *The Yellow Sound* defies facile analysis. An eerie, kaleidoscopic blend of color, music, and movement, the work not only operates with so few intelligible words as to be virtually wordless, but also insinuates the insufficiency of spoken speech as a dominant theme. Individual or group bodily movement, together with color and music with which the movements of people are variably in or out of synch, carry the expressive weight of the composition. Although in principle no single element of *The Yellow Sound* was intended to be dominant, Kandinsky was so deeply concerned about integrating color into the integrated work of art (*Gesamtkunstwerk*, in German) that his composition seems above all an extraordinary experiment in the expressive use of color and light on stage. Too long examined exclusively in light of Kandinsky's own ideas on stage composition, *The Yellow Sound* should be set as well in the context of the fascination with nonverbal theater of the early modernist period.

The Retreat from Speech in the Drama

Although it would be convenient to be able to chart a pattern in the development of a trend in the arts, events rarely occur in a neat succession. More often, they happen more or less simultaneously, responding to a variety of stimuli and making it extremely difficult to precisely determine causes. And so it is, for the most part, in the emergence of modernist nonverbal theater. I chose to begin this book with the cultivation of pantomime in turn-of-the-century Europe in order to make as strong a point as possible about the nexus between wordless theater and the modernist physical imperative. However, any chronology for pantomime and retreat from speech in drama during the late nineteenth and early twentieth centuries would be difficult due to their untidy patterns of development. Hence, what I propose to do in this section is consider a few representative dramatic texts by several well-known writers of the period in which a conscious effort is made to undermine the role of traditional dialogue in the play or in which questions about the validity of such dialogue are insinuated. The dramatists are Maeterlinck, Chekhov, Hofmannsthal, Schnitzler, Lev Lunts, and Gertrude Stein.

Maeterlinck. At the outset of his career as a dramatist, Maeterlinck clearly sought a revolutionary transformation of the contemporary stage. Although a prolific essayist as well as a dramatist, it was principally by means of his short "plays for marionettes" of the early 1890s—*L'Intruse* (*The Intruder,* 1890), *Les Aveugles* (*The Blind,* 1890), *L'Intérieur* (*On the Inside,* 1894)— that Maeterlinck hoped to validate a new type of static, metaphysical drama built around the inevitable confrontation with death. Since I have examined *On the Inside* elsewhere in the context of the great interest in the puppet figure in turn-of-the-century Europe, I would like to build my present case around Maeterlinck's first play, *The Intruder*.[48]

First produced in 1891 at a Paris benefit for the poet Paul Verlain and the painter Paul Gauguin, the play is set in an old Flemish country house on a Saturday night in the nineteenth century. For maximum universality, Maeterlinck's plays usually have vague, indeterminate settings both in space and time. In a dimly lit room with a large Dutch clock, a blind old grandfather worries about his daughter, who is lying ill in another room from a difficult childbirth. Darkness or dim lighting function symbolically in Maeterlinck and establish an atmosphere of spiritual mystery and dread. The blindness of the grandfather, which is revealed only about midway through the play, operates as a corollary to the diminished role of speech in the play. Just as Maeterlinck believed that deep emotion cannot be verbalized and that words if anything betray feelings, so, too, did he use blindness to suggest that the material world is but a distraction from man's inner, spiritual life, for which physical sight was unnecessary and even an encumbrance.

It is because he is not distracted by the material world around him that the blind grandfather senses the growing danger to his daughter. The other, sighted, members of the family, lacking the grandfather's intuitive power, believe that the daughter is recovering. They are if anything more concerned over the health of the child, who has not uttered a single cry since birth. The grandfather predicts that he will be deaf, and perhaps dumb, the result of cousins marrying cousins.

As the family awaits the arrival of a nun, the ill woman's sister-in-law, everything on the outside seems to grow still as if in hushed expectation of the nun's coming. But the sudden silence of the nightingales in the trees, and the agitation and odd behavior of the swans and fish in a nearby pond, cause one of the ill woman's daughters to surmise that someone has come. It is, to be sure, not the nun who is approaching but Death, which only the blind grandfather can sense. As the other members of the household speculate on what might be causing such consternation among the animals, they begin feeling cold coming into the house and move to shut the door. But for some reason, they are physically unable to. In symbolic terms, this means that ordinary mortals cannot prevent the passage of Death into the house. When the sounds of the sharpening of a scythe are heard next, the symbolism becomes obvious—at least, one assumes, to the audience; except for the grandfather, the people in the house believe that it is the gardener at work even though it is a weekend night.

As the others talk unfeelingly, and even disparagingly, of the grandfather's blindness and strange behavior, other small but portentous events occur. As the atmosphere of dread deepens, the grandfather is convinced that his daughter has taken a turn for the worse; moreover, he is sure that someone else has entered the room, which the rest of the family of course deny, regarding the old man as now out of his wits. When the grandfather asks how many are in the room, the other members of the family, all seated around a table, identify themselves. But the old man is sure that there is another presence in the room that the others cannot see. Then, although the windows are shut, the lamp goes out and the room is thrown into darkness. In need of air in the stifling room, the grandfather asks that a window be opened. When it is, they are all amazed at the silence all around, a silence so great that they believe they hear the leaves falling on the terrace. At the stroke of midnight, the grandfather hears the sound of someone rising hastily. A moment later, a terrible wailing comes from the grandchild's room. To accentuate the dread of the play's finale, Maeterlinck calls in a stage direction for the wailing to continue, "with gradations of terror," to the end of the scene. As they all get up to investigate, a hurrying of heavy steps is heard on one side of the room followed by a "deathly" stillness. Death, in other words, has left with his latest victim.

Up to this point, the play's minimalist dialogue, accompanied by sounds at certain intervals, serves primarily to create mood. There is at least as much reference to silence and actual stillness in the play as there is speech.

Dialogue is vastly reduced, as is physical action, in keeping with Maeterlinck's aim of diminishing the significance of both while heightening that of silence and the presence of the supernatural. Since Maeterlinck believed that spoken speech and physical action belong to the phenomenal world, and thus hinder the perception of spiritual forces, he thought their presence must be reduced to a bare minimum. Physical action—where it occurs—is highly stylized and the perfect accompaniment to the repetitive, incantatory dialogue. For maximum effect, at a key juncture Maeterlinck may employ purely mimed action, as he does, for example, at the end of *The Intruder*. When the dying woman's husband and brother rush to the room from which they hear the child's wailing, this is what they encounter:

> At this moment heavy steps are heard hurrying in the room on the left.—Then a deathly stillness.—They listen in mute terror, until the door opens slowly, and the light from the room next door falls into where they are assembled. The Sister of Charity appears on the threshold, in her black garments, and bows as she makes the sign of the cross, to announce the death of the wife. They understand, and, after a moment of hesitation and fright, silently enter the chamber of death, while the uncle politely effaces himself at the doorstep, to let the three young girls pass. The blind man, left alone, rises and gropes nervously about the table in the darkness.[49]

Chekhov. Although influenced by Maeterlinck's views on static drama and silence, Chekhov never went as far as the Belgian writer in dispensing with the trappings of realism. But while retaining the outward form of the traditional play, Chekhov operated with it subversively. Plot structure in any conventional sense is absent in his major plays. Rather than advancing action, dialogue is used primarily to reveal character. Often fragmentary, its importance is less in what is spoken than what is unspoken. Chekhov uses speech *against* itself, to demonstrate the inadequacy of words to convey emotion. If physical action is also a diminished presence in his plays—though not to the extreme that we find in the early Maeterlinck—gesture language is often employed as a vehicle of communication where spoken speech fails. These properties of the Chekhovian play are splendidly exemplified in the last, and perhaps the best, of his full-length works, *Vishnyovy sad* (*The Cherry Orchard*, 1904).

The Cherry Orchard is a play about loss, both in the physical and spiritual sense. The most obvious immediate loss is that of the cherry orchard, the pride and joy of the estate on which Madame Ranevskaya and her brother, Gaev, grew up. Representatives of the old landed gentry, Ranevskaya and her brother are relics of the past. They can neither adjust to change nor keep up with it. When their estate and the cherry orchard that belongs to it are bought at auction by Lopakhin, the son of a former serf on the estate who is now a well-off businessman, the change of hands of the property signals the end of an era. As an up-and-coming real estate developer, Lopakhin intends to cut down the orchard and subdivide the property into lots for cottages for summer vacationers. Although barely able to control his desire to take the estate into his own hands, the boorish Lopakhin is also sentimental and tries, out of kindly feelings toward Ranevskaya and Gaev, to help them retain it. But his efforts are in vain. They do not understand the world of business and lack the inner resolve to take the steps necessary to keep their property. And so in the end, Lophakin wins.

The scene in which Gaev and Lopakhin return from the auction after the sale of the estate to Lopakhin occurs in Act II. It is a high point of the play. For the sake of ironic contrast, Chekhov brings the bearers of ill tidings into the midst of a party being held in the ballroom. Although Ranevskaya opines at one point that perhaps the time is not right for a party because the status of the estate has not yet been settled, the dance goes on anyway. In order to maximize the contrast between the mood of the dance before the arrival of Gaev and Lopakhin and what follows, Chekhov gives free rein at the outset of the act to the play's most ludicrous characters—the boorish, impecunious landowner, Simeonov-Pishchik; the stumbling clerk, Yepikhodov; the faintly absurd German governess, Charlotta; the senile old servant, Firs; and the irritating perpetual student, Trofimov. Although Ranevskaya and her adopted daughter Varya express anxiety over the outcome of the auction and Ranevskaya must decide whether or not to return to her lover in Paris, the dance scene has a patently comic character. This is established both by the dialogue of the characters and the physical play between them. The actions of the characters and accompanying sound effects are as important as the dialogue in building the mood before Gaev and Lopakhin appear.

How Chekhov shifts the semantic weight from speech to gesture in order to suggest the breakdown of speech when confronted with deep emotion is handsomely illustrated in *The Cherry Orchard* when Gaev and Lopakhin finally return from the auction. Lopakhin is the first to appear. Ranevskaya, agitated, hurls rapid-fire questions at him: "Well? The sale took place? Talk!"[50] Unable to answer her straightaway, Lopakhin deflects her questions: "The auction ended at four o'clock . . . We missed the train and had to wait until nine thirty . . . Whew! I'm a bit dizzy" (312). But Lopakhin's facial expressions tell the whole story. Thrilled that he now owns the estate on which he was raised as the son of serfs, Lopakhin, out of compassion for Ranevskaya, who had always been kind to him, cannot bear to tell her the truth. He must instead buy time through dialogue that skirts the issue while at the same revealing his conflicting emotions through body language. The stage directions call for him to look "embarrassed, fearful of betraying his joy."

When Gaev enters, his gestures disclose the truth before a word is spoken. He is holding parcels in his right hand while with his left he wipes tears away. Suspecting the worst at this moment, Ranevskaya, impatiently, tearfully, fires questions at him as fast as she had at Lopakhin: "Lenya, what happened? Lenya, well? Come on, for God's sake . . ." Like Lopakhin, Gaev cannot bear to tell her the truth immediately and similarly skirts the issue. Weeping, he says to the servant Firs: "Here, take these . . . Anchovies, herrings . . . I've eaten nothing all day . . . What I've been through" (313)! Just then the door to the billiard room opens and Gaev hears Yasha's voice, "Seven and eighteen!" Welcoming the chance now to extricate himself from a difficult situation, Gaev is only too happy to retreat into his favorite refuge from reality—billiards. His facial expression changes, and he stops weeping. The transition of mood is effected wholly by physical means.

After Gaev leaves the room, Ranevskaya, joined now by Pishchik, asks Lopakhin about the outcome of the auction. This time, Lopakhin cannot put off telling them the truth any longer. But his reply is a single word, "Sold." And when Ranevskaya wants to know who bought it, he again answers as simply as possible: "I bought it." In each case in the original Russian, Lopakhin's reply picks up from the last word of the question put to him, as if further weakening the power of speech here.

Ranevskaya's reaction to the blow is too great for verbalization. All she can do is appear to collapse and keep herself from falling to the floor by leaning against a nearby table and chair. Until the end of the act she remains speechless, revealing her feelings only through gestures. She sinks into the chair and weeps bitterly, the dance band in the background striking up at an inopportune moment, heightening the ironic contrast established at the beginning of the act.

Ranevskaya's reaction to the news of the estate's sale to Lopakhin is purely gestural and passive. Her adopted daughter Varya's reaction to the ill tidings is similarly gestural, but defiant. The stewardess of the estate in Ranevskaya's absence, she takes the keys she wears on her belt and flings them to the floor in the middle of the room, then stalks out. His previous reticence gone now, and the ownership of the estate symbolically transferred to him when Varya tosses the keys onto the floor, Lopakhin explodes in an outburst of incredulity (that the estate is his) and boastfulness (his bidding skill at the auction). The gestures accompanying his torrent of words are every bit as expressive: he laughs uproariously, stamps his feet, retrieves the keys from the floor, jingles them, then calls for the band to resume playing. Lopakhin's joy in the acquisition of the estate may be understandable, but he is at this point the consummate boor, the peasant who may have made money but on some level has never ceased being a peasant. His boastful, insensitive account of the auction can only be hurtful to Ranevskaya, who is still present. And when at the end of his tirade he summons the musicians to play in celebration of his coup, his words can only wound Ranevskaya deeper: "Hey, musicians! Play! I want to hear you. Everybody come see how Yermolay Lopakhin's going to take the ax to the cherry orchard, how the trees are going to fall to the ground! We'll build summer cottages, and our grandchildren and great grandchildren will have a different life here . . . Let's have music! Play!" (314).

At the end of the play, when Ranevskaya and other members of her household are about to leave the estate forever, there is another fine instance of Chekhov's preference for gesture language over speech to communicate emotions. It involves Varya and Lopakhin. She loves Lopakhin and wants to marry him; though attracted to her, he finds it difficult to propose despite Ranevskaya's prodding. When Lopakhin asks Varya where she intends going, she tells him that she has agreed to be the housekeeper on an estate about fifty miles away. He replies: "That's in Yashnevo, isn't it? 'Bout fifty miles from here. (*Pause.*) I guess life in this house has really come to an end" (322). Since his remarks touch a raw nerve in Varya, she does not answer directly. Instead, Chekhov has her continue fussing with her baggage, as if suggesting thereby her reluctance to leave and her uncertainty as to the future. Her mind seems to be fixed on some object she has apparently misplaced, when Lopakhin breaks her concentration by asking her what her plans are. Distracted, she does not reply to his question immediately but continues the business with her baggage: "Where can it be? . . . Maybe I put it in the trunk . . ." As if coming to, hesitatingly, she finally responds to Lopakhin: "Yes, life in this house has come to an end . . . there won't be any more." Lopakhin then announces that he is leaving for Kharkov on the next train. Time is fast running out on them. Lopakhin must declare himself now or give up any thought of marrying Varya. The last words between them are irrelevant, hesitant, a slow dance around the unspoken subject on both their minds. When a voice from outside summons Lopakhin, presumably to tell him his train is arriving, Lopakhin replies hurriedly, "This minute!" and rushes from the stage. The stage direction calls for the actor playing Lopakhin to reply to the call from outside "as if he had been waiting for the call for a long time" (322). Lopakhin, clearly, has had no intention of proposing to Varya and simply cannot get away fast enough. Crushed, Varya at this point says nothing, but her actions speak volumes. Deflated, she sits on the floor, rests her head on a bundle of clothes, and sobs softly.

There is another superb example of Chekhov's understatement and indirectness—insinuating again the inadequacy of speech to render emotion—when Ranevskaya enters a moment later. Her first word is the interrogatory *"Chto?"* ("Well?" or "What's happening?"), which is followed by a pause as Ranevskaya quickly takes stock of the situation. She then says, in a terse, businesslike tone, "It's time to go." Taking her cue from Ranesvakaya, Varya says nothing about the last meeting with the man she had hoped to marry. No longer crying, wiping her tears away, she replies to Ranevskaya in the same matter-of-fact tone: "Yes, it's time, Mama. If I don't miss the train, I'll make it to the Ragulins' today . . ." (322).

Hofmannsthal. If Chekhov conveys his sense of the limitations of speech by operating subversively with dialogue while elevating the semantic role of gesture, as in *The Cherry Orchard,* Hofmannsthal—who turned to pantomime and ballet in part because of a genuine crisis of language—made his skepticism about speech a focal point of one of his finest plays, *Der Schwierige (The Difficult Man).* The comedy was completed in 1918; published in *Die Neue Freie Presse,* the leading Vienna newspaper, in 1920; and staged at the Residenztheater in Munich on November 8, 1921, also the year in which it appeared in book form.

A caustic look at upper-crust Viennese society in his own time, *The Difficult Man* is to that extent a comedy of manners. The title of the play derives from its central figure, Hans Karl Bühl, an intriguing study of a sophisticated aristocrat who has returned to polite society from frontline service in World War I, where he was shellshocked. Ill at ease and more aware than ever of the superficialities and hypocrisies of his world, Hans Karl tries to distance himself from it as much as he can, even at he risk of walking away from the young woman (Helen Altenwyl) whom he obviously loves and who has for a long time loved him. Uncomfortable with his own emotions, which he tries to suppress, fearful of the "odious confusions . . . a man exposes himself to who mixes with people"—as he confides to his sister, Crescence, at one point—Hans Karl seeks to resolve inner contradictions through flight from himself. But Helen's love overcomes his doubts and hesitancy. Without spelling it out in so many words, it is she who proposes marriage to him, which we know for sure he has accepted when he announces to his sister that he is engaged.

Much of Hans Karl's skewed attitude toward the world, or at least toward the world of aristocratic Viennese society, derives from his disdain for social converse. He professes, in fact, to find more meaning in the performance of a circus clown than in the company of members of his own social milieu. Helen shares his attitude toward conversation, as she declares to her boorish suitor, Baron Neuhoff, in act II, scene 1: "We have every reason, we younger people, to feel that if there's anything in the world we're in dread of, it's conversation—words that flatten everything real and soothe it with prattle."[51] And her father, Count Altenwyl, backs her up:

> In my view, no one knows what conversation is any more. It most assuredly does not consist in gushing like a waterfall oneself, but in prompting others to join in. In my day, people used to say: when somebody comes to me, I have to conduct the conversation in such a way that when his hand is on the doorknob, he'll fancy himself clever, then on the way out consider me clever. Nowadays, pardon the crudeness, no one understands how to make conversation or how to keep his mouth shut. (48)

Hans Karl's condemnation of speech, of the excessive universal trust in its efficacy, and of its failure to communicate the inexpressible, is stated unequivocally in this scene with Helen in act II, scene 14:

> HANS KARL: I have something to say to you.
> HELEN: Is it something very serious?
> HANS KARL: It seems that that's what one expects. That everything in the world is accomplished through speech. In any case, it's rather ridiculous to imagine that just with well-chosen words it's possible to exert heaven knows how great an influence in this life where in the final analysis everything depends on the inexpressible. Speech is based on an indecent excess of self-esteem. (72)

A little later in the same scene, when Hans Karl confesses the difficulty he experiences trying to make himself understood to her, he voices Hofmannsthal's own conviction of the superiority of silence to speech: "Naturally you can't understand me. I understand myself much worse when I speak than when I am silent. I can't even try to explain to you; it's just something I learned when I was away—that there is something written in people's faces"(75).

Hans Karl's fear of speech also motivates his desire to extricate himself from the soirée at the Altenwyls, where his decisive meeting with Helen takes place. Besides wishing to avoid an emotional confrontation with Helen, Hans Karl is desperate to leave before her father can corner him to press his plea that Hans Karl deliver a speech in the Upper House of Parliament on behalf of their club. As he confides to Antoinette's husband, Hechingen: "Am I supposed to stand up and make a speech about people learning to get along with each other and peace among nations—I, a man whose strongest conviction is that it is impossible to open one's mouth without causing the most God-awful confusion?" And when Hechingen begs to protest, Hans Karl adds: "But everything one utters is indecent. The simple fact of expressing anything is indecent" (820).

Lunts. A diametrically different approach to the matter of dramatic action than Chekhov's was taken by the early Soviet writer Lev Lunts. A gifted writer of prose and drama, Lunts died of illness at at the age of twenty-three (he was born in 1901) while on a trip to Hamburg to visit his parents. A member of the Serapion Brotherhood of Soviet writers, who demanded greater autonomy for the Russian artist in the aftermath of the revolution, Lunts established his reputation as a fiercely independent dramatist and theorist of drama on the basis of four plays and a few essays written and published in the 1920s. His plays include *Vne zakona* (*Beyond the Law*, 1920), *Bertran de Born* (1922), *Obezyany idut!* (*The Apes Are Coming!*, 1923), and *Gorod pravdy* (*The City of Truth*, published posthumously in 1924). His most important theoretical writings on drama were a speech titled "Na zapad!" ("To the West!"), which he delivered at a meeting of the Serapion Brotherhood on December 2, 1922, and the afterward to his play *Bertran de Born.*

Lunts's ideas on the drama can be summarized as succinctly as he wrote them. He believed, for example, that Russian literature, and Russian drama in particular, had for too long been hobbled by the preoccupation of writers with psychology and verisimilitude. This excessive concern with psychological portraiture and "realism"—a term Lunts disparages at every opportunity—came at the expense of plot (*fabula*, in Russian). This was the major reason why, in Lunts's opinion, the Russians had never really been able to develop an authentic tragic drama compared with the West. Professing great esteem in "To the West!" for such Western masters of adventure as Arthur Conan Doyle, Alexandre Dumas, James Fenimore Cooper, Ryder Haggard, Blasco Ibañez, Rudyard Kipling, Jack London, Robert Louis Stevenson, and H. G. Wells, Lunts calls on his fellow Russian writers to learn from the West and create, above all, a Russian drama in which dialogue and character are subordinate to plot. His point of departure in "To the West!" is the phenomenal popularity of the novel *Atlantida* (1919) by the young French writer Pierre Benois. Only contemporary Russian critics remain indifferent to it, claims Lunts, dismissing it as proof of the collapse of Western bourgeois culture. Striking a chord heard often in the years immediately following World War I, Lunts maintains that weariness with the war created an appetite for literary works of an exotic and adventurous character.[52] While cautioning that Benois was still a young writer and that *Atlantida* was in some ways flawed and derivative, Lunts nevertheless re-affirms the importance of the novel as an example.

Lunts urges his fellow Russian writers, as well as critics and the reading public, to overcome their long-held and deeply rooted prejudice against adventure stories as neither serious nor suitable for adult readers. What the West has long regarded as classic has been dismissed in Russia as childish amusement. The slogan must now be: "*Plot!* The ability to handle com-plicated intrigue, to tie and untie knots, to weave and unravel—this is achieved by many years of painstaking effort, created by a sustained and beautiful culture."

Although the situation in contemporary Russian prose, according to Lunts, is bad enough—even the lessons regarding plot structure to be learned from such masters of the Russian realistic novel as Turgenev, Dos-toevsky, and Tolstoy, who created plot, however weakly, have been largely forgotten—Lunts reserves his harshest criticism for the Russian theater:

> A Russian theater does not exist. There is none now nor has there ever been one. There have been five to seven exemplary outstanding comedies, a few good comedies of manners in part forgotten . . ., but they don't count because they never created a *system*. Great theatrical authors always appear as a pleiad and form a school. So it was in England in the sixteenth and seventeenth centuries, in Spain during the same period, in France in the seventeenth and nineteenth centuries. But in Russia nothing similar took place. That is why we do not pos-sess even a *single* tragedy.

Lunts's answer for this state of affairs is simple: "On the stage, intrigue, action, are what matter" (206).

Rather than concentrate on intrigue, the Russian theater, contends Lunts, has pursued above all social motifs, psychological truth, and every-day life.[53] By ignoring intrigue, the Russian theater does not exist. Brash as well as provocative in his views, Lunts dismisses such Russian dramatists as Turgenev, Chehov, and Gorky as the authors of "unique plays *for read-ing*" (207). Referring to the "crisis of the theater" that was so hotly debated in Russian theatrical circles at the turn of the century, Lunts remarks that "nobody sheds any tears over the fact that among us nobody knows how or, more important, wants to know how to handle intrigue, to learn techniques of plot. Nobody knows and, more important, nobody wants to know that before slice of life [*byt*], before psychology, before language—before everything else—the simplest laws of scenic action must be mastered" (207).

This remark about language has to be set in the context of Lunts's brief against the populists (*narodniki*), who in his view had come to dominate Russian literature. The goal of the populists was to portray Russian peasant life as faithfully as possible, and this implied an accurate reproduction of folk speech. This was the Russian equivalent of the German dramatist Gerhart Hauptmann's original version of his play *Die Weber* (*The Weavers*) in Silesian dialect. A second version of the drama had to be written in standard German before the play could be performed in theaters outside the Silesian dialect area, precisely the kind of theatrical verisimiltude that Lunts decried.

Apart from the essay "To the West!" Lunts reiterated his views on the drama in the afterward to his play *Bertran de Born*. "Nowhere have psychology and realism exerted such destructive influence as on the stage," he declared. By its very nature, he continued, "the theater is alien to trifling scenes of everyday life and subtle psychology. Theater exists in *action*. But in Russia, they teach that one should strive for a faithful representation of real everyday feelings, of "real" people." In yet another swipe at Chekhov and the Chekhovian play, Lunts fulminates: "And so, instead of Shakespeare, Racine, and Hugo, our theater is dominated by the most subtle, the most tedious psychological cud of Chekhov. It is 'true,' it is 'fair,' and it—and none other!—has brought the theater to ruin. Everyone laments the crisis of dramaturgy—and everyone presents wise dramas without the slightest action constipated with manners and mood" (141).

In an effort to reverse this trend in Russian drama, Lunts determined that when approaching the writing of a play "in a country where they do not know and do not want to know theater," he would go to the opposite extreme of Chekhov. Instead of a theater of moods, of naked everyday life, of "cheap tricks," he would create a theater of pure movement. To see how well he succeeded in creating an anti-Chekhovian drama of action, in which speech neither creates mood nor subverts emotions nor serves any other purpose than to advance the intrigue, let us have a look at his first play, *Beyond the Law* (1920).

Set in Spain in an indeterminate time and place—the setting is the generic Ciudad ("city," in Spanish)—Lunts makes it clear in a short preface that "Spain" is just a convention and that the spectator or reader should not look for any specifics of Spanish life. "For me," he declares," it is not the literary aspect of the play that is important, but its theatrical aspect" (42). The central idea of the play is that society cannot function without law, that no man is above the law, and that complete social equality is an impossible goal. The truly egalitarian society could be achieved only at the cost of individuality and human dignity, neither of which the Serapions were willing to see compromised in a postrevolutionary, proletarianized Russia. But rather than advance his views in a "thesis" play, Lunts wrote a deceptively simple play of action and intrigue.

The person who appears "beyond the law"—in the sense that the law will no longer protect him from anyone with a grudge against him—is the robber Alonso, who has earned the wrath of Rodrigo, chancellor of Ciudad, by giving Rodrigo's son a well-deserved thrashing beneath the windows of the chancellor's home. Alonso is intoxicated with what he believes to be his new freedom: he will be free to romance other men's girlfriends and wives because he is beyond the law, and he will be free of his own wife since his marriage vows will no longer have any meaning.

With a light and repetitive dialogue, in the style of vaudevillean banter, and with entr'acte sideshows in the form of short, amusing scenes played on the right and left sides of a tripartite stage, *Beyond the Law* at first seems to be a comic play. But the mood darkens, and vaudeville gives way to tragedy when Alonso is cleverly manipulated by Rodrigo's ambitious mistress, Clara, into fomenting a plot against Rodrigo and Philipp, duke of Ciudad. Clara at first convinces her lover that he should topple Philipp, whom Rodrigo holds in contempt, and become duke himself or perhaps even king. But when Rodrigo refuses to consider marrying Clara and seating her on the throne alongside him, Clara persuades Alonso that he and his men should overthrow Rodrigo and install Alonso as their new leader once Rodrigo has overthrown Philipp.

At first, Alonso sees the overthrow of Philipp and Rodrigo as the chance to topple the order of privilege and make the people king. He will do away with all laws and thus no man will be able to rule over another. As he confides to his friend Ortuño: "Tomorrow night we'll overthrow Duke Philipp, arrest Rodrigo and all his accomplices, and get rid of the laws. All of Ciudad will be beyond the law" (77). Although his intentions are initially honorable—Alonso forbids anyone to kill, pillage, or rape—the revolt that finally erupts turns into a bloodbath. Wildly hailing Alonso as their leader—which Alonso tries in vain to discourage—the crowd becomes a rampaging mob, destroying everything in its path. Seeing his vision of a classless, truly egalitarian society made a mockery before his eyes, Alonso now vows to become the leader like the one the people hail in order to restore order: "Beyond laws. Here's what will be beyond laws: fire, murder, and blood. Now and forever. . . .I will be the duke. I will again be beyond the law, and I will introduce laws. I will make the people happy with just laws, and they will celebrate my name in song. Enough stupidity and games!"(94).

One of Alonso's first orders as the new authority in Ciudad is to have his wife killed. For Alonso, there are now no more laws of honor (the only laws he recognized once he was beyond the law). The finale of the play fulfills Clara's prophecy that whatever law Alonso may be beyond, the one law he cannot escape is that of woman. When Alonso tells Clara almost boastfully that he has had his wife killed because she bothered him, he is clearly in ecstasy over his new sense of power: "Oh, Clara! Today I am free! I will be a king! I am no longer a peasant. I am a duke, I am a king" (96)! Carried along by the same wave of self-glorification, he vows to unite with a ruling family and toward that end will marry Inessa, Duke Philipp's daughter. When Clara reminds him that he told her he loved her and wanted to marry her and share his power with her, he falters, as did Rodrigo before him: "What do you need a title for? Isn't it all the same whatever you're called? I love you. But that little Inessa . . . She'll be, well . . . just for appearance, the empress! (Carried away.) I will be emperor! Over the whole earth . . . I will never forget you . . . The pope will crown me. The pope! Where Charles the Great was crowned . . . Ha, ha" (97)!

Clara cannot control her inner rage at this second rejection and stabs Alonso. As he falls dying, she taunts him: "What is it, my duke, my king, my emperor? Will you agree now to make me your wife? Die like a dog. And a dog you are. I thought you were a prince, but you're nothing but a peasant!" Delivering a second, fatal blow, she closes the play with the bitterly ironic words: "You wanted to be beyond the law. Now die according to the law!" (97).

As a student of Romance languages and literatures, Lunts had a good knowledge of Spanish literature and would seem to have learned well the lessons of the old Spanish comedia de capa y espada (comedy of cape and sword) in which plot was paramount and all other elements of the play subordinate to intrigue. Lunts followed this pattern in Beyond the Law, which he wrote as an action-oriented, anti-Chekhovian play that he thought would point the way to a new type of Russian drama sure to breathe new life into the moribund Russian theater of his time. Although Alonso is by no means devoid of psychological interest, there is little introspection in the play and character interaction is fueled primarily by the intrigue. Since Lunts is disinterested in psychology and realism, the dialogue in *Beyond the Law* is wholly anti-Chekhovian and neither builds mood nor reveals depths of feeling. Baldly comic in the vaudevillean scenes, dialogue is employed solely for the sake of action in the rest of the play. Very different in its aims than Maeterlinck's in its exclusive service to humor or intrigue, *Beyond the Law* can still be regarded as minimalist, as in the opening scene of the play, which builds comic suspense and sets the tone for the lighter scenes:

> DON GONZALO (*running in*): Don Benigno! Don Benigno! Have you heard?
> DON BENIGNO: What's up?
> DON GONZALO: Have you heard?
> DON BENIGNO (*circling him*): What? What's happened?
> GONZALO: Just now on the main street of Ciudad . . .
> ALL: Come on, come on!
> GONZALO: On the main street . . .
> ALL: So out with it!
> GONZALO: In broad daylight!
> BENIGNO: So what happened there?
> GONZALO: Under the windows of Rodrigo, the chancellor's house!
> BENIGNO: Go 'head, go on.
> GONZALO: Under the chancellor's windows!
> MENGO: Well, you won't get anything out of this idiot! (44)

What took place on the main street of Ciudad before Chancellor Rodrigo's windows, and Alonso's part in it, will still be kept from the audience for several more lines. This pattern of comic suspense characterizes virtually all the short entr'actes that take place on both sides of the split stage. The scene in which Clara plants in her lover Rodrigo's mind the idea of overthrowing Duke Philipp and seizing rule of Ciudad exemplifies Lunts's use of similarly spare dialogue to propel the intrigue:

> RODRIGO: I'm not afraid of anything. Kiss me, Clara . . . That's it . . . Harder. But I'm just sick and tired of working for others. If these were my beasts! I have to tame them for someone else. For this duke, this old idiot! And I have to work for the likes of him! Why is he duke and not I? Why are thrones just for fools? Oh Clara, if I were duke!
> CLARA: But aren't you omnipotent as it is, Rodrigo?
> RODRIGO: That's not it. Every day to have to go to a crowned old fogey, bow to him, abase myself, when you know that you're greater and more powerful than he is.

CLARA:. Then why don't you become duke, Rodrigo?

RODRIGO: I? Duke?

CLARA: Yes, duke! Why don't you overthrow Philipp? You could, after all. The army recognizes only you. It never obeys the duke.

RODRIGO: Come to your senses!

CLARA: You'll be a duke, a great duke! Look at our city. It's small and trivial. Become duke, oh do! And our duchy will become the leading one!

RODRIGO: Betray the sovereign?

CLARA: What kind of a sovereign is he? Rodrigo, be a man! You must overthrow Philipp, you must . . . (65)

Stein. Although they retained spoken speech in their plays and wrote with very different aims and with very different audiences in mind, dramatists such as Maeterlinck, Chekhov, Hofmannsthal, Schnitzler, and Lunts nevertheless shared a common disdain for traditional dramatic dialogue and sought either to undermine it or to reduce its primacy. Hofmannsthal and Schnitzler struck cautionary notes, albeit for different reasons, regarding speech; Maeterlinck, at least in his early plays, approached it in a minimalist way, turning it wholly into an instrument of mood; Chekhov used speech to demonstrate its inadequacy as a means of communicating emotion; Lunts, rebelling against what he interpreted as Chekhov's obsession with psychology and realism, created a novel stage idiom that reduces speech to a mere mechanism of intrigue. Collectively, these dramatists sounded a retreat of speech in the drama that paused just short of total surrender to gesture.

The modernist subversion of the traditional function of speech in drama, exemplified by the dramatists examined above, occurred within recognizable boundaries of dramatic composition. What I mean by this is that these dramatists were acknowledged dramatic writers, with a deep and abiding interest in the stage, who sought, in different ways, to breathe new life into what they regarded as old and tired theatrical forms. But there were other writers whose apparent disinterest in theater and singular lack of concern for even the outward appearance of dramatic form inclined them to a yet more radical form, demolishing both traditional dialogue and play structure. Gertrude Stein is a case in point. Although this book deals with topics in European cultural history, Stein, an American expatriate, warrants inclusion on the grounds both of the European locus of her creativity and her proximity to the great changes that took place in the arts in Europe in the first three decades of the twentieth century. Modernism and the avant-garde swirled about Stein and were absorbed—and reflected—by her in ways not always immediately apparent.

Long disclaiming any serious interest in theater, Stein nevertheless wrote a large number of works she called "plays" and "operas" from 1913 to 1946. Surprisingly, given their playful flouting of nearly all the conventions of dramatic composition, at least three dozen "plays" and "operas" by Stein have been performed since 1934, mostly in the United States but also in England, France, and Germany. Lest it appear, however, that Stein has somehow miraculously become a staple of the American stage, some qualifications are in order. With very few exceptions, productions of Stein's "plays" and "operas" have taken place in small, by and large nonprofessional theaters, a number of them on college and university campuses. Thus it would not be unfair to characterize the interest in Stein's "plays" and "operas" as predominantly elitist in nature. It is also true that beginning with the 1934 production of *Four Saints in Three Acts* at the Wadsworth Athenaeum in Hartford, Connecticut, the works by Stein that have most attracted production are those for which musical scores and/or ballet choreography have been composed.[54] These include *Capital, Capitals* (written in 1922), *Four Saints in Three Acts* (written in 1927), and *The Mother of Us All* (1946), for which Virgil Thomson wrote the musical scores, and *Doctor Faustus Lights the Lights* (1938), the most conventional (relatively speaking) of Stein's "plays" and "operas," which was written as an opera with ballets. Arguably the most successful of Stein's nonmusical plays was one of her last, *Yes Is For a Very Young Man* (1946). It deals with the French Resistance during World War II and draws on Stein's own experiences (which she writes about it in *Wars I have Seen*) as an exile in the French countryside during the conflict.

If Stein came around to introducing more conventional elements of dramatic composition in works of the 1930s and 1940s, her early "plays"—those written in the teens—collectively represent an outrageous mockery of conventional play structure wholly in the spirit of modernist revisionism. Besides lacking (usually) any discernible beginning, middle, and end, these works either completely abandon the traditional division of the play into acts and scenes or reduce them to single lines or words in the manner of the *sintesi* (syntheses) of such Italian Futurists as Umberto Boccioni, Paolo Buzzi, and Francesco Cangiullo. Perhaps the best example of this occurs in *Counting Her Dresses* (1917). The "play" is divided into forty-one "parts" containing anywhere from one to six "acts." By using each "act" to accommodate for the most part just a single short line, as in Part XXI, Stein only underlines the arbitrariness of such terms as "act" and "scene" as units of composition:

Act I
   Have you any way of sitting.
Act II
   You mean comfortably.
Act III
   Naturally.
Act IV
   I understand you.[55]

The minimalist act structure is paralleled, of course, by the minimalist dialogue. In *I Like It to Be a Play* (1916), acts are abandoned entirely and the short work consists of eleven "scenes" made up of short lines of dialogue.

Other casualties of Stein's attack on traditional play form are worth noting. Setting as a rule is never established. In rare instances, it may be inferred from the dialogue, as in *I Like It to Be a Play*, one of several works written in Mallorca in 1916 where Stein and Alice Toklas took refuge during World War I. Although this would change somewhat in her later works, Stein also almost never identifies speakers in her early "plays." Two of the rare exceptions are *Do Let Us Go Away* (1916) and *Please Do Not Suffer* (1916). In her first "play," the five-act *What Happened* (1913), speakers are identified by number from "one" to "four." *White Wines*, which was also written in 1913, divides the speakers into three groups: "All together," "Witnesses," and "House to house (5 women)." By generally eliminating both a defined setting and characters immediately identifiable by name, Stein compels the reader or spectator to hear all the more intently the speaking voices, to concentrate on the moment in time, on the present (since virtually no other time exists in Stein). By abandoning such "distractions" as place and characters' names, Stein is free to focus wholly on speech, which in its radical departure from theatrical tradition calls into question the very purpose and style of dramatic dialogue. That this was indeed Stein's purpose—pursued with obvious delight—in her early "plays" seems obvious from the following lines from the aptly titled *I Like It to Be a Play*:

     In a sort of prelude or preface:
I liked it to be a play and so cleverly spoken.
Americans are very clever.
So are others.
Yes indeed.
And all men are brave. (286)

In the great majority of Stein's "plays," dialogue does not advance action in the usual sense (since the "plays" are lacking in such action). Moreover, the independence of dialogue from recognizable speakers establishes language — as spoken speech — as the area of Stein's greatest interest. Dialogue, strictly speaking, does not really exist in Stein's plays, its place taken by monologic utterances of a fragmentary, disconnected, isolated, and static nature.

Rather than propel dramatic narrative or explore the states of mind of characters and their evolving relationships, the speech of Stein's "plays" repudiates motivational and descriptive roles in favor of immediacy. All that exists in the Stein "play" is the present moment, however the reader or spectator reacts to it, puzzling over Stein's frequent illogicality or pushing through this barrier to a sense of different voices and the rhythms of words. By writing plays primarily for herself, at least certainly up to the 1930s, rather than for actors and anticipated stage production, Stein felt no obligation whatsoever to honor any of the formal conventions of play composition, above all in the use of language. By eliminating the environment in which theatrical speech generally occurs, Stein highlights speech itself, as virtually a thing unto itself. This deliberate deconstruction of the literary dimension of dramatic dialogue additionally underscores the antiliterariness of the "play" as a whole. What the reader or spectator confronts is not a play text — which the works by Maeterlinck, Chekhov, Hofmannsthal, and Lunts examined above still represent — but the score, if you will, of a performance in which the sole star is living speech as sound and rhythm. Without necessarily realizing the ramifications of her innovations, Stein came closest to that other outstanding performance genre of her time — pantomime — in which the literary text serves merely as the pretext for the "pure" performance of the human body.

THREE

The Dance Phenomenon

I spit upon the dancers painted by Degas. I spit upon their short bodices, their stiff stays, their toes whereon they spin like peg-tops, above all upon that chambermaid face. They might have looked timeless, Rameses the Great, but not the chambermaid, that old maid history. I spit! I spit! I spit!

WILLIAM BUTLER YEATS, *The Death of Cuchulain*

The Dancers

The American Role. The impatience with tradition and the desire to expand into less inhibited and restricted forms of expression that was characteristic of the turn of the century show up clearly in the emergence of the modern dance phenomenon. Although far-reaching experimentation was undertaken on both sides of the Atlantic, not surprisingly the greatest early innovators were American women. The newness of America, its freedom from the weight of tradition, made their transition from classical dance forms to the more expressive modern dance easier; the baggage that Europeans carried was ever so much heavier.

The three outstanding American dance innovators of the early modernist period were Loïe Fuller, Isadora Duncan, and Ruth St. Denis. Apart from their own important and unique contributions to dance in the twentieth century, these pioneers attracted the attention of contemporary artists in other fields who were similarly striving to loosen the bonds of the traditional and conventional. For the first time in any significant way, dance itself became the subject of art.

The readiness of American artists to break new ground seems not to have been paralleled by the readiness of American society to accept such experimentation. If the European artist had to contend with the more intimidating burden of the past, European audiences at least evidenced a greater willingness to give the innovations of the American dancers a sympathetic hearing. Thus the early successes of Fuller, Duncan, and St. Denis came not in their own country but in Europe, where before long all three dancers became celebrated. Their fame served as a stimulus to young European dancers, above all in the German-speaking world where their impact was greatest, to follow their lead in spurning tradition and exploring new paths. While the different approaches to the body of the Americans and their European counterparts have been commented on extensively in the literature on modern dance, they must also be viewed as a dimension of the culture of the physical in the modernist period.

Apart from her solo dancing and strong preference for subjects drawn from nature, Loïe Fuller commanded attention above all for her integration of a dazzling array of lighting effects, many of her own invention, and costumes, also of her own design, consisting of hundreds of yards of delicate silk. Responsive to the technical innovations of her time, Fuller experimented with electrical lighting, which was then quite new, and with the different color effects with which contemporary painters were increasingly becoming involved. For example, in her *Fire Dance* (1895), which she performed to the music of Wagner's "Ride of the Valkyries," Fuller made extensive use of "underlighting" by standing on a panel of frosted glass illuminated from beneath. Her friendship with the Curies, the discoverers of radium, resulted in her famous *Radium Dance*, which simulated the luminosity of the element. Fuller's most visually arresting effects were achieved through the projection of colored lights on her own billowing costumes, which she animated into continually changing forms and shapes through rhythmical movement. The dynamic combination of color and costume in motion captivated audiences and inspired artists who attempted to capture the unique qualities of her dance in various media. Among the most unusual of these tributes to Fuller were four gilt bronze table lamps by the French sculptor François-Raoul Larche.[1]

The Paris Exposition Universelle of 1900, which came to play such an important role in the shaping of modernist trends in the arts, served as a showcase for Fuller's talents. Besides her own theater of dance at the exposition, she presented pantomimes by the Japanese actress Sada Yacco, who surmounted the language barrier to become an international celebrity throughout turn-of-the-century Europe. The cooperation between Fuller and Sada Yacco in the area of pantomime further illuminates the remarkable revival of interest in nonverbal theater at the time. Fuller is also remembered for her encouragement of other dancers such as Isadora Duncan, whose first European appearances she sponsored. And among the visitors to her theater at the Paris Exposition was Ruth St. Denis, who was attracted to Fuller's technical experiments as well as to the Orientalism embodied in the performances of Sada Yacco, which was becoming a major source of inspiration to Western artists.

Isadora Duncan's break with the past was broader in scope than Loïe Fuller's. Like Nora in Ibsen's *The Doll House,* Duncan sought a redefinition of the role of woman in society, of the place of woman in the family, and of traditional attitudes toward female sexuality at a time in American life when such issues were coming to the fore.[2] As a serious creative artist, Duncan placed her deepest trust in instinct, which created a bond between her and those trends in contemporary philosophy (Nietzsche, Bergson) and psychology (Freud) that were also willing to attribute cognitive value to instinct. Duncan's art and personal life style were validated by nature: what was natural was good, true, and ultimately, beautiful; what defied the natural or compromised it was to be avoided. Her attitude toward performance costume was dictated by these beliefs and reflected not only artistic choices but the contemporary movement toward a reform of women's attire. To liberate the feet, sandals rather than traditional dancer's footwear were worn, or the feet were left entirely bare, giving rise to the popularity of the "barefoot dancer." In order to allow her body the greatest possible freedom of movement, Duncan eschewed anything binding or form fitting, choosing instead a loose gown or a tunic inspired by classical Greece.

The enthusiasm for ancient Greece among the Symbolists, who found new inspiration in Greek tragedy and in the Greek concept of the hero, further validated Duncan's preference for the garb of ancient Greek women, known to her from the statues and artifacts preserved in museums.[3] Duncan's public appearances in her Greek-style tunic and sandals or bare feet in turn gave further encouragement to the emulation of classical models among artists of her time.

With the free and natural as her guide, Duncan strove for a high degree of simplicity in all her dance. Scenery, costume, special effects, and story were reduced to a minimum. Attention was to remain fixed on the dancer and the universal truths being revealed in dance; anything that threatened to divert the spectator's concentration was regarded as intrusive and superficial and had no place in her art.

Duncan's career in Europe owed most to the impetus given it by Loïe Fuller, whom she met in 1902. It was Fuller who sponsored her independent concerts in Vienna and Budapest. Duncan was generally well received by Europeans, with the exception of the French, who kept their distance from her until 1909 when she returned to Paris shortly after her memorable performances of Gluck's *Iphigenia in Aulis* at the Metropolitan Opera House in November 1908.[4] Although this engagement marked the pinnacle of her American career, much of Duncan's fame had, in fact, grown out of her activities in Russia. She made her first trip there in 1904 and attracted the attention of such prominent figures in the world of Russian dance at the time as Michel Fokine and Sergei Diaghilev. Liberal in her social and political outlook, she understood the gravity and promise of the revolution of 1905. That promise seemed fulfilled in the Bolshevik coup d'etat of 1917. Recalling Duncan's earlier visit to Russia and eager to promote modern dance as a popular art form capable of reaching out to mass audiences, the Soviet authorities invited her to return to the country and establish a school there in 1921. Duncan accepted the Soviet invitation enthusiastically and organized a school, drawing on the experience of the school of dance she had organized at Grünewald, Germany, in 1904. Once her Russian school was established, Duncan entrusted the actual management of it to a graduate of the Grünewald school and one of her adopted daughters by the name of Irma. The school performed on a number of occasions in Russia and abroad and was highly regarded.

Tragedy pursued Duncan most of her adult life and moderated the carefree exuberance and joy of her art. Her two children were drowned in a freak automobile accident in Paris in 1913. Her marriage to the flamboyant, hard-drinking Russian poet, Sergei Esenin, cost her the affection of the American public, who took the marriage and her travel with Esenin through the United States as evidence of her affection for bolshevism. After the breakup of her marriage and her problems with weight control, Duncan sought more and more relief in alcohol and sexual promiscuity. Her own death in 1927 came in an automobile accident even more freakish than the one that took the lives of her children. As she began driving off in an open sports car, her scarf trailed away from her neck, got caught in the spokes of a wheel and strangled her to death.

The fame of Ruth St. Denis, the youngest of the American pioneers of modern dance, owed much to the Eastern exoticism of her numbers.[5] An ardent exponent of feminism and liberated women's dress and attitudes, St. Denis (who was born just Ruth Denis in New Jersey) had been exposed to a measure of Hinduism in the jumble of Theosophy and Christian Science in which she was raised. Once she launched her career as a dancer, St. Denis was quick to recognize the potential of the early twentieth-century fascination with the East. Her first success along these lines was her dance *Radha*, which she created in 1906. Performed to the music of Delibes's Indian opera, *Lakmé*, *Radha* is based on the love between the god Krishna and the milkmaid Radha. In St. Denis's interpretation, Radha became a temple goddess celebrating a ritual of the five senses. While borrowing no more than the trappings of Indian culture and art, St. Denis satisfied an audience's sense of Eastern exoticism through her costuming and the extraordinary sinuousness of her style. Two of the other famous "Indian" dances in her repertoire included *The Incense*, at which spectators were enthralled by the uncanny rippling effects she achieved with her arms, and *The Cobras*, in which she again captivated audiences by means of the great dexterity of her arms, each of which now took on the aspect of a twisting, lunging snake.

Following the examples of Fuller and Duncan, St. Denis went to Europe in 1906. Like her fellow Americans, she too became celebrated and sought after. Of the artists who entered her orbit, the most prominent was Hugo von Hofmannsthal, whose relations with St. Denis are discussed later in this chapter.

St. Denis took advantage of her travel in Europe to broaden her knowledge of Indian art by studying museum collections. In 1908 she unveiled the first of her new dances attributable to this research. It was called *The Nautch* and featured the lead figure of the Indian street dancer, about whom St. Denis was to create additional dances. Harry Kessler's praise of it in a letter to Hofmannsthal on February 6, 1908, was typical of the way the work was received: "Her new dance of the Nautch-girl is the wonder of wonders—the most fantastic in intensity, austerity, sensuality, and tempo that she has ever done" (175)! The dominant features of the street dancer, as interpreted by St. Denis, were rhythmic stamping of the feet accentuated by ankle bells, the whirling about of the body, and the same sinuousness of arms and head for which St. Denis was already famous. As Susan Au points out, St. Denis incorporated into later versions of the dance a spoken patter in pseudo-Hindi and a demand for alms, followed by an elaborate mime of the dancer's contempt upon receiving none from the audience.[6]

As the story goes, St. Denis had been fascinated by ancient Egypt from the time she saw a poster for Egyptian Deities cigarettes featuring an enigmatic Egyptian goddess. However, the dream of creating a great dance work built around the ancient Egyptian theme had to wait until 1909, after St. Denis had returned to the United States. When it was ready, *Egypta* was an impressive full-length production performed by a cast of dancers and musicians led by St. Denis playing the multiple roles of Egypta, the goddess Isis, and a palace dancer.

St. Denis's enthusiasm for dances inspired by ancient India and Egypt continued after she and her new partner and husband, Ted Shawn, whom she first met in 1914, established their renowned Denishawn school of dance in Los Angeles in 1915. The curriculum of the school consisted of ballet (which was performed bare-footed), free-flowing arm and torso movements, ethnic and folk dances, Dalcroze eurythmics, and Delsarte exercises. St. Denis also gave lectures on the history and philosophy of dance.

The first major production of the school—A *Dance Pageant of Egypt, Greece, and India*—attested to St. Denis's ability to draw inspiration from the ancient world. It was performed with great success at the Greek Theatre pageant in Berkeley. As Shawn was able to exert greater influence over their productions, dances inspired by the ancient East were complemented by others of North African, Spanish, Native American, and American origin.

The European Contribution. The stimulus of such American innovators as Fuller, Duncan, and St. Denis bore fruit in the emergence of a European modern dance movement. Its strongest roots were in Germany, where it came to be known primarily as *Ausdrucktanz* (expressive dance), and the dancer most closely identified with expressive dance was the German, Marie Wiegman, who became better known under the Anglicized name of Mary Wigman.[7] But Wigman's contribution to modern dance cannot be separated from the pioneering theoretical work in rhythm and movement of her teachers, Émile Jaques-Dalcroze and Rudolf Laban.

A professor of harmony at the Music Conservatory in Geneva, Dalcroze is most widely known as the founder of "eurythmics," a technique originally designed to heighten musical sensitivity by relating music and movement.[8] Before long, the adaptability of eurythmics to choreographical improvisation was recognized, and Dalcroze was looked to by dancers as a guru. Wigman first studied with Dalcroze at the institute he established in 1910 in Hellerau, a planned workers' community near Dresden. But it was not dance that first brought Dalcroze to Hellerau. The model community with its gardens and spacious distribution of homes had been founded by the Deutsche Werkbund, an organization imbued with a utopian vision of a new kinder and gentler industrial culture. Convinced after seeing a demonstration of Dalcroze's method that eurythmics could be meaningfully integrated into the life of the Hellerau community and its liberal educational system, the Deutsche Werkbund invited him to become director of the newly established Bildungsanstalt für Musik und Rhythmus (Educational Institute for Music and Rhythm). Dalcroze accepted the offer.

Before long, the fame of the institute attracted enthusiasts of body culture from Germany and beyond, as well as dancers excited about the possibilities of eurythmics. Wigman studied with Dalcroze in Hellerau from 1910 to 1912. Dalcroze himself remained in Germany until 1914, when he left to open the Institute Jaques-Dalcroze in Geneva. At the peak of its fame, there were five hundred students enrolled at the Educational Institute for Music and Rhythm, and branches of the school were established in several European cities, among them Prague, Warsaw, Kiev, and St. Petersburg. The outbreak of World War I and Dalcroze's negative feelings toward Germany ended his ties to Hellerau. Both the city and its once famed institute became casualties of the war.

Wigman's next mentor was the immensely influential Rudolf Laban, the person generally credited with originating Ausdrucktanz.[9] Laban eventually became renowned as a teacher, a theorist of dance, and the creator of the system of dance notation named after him, Labanotation, which, with some modifications, is still in use today. At the height of his influence, he operated a network of schools in such cities as Basel, Stuttgart, Hamburg, Prague, Budapest, Zagreb, Rome, Vienna, and Paris. Laban's experiments were conducted mostly at the Schule für Lebenskunst (School for the Art of Life) that he founded in 1913 in the bohemian art colony at Monte Verità near Ascona, Switzerland.[10] When World War I erupted, he moved to Ascona, where he remained until 1918, preoccupied mainly with developing his system of dance notation (*Bewegungsschrift*, as he called it) and furthering his research into the art of movement.

Laban's most significant choreographic work came in the 1920s and early 1930s, beginning with his production in Hamburg in 1922 of *Swinging Cathedral*. By 1923 dance schools bearing his name and directed by former master pupils had been established in nine major European cities. Shortly thereafter, he opened a Choreographic Institute in Würzburg, Germany; in 1927, it was relocated in Berlin. That same year, Laban produced the dance spectacle *Titan* for the First Dancers' Congress held in Magdeburg, but while dancing the lead role in his "Don Juan," he suffered an injury that ended his dance career and that of his company. Laban devoted much of his energy after his accident to his system of dance notation, which was published under the title *Schrifttanz* in late 1928. The next year was an especially big one for Laban. The Choreographic Institute moved again, this time to Essen, where it merged with the dance department of the Volkswangschule, a prestigious municipal center for professional training in the arts. It was directed at the time by Kurt Joos, a former pupil of Laban's.[11] For the Crafts and Guilds of Vienna, Laban directed a monumental pageant in which twenty-five hundred performers participated before as many as a million spectators.

In 1930, Laban moved to Berlin, where he served for four years as director of the Prussian State Theaters. Never entirely trusted by the Nazis after they came to power, Laban nevertheless did well as the director of the Deutsche Tanzbühne (German Dance Stage). By laying greater emphasis on the Germanness of Ausdrucktanz and advocating a new German theater based on myth, he clearly sought to please Germany's new masters by accommodating their nationalist ideology. But his efforts to stay afloat in troubled waters ended during the Eleventh Olympic Games, held in Berlin in 1936. Laban was placed in charge of the dance part of an arts program to be presented in conjunction with the athletic events. With a thousand participants from all over Europe, Laban mounted a pageant called *Vom Tauwind und der neuen Freude* (*Of the Warm Wind and the New Joy*). It was performed on June 20, 1936, in a new stadium built to accommodate the Olympics as a kind of dress rehearsal for a repeat performance during the games themselves. But Minister of Propaganda Goebbels, who was with other government officials in the audience of some twenty thousand, decided that it should not be repeated despite its otherwise warm reception.

Laban's work was now branded *staatsfeindlich* (hostile to the state), and he himself was denounced and placed under virtual house arrest. His career in Germany was over. He eventually managed to emigrate to England in 1938 and there joined the dance school being run by Kurt Joos and Sigurd Leeder at Dartington Hall, Devonshire, a combination progressive school, agricultural station, and arts center founded by Leonard and Dorothy Elmhirst. The complex boasted of outdoor stages as well as an intimate theater designed by Walter Gropius. Laban remained there as an instructor until July 1940, when he and another former student, Lisa Ullmann, who had established the first movement choir in England, moved to London. Until his death in 1958, Laban taught and lectured widely, generally in close collaboration with Ullman. For several years he and a Manchester industrialist also worked closely, and by and large successfully, on the adaptation of movement notation to industrial needs.[12] In 1948, Laban published *Modern Educational Dance*, the most widely read and arguably the most influential of his writings on movement and dance.

Mary Wigman's studies with Laban began when she joined his circle of dancers on Monte Verità. Laban had opened a school in Munich in 1912 and from 1913 began running summer programs on Monte Verità. With the outbreak of war, Laban and his dancers, Wigman among them, left Munich for Ascona, which became a refuge as well for other artists fleeing the conflict. Although Laban also put much emphasis on improvisational training, he was less rigid than Dalcroze on the matter of musical accompaniment and permitted his dancers to express themselves in movement with or without music, or to the accompaniment of speech and percussive sound. As Mary Wigman herself recalled:

> We danced with music and without it. We danced to the rhythms of poetry, and sometimes Laban made us move to words, phrases, little poems we had to invent ourselves. Although these experiments did not and could not lead to a definite artistic form, they opened up another part of the magic land and helped deepen our emotional background. . . .
>
> Laban had the extraordinary quality of setting you free artistically, enabling you to find your own roots, and thus stabilized, to discover your own potentialities, to develop your own technique and your individual style of dancing.[13]

Wigman remained in Ascona until 1919. Her first public performances under Laban's auspices came in 1914. The debut included the first sketch of her grotesque *Hexentanz I* (*Witch Dance I*), most of which was danced in a seated position.[14] She wore a mask during the performance, which she described as a demonic translation of her own features. The dance conveyed a sense of evil and animality through the dancer's grasping, clawlike gestures and the earthbound heaviness of her body. Wigman wrote about *Witch Dance* in her book *The Language of Dance* (1963), confessing that she herself was at first disturbed by the suppressed emotions she unleashed in choreographing this dance.

Wigman's first appearance in a large public theater came on June 18, 1917, in the Pfauen Theater of Zurich. After 1918, she made a decisive move away from the representational and pictorial. Whatever her initial uneasiness with *Witch Dance*, Wigman pursued grim aspects of life in subsequent dances—the horrors of war, aging, the inevitability of death—and these became as characteristic of her art as the Oriental exoticism of the dances of Ruth St. Denis.

Her most creative period was the decade of the twenties, when she choreographed and performed in both solo and group dances. She founded her own school of dance in Dresden in 1920, numbering among her students such prominent figures in the modern German dance movement as Hanya Holm, Yvonne Georgi, Gret Palucca, Max Terpis, Margarethe Wallmann, and Harald Kreutzberg. After her successful solo dances in 1920–21, the Frankfurt Opera House invited her to introduce a new work. This was a "dance-poem" composed earlier on Monte Verità but previously unperformed and unpublished.[15] Based on the Salome theme that had inspired a number of dancers at the turn of the century, but incorporating original elements of plot and interpretation (Herod, for example, represented by a large puppet; a group of female dancers as an onstage audience), *Die sieben Tänze des Lebens* (*The Seven Dances of Life*, 1921) became one of Wigman's most notable ensemble works. Besides confirming the future direction of Wigman's choreography toward group as opposed to solo dance, *The Seven Dances of Life* also prefigured Wigman's elimination of the masculine element (at least until 1930) and her concentration on the feminine. With her next ensemble dance, *Szenen aus einem Tanzdrama* (*Scenes from a Dance Drama*, 1924), Wigman not only took further aim at the narrative element in dance (hence the irony of the dance work's title since there is no "drama" in it) but, by increasing the all-female ensemble from four to eighteen dancers, introduced, as Susan Manning puts it, "the utopia of the all-female dance group."[16]

Wigman choreographed five more works before the breakup of her company in 1928, three of which are of particular interest for the adaptation of the mask from Wigman's earlier solo dances to the larger ensemble work. *Das Tanzmärchen* (*Dance Fairy Tale*, 1925), the first, was conceived very much in the nature of a parody of the conventions of the nineteenth-century story ballet. *Totentanz* (*Dance of Death*, 1926) had its origins in a scenario that Wigman had written while on Monte Verità. It was performed entirely with masks and featured the interplay between six figures wearing identical masks and costumes and two others costumed differently, one as Death and the other, danced by Wigman herself, as an "alien body, like someone who perhaps only came to pass through, as a plaything of irrational happenings. With this masked face acquiring human features, the entire figure experienced movement impulses from time to time which recalled a once-lived existence."[17] The last of Wigman's group dances before she disbanded her company, *Die Feier* (*Celebration*, 1927–28), was also the most ambitious she had yet undertaken, running an entire evening at the Second Dancers' Congress in 1928. Abandoning masks and narrative elements and recapitulating motifs from earlier works, *Celebration* also explored the shifting dynamics of the relationship between the choreographer as solo performer and the group, between the authoritarian figure and the autonomous mass subordinate to it.

After Wigman disbanded her group of female dancers (largely out of financial considerations), she returned to solo performance. Her major work on the threshold of the momentous 1930s was the sequence *Schwingende Landschaft* (*Shifting Landscape*, 1929), which consisted of seven solo dances. "Gesicht der Nacht" ("Face of Night"), the only "dark" solo of the seven, was a tribute to the German soldiers killed in World War I. She memorialized them even more explicitly in the controversial *Totenmal* (*Call of the Dead*, 1930), on which she collaborated with Albert Talhoff and which, Susan Manning argues, "set a precedent for Nazi dramaturgy" (149), despite the fact that the essentially ambivalent nature of the work inclined most observers to regard it as pacifistic in intent.

Wigman and her dancers made three tours of the United States between 1930 and 1933. Interest in German Ausdrucktanz was now so strong in America that Wigman was persuaded to establish a school in this country. With that purpose in mind, she sent her student, Hanya Holm, to New York in 1935. It was thus that German modern dance was brought to America—a fair exchange, one might say, for the early pioneering work in Europe of Fuller, Duncan, and St. Denis. Although the Wigman school in New York was a success, anti-German feeling ran so high in the United States after the Nazis came to power in Germany that the school could no longer operate under its original name, and Wigman instructed Hanya Holm to name it after herself.

Wigman made her own kind of peace with the Nazis and remained in Germany through the end of the war. In the early years of Nazi rule, from 1933 to 1936, Wigman seemed in certain respects to position herself artistically as a supporter of the regime. Her emphasis on the expressive abilities of the body as opposed to the limitations of the mind accorded comfortably with the Nazi appeal to the irrational and anti-intellectual. Wigman's honeymoon with the Nazis, which in a sense culminated in her participation in an opening-night festival for the Berlin Olympics of 1936, *Olympische Jugend* (*Olympic Youth*), ended in 1937. Philosophical differences with the Cultural Ministry, headed by Josef Goebbels, over the role of the individual artist versus the social collective led to her disinvitation to choreograph the First German Art Exhibition in Munich that year. Greater Nazi attempts to shape the curriculum of dance schools and directives aimed at limiting improvisation widened the distance between Wigman and the regime. With no further state commissions for group choreography, Wigman retreated into solo performance, which further accentuated her artistic differences with Goebbels and his ministry. The broader implementation of Nazi racial policies also drastically affected the enrollment in Wigman's school. A significant percentage of her students were Jewish and a number were also foreigners. Although Wigman tried to preserve the integrity of the institution, time was against her. She held on as best she could until 1942, when she finally retired and had to sell her school.

Notwithstanding the hardships she and her school experienced from

1937 to 1942, Wigman herself was never in jeopardy. She continued to be acknowledged as at least the symbolic head of the German dance movement and was able to remain in Germany throughout the war in relative security, still able to function modestly as a dance teacher.[18] After the war she reopened her school, first in Leipzig (in what soon became the German Democratic Republic) and then in West Berlin in 1949, and resumed choreography until 1961. She continued to teach until 1967, the year she closed her school. One of stellar figures in the history of modern dance, Mary Wigman died in 1973.

The Dance in the Drama

The incorporation of dance scenes in modernist drama, the appropriation, if you will, of dance by the drama, would seem at first glance to have been an accommodation by dramatists of Wagner's ideas on the *Gesamtkunstwerk*, the "total work of art," in which elements of the performing, auditory, and visual arts are brought together in a single unified whole. While not discounting the role of Wagnerian thought, I prefer to interpret the prominence of dance in modernist drama as further evidence both of the movement away from the verbal to the gestural and of the cohering modernist cult of physicality. There is also the overwhelming impact of the modern dance phenomenon and the celebrity of such dancers as Fuller, Duncan, St. Denis, Wigman, Grete Wiesenthal, and others with whom dramatists in some instances were on close personal and professional terms. It would hardly be an exaggeration to regard modernism as the great age of the dancer. Therefore, finding a marked presence of dance elements in the drama of the period should come as no surprise. Dance came to be regarded as a kindred performance art, indeed, one whose own development under the aegis of modernism ran parallel to that of the drama. It was wholly natural for dramatists to be interested in dance and dancers and to find ways to give greater prominence in their works to the enhanced place of dance in the new artistic revolution. The plays examined below are representative of the extent to which dance permeated modernist drama; they are grouped into thematic categories.

Dance as Liberation: Ibsen, Strindberg, Sologub, Hofmannsthal. A defining moment in Ibsen's *The Doll House* (1879) comes very near the end of the second act. Nora is terrified of what will happen when her husband, Torvald, retrieves the letter the bank clerk, Krogstad, has left in his mailbox. The letter exposes Nora's forgery of her dying father's signature on the promissory note for which Krogstad lent her the money to take her then ailing husband to Italy for his health. Krogstad has been trying to use the letter to blackmail Nora into interceding with Torvald, a man of firm principles, to save the shady Krogstad's position at the bank. In order to keep Torvald from opening his mailbox for as long as possible, Nora diverts his attention by pleading for his help for her preparations for the upcoming costume party at the Stenborgs'. Torvald wants her to go as a Neapolitan peasant girl and dance the tarantella she learned on Capri. Feigning extreme nervousness about her lack of practice, Nora gets Torvald to play the piano while she rehearses. Her dance quickly becomes so wild and frenzied that Torvald urges her to slow down. When she insists that she cannot dance otherwise, Dr. Rank, the close family friend, takes Torvald's place at the piano while the latter stands to a side and gives her directions. But Nora seems not to hear them; her hair becomes undone and falls over shoulders; she does not notice, but continues dancing until Torvald in exasperation shouts for her to stop.

Although Nora's tarantella does not last long, it is multilayered in meaning. It is intended, initially, to deflect Torvald's attention from Krogstad's damning letter. But the significance of the dance does not end there. Nora is terrified over the revelation of the contents of the letter and her dance expresses that dread. As an Italian peasant dance, the tarantella is uninhibited and provides Nora, for as long as she dances it, a needed emotional release. The dance is also one of anticipation. When her old friend, Kristine Linde, offers to help her with Krogstad, with whom she had a relationship in the past, Nora urges her not to, saying, "Don't try to stop anything now. After all, it's a wonderful joy, this waiting here for the miracle."[19] Her enigmatic statement is illuminated only in the next act. The miracle Nora refers to is her husband Torvald's understanding and support once the contents of the letter are revealed. In this light, the tarantella can be viewed as a dance of joy, a celebration in advance of Torvald's reaffirmation of his love for her. For Nora, the dance is also life itself. When Kristine leaves her at the end of Act 2, she counts the hours to the end of the party at midnight the next day. When the dance is over, her fate will be decided.

As we know from the final act, Torvald fails to live up to Nora's expectations. Nora resolves to leave him, their children, and their house, in which she has truly been no more than a doll for her husband's amusement, bereft of a life of her own as a human being. Although a reconciliation between Kristine Linde and Krogstad results in the note being returned to Torvald and Nora and in Torvald regaining his equilibrium, the miracle Nora had hoped for does not materialize. The only recourse open to her is flight and independence. By embodying Nora's most intense, most passionate moment in the play in an improvised dance of Italian folk origin, Ibsen anticipated and in a sense pointed the way, on the threshold of the modernist movement, to the greater entry of dance into the drama.

Folk dance as release, as liberation, occurs yet more powerfully in Strindberg's famous one-act play, *Miss Julie* (1888). The ill-starred relationship between Julie, the daughter of a count, and her father's valet, Jean, cannot be separated from the context of the midsummer's eve dance in which it develops. A natural rebel brought up by her commoner mother to believe in social equality and women's rights, Julie feels constrained by what she regards as the artificial social barriers separating her from the folk who work on her father's estate. But she dares not defy her father. This changes the moment his affairs carry him away from the estate as the play opens. Hardly has he departed for the train when Julie rushes to embrace the folk as if partaking of forbidden fruit. The pretext for this symbolic defiance is the dance being held in celebration of midsummer's eve. Since this is a dance of the folk on her father's estate, Julie would ordinarily be forbidden by her father's social code from participating in it. But with her father absent, Julie is free to respond to her own instincts, which she does with a vengeance, both by joining in the folk dance and then by initiating the romantic relationship with the virile manservant, Jean.

It was clearly Strindberg's intention to link the count's departure and Julie's behavior at the folk dance at the very outset of the play. Jean has just returned from the train station, where he has taken the count, and he describes to Kristine, the count's cook, what he saw in the barn when he stopped off for a dance: "I took the Count to the station and when I returned past the barn I stopped in for a dance. Who do I see but Miss Julie leading off the dance with the gamekeeper! But as soon as she saw me she rushed over to ask me for the next waltz. And she's been waltzing ever since—I've never seen anything like it. She's crazy!"[20]

It is, in fact, with Jean's first reference to Julie's "craziness" that the play begins. The count's servants have for some time regarded Julie as odd. Obviously chafing under the yoke of the code governing relations on her father's estate, and atypical of young women of the landed gentry of her generation by virtue of her mother's upbringing, Julie would naturally strike the folk on the estate as "crazy," the more so since the recent breakup of her engagement. But the craziness Jean speaks of relates directly to Julie's unprecedented behavior at the dance. Throwing convention, and caution, to the winds in her father's absence, Julie is not only present at the servants' dance but joins in it, dancing with the count's servants, above all with his valet, Jean. It is this violation of the social code that sets in motion the train of events culminating in Julie's suicide at the end of the play. Once having crossed the line, by both participating in the dance and initiating a romance with Jean, Julie cannot recross it. With a life with Jean in another country essentially impossible, despite their plans to flee before the count returns, and no resumption of her former way of life possible, death is Julie's only solution. From the moment she enters the midsummer's eve folk dance, Julie is doomed.

The importance Strindberg attached to *Miss Julie* as a departure from the norms of contemporary dramatic writing, especially in the genre of the one-act play, is evident in the lengthy preface he wrote for it. Although he discusses every facet of the play, Strindberg's remarks on the technical aspects of composition are particularly germane to any consideration of the move away from verbal theater in the late nineteenth century. Strindberg hoped that with greater experimentation he eventually would be able to educate audiences enough so that they could sit through a one-act play that lasts an entire evening. "Meanwhile," he writes in the preface to *Miss Julie*, "in order to relax tension for the audience and the actors, without breaking the illusion for the audience, I have used three art forms traditionally associated with drama: monologue, mime, and ballet. The original association was with the tragedy of antiquity, monody having become monologue, and chorus, ballet" (58).

Aware that monologue was discredited by "our realists," Strindberg nonetheless justifies his use of it, but concedes that there are times when a monologue might seem implausible. In such cases, he has replaced monologue with mime, as in what may be regarded as the second scene of *Miss Julie*, designated as "Mime," in which the rather long introductory stage direction outlines the actions Kristine the cook will mime. Strindberg expresses a certain enthusiasm over the return of some contemporary Italian theaters to improvisation, opining that this could be "the beginning of a fertile new art form, something worthy of the name *creative*" (58). In this spirit, he has allowed the actress playing the role of Kristine to improvise the actions called for in the stage direction to "Mime," affording her "even greater freedom to be creative—and to win independent acclaim."

The next mimed scene of the play is entitled "Ballet." It begins with servants and farm people entering, led by a fiddler. Bedecked with flowers, they place a small barrel of beer and a keg of schnapps on a table and start drinking. A dance circle is then formed, and they all join in singing the song, "The Swineherd and the Princess," which mocks the waltzing in public of Julie and Jean.

When the various elements of dance and mime in *Miss Julie* are taken together, the play can easily be related to the evolution of modernist non-verbal drama. Strindberg deliberately introduced mime in the play as a way of getting around situations in which monologue would be implausible. But he was also aware, in doing so, of the greater willingness of directors to allow actors and actresses greater interpretive control of their roles through the improvisation of physical action. Dance is pivotal in the play in two respects. The dance the count's servants and farm people perform on mid-summer's eve and later in the "Ballet" is a folk dance, hence a link between Strindberg and other European dramatists of his time who were receptive to folk culture. But the dance is also important sociologically and psychically. By participating in the servants' dance, Julie has defiantly crossed from one world into the next; she has stepped across a line, which now makes possible the previously unthinkable relationship with her father's valet. But for the reasons Strindberg the Naturalist has amply elucidated in the play—Julie's mother's liberal upbringing, her preference for the common people, her attitude toward men, and so on—Julie's rush to join in the dancing of the servants and farmhands the moment her father leaves is a psychological and emotional imperative. Whatever the consequences, she responds to an inner compulsion to join the dance. The die has long been cast.

Dance and folk culture also come together, though in a much lighter spirit, in the Russian writer Fyodor Sologub's play *Nochnie plyaski* (*Nocturnal Dances*, 1908). A Symbolist, whose real name was Fyodor Kuzmich Teternikov, Sologub had a strong interest in folk culture and based *Nocturnal Dances* on a fairy tale in a well-known collection of Russian folk tales (*Narodnye russkie skazki*) published in 1897 by A. N. Afanasev. The action takes place in the land of King Politovsky. The king has twelve daughters but laments the fact that with the passing of his wife, his daughters are not the source of joy to him that they should be. They have no interest in get-ting married, shun the company of other young people, and show no one any affection. Their answer is that they love only their father, the king, and that all other people are repugnant to them. Further troubling the king is that his daughters seem to sneak out somewhere every night, but he has no idea where. When they demur that they sleep at home and can be seen in their beds, he tells them that they do, in fact, sneak out but leave dummies of themselves behind.

The truth of the matter is that, like Ibsen's Nora and Strindberg's Julie, the princesses seek liberation from the conventions and rigidities of their environment. Regarding the king's court as a prison, they yearn to be among the folk at their fairs and bazaars, simply attired and barefoot, free to dance the dances and sing the songs of the folk. In fulfillment of their wishes, the princesses enter the underground kingdom of an "accursed ruler," where they dance to their hearts' content wearing simple gowns cut from their bedclothing. The scene is illuminated only by the light of the moon.

The king, in the meantime, has accepted the offer of a young poet to spy on the princesses in order to discover the secret of their nightly disappearances. Wearing the *shapka nevidimka* of Russian folklore, the cap that makes its wearer invisible, the poet follows the princesses and becomes an unseen witness to their nightly ritual. In the tongue-in-cheek manner of Sologub's play, the poet reports back to the king that every night the princesses "dance all night, executing dances in the style of the famous Isadora Duncan to the music of great composers of different lands and ages."[21] Confronted with the accuracy of the poet's account and objects he has brought back from the enchanted kingdom, the princesses confess the truth. As a reward, the poet is ordered to choose whichever of the twelve princesses he would like as a wife. The play ends with the king ordering preparations for the forthcoming wedding of one of his daughters.

For all its entertaining dialogue in folkish prose and verse, Sologub's *Nocturnal Dances* conveys a message wholly compatible with the Symbolist outlook. Quoting the words of the king of the underground kingdom to the princesses as they are about to begin their nightly dances, the young poet relates:

> Forget the dream of day. There,
> Beneath the sun, are only masks.
> Here riddles are resolved. When
> Masks come off, the faces underneath
> Are holy; all is holy before me.
> So leap, sisters, rejoice in light dance.
> Fairy tales dance together with us
> Here beneath the magic moon. (261)

The world of day, the phenomenal world, is naught but mask, illusion. But in the realm of fantasy, the realm conjured up by the fairy tale, by the songs and dances of the folk, masks fall away, the authentic countenances beneath them, revealed by the light of the moon, are revered, and mysteries are solved. Significantly, and in line with what we have already observed in Ibsen and Strindberg, Sologub uses dance, and the dance of the folk in particular, as the expression of joyful release, of ecstatic liberation from the inauthenticity of mundane existence.

Electra (1903) was the earliest work by Hugo von Hofmannsthal to manifest his serious interest in dance. Although it may have proven more durable as the libretto for Richard Strauss's opera (1909) of the same name, it was written a few years earlier (1901–3), staged by Reinhardt in his Kleines Theater in Berlin (October 1903), and published before Strauss composed the music for it. Notable principally for its portrait of a frenzied, animal-like Electra, raging with lust to exact vengeance on her mother, Clytemnestra, and her mother's new spouse, Aegisthus, for the murder of her father, Agamemnon, *Electra* was written at a time when Hofmannsthal, like other contemporary artists, sought inspiration in classical Greek myths, in part under Nietzsche's influence. *Electra* was followed by *Öedipus und die Sphinx* (*Oedipus and the Sphinx*, 1905), which Reinhardt staged at the Deutsches Theater in Berlin in 1906, and an adaptation of Sophocles' *Oedipus Rex* (1906), which Reinhardt again staged, at the Neue Musikfesthalle in Munich in September 1910. Hofmannsthal also had in mind a play devoted to Orestes, but abandoned it along with other planned studies of myths, which have been preserved in sketches for *Leda und der Schwan* (*Leda and the Swan*, 1900–1904), *Jupiter und Semele* (*Jupiter and Semele*, 1901), and *Pentheus* (1904). It was only in 1911 that he returned in part to classical Greek subjects, completing his play *Ariadne auf Naxos* (*Ariadne on Naxos*) in 1911.

The dance motif in *Electra* is introduced early in the play when Electra, grieving for her murdered father, vows to him that when their vengeance is exacted against his murderers, she, her sister Chrysothemis, and her brother Orestes

> will dance around your grave:
> and above the dead men I will lift my knee
> high in the air, step by step, and they
> who will see me dance, yes, even they
> who will see my shadow only from afar
> dancing so, they will say: for a great king
> this royal pageantry is being held
> by his flesh and blood, and happy is he
> who has children that dance such royal dances
> of victory around his noble grave![22]

Electra's moment of triumph comes at the end of the play. Orestes, first reported as dead, returns alive and carries out the murder first of Clytemnestra, then of Aegisthus. When the deed is done, Electra hears shouts of joy and sees torches in the distance. She knows that all are now waiting for her:

> I know very well that they are waiting for me,
> because I must lead the dance, and I cannot;
> the ocean, the enormous twentyfold ocean,

buries my every limb with its weight, I cannot
raise myself. (76)

But when she hears her sister, Chrysothemis, shouting from excitement
that Orestes is being borne in triumph, Electra summons her last drop of
energy to begin the dance she knows she must perform: "*Electra has risen.
She comes striding down from the doorsill. She has thrown back her head
like a maenad. She flings her knees up high, she stretches her arms out wide;
it is a nameless dance in which she strides forward.*" When Chrysothemis reappears followed by torchbearers and a throng of men and women, Electra
urges her to say nothing and to follow her in dance:

> Be silent and dance. All must
> approach! Here join behind me! I bear the burden
> of happiness, and I dance before you.
> For him who is happy as we, it behooves him to do
> only this: to be silent and dance!

The moment is not for the poverty of words, but for the expressiveness
of dance. After a few more steps, Electra collapses, dying. She is at last free
from the terrible passion, indeed madness, of hatred and revenge that have
consumed her life.

Oscar Wilde and William Butler Yeats: Dance as Myth and Legend. Oscar
Wilde's celebrated *Salomé*, which he wrote originally in French, was first
published in 1892. Its premiere was held on February 11, 1896, in the Théâtre de l'Ouevre in Paris, under the direction of its talented and risk-taking
director, Aurélien Lugné-Poe. Censorship (because of its handling of a biblical subject) kept the play from the London stage until May 1905, when
Lord Alfred Douglas's translation served as the basis of the production by
the New Stage Club at the Bijou Theatre. Written, therefore, shortly before
Maeterlinck first attracted attention as a dramatist with his short "plays for
marionettes," *Salomé* is easily reconciled with turn-of-the-century symbolism. Its biblical subject is typical of the popularity of the Old and New Testament among early modernist artists attracted to the "authenticity" of early
Christianity (to some extent influenced by Renan's "reconstruction" of the
historical Jesus) or involved in the Christian revisionism of the period. The
eroticism of the work, coupled with the figure of the demonic seductress
whose passion turns into blood lust, further substantiates the time frame.
So, too, does its shimmering imagery (as in Herod's long monologue near
the end of the play when he tries to persuade Salome to take magnificent
jewels instead of Jokanaan's head) and its lavish use of color, particularly

red, as when Salome describes Jokanaan's mouth ("Thy mouth is redder than the feet of those who tread the wine in the wine press," and so on).[23]

Although it occurs late in the play, Salome's dance of the seven veils before Herod can fairly be regarded as the highlight of the work. Preceded by the tetrach's entreaties that she dance for him, his promise to grant whatever she wishes so long as she dances, and Herodias's urging that her daughter not dance for Herod, interest in the dance is built up more than virtually any other aspect of the play. Salome's dancing barefoot is a small but not unimportant point in establishing the periodicity of Wilde's play. Although the premier exponents of modern dance—Loïe Fuller, Isadora Duncan, Ruth St. Denis, Mary Wigman—first attracted public attention after *Salomé* had been published, the neo-Greek classicism of the turn of the century had already prepared the way for the new, more expressive dance of easy flowing tunics and bare feet. If barefoot dancing seems appropriate to the biblical setting of *Salomé*, Wilde nevertheless felt strongly enough about this feature of the dance to call attention to it. When slaves bring perfumes and the seven veils that Salome will use in her dance, they also remove her sandals. Herod notices this and remarks: "Ah, you are going to dance with naked feet. 'Tis well! 'Tis well. Your little feet will be like little white flowers that dance upon the trees" (340).

Although Oscar Wilde's *Salomé* would seem to have little in common with Ibsen's *Doll House*, they share one significant feature—the improvised nature of the dance the lead female in each play performs. Nora's symbolically loaded dance is an improvised Italian tarantella. In *Salomé*, the actress playing the part of Salome is given free rein in the improvisation of the dance. All the reader of Wilde's play knows of it is the simple stage direction, "Salome dances the dance of the seven veils." The specific nature of the dance, and its duration, are left to the reader's imagination. But the audience beholds an obviously voluptuous dance fashioned out of the collaboration of actress and director. The success of the dance can be measured by Herod's enthusiastic response to it: "Ah! wonderful! wonderful! You see that she has danced for me, your daughter. Come near, Salome, that I may give you your reward" (341). Her reward, as we know, is the head of Jokanaan delivered on a silver platter.

Since Wilde had no opportunity to work with a dancer in the interpretation of Salome's climactic dance, he was unable to establish a precedent for the way the dance ought to be performed. His fellow Irishman, William Butler Yeats, was more fortunate with respect to his own dance plays. This cycle of four short works comprises *At the Hawk's Well* (1917), *The Only Jealousy of Emer* (1919), *The Dreaming of the Bones* (1919), and *Calvary* (1920).

Attracted, like the Symbolists, to poetic drama inspired by myth, Yeats wrote the first two works as one-act verse plays related to the Cuchulain cycle—about the youthful hero of Irish legend—which he began with *On Baile's Strand* in 1904. The well in which the waters of eternal life appear at mysterious intervals is sought out by Cuchulain in *At the Hawk's Well*. He finds an old man at the well who has kept a vigil there for fifty years waiting to drink of the waters of immortality that forever elude him. The well is guarded by a woman whose dress resembles a hawk and who cries like a hawk to frighten away those who would approach the well. Influenced by the austere ritualism of Japanese Noh drama (Yeats, in fact, wrote an essay on "Certain Noble Plays of Japan")—a reflection of the impact of Oriental art on the Western consciousness at the turn of the century—Yeats's plays for dancers are highly stylized (in a manner somewhat reminiscent of Maeterlinck) through the use of mask and integrated music and dance. Both the masks and the music for *At the Hawk's Well* were created by the artist Edmund Dullac. The setting is spare and suggestive. A folded black cloth with a gold pattern on it suggesting a hawk is carried in by one of three musicians. While the cloth is being spread out, the Guardian of the Well enters, covered entirely by a black cloak. Beside her lies a square blue cloth representing a well. In the familiar pattern of Symbolist poetic drama, music (in this case that of a gong, drum, or zither) accompanies movement, which is highly stylized and gives the impression of having been choreographed.

Dance, indeed, is the most prominent element in the play's structure; in the first performance of *At the Hawk's Well*, in Lady Cunard's London drawing room, it was choreographed by a Japanese dancer named Itow, who also danced the part of the Guardian of the Well. The musicians and the Guardian of the Well are spoken of as dancers by the Old Man, dancers whose purpose is to so entrance those who would seek out the magic waters of the well that they are never awake or conscious when the well contains water. As the Old Man explains to Cuchulain:

> I came like you
> When young in body and in mind, and blown
> By what had seemed to me a lucky sail.
> The well was dry, I sat upon its edge,
> I waited the miraculous flood, I waited
> While the years passed and withered me away.
> I have snared the birds for food and eaten grass
> And drunk the rain, and neither in dark nor shine
> Wandered too far away to have heard the plash,

And yet the dancers have deceived me. Thrice
I have awakened from a sudden sleep
To find the stones were wet.[24]

When the Old Man believes the water is returning to the well, and he and Cuchulain prepare to drink what drops they can, they attract the gaze of the Guardian of the Well, who throws off her cloak and stands menacingly in a dress suggesting a hawk. Defiant, Cuchulain refuses to leave the well. The Guardian of the Well then begins a dance, which, like that of Salome in Wilde's play, is left to the interpretation of the actress performing the part. Unlike Wilde, however, Yeats had not only the collaboration of the Japanese dancer Itow but also that of the gifted dancer and choreographer Dame Ninette de Valois (real name, Edris Stannus). Born in Ireland, Valois established a career as a dancer mainly in England and in 1926 became choreographic director of both the Abbey Theatre in Dublin and the Old Vic in London. In 1931 she established the celebrated Sadlers Wells Ballet School (later, the Royal Ballet); her contributions to dance were honored when she was made a dame of the British Empire in 1951.[25] After losing Itow to a New York theater, Yeats found another dancer for *At the Hawk's Well*— as well as for his other dance plays—in the person of Ninette de Valois. As she recalls in her memoirs, *Come Dance with Me: A Memoir 1898–1956*:

> In the late twenties, W. B. Yeats found another dancer for *The Hawk's Well*, for I danced this role myself. I was the first to achieve this distinction after Mr. Itow— and I even succeeded in wearing his costume. Yeats re-wrote *The King of the Great Clock Tower* and *The Only Jealousy of Emer* so that the "Queen" in the former and the "Woman of the Sidhe" in the latter could be interpreted by me in dance mime, wearing masks for both roles.[26]

The dance of the Guardian of the Well continues for some time and Cuchulain gradually succumbs to its spell. The First Musician announces the coming of the waters of immortality, but neither Cuchulain nor the Old Man are present to drink from the well. When Cuchulain enters, he reports that the Guardian "has fled from me and hidden in the rocks. The Old Man apprises him of what has actually happened: "She has but led you from the fountain. Look!/ Though stones and leaves are dark where it has flowed,/ There's not a drop to drink" (218).

The magical properties of dance are again the focus of *The Only Jealousy of Emer*. Emer, Cuchulain's wife, crouches beside his near-dead body, which she and his mistress, Eithne Inguba, whom Emer has called on for help, try in vain to resuscitate. Bricriu — "Maker of discord among gods and men,/ Called Bricriu of the Sidhe" (287)—enables Emer to see the Ghost of Cuchulain. But he will be unable to respond to her unless Emer renounces her love for him. A Woman of the Sidhe then enters and performs a dance around the crouching figure of the Ghost of Cuchulain. She is accompanied by string, flute, and drum played by the same masked musicians from *At the Hawk's Well*. In a stage direction, Yeats indicates that the Woman of Sidhe's mask and clothes "must suggest gold or bronze or brass or silver, so that she seems more an idol than a human being. This suggestion may be repeated in her movements. Her hair, too, must keep the metallic suggestion" (291). As the Woman of the Sidhe dances, the Ghost of Cuchulain awakens and believes he recognizes the woman as the Guardian of the Well. The woman then urges Cuchulain to kiss her mouth "for at my kiss/ Memory on the moment vanishes:/ Nothing but beauty can remain" (292). But the memory of Emer keeps Cuchulain from kissing the Woman of the Sidhe, who now mocks him as she recalls his infidelities. As the Ghost of Cuchulain pursues the Woman of the Sidhe, crying, "Your mouth, your mouth!" Bricriu urges Emer to renounce Cuchulain's love forever. When she at last relents, this way hoping to break the spell of the Woman of the Sidhe, Eithne Inguba enters to tell her that it is she who has revived Cuchulain. But when Cuchulain, again wearing the heroic mask, appears, he has no memory of Emer and calls only for his mistress, believing that she is the one who saved him from the Woman of the Sidhe: "Your arms, your arms! O Eithne Inguba,/ I have been in some strange place and am afraid" (292).

Although the masked musicians from the two previous "plays for dancers" reappear in *The Dreaming of the Bones* bearing their instruments and their cloth, the play stands apart from the Cuchulain cycle and is set in the time of the Irish Easter Rising of 1916. Stylistically similar, however, to the other "plays for dancers," it was choreographed by Ninette de Valois to the music of Dr. J. F. Larchet, the musical director of the Abbey Theatre. Mixing ancient and contemporary Irish history, the play recounts the chance meeting between a Young Man—a participant in the Easter Rising—and a Stranger and a Young Girl "in the costume of a past time" and wearing "heroic masks." The Young Man is the only figure in the play who is unmasked. It soon becomes apparent that the Stranger and the Young Girl are ghosts, the shades of two lovers, Diarmuid and Dervorgilla, who betrayed Ireland to the Normans seven hundred years earlier. As punishment, they are kept from each other's arms until someone is willing to pardon them for their crime.

As they climb the summit of a mountain where the soldier will take refuge from the pursuing English, he notices that the Stranger and the Young Girl dance, and he asks:

> Why do you dance?
> Why do you gaze, and with so passionate eyes,
> One on the other; and then turn away,
> Covering your eyes, and weave it in a dance?
> Who are you? what are you? you are not natural. (443)

It is then that the true identity of the ghostly pair is revealed ("Seven hundred years our lips have never met," confides the Young Girl). As the play draws to an end, the soldier describes the eerie dance of the lovers condemned to be apart for all eternity:

> The dance is changing now. They have dropped their eyes,
> They have covered up their eyes as though their hearts
> Had suddenly been broken—never, never
> Shall Diarmuid and Dervorgilla be forgiven.
> They have drifted in the dance from rock to rock.
> They have raised their hands as though to snatch the sleep
> That lingers always in the abyss of the sky
> Though they can never reach it. A cloud floats up
> And covers all the mountain-head in a moment;
> And now it lifts and they are swept away. (443)

Confessing that he was almost tempted to forgive the star-crossed couple, the soldier leaves the stage to the accompaniment of the musicians who conclude each of the "plays for dancers."

The same musicians (their faces now made up to resemble masks) appear once again in the fourth of the plays for dancers, *Calvary*. This time, Yeats has not only parted company with the Cuchulain cycle, but also with Ireland. The scene is set in Jerusalem at the time of Christ's crucifixion. Apart from the musicians, the only other characters in the play are Christ, Lazarus, and Judas—all wearing masks—and three Roman soldiers who, like the musicians, have their faces made up to resemble masks. Reminiscent of *The Dreaming of the Bones* in this respect, dance figures very near the end of the play but is structurally and otherwise less significant. After Lazarus and Judas both fail in their pleas for Christ to save them from His love and power (Lazarus through death, Judas through forgiveness for betrayal), Christ is raised onto the cross. Before they begin to gamble for Christ's cloak, the Roman soldiers announce that they will dance the dance of the dice-throwers for Christ's benefit "for it may be/ He cannot live much longer and has not seen it" (456). That the dance is short is apparent from the words of the Second Roman Soldier:

> In the dance
> We quarrel for a while, but settle it
> By throwing dice, and after that, being friends,
> Join hand to hand and wheel about the cross. (456)

Yeats's interest in dance continued well beyond the "plays for dancers" of the period 1917–20. Such plays as *The Resurrection* (1931), *A Full Moon in March* (1935), *The King of the Great Clock Tower* (1935), and *The Death of Cuchulain* (1939) all feature elements of dance. Of minimal interest in *The Resurrection,* dance forms only a small part of the wild antics of the worshippers of Dionysus. Both *A Full Moon in March* and *The King of the Great Clock Tower* (which Yeats, by the way, dedicated to Ninette de Valois) are variations on the Salome theme. In the first play, the Swineherd hopes that his singing will be the best the Queen has heard and that he will win her as wife. But his irreverent manner angers the Queen, who orders him out of her sight before he can sing. After the inner curtain is closed and then opened, the Queen appears holding the severed head of the Swineherd, her hands red with blood. She dances to the accompaniment of drum taps and lays the head on her throne. As attendants sing the parts of the Queen and the severed head, the Queen herself continues to dance, at one point taking up the head and laying it on the ground. She then dances a dance of adoration around it. In a scene reminiscent of Wilde's *Salomé,* the Queen "takes the head up and dances with it to drum-taps, which grow quicker and quicker. As the drum-taps approach their climax, she presses her lips to the lips of the head. Her body shivers to very rapid drum-taps. The drum-taps cease. She sinks slowly down, holding the head to her breast" (629).

In *The King of the Great Clock Tower,* a character identified as the Stroller tells the King that he heard the king had married a woman called the most beautiful of her sex. From that day forth, the Stroller, who says that he is a poet, put her in his songs, after which she grew more beautiful with every passing day. But he has never seen her face and would now like to see it. The King permits him to behold the Queen, then orders him to leave. But the Stroller says he swore that the Queen would dance for him and him alone when first he saw her. Outraged at the Stroller's insolence, the King orders him decapitated. When he returns with the severed head, he places it on a throne and orders the Queen to dance:

Dance, turn him into mockery with a dance!
No woman ever had a better thought.
All here applaud that thought. Dance, woman, dance!
Neither so red, nor white, nor full in the breast,
That's what he said! Dance, give him scorn for scorn,
Display your beauty, spread your peacock tail. (639)

When the Queen dances and, taking the severed head, places it on a shoulder, an attendant, as in *A Full Moon in March*, sings as the head. In the play's finale, when the clock in the Great Clock Tower sounds (represented by blows on a gong by an attendant), the Queen dances, thereby fulfilling the prophecy made the Stroller by the "great Aengus" of the Boyne Water that at midnight when the old year dies, "upon that stroke,/ the tolling of that bell," the Queen would kiss the Stroller's mouth. At the end of her dance, as the last gong sounds, the Queen presses her lips to those of the severed head, then lays it on her breast. The King rises in anger with drawn sword, but instead of striking the Queen, he kneels before her and places the sword at her feet.

The Death of Cuchulain, written in 1938 and staged for the first time only eleven years later, reveals Yeats's lighter side and capacity for self-mockery. As the end of his own life approached (he died in 1939), Yeats may have had Cuchulain as well as his own inevitable end on his mind and sought to complete the cycle. The first character who appears on stage is an old man "looking like something out of mythology." He introduces himself with these words:

> I have been asked to produce a play called *The Death of Cuchulain*. It is the last of a series of plays which has for theme his life and death. I have been selected because I am out of fashion and out of date like the antiquated romantic stuff the thing is made of. I am so old that I have forgotten the name of my mother and father, unless indeed I am, as I affirm, the son of Talma, and he was so old that his friends and acquaintances still read Virgil and Homer. (693)

Among the ingredients in this play, the Old Man promises dance. On one of the rare occasions when Yeats expresses himself on the matter of words and dance, his character declares: "I wanted a dance because where there are no words there is less to spoil." He continues, with reference to the previous Cuchulain and Salome-inspired plays, and with a solid dig at classical ballet and its painterly admirers, chief among them Degas:

> Emer must dance, there must be severed heads—I am old, I belong to mythology—severed heads for her to dance before. . . . But I was at my wit's end to

find a good dancer; I could have got such a dancer once, but she has gone; the tragicomedian dancer, the tragic dancer, upon the same neck love and loathing, life and death. I spit three times. I spit upon the dancers painted by Degas. I spit upon their short bodices, their stiff stays, their toes whereon they spin like peg-tops, above all upon that chambermaid face. They might have looked timeless, Rameses the Great, but not the chambermaid, that old maid history. I spit! I spit! I spit! (694)

The dance promised by the Old Man is realized after Cuchulain is slain. The Morrigu places Cuchulain's severed head on the ground and leaves, after which Emer enters and begins to dance. Her dance seems to rage against the severed heads of those that had wounded Cuchulain and have been placed on the ground in a circle. After dancing three times around these heads, Emer moves again toward that of her husband "in adoration or in triumph." As she appears to prostrate herself before it, she rises, looking up as if listening to something. Only faint bird notes break the silence, but as the stage slowly darkens, loud music, typical of an Irish fair of Yeats's day, effects the transition from the myths of the past to those being forged in the present. The three musicians of past plays now appear in ragged street-singers' clothes. As two of them begin to pipe and drum, the Street-Singer connects the ancient Ireland of Cuchulain to that of the Easter Rebellion:

> What stood in the Post Office
> With Pearse and Connolly?
> What comes out of the mountain
> Where men first shed their blood?
> Who thought Cuchulain till it seemed
> He stood where they had stood?
> No body like his body
> Has modern woman borne,
> But an old man looking back on life
> Imagines it in scorn.
> A statue's there to mark the place,
> By Oliver Sheppard done.
> So ends the tale that the harlot
> Sang to the beggar-man. (704–5)

Trivialized by the calamities of his own time, ancient Ireland and its myths seemed to lose their spell and in *The Death of Cuchulain* Yeats gave them fitting burial.

Dance and the Life Force: Gerhart Hauptmann. Und Pippa tanzt! (And Pippa Dances!, 1906), by the great German dramatist Gerhart Hauptmann, is usually grouped with *Hanneles Himmelfahrt (Hannele's Assumption,* 1893) and *Die versunkene Glocke (The Sunken Bell,* 1896) as his leading "Symbolist" plays. Subtitled "Ein Glashuttenmärchen" ("A Glass Works Fairy Tale"), *And Pippa Dances!* clearly stands at a far remove from such early naturalistic plays as *Vor Sonnenaufgang (Before Sunrise,* 1889) and *Die Weber (The Weavers,* 1892) that established Hauptmann's reputation.

A curious, in some ways puzzling play, not usually reckoned among Hauptmann's best, *And Pippa Dances!* equates dance with the life force. In this respect, it may be regarded as one of the more important early twentieth-century texts generated by the dance phenomenon. The principal bearers of the idea of dance as the life force are Pippa and Huhn. The two characters at first glance are as different as night and day. Pippa is the young daughter of an unsavory Italian master glassblower, Tagliazoni, who practices his craft in a new factory in the Silesian mountains but is killed at the end of the first act when he is discovered cheating at cards. Huhn, a retired glassblower, is a giant of a man with long red hair, red bushy eyebrows, and a red beard, covered entirely in rags. As the play develops, dance forges an unlikely but powerful bond between Pippa and Huhn. Except when she dances, Pippa is passive and detached, barely aware of her surroundings. In dance, however, she is life itself. Looked upon admiringly, even covetously, especially by the manager of the glass factory, Pippa is a source of entertainment to the men who congregate in Wende's tavern. They enjoy watching her dance, above all with old Huhn, to the music of an ocarina. The magnetism between Pippa and Huhn, whom Pippa otherwise regards with revulsion, is established in the first act when she finally yields to his unverbalized entreaties that she dance with him:

> Suddenly, beginning with a slap, she jingles the tambourine and glides up to Huhn in a dancing motion, as if intending to elude him by dancing right past him. The ocarina starts up and the old man also begins the dance. It consists in the effort of something clumsy and gigantic to catch something beautiful and nimble; rather like a bear in pursuit of a butterfly which with dazzling colors flutters all about him. As often as the girl eludes him, she utters a loud, bell-like laugh. Sometimes she wrests herself away from him, spinning about herself and so entwining herself in her own reddish gold hair. When pursued, her throat gives off sounds like "ai" in the manner of a childish squeak. The old man hops about as grotesquely and ridiculously as a captured bird of prey. He lies in wait for her, lunges at her but misses, and pants, more and more excited, growling

louder and louder. Pippa dances ever more ecstatically. The lumberjacks have come to their feet. The card players have interrupted their game and watch intently. . . . Now it seems that Pippa can no longer elude the monster; she emits a loud shriek. [27]

Grotesque and erotic at the same time, the dance in a sense extends and animates the previous veiled eroticism of the conversation between the factory manager, who is in his forties, and Pippa. In the melee that breaks out in the aftermath of the discovery of Tagliazoni's cheating, the manager declares that for her safety Pippa can no longer stay in the tavern and proposes taking her with him. But as if his romantic rival, Huhn snatches Pippa when the director's attention is momentarily diverted and races off with her to his own hut.

Alone with Huhn in act 2, Pippa is fearful but grows calmer as the old man treats her gently. The action of the play then shifts to two characters who owe most to the fairy-tale tradition, the poetic young traveling journeyman, Michel Hellriegel, who has found Pippa in Huhn's hut and escapes with her, and the "mythic personality" Wann, a man in his nineties who appears remarkably youthful and is regarded as something of a sage. Like an anxious lover, the factory manager comes to Wann to seek his help in finding Pippa. Wann then seems to summon Pippa by magic when he ties a silk kerchief around his mouth and claps his hands loudly. Immediately, Pippa rushes into the cabin, half-frozen and struggling to catch her breath. The conjuring of Pippa may actually owe more to optics than magic; Wann has a telescope through which he surveys the surrounding woods and mountains and had been observing Pippa and Hellriegel making their way toward his cabin. As they all rush out to rescue Hellriegel, who has become trapped in snow, Huhn, who has arrived in the meantime, sneaks into Wann's cabin. When Wann discovers Huhn at the end of the third act, the two men struggle and Huhn is overcome.

The last act of the play brings Pippa and Huhn together for a final dance. Left alone in Wann's cabin for a while with the barely conscious Huhn, Pippa and Hellriegel feel pity for him and Pippa begins to respond to his audible heart beats. As they give him wine, Huhn deliriously raves about the magnificent glassware he has created and about a single small spark he once poked out of a cold ashpit and now imagines himself dancing with. To Huhn, Pippa is that spark, a creation of his own dance in the forge with the forge hammer. The longer Pippa keeps her hand on Huhn's beating heart, the more the beating resembles powerful blows striking from deep down at the earth's surface. Pippa identifies with the spark, as if she herself were being born anew from fire, and she is overcome by an irresistible urge to dance. So great is Pippa's need to dance at this point, she declares that she will die unless she dances. Again together, Pippa and Huhn dance a symbolic reenactment of Creation in all its convulsive fury:

> To the tones of the ocarina, which Michel plays, Pippa makes painfully extended dance movements which have something convulsive about them. Gradually, the dance becomes wilder and more bacchantic. A rhythmic trembling animates the body of old Huhn. At the same times he drums his fists in a frenzied kind of way, following the rhythm of Pippa's dance. As he does so, he seems to be shaken by an overwhelming chill, like someone who comes from the bitter cold into warmth. From the very depths of the earth come muffled sounds: rumbling thunder, triangles, cymbals, and drums being struck. (75)

When Wann intrudes on the scene, Huhn, a look of hate on his face, declares: "I can make glasses! I sure can . . . I can make them and I can break them! Come—with—me—into the dark—little spark." As he pronounces these words, he crushes the drinking glass he is still holding in his hand; the broken pieces tinkle. Just then a tremor passes over Pippa and her body stiffens. She manages to call out Hellriegel's name before falling dead in Wann's arms. Looking Wann triumphantly in the eyes, Huhn summons up his last bit of energy, cries out the evocative (but otherwise meaningless) "Jumalaï," and slumps back, dead, on the bench he had been lying on before. Blinded by the brilliance of the winter light when he leaves Wann's cabin to get ice to revive Huhn early in the act, Hellriegel has no idea what has happened to Pippa. Rejoicing over the defeat of Huhn, he rhapsodizes, to Wann's encouragement, over the trip he and Pippa will now be able to make to the city of their dreams, golden Venice. "Marrying" Pippa and Hellriegel, Wann sends them on their way. Taking up his ocarina, and delighting in the prospect of playing for people in Venice with Pippa at his side dancing, Hellriegel sets out on his journey, a blind man's staff in his hand placed there by Wann. The play ends with the "sad, heartbreaking melody" Hellriegel plays on the ocarina as he gradually fades into the distance.

The various strands from which *And Pippa Dances!* were woven are of sufficient interest to merit comment. A native Silesian, Hauptmann had a firsthand knowledge of the Riesengebirge region in which his play is set. Apart from its lore, which *And Pippa Dances!* reflects, Hauptmann was also attracted to the region because of its glassworks. This provided the link with Venice, in which Hauptmann had a twofold interest. The future dramatist had lived and worked as a sculptor in Rome from October 1883 to March

1884. Although he contracted typhoid fever while there and had to return home, he never lost his affection for Italy and traveled there on several occasions later in his career. The particular attraction for Venice, the home of Tagliazoni and Pippa and the almost magical land of which Michel Hellriegel dreams, has its own traceable sources. The neo-Byzantine strain of turn-of-the-century European art became fixated on the city of Venice, which exerted its own fascination both because of its Byzantine elements and the role of carnival in Venetian social life. The city seemed to be one of masks, of hidden meanings and secrets, of the interplay between illusion and reality. So great was the fascination with Venice among European artists in the late nineteenth and early twentieth centuries (Thomas Mann's *Death in Venice*, for example) that it would not be inappropriate to speak of a "Venetian theme" in turn-of-the-century literature and art. But Hauptmann had another, purely Silesian, reason for his strong interest in Venice, namely the fact that Venetian-Silesian glassmaking ties have a long history to them, something reflected even in the folklore of the Riesengebirge region.[28]

The elements out of which *And Pippa Dances!* was fashioned—including Hauptmann's infatuation with the sixteen-year-old actress Ida Orloff (whose real name was Ida Margarete Weissbeck), who played the lead role of Hannele in *Hannele's Assumption* at its premiere in 1893—are upon analysis incidental to the prominence in the play of dance and its significance. Whatever the projection of Hauptmann's romance with Ida Orloff in the grotesque relationship between Pippa and Huhn, the emphasis is above all on dance as the nonverbal expression of powerful emotions buried deep in the human psyche. The dancing between Pippa and Huhn is erotic and elemental. In Nietzschean terms—and Nietzsche's influence on Hauptmann in *And Pippa Dances!* and elsewhere has to be taken into consideration—it is Dionysian. Viewed in this light, the hatred between the physical, almost nonverbal, animal-like Huhn and the learned and philosophical Wann lends itself to interpretation in terms of the Dionysian-Apollonian dichotomy.[29] Progressing from realism and naturalism to symbolism and fantasy, Hauptmann moved to embrace the irrational power of the Dionysian, which he encapsulated in the dance relationship between Pippa and Huhn and in their deaths near the end of the play.

That Hauptmann's interest in dance was not confined just to his writing of *And Pippa Dances!* is manifest in his later desire to meet such renowned personalities as Ruth St. Denis and Isadora Duncan. Warren Maurer also speculates that Pippa's surname, Tagliazoni, may have been suggested by

Maria Taglioni, a celebrated Italian dancer whose name at the turn of the century "was still synonymous with the dance."[30]

Myth and Mockery: Georg Kaiser and the Modern Dance Phenomenon. Although it would appear to be another dramatic work inspired by the dance craze of the early twentieth century, Georg Kaiser's *Europa: Spiel und Tanz in fünf Aufzügen (Europa: Play and Dance in Five Acts, 1914–15)* is more in the nature of a spoof of the whole dance phenomenon. It also has a more direct relevance for the central proposition of this book, as we shall soon see.

The plot of *Europa* is easily summarized. It is based on the classical myth of the abduction of Europa, the daughter of King Agenor of Phoenicia and Thelephassa, by the god Zeus. Transforming himself into a white bull, Zeus charms Europa, who climbs on his back and is borne away by him to Crete. She later has three sons by him. Kaiser has used the basics of the myth to deflate the universal obsession with dance in the late nineteenth and early twentieth centuries.

The two principals of the play, Zeus and Europa, both suffer from extreme boredom. Accompanied by the sprightly Hermes, Zeus has descended to earth seeking adventure because, as he says, "Der Mensch ist das süsse Abenteuer ("Man is sweet adventure")."[31] Europa, meanwhile, languishes from her inability to find an appropriate suitor. Since she herself is portrayed as a divine dancer, King Agenor hopes that she will find a suitable husband from among a number of dancers who are brought to perform before her. The king is beside himself, fearing that since the mysterious disappearance of his son, Cadmus, the future of his throne rests with Europa, who continues to resist his efforts to find her a mate. Intrigued by what he has heard of Europa from rejected suitors, Zeus resolves to seek Europa's hand. With Hermes acting as his spokesman, Zeus will present himself at a great dance evening at which his superiority over all other dancers will leave Europa no choice but to accept him in marriage.

Before the events of the dance unfold, Zeus and Hermes have a chance to learn more about Agenor's kingdom. And it is here that Kaiser's underlying purpose of deflating dance in *Europa* becomes clear. His kingdom, which Agenor describes to Hermes in the second act, is one of "undisturbed peace" (601). It has been ages since its borders have been violated. It no longer has enemies, and its armaments are covered with rust; King Agenor confesses that he no longer knows what a sword, spear, and shield are. Further enhancing the peacefulness of his kingdom is the prohibition of loud noise. Haste is slowed and clumsy gestures are smoothed out. Agenor's kingdom, in other words, is a utopia. And that is precisely what Kaiser has against it. Or, treating *Europa* as an allegory, what Kaiser is decrying is a world, a state, a society free of tensions, conflicts, struggle, challenges to manliness. In light of its time period, the outset of World War I, Kaiser's brief seems to be with pacifism, a pacifism that would appear to be beneath the dignity of a man. The emblem, if you will, of King Agenor's utopia is dance. As the king himself declares to Hermes: "Dance is the last stage. Whatever remains of our coarseness is dissolved in dance down to the last kernel. Dance is the expression of the total moderation of the emotions" (602).

Dance is not only the means for the refinement of mores, to which King Agenor attributes the success of his utopia. It has also become the instrument for the psychic emasculation of the men of the kingdom. Dance has rendered them so effete that they have become women; hence Europa, now tired of the effeteness brought on by dance, cannot find a suitable partner from among them.

The great dance evening, arranged by Agenor in a last, desperate effort to find a suitor for Europa, occurs in the third act at the play's high point. It begins with much fanfare, but is soon reduced to a shambles. After one or two unimpressive performances, the dancers refuse to continue, upset over the fact that Agenor has permitted a new dancer to participate in the competition. The new arrival, of course, is Zeus. Despite their objections, Agenor orders the dance evening to continue. A gaily attired Hermes comes out and executes some dance steps, but announces that he is merely a prelude to the dancing of his "young master," whom he will accompany musically on a flute. But Zeus's dance is a failure:

> Zeus emerges. A blue cloak flaps wide and heavy on him. His hair is tied around with a dullish yellow cloth. His dance: Hindered in his free movement by the weight of his cloak, his dance steps are slow and sparse. Several times he tries to raise his knees and arms more nimbly. In this way, he draws nearer the side where Europa is sitting. He wants to put a foot under the lowest step, but the resistance of his robe is too strong. With gestures of sad resignation, he turns around and drags himself to the opening and disappears. (618)

Zeus's second appearance is no more successful:

> Zeus in yellow robe, but it is shorter and of lighter material. Hair and forehead bound in blue. He enters with agile steps. His dance is alternatingly jubilant and melancholy. On one occasion he ascends half way up the steps leading to Europa. But then he turns around, shaking his head. He makes another try at

rushing up to Europa, but again turns back. He tugs annoyingly at his cloak, which tires him prematurely and he withdraws. (619)

I have quoted these two scenes from the play to show that in his deflation of the modern dance phenomenon Kaiser has incorporated some of the play's funniest moments in wordless dance scenes. This is also true of the scene in which Zeus, all dressed in white, his hair gold, dances in a way that brings astonished praise from the other dancers and boundless joy from King Agenor, who sees that at last a man has appeared who is worthy of Europa. At the height of his triumph, Zeus bounds up the steps toward Europa and then throws himself at her feet. As Agenor rushes to bring Zeus and Europa together, Europa tries to talk but instead breaks out in hysterical laughter. Zeus turns red from embarrassment, but when Agenor tries to placate him by telling him that Europa is just laughing from joy at her impending wedding, a storm of laughter engulfs the hall.

The famous abduction of Europa by Zeus in the guise of a bull occurs not long afterward. As Hermes and a disgusted Zeus repose in the woods near a bay, Hermes catches sight of Europa and her retinue of young women approaching. They both take cover behind a willow tree. Encouraged by the other women, Europa agrees to dance her answer to Zeus's proposal of marriage at the conclusion of the dance evening. She will dance around the willow tree, which she declares will represent the person to whom her answer applies. Her seductive, teasing dance is interpreted by Zeus as defiance. He vows to teach her a lesson and accordingly transforms himself into a huge, powerful bull. His intention is to frighten Europa out of her wits and then gloat over her mad flight from him. When Europa and her retinue reappear after going off in search of flowers and are about to resume their dancing, Zeus appears as the bull. All the women flee in terror, but Europa holds her ground and even begins talking to the bull tenderly, flirtingly. She tells him about the dance evening and Zeus's strange disappearance after his last dance and wonders aloud why he could not dance as nicely as the bull does under her guidance. After making him her "captive" by tossing a chain of flowers around him, she praises his strong body then clambers onto his back. At a certain point, the bull rises to his full height and dashes, bellowing, into the bay with a fearful yet delighted Europa clinging to his back.

When Agenor despairs over Europa's abduction, emissaries from Cadmus arrive at his court. They are a troop of powerful armed warriors of a type Agenor has never before seen. Agenor doubts that their king is really his lost son, Cadmus, whom he believes is dead, but the warriors inform

him that Cadmus is indeed their king and that he left Agenor's realm because without arms it was no longer a manly kingdom, no longer a kingdom
he wished to rule over after his father. And so he went off and eventually
became ruler of a land of warriors who are literally his creation since, as
they explain to King Agenor, they are the issue of dragon teeth—the bare
teeth of Cadmus's dragon-strong will—planted by him in fields whence
they sprang already armed with swords and spears. Before they take their
leave of Agenor, Cadmus's warriors have a request to make of him. Since
they were not born of women, and there are no women in their realm, they
ask Agenor to supply them with women to take back with them. It is at this
point that Europa returns. When Cadmus's warriors burst in on the reunion
between Europa and Agenor, she is delighted to behold real men, and
when they inform her that they are from Cadmus and that they have been
ordered to return with women, Europa volunteers to go with them and to
bring her retinue of ladies-in-waiting with her. But the leader of the warriors
now declares that if Europa follows them, they cannot return to Cadmus's
realm because the king's sister must rule over her own land. Hence they
will go in search of a new land that will be named for their new queen,
Europa. Fearful that his own kingdom will go under without an army to
preserve it, Agenor calls out to his own men to take up arms and become
real men. They dash out and return with peasant girls who, they promise
Agenor, will bear them the strong men of the future. Agenor's final words
to the assembly of his own men and Cadmus's warriors make the point with
which Kaiser wanted to leave his audience: "Struggle for life, which alone
survives; real life is strong life, and the strongest is the best" (651).

In responding to the dance phenomenon of his own time, Kaiser wrote
a play in which dance figures prominently but is used against itself as symptomatic of an effete culture that can survive only through strength and
struggle. It was a message wholly in line with the growing cult of manliness
and physical strength of early twentieth-century Europe.

The Dance Phenomenon:
Its Impact on Literature

The commanding modernist interest in dance in general and in the modern dance phenomenon can also be seen in poetry and prose fiction. Beginning with the French Symbolists Stéphane Mallarmé and Paul Valéry in
the late nineteenth century, the evidence is striking. An enthusiast of music
and theater, deeply concerned with the relationship between literature and
the performing arts, Mallarmé concentrated his thoughts on dance in a few
short essays in *Crayonné au théâtre* (*Scribbled at the Theater*, 1887).[32]

To Mallarmé, poetry was the source of all beauty, and dance—poetry in motion, universal in its wordlessness, at once theatrical—was poetry transposed to the stage, its most perfect scenic realization. Since dance was no mere reproduction on stage of everyday movements and gestures, it was symbolic, abstract, impersonal, and as universal as music, like the poetry Mallarmé sought to create. In dance, the dancer ceased to be an individual, a distinct entity, and became an emblem, a sign, its meaning to be determined by the spectator's imagination:

> This means that the dancer *is not a woman dancing*; that, by reason of these juxtaposed motives, *she is not a woman*, but a metaphor symbolizing one of the elemental aspects of our form—sword, cup, flower, and so on, and that *she does not dance* but instead suggests through the wonder of leaps and shortcuts, with a bodily writing, what one would need several paragraphs of dialogue or descriptive prose to express in writing. Hers is a poem free of all the writer's tools.[33]

In his writing on dance, as on music, Mallarmé never parted company with the domain of literature, regarding dance, like music, as another form of writing. Unlike literal writing, however, the text produced by dance is the dance itself. The dancer evaporates, as it were, in the dance, which becomes its own subject. It is self-contained, physical and immaterial at the same time, and impermanent. As Mary Lewis Shaw puts it so aptly: "The absence-in-presence of the dancing figure implies a presence-in-absence of the literary text."[34]

Although he grew up on and greatly admired traditional ballet—which shaped most of his views on dance—Mallarmé appreciated the innovative and was attracted, like so many in his time, to Loïe Fuller. The American dancer had come to Paris in 1892 with the ambition of dancing at the National Academy of Choreography. When she was offered only four performances at the Opera, she accepted a lucrative engagement at the Folies Bergères. After resolving a misunderstanding over another dancer performing under her name, Fuller went on to dance at the Folies and became an outstanding success.

Mallarmé saw Fuller on more than one occasion and probably sketched his short essay, "Autre étude de danse: les fonds dans le ballet, d'apres une indication récente" ("Another Dance Study: Subjects in the Ballet, According to a Recent Indication"), during an actual performance in 1893. In his essay, Mallarmé draws particular attention to Fuller's trademark—the yards of illuminated fabric with which the dancer filled the stage and succeeded in keeping aloft by the amazing manipulation of her body: "This transition from sonorities to fabrics (or, better said, Music resembling gauze!)

is, uniquely, the sortilege that Loïe Fuller operates . . . . The enchantress makes the ambiance, draws it from herself and suppresses it in herself, by means of silence palpitating with crêpes de Chine." [35] Consonant with his views on silence expressed elsewhere, Mallarmé insists on the ineffability of much of Fuller's art: "So much must be tacit! To proffer a word about her, while she performs, even very quietly and for the edification of those near, seems impossible" (309).

Fascinated with pantomime, as his short essay "Mimique" ("Mime") in *Crayonné au théâtre* makes clear, Mallarmé addressed the need to keep dance and mime distinct. He felt that both shared the common feature (and virtue) of silence, and in this regard related to and competed with one another. But, as he cautioned in another essay, "Ballets," dance and panto-mime should not be mixed:

> Drama is the historic art of the stage; although it shares the stage, ballet is dif-ferent, symbolic. Allied, but not to be confused. Two attitudes that are jealous of their respective silences should not be yoked haphazardly and with com-mon treatment. Mime and dance become suddenly hostile if they are forcibly brought together . . . . This distinctive trait of each theatrical genre, in contact or opposition with the other, becomes the controlling element of the work that employs the disparity for its very structure. But a communication still remains to be found. Ordinarily, the librettist does not grasp that the ballerina expresses herself with steps, and knows no other eloquence, not even that of gesture.(306)

Despite its brevity, "Mime" is an intriguing piece. It was occasioned by the macabre pantomime, *Pierrot Assassin de sa Femme* (*Pierrot, the Mur-derer of His Wife*, 1881), by Mallarmé's cousin, Paul Margueritte. A writer of pantomimes and other literary works, Margueritte was also one of the founders of the Cercle Funambulesque (1888–98), a highly successful ama-teur group devoted to all aspects of mime and intent on continuing the tradition of the Théâtre des Funambules of the 1830s.[36] Finding a paral-lel with writing, as he does, for example, in his pieces on dance, Mallarmé likens the silence of mime, which is the absence of language, to the blank-ness of a page on which nothing has yet been transcribed. But mime as a blank page acquires a text, in a sense, through performance, a form of cor-poreal writing. Of particular interest in the Margueritte pantomime is its ideal silence. Only the "idea" is illustrated on the stage since there is no "effective action"—the pantomime consists in the main of Pierrot's night-time *memory* of the murder of his wife, Columbine, by tickling her to death. The actual deed, however, is not mimed, only Pierrot's reenactment of it with himself playing victim and murderer. In the end, a hallucinating Pierrot dies of a seizure after some mysterious force seems to be tickling his own feet and he accidentally sets his bedroom on fire. Mallarmé quotes Margueritte's own words at this point: "This is how the Mime works, wherein the play is limited to a perpetual allusion without the glass being broken. There is thus established an atmosphere of pure fiction" (310).

Paul Valéry's interest in dance went back at least to the beginning of the century. In a letter to Claude Debussy in 1900, for example, he alluded to their possible collaboration on a ballet.[37] The ballet never materialized, but Valéry did incorporate his thoughts on dance in the well-known dialogue, L'Ame et la danse (The Soul and the Dance), which first appeared in La Revue Musicale on December 1, 1921.[38] As a banquet attended by Socrates, Phaedrus, and the physician Eryximachus (all three drawn from Socrates' The Symposium) draws to an end, dancing girls appear, and the men comment on the exquisiteness of their performance, especially that of Athikte. As Eryximachus observes in wonderment: "Her whole being becomes dance, and wholly vows itself to total movement!"[39] Socrates then directs the conversation to the meaning of dance itself. Erixymachus's answer recalls Mallarmé's view that the dance has no referent beyond itself:

SOCRATES: O my friends, what in truth is dance?

ERIXYMACHUS: Is it not what we see?—What clearer expression of dancing do you want than dancing itself? (308)

In her dancing, Athikte seems to be respond to unconscious forces within herself, as if possessed. As Socrates declares: "A cold eye would without difficulty see her as demented, this woman strangely uprooted, who wrests herself away from her own form, whilst her limbs—gone mad—seem to dispute earth and air; and her head, thrown back, trails on the ground her loosened hair; and one of her legs takes the place of that head; and her finger traces I know not what signs in the dust!" (310).

As to whether or not Athikte represents anything in dance, Socrates comments: "Nothing, dear Phaedrus. But everything, Eryximachus. As well love as the sea, and life itself, and thoughts . . . . Do you not see; she is the pure act of metamorphosis?" (312). He further elaborates on Athikte's singularity in the most renowned passage of the dialogue, wherein he compares the dancer in her all-consuming ecstasy to a salamander living "completely at ease, in an element comparable to fire":

Well, then, does it not seem to you, Eryximachus, and to you, my dear Phaedrus, that the creature that is quivering over there, fluttering adorably within our gaze, that ardent Athikte, who divides and gathers herself together again, who rises and falls, so promptly opening out and closing in, and who appears to belong to constellations other than ours—seems to live, completely at ease, in an element comparable to fire—in a most subtle essence of music and movement, wherein she breathes boundless energy, while she participates with all her being in the pure and immediate violence of extreme felicity?—If we compare our grave and weighty condition with the state of that sparkling salamander, does it not seem to you that our ordinary acts, begotten by our successive needs, and our gestures and incidental movements are like coarse materials, like an impure stuff of duration—whilst that exaltation and that vibration of life, that supremacy of tension, that transport into the highest agility one is capable of, have the virtues and the potencies of flame; and that the shames, the worries, the sillinesses, and the monotonous foods of existence are consumed within it, making what is divine in a mortal woman shine before our eyes? (319)

In an essay on "Poet and Dancer before Diaghilev," Frank Kermode expresses his belief that when Valéry wrote the above passage in *The Soul and the Dance*, he specifically had Loïe Fuller in mind: "Fuller with her long sticks, her strange optical devices, her burying the human figure in masses of silk, achieved impersonality at a stroke. Her world was discontinuous from nature; and this discontinuity Valéry, speaking of his Symbolist ancestry, described as 'an almost inhuman state.'" [40]

Athikte's dance is understood, finally, as an act of utter self-possession. As Socrates explains, "the body which is there wishes to attain to an entire possession of itself, and to a point of glory that is supernatural" (321). That point of glory, wherein Athikte appears about to penetrate into another world, is the culmination of her dance. Following it, she falls lifeless, but she is not dead and soon recovers. At the moment of supreme ecstasy, she was, as Socrates had opined to Phaedrus and Eryximachus, resting motionless "in the very center of her movement. Alone, alone to herself, like the axis of the world" (324). Drawing the lesson from the mystery of performance embodied in Athikte's dance, Socrates acknowledges the ultimate supremacy of body over mind: "A body, by its simple force, and its act, is powerful enough to alter the nature of things more profoundly than ever the mind in its speculations and dreams was able to do!" (324).

Commenting on his dialogue in a letter to Louis Séchan (who devotes a chapter to *The Soul and the Dance* in his own book, *La Danse grecque antique* [Paris, 1930]) Valéry stressed the physiological: "The constant thought of the *dialogue* is physiological—from the digestive difficulties of the opening to the final fainting-spell. . . . As for the form of the whole, I tried to make all the dialogue itself a kind of ballet in which the Image and the Idea are in turn the ballerinas. The abstract and the concrete lead by turns and are united in the final vertigo."[41]

Dance as possession, the possession of the dancer by his or her body, is the subject of one of the best short works of fiction by the German writer Alfred Döblin. A Berlin physician-become-writer whose international repute owes most to his novel *Berlin Alexanderplatz* (1929), Döblin began his literary career with short stories that he began publishing in 1910 in Herwath Walden's Expressionist journal *Der Sturm* (*The Storm*). The first collection of the stories appeared in 1915 under the title *Die Ermorderung einer Butterblume und andere Erzählungen* (*The Murder of a Butterfly and Other Stories*). The collection includes "Die Tänzerin und der Leib" ("The Dancer and the Body"), arguably the most intriguing of Döblin's short stories and the first he published in *Der Sturm*.

A reflection of the influence on Döblin's early writing of the Symbolist movement's preoccupation with abstract questions of art, "The Dancer and the Body" explores the strange relationship between a young dancer and her body. Gifted by nature, the girl became a dancer at the age of eleven. So superb was her command over her body, so masterful her control of her medium, that she succeeded "in sprinkling cold on the most voluptuous dance."[42] By the age of sixteen, she was to all intents and purposes "loveless, paid close attention to her less talented colleagues, and became bored with their complaints" (16). But disaster befell her when she was nineteen. She contracted a serious illness that made dancing progressively more difficult. Although she made every effort to continue with her art, she finally gave in to her mother's insistence that she enter a hospital. Bitter over her helplessness, she turned to berating the body that had let her down and refused to cooperate with her doctors and nurses. The tension between the dancer and her body was further aggravated by the doctors' primary concern with it, as if indeed it had become a thing unto itself. But then her attitude changed. Now regarding her body as the home in which she lived, she became resentful of the physicians' intrusions, as if they were thieves stealing a part of her every time they came. Overcome by weakness, unable to resist any longer, she again distanced herself from her body, treating it as a separate entity, more like another person:

> The body lay beneath her like a piece of carrion. No longer did she concern herself with its pains. When it stabbed and tormented her at night, she said to it: "Be calm until the doctors' visit in the morning. Complain to them, to your

doctors, but leave me alone." They kept separate house, and the body could see how it had come to terms with the doctors. "They'll soon be taking notes again." At that, she cut off further pestering. (18)

Stirred by the march music of soldiers passing the hospital one afternoon, the dancer told her nurses that she wanted to embroider and demanded the appropriate materials. Clutching a pencil, she furiously drew a curious picture on the cloth: a round, shapeless body on two legs, without arms and head,

> nothing but a thick, two-legged ball. Next to it, towered a large, gentle man with a huge pair of spectacles who was stroking the body with a thermometer. But while he was seriously preoccupied with the body, a small girl, who was hopping on bare feet, made a long nose at him with her left hand while with her right she was jabbing the body from beneath with a sharp pair of scissors until it began running out in a thick stream like a punctured barrel. (19)

The drawing became an act of catharsis after which the dancer again wanted to dance, to dance above all a waltz with him who had become her master, with her body. With one final exertion of her will, she believed, she could seize him by the hands and throw him about and down until he was no longer her master. Driven by intense hate, she wanted to roll him on the floor, like a barrel, and stick his face in the sand. But with a voice that had suddenly become hoarse, she called for her doctor. As he was leaning over her to examine her, she tossed off her blanket and plunged the sewing scissors into her chest. "Even in death," Döblin writes at the end, "the dancer had the same cold, contemptuous twist to her mouth" (19).

In a highly compressed (three-and-a-half-page) story—remarkable in its brevity for a writer known for the length of his novels—Döblin drew an eerie picture of the relationship between the artist and his art. Rejecting the view that art resided within the artist, Döblin uses the ultimately fatal relationship between a dancer and her body to demonstrate that just when the dancer was at the height of her power, when she wielded her body as if it were no more than a plaything subject to her will, the body exerted its own power, asserted its own autonomy, and toppled her from her lofty peak. Only by destroying herself and her body at the same time could the dancer at last find peace and release from the torment of her awareness that the body had become her master.

So productive was Hugo von Hofmannsthal's involvement with dance and dancers that he can be regarded as paradigmatic of the extent to which the dance phenomenon could impact on the consciousness of the modernist artist. In personal terms, Hofmannsthal's enthusiasm for dance is best seen in his relations with two of the leading dancers of his time, the American Ruth St. Denis and the Austrian Grete Wiesenthal. These artistically productive relations were preceded by Hofmannsthal's deepening interest in nonverbal art, as we have already seen.

Hofmannsthal actually began writing nonverbal drama as early as 1900, a year before the composition of *The Letter* (1901). This is significant insofar as it establishes that Hofmannsthal's turning from verbal to nonverbal theatrical writing did not come as a consequence of the crisis described in that work. Indeed, he had already begun to experience a certain dissatisfaction with verbal art before venting his thoughts on the matter in *The Letter*. Between March 1900 and July 1901, he had written the libretto for the ballet *The Triumph of Time* and the text for the pantomime *The Pupil* (1901). These were the first in a long succession of dance libretti and pantomimes, extending to the opera libretto *Achilles on Skyros* in 1925.

Much of the impetus to Hofmannsthal's composition of libretti and pantomime came from his association with Ruth St. Denis and Grete Wiesenthal. It was Count Henry Kessler who first became smitten with St. Denis after he saw her perform in *Radha*. In a letter to Hofmannsthal from Berlin on October 6, 1906, Kessler, always on the lookout for rising stars, mentions that "a certain dancer, St. Denis," who "achieves what Duncan would like," is visiting from Paris. He then recommends that his friend see her at the first opportunity, and he describes her in these ecstatic terms: "It as if she stepped out of a Grecian vase, extraordinary in her movements, beauty, and rhythm."[43] A little over a month later, on November 20, Kessler reports to Hofmannsthal that he had St. Denis over for breakfast together with the dramatist Gerhart Hauptmann and that Hauptmann was impressed with her to the extent of intending to write a play for her to be produced by Reinhardt's Kammerspiele. Hauptmann later told Kessler that he was going to do a pantomime for her (139). Following a special matinee performance at the Theater des Westens in the Charlottenburg district of the German capital, the dancer was whisked away to a lunch hosted by Kessler at the exclusive Automobile Club of Berlin for the purpose of introducing his latest "discovery" to his coterie of artists.[44] Kessler's enthusiasm for St. Denis at this time bordered on the ecstatic. "Every moment with her," he wrote Hofmannsthal, "is pure joy for she always grasps the essence of everything" (134). Noting that St. Denis was then preparing new dances based on ancient Egyptian motifs, Kessler mentions that he and the dancer were going to make the rounds of Berlin's museums for material. In closing his letter to Hofmannsthal, Kessler urges him to make her acquaintance when she comes to Vienna, probably in January 1907.

Hofmannsthal saw St. Denis for the first time in a performance of *Radha* in Berlin in November 1907. Not long afterward, he wrote an essay of glowing praise under the title "Die unvergleichliche Tänzerin" ("The Incomparable Dancer"). Describing his response to her dancing, Hofmannsthal declared: "I feel this performance impregnated in the extreme with the single solitary moment in which we live. I feel how something incendiary has penetrated the real sensual life that has been present in the ghostly sphere of intellectual enjoyment for only a few decades."[45] It was, he went on, "the dance as such, the mute music of the human body." But true to his convictions now concerning the inadequacy of language, he declined any further attempt at defining the essence of St. Denis's art:

> Yet I shall hardly attempt to describe her dancing. Whatever one could describe in a dance would never be more than the incidentals: the costume, the sentiment, the allegory. Here nothing is sentimental, nothing allegorical, and even the costume, that glittering drapery which amid the enchantment of rhythmic, gradually intensifying movements suddenly yields to sudden nudity, the vision of which is rendered mysterious by the strange coloring of the light, and grave, severe as the vision of an undraped sacred statue in the enclosed space of a temple—this costume embroidered with gold (or whatever else she might wear on other occasions) is of incomparably small importance. (497–98)

Cognizant of St. Denis's indebtedness to Eastern art, Hofmannsthal attempted to set her in the appropriate context, beginning with her inscrutable smile:

> a mysterious smile always present in her motionless eyes: the smile of a Buddha statue. A smile not of this world. An absolutely unfeminine smile. A smile somehow related to the impenetrable smile in pictures by Leonardo. A smile that attracts the souls of uncommon persons and, from the first moment, but lastingly, alienates the hearts of women and the sensual curiosity of very many men.—And now the dance begins. It consists of movements. It consists of movements that merge with the next in an unceasing rhythmic flow. It is the same as what one saw the little Javanese girls dance in Paris in 1899, and this year the dancers of the King of Cambodia. Naturally it is the same thing to which all Oriental dancers aspire: the dance itself, the essential dance, the silent music of the human body. A rhythmic flow of incessant, and, as Rodin says, of right

movements. . . . That then is how she dances. It is the most intoxicating chain of gestures not one of which verges on a pose. They are constant emanations of absolute sensuous beauty, not *one* of which is convention, at least not European convention but instead the convention of the highest, most austere, ancient style. The progress of this dance is indescribable. A description would consist of details that are entirely insignificant and the picture would be distorted. (499–500)

After Berlin, St. Denis went on to Vienna, where she introduced such new dances as "The Yogi" and "The Nautch" at the popular (and venerable) entertainment palace, Etablissement Ronacher, in the heart of the imperial capital. This gave her ample opportunity to get together with Hofmannsthal and to plan some collaborative undertaking. Much impressed by Oscar Wilde's *Salomé*, Harry Kessler proposed to Hofmannsthal that he create a new Salome for St. Denis. Originally, she was supposed to appear in the role as a guest artist in a production of Wilde's *Salomé* scheduled for Max Reinhardt's Kammerspielhaus for the 1907–8 season. But her interest in playing Salome notwithstanding, she backed out of the production because of what she regarded as the secondary status of the dance in Wilde's play. When Kessler learned of her decision, he lost little time in persuading Hofmannsthal to rewrite the role as a showcase for St. Denis's talents. In a letter to the poet, Kessler described St. Denis's interpretation of the setting of Salome's dance and its effect principally on Herod:

> Immediately preceding the dance, a short, but highly dramatic and poetically compelling scene is needed, involving Herod and Herodias, and possibly also John, which results in Herodias allowing Salome to dance. In preparation for Salome's entrance and the dance, the lights on the table will gradually dim, so that the circle wherein she will dance becomes illuminated. This should take place through some sort of "natural" occurrence that is somehow motivated in the scenery (moonlight through an opening or window, or something similar). Salome's dance is now the important thing. She performs various dances, one after another, which makes Herod wilder and wilder, until finally, in a utter frenzy, he makes his vow. *During* the dance, the lights continue to grow dimmer, and the table gradually becomes completely dark; only the faces of the guests shine out of the darkness. Finally, just the pathologically distorted faces of Herod and Herodias, seated facing each other at either end of the table, at the *relatively* brightest spots, are visible. Out of this eerie darkness Herod utters the vow. The curtain closes almost immediately, and then reopens on a bleery-eyed dawn, and Salome enters with the head of the Baptist.[46]

Kessler also conveyed to Hofmannsthal St. Denis's desire that the poet write a twenty-minute narrative to precede her solo dance. "The basic idea," Kessler wrote, "is, in any case, that the poetry remain throughout a frame for the dance. It seems to me that this project is perfect for you. The scene before the dance can and must be very strong poetically, captivating in beauty of language and tone, so that the dance blooms from it as a flower of poison, blooms from this grandiose biblical speech and scenery and then overshadows everything" (136–37). But the plan never reached fruition. St. Denis may have been put off by Hofmannsthal's intention to include spoken scenes in it in a combination of dance and drama. St. Denis's biographer, Suzanne Shelton, speculates additionally that the project fell victim to the dancer's budding relationship with Hofmannsthal's brother-in-law, the artist Hans Schlesinger, who spent most of his time in Italy and who was shunned by both Hofmannsthal and Kessler. In fact, despite their creative mutual attraction, the Austrian writer never actually succeeded in creating a work for his American friend. Her influence, however, expressed itself in other ways. Besides encouraging his inclination toward nonverbal drama, St. Denis may also have been on Hofmannsthal's mind when he wrote the short dialogue *Furcht* (*Fear*, 1907), a work that also brings to mind Valéry's *The Soul and the Dance*. Hofmannsthal's dialogue takes place between two Greek dancing girls, Laidion and Hymnis. Laidion in particular is tired of entertaining men and of entering into relationships with them that usually lead nowhere. She yearns to be far away and is intrigued by a sailor's story about a strange barbarian island whose inhabitants dance just once a year in an annual rite of patently orgiastic character. As she tells Hymnis:

> They dance only once in the year. The young men crouch on the ground and the girls of the island stand in front of them, all together, in such a way that their bodies become one body. That's how motionless they stand. Then they dance, and at the end the girls give themselves to the boys, with no choice involved. The girl belongs to whomever seizes her. They do it for the sake of the gods and the gods bless them.[47]

Although Hymnis dismisses this as shameless, Laidion envies the girls of the island because they are without fear. Life has taught her that fear comes from hope which in turn springs from desires destined to be thwarted. It is, in fact, fear that makes young women such as Laidion and Hymnis dance; they are like puppets on strings being manipulated by fear. Hymnis cannot understand her. When she herself dances, men tear their wreaths from their heads and throw them at her feet. At such moments she feels herself fulfilled. To her insistence that she experiences no fear, Laidion replies that she has desires, and desires are fear, that all her dancing is nothing more than desire and striving. Since desire, striving, and hope breed fear, the person who is truly happy is the one who knows no hope. Hence Laidion's envy of the women on the island who lack personal desires and fears. There then follows a wordless scene in which Laidion begins dancing as if surrounded by the women of the mysterious island who join her in a frenzied dance in which they become the conceivers and conceived of the island, "the bearers of death and of life" (367). Laidion is completely transformed under the spell of the dance, her countenance becomes that of a "barbarian deity." When she comes to after falling exhausted onto a bed (recalling the faint into which the dancer in Valéry's dialogue falls), she complains bitterly of knowing that the satisfaction of being happy without hope exists in the world but that she herself does not possess it. It seems likely, given the chronology of *Fear* and Hofmannsthal's relations at the time with St. Denis, that he saw her as the embodiment of the principle of pure dance as he portrays it in his story.

Hofmannsthal's relationship with another dancer, his fellow Viennese Grete Wiesenthal, proved more productive than with Ruth St. Denis. The poet and the dancer met for the first time in 1907, not long after Hofmannsthal was introduced to St. Denis by Count Harry Kessler. The oldest of the seven children of the academic painter Fritz Wiesenthal, Grete, soon followed by her sister, Elsa, began studying ballet at the age of ten in the imperial court opera theater.[48] In May 1907, the year in which she met Hofmannsthal, Grete Wiesenthal and Elsa left the court theater and struck out on their own in a program of light dances composed by them.

The public career of the Wiesenthal Sisters, as the troupe of Grete, Elsa, and another sister, Bertha, became known, was launched on January 14 at the opening night of the most famous cabaret in Vienna's history, the Fledermaus ("Bat").[49] This led in turn to Max Reinhardt's invitation to them to come to Berlin to perform dance matinees in the theater hall of the Künstlerhaus (House of Artists). Other invitations followed and before long the sisters were international celebrities, dancing before enthusiastic audiences from Russia to the United States.

The focus of the collaboration between Hofmannsthal and Grete Wiesenthal was their common interest in pantomime. Hofmannsthal wrote his first pantomime, *The Pupil*, as early as 1901. In 1907, when the poet and the dancer first met, Grete and Elsa Wiesenthal danced in the pantomime *The Dancer and the Marionette*, based on a work by Max Mell. Three years later, in 1910, the three Wiesenthal sisters performed in Max Reinhardt's production of *Sûmurûn*. Hofmannsthal's own interest in pantomime, which had been growing steadily since his relationship with Ruth St. Denis, converged with that of Grete Wiesenthal in 1910. In the summer of that year she read Hofmannsthal's recently completed pantomimes, *Amor and Psyche* and *The Strange Girl*, and danced in them in Berlin in the autumn. The latter work in particular proved a considerable success and was made into a silent film under the same title. Shot mostly in Sweden, Grete Wiesenthal played the lead role in it. The film had its premiere in the Cinés-Theater in Berlin in September 1913. It opened in Vienna in January 1914 and in London that same month as *The Strange Girl*.

Prior to her collaboration with Hofmannsthal, Grete Wiesenthal drew the inspiration for her dances primarily from music. Narrative action played no role or at best a very limited one. But this changed once she and Hofmannsthal began working together. This is not to suggest that Grete Wiesenthal discovered pantomime only within the context of her relationship with Hofmannsthal. At the beginning of her career she had worked as a dancer and choreographer in pantomimes under Max Reinhardt's tutelage at the Berlin Deutsches Theater. These "exercises" provided her the opportunity to experiment with ways of freeing herself from conventional gesture language and stereotypical sign language. But she came to appreciate the full potential of dance pantomime in her collaboration with Hofmannsthal. She acknowledges this, and his role in her development as a dancer, in a reminiscence she wrote, "Amoretten, die um Säulen schweben" ("Cupids Floating about Columns"), for a volume of commemorative pieces published in 1949 on the twentieth anniversary of Hofmannsthal's death:

> In our talks on the essence of dance and pantomime, I felt him to be a true spiritual dance partner with a rare intuitive understanding that I never experienced later with any other. The sublime dance works Hofmannsthal created for me—*Amor and Psyche* and *The Strange Girl*—arose from these talks. I then took them with me to Berlin to give them life on the stage.[50]

FOUR

The Man of Letters

as Man of Action:

From Teddy Roosevelt

to Saint-Exupéry

I thought about Tolstoi and about what a great advantage an experience of war was to a writer. It was one of the major subjects and certainly one of the hardest to write truly of and those writers who had not seen it were always very jealous and tried to make it seem unimportant, or abnormal, or a disease as a subject, while, really, it was just something quite irreplaceable that they had missed.

ERNEST HEMINGWAY, *Green Hills of Africa*

We have examined the shift from the verbal to the nonverbal in the theater and the emergence of the modern dance phenomenon and its resonance in other arts as a further response to this transformation. The present chapter considers the impact of the modernist physical imperative on the writer, reflected in the activist pursuit of physical challenge and danger, the new thematics of war and sport, and, where relevant, the cultivation of an appropriate literary idiom.

The widening reaction against bourgeois society, on the one hand, and the inertia of intellectual culture, on the other, resulted in many writers yearning for direct participation in life. Inventing action was one thing; living it, something else entirely. The greater the danger and the greater its proximity, the more one lived life to the fullest. This quest for the life of action, and the almost transcendent exultation in it, typified the outlook of a number of writers in the decades both before and after World War I. By transforming himself from a man of letters into a man of action, the writer stood a better chance of fulfilling himself both as an artist and as man. I am deliberately not using "man" in the generic sense here. The phenomenon I am addressing was, to all intents and purposes, distinctly masculine. The figures I am writing about were men; their passion for action, in the physical sense, was understood as "masculine"—women either had no place in this cult of masculinity or at best were assigned secondary or marginal roles in it. This does not mean that the writers being considered were indifferent or in any way hostile to women; some certainly were, but often quite the contrary was true. It is just that they viewed their embrace of action, and danger, as an authentication of themselves as men first and foremost. Theirs was a world of physical challenge, the willingness to look death in the face, the company of like-minded men. It was a world that was homosexual in the anerotic sense of the term. Sex, where it asserted itself, was no more or less than another aspect of male self-realization. Yet in its marked masculine exclusivity, this was a world that was irrefutably gender biased.

Apart from exotic travel, which was much in fashion during the modernist movement and had broad ramifications, from philosophical interests to poetic style, the greatest opportunity for the man of letters to realize himself as a man of action, or for the man of action to become a man of letters, was afforded by World War I. Occurring within the time frame of modernism, the war must be viewed within the context of the widespread desire to shape a new postbourgeois Europe. In the aftermath of the defeat of the Central Powers, the political map of Europe was transformed. By 1918, the old order was gone in more than just the political sense. The great empires of nineteenth-century central and eastern Europe had crumbled. Germany in defeat was in shambles, and the Weimar Republic that arose from the rubble proved too fragile to withstand the assault on it from Right and Left alike. The Austro-Hungarian empire of the Habsburgs disintegrated even more ignominiously and was replaced by a tiny Austrian state first known as German-Austria (*Deutsch-Österreich*), to distinguish it from an independent Hungary and the new or reborn Slavic states that were carved out of the old Habsburg empire: Czechoslovakia, Poland, and the Kingdom of the

Serbs, Croats, and Slovenes (later Yugoslavia). The empire of the Russian tsars was another casualty, replaced after 1917 by the new Bolshevik state of the Union of Soviet Socialist Republics.

The collapse of the old imperial structures saw also the collapse of bourgeois society as it had existed in the nineteenth century. Loathed and contested by artists and intellectuals, besieged by revolutionaries at both ends of the political spectrum, the traditional bourgeois order had scant hope of survival in the 1920s and 1930s. Totalitarianism, both on the Right and the Left, made sure of that.

The almost mindless enthusiasm for the first "world war" was fueled, to a great extent, by the expectation that Europe would not, could not, emerge from it as it had been. The pent-up claustrophobia, the sense of sterility of the nineteenth century, desperately needed release through change, and the more cataclysmic the change—so the feeling went—the greater the possibility of a truly new age dawning. Europe may have stumbled into war because of an entangling network of alliances, but once in it, the passion for soldiering and combat bordered on the irrational. If the war was destined to change the political and economic map of Europe, it was also destined to change its literary landscape.

As examples of the different ways the creative personality responded to the war, and to the risks and challenges of high adventure in general, I propose to consider the cases of seven writers: Gabriele D'Annunzio and Filippo Tommaso Marinetti, both Italian; Nikolai Gumilyov, Russian; Ernst Jünger, German; Ernest Hemingway, American; and two Frenchman, Henry de Montherlant and Antoine de Saint-Exupéry. Although too young to participate in World War I (he was born in 1900), Saint-Exupéry exemplifies no less handsomely the writer whose passion for adventure and fearlessness in the face of great danger began at an early age and demanded an active role in World War II despite the fact that by then he was considered too old for combat. Other figures might also have been introduced, but the writers I discuss represent sufficient literary as well as geographical diversity for the purposes of this study.

The figure of the artist as activist was hardly an innovation of modernism. The type has existed for a long time; one need reach no further back in history than the Romantic movement and Byron's embrace of the Greek liberation struggle, which led to his death at Missolonghi in 1824, or the Pole Adam Mickiewicz's formation of a legion of Polish volunteers in Italy to fight against Austria in 1848. It is, however, the convergence of cultural and social factors in the modernist period that all but impelled the man of letters to don the mantle of action.

If the twentieth century was destined to become, as some have suggested, the American century, perhaps it was proper that the first president of the new century, Theodore Roosevelt (in office 1901–9), should exemplify love of action and conflict, enthusiasm for physical fitness, the great outdoors, blood sport, and the ability to commit his adventures to literary form. Unlike Kipling, who glorified derring-do and combat but had little firsthand experience, Roosevelt seemed never more fulfilled than when he traded the role of politician for that of explorer, hunter, and fighter.

In order to overcome childhood frailty, Roosevelt had embarked on a program of vigorous physical training from which he emerged an exemplar of physical as well as mental self-discipline and self-reliance and a dedicated outdoorsman and hunter. When hardly into his teens, he sought to find literary expression for his forays as a budding naturalist and small-game hunter in the Adirondacks and White Mountains.[1] Specimen collecting and further refinement of his skills with a rifle followed on a family trip to Egypt, the Holy Land, Syria, and Greece in the winter of 1872–73. Ten years later, he visited the Dakota Territory, thereby beginning his long fascination with the vast expanses of the American West and the great opportunities for big-game hunting it offered. Challenged and exhilarated by everything he experienced in the West, Roosevelt endeavored at the same time to recount his adventures with a more mature style of writing intended to effectively convey the emotions he experienced in the field and to give the reader a sense of genuine participation. His books from this period—*Hunting Trips of a Ranchman* (1885), *Ranch Life and the Hunting Trail* (1888), and *The Wilderness Hunter* (1893)—were enormously successful and inspired readers drawn to the outdoor life for decades. More than a mere recorder of his own adventures, Roosevelt had a superb power of observation and the gift for describing even the ordinary with a keen eye for detail. His writing was lucid, spare, and often vivid. Thrilled by everything he had experienced in the West—his adventures as explorer, rancher, and hunter, which he believed shaped him as a man—Roosevelt was prompted to write arguably his finest literary work, the four-volume *Winning of the West* (1889–96), an exceptionally felicitous combination of sound historical scholarship and narrative power. As Roosevelt's biographer, William Henry Harbaugh, characterizes its achievement: "It stamped its author as a historian of genuine distinction: of brilliant, though uneven, literary power; of broad, and often acute, comprehension; and of extraordinary narrative force."[2]

By now a recognized authority on big-game hunting, Roosevelt wrote of his experiences with a variety of animals and weapons with professionalism, free of remorse and balanced by a deep feeling for the beauties and challenges of nature. These qualities are plainly in evidence in the series of books he wrote or edited for the Boone and Crocket Club, including *Trail and Campfire* (1897), about hunting in the Rocky Mountains; *American Big Game Hunting* (1893), the first of three volumes he coedited for the Boone and Crocket Club series; and *Hunting in Many Lands* (1895). But whatever the subject of his subsequent books of exploration and hunting— *Hunting Trips on the Prairie and in the Mountains* (1900), *African Game Trails* (1910), and *Through the Brazilian Wilderness* (1914)—no episode as an outdoorsman compared with his exploits during the Spanish-American War of 1898 for the sheer thrill and sense of manhood that he achieved.

Carried along on the near-hysterical wave of war fever that gripped most Americans in the wake of the mysterious sinking of the U.S. battleship *Maine* in Havana harbor on February 15, 1898, Roosevelt resigned his post as assistant secretary of the Navy, accepted a commission as lieutenant colonel, and set about organizing a regiment of volunteer cavalrymen. Officially known as the First Volunteer Cavalry Regiment, the regiment covered itself with glory and entered American popular lore as the Rough Riders. Formally under the command of Colonel Leonard Wood, a professional military man and a good friend of Roosevelt's, the Rough Riders were swamped with applications from all over the country. Finally consisting of 23,000 handpicked men, the Riders' finest hour was the charge up San Juan Hill in the battle of Santiago. Roosevelt himself led the charge, which delivered a crippling blow to the Spaniards. The event has been immortalized in Frederic Remington's painting, "The Charge Up San Juan Hill," which shows Roosevelt as the sole figure on horseback, leading the assault. For Roosevelt personally, the event was, in his own words, "the great day of my life." The Spanish-American War catapulted Roosevelt to even greater national fame as a genuine American hero, as the embodiment of manly virtues, and as the ideal candidate for the governorship of New York. His successful run for that office led in just a few years to the White House, in which he served first as William McKinley's vice president and then as president following McKinley's assassination in 1901.

Even before he left the White House in 1909, Roosevelt had his heart set on what he felt would be the greatest hunting expedition of his life— going after the great animals of the African plains. With the backing of the Smithsonian Institution, to whose National Museum's collections of African natural history he made major contributions, Roosevelt set off on his grand safari on March 23, 1909. He was accompanied by a U.S. Army naturalist, Dr. Edgar Mearns; Alden Loring, another naturalist; Edmund Heller, a twenty-six-year-old professor at the University of California with whom

Roosevelt would in 1914 author the two-volume *Life Histories of African Game Animals*; a group of professional big-game hunters; and some two hundred natives.[3] Once on the African continent, the expedition lasted from April 9, 1909, to March 30, 1910, and followed a route from Aden to Mombassa, Port Florence, Entebbe, around Lake Victoria, and Gondokoro in British East Africa, thence to Khartoum (Sudan), Wadi Halfa (Egypt), Aswan, and finally Cairo, from which Roosevelt proceeded to a ceremonial tour of several European capitals. In early June 1910, he was back in New York, where a parade was held in his honor.

The African safari was Roosevelt's grandest adventure as a hunter, and the book to which it gave rise, *African Game Trails*, was a splendid tribute to the magnificence of the great beasts Roosevelt found in abundance and the strangeness and wonder of the African landscape. A huge success — from the hunter's point of view — in terms of the number and variety of game bagged, there is hardly a nuance of the safari that is not described with vividness and admirable fidelity to detail. Avid hunter though he was, Roosevelt respected the animals he killed and was sincerely concerned about the preservation of species. Although he never sanctioned the whole-sale slaughter of wildlife, he believed that nature was incapable of sustaining the uncontrolled growth of herds and so he approached the disciplined "thinning" of them with a consistent lack of sentimentality. In this respect, as well as in his great love for hunting and the connection he drew between it and manliness, he anticipated Hemingway's African safaris of the early 1930s and their greatest literary fruit, the nonfictional *Green Hills of Africa* (1935). In their shared love of the kill, their instinctual need of action as a fundamental component of manliness, and their ability to translate their adventures into virile and compelling writing, Roosevelt and Hemingway were cut from much the same cloth.

Gabriele D'Annunzio:
The Symbolist as Conqueror

D'Annunzio was without question the leading Italian writer of his day. A gifted, prolific writer, as well known for his prose fiction as for his poetry and plays, D'Annunzio contributed greatly to his own cult. Short, slight, bald-headed in adult life, eventually blind in one eye, he was anything but an ideal masculine type. But what he lacked in looks he more than made up for in intelligence, seductive personal charm, flamboyance, and self-promotion. His reputation as a lady-killer was legendary, as was his romantic liaison with the world-famous Italian actress Eleanora Duse.[4]

D'Annunzio's lush verbal style, his typical fin-de-siècle aestheticism, would hardly seem compatible with a flair for military adventure and high political drama. But World War I provided the poet with an unparalleled opportunity to show the stuff he was made of as a man, soldier, and patriot.

Reared like so many of his contemporaries on the writings of Nietzsche, Bergson, and others, D'Annunzio enthusiastically welcomed Italy's declaration of war against the Central Powers on May 24, 1915. He was fifty-two years old at the time, but his age did not deter him either from racing about Italy giving impassioned speeches in favor of Italian intervention in the war on the side of the Allies (Britain, France, Russia) or from asking permission to be a combatant himself. Given an appropriate officer's rank commensurate with his stature as a man of letters, D'Annunzio hurled himself into battle with unrestrained zeal. A flyer before the outbreak of the war, a fact reflected in one of his best novels, *Forse che sì, forse che no* (*Maybe Yes, Maybe No*, 1910), he took part in a number of aerial missions against Trieste, Duino, Pola, and Cottero, dropping bombs and propaganda leaflets. Undoubtedly his most sensational exploit in the sky was his participation in a bold, nonlethal raid by seven Italian aircraft from Treviso over Vienna on August 9, 1918, when he dropped red, white, and green leaflets on the Habsburg capital that called for its citizens to surrender. Six months before, in February, D'Annunzio had also left behind leaflets during a torpedo boat excursion into Buccari harbor near the Adriatic port of Fiume on the Dalmatian coast, where an Austrian vessel was torpedoed and sunk. D'Annunzio's passion for flying was paralleled, as we shall see, by that of Marinetti and the Futurists, whose enthusiasm for the machine and modern technology placed them in the vanguard of aerial enthusiasts. As late as 1935, Marinetti was still publishing such paeans to aviation as *L'Aeropoema del Golfo della Spezia* (*Aeropoem of the Gulf of Spezia*).

However dangerous and adventurous D'Annunzio's experiences in the air and on the sea were during the war, they pale in flamboyance when compared to his takeover of the Adriatic coastal city of Fiume shortly after the war. Like other states created out of the wreckage of the Austro-Hungarian empire after World War I, a new South Slavic state comprising principally Slovenes, Croats, and Serbs was also planned. This new state had no greater supporter than the influential American president, Woodrow Wilson, who played a major role in the postwar peace negotiations. Italy's claims on towns and cities along the Dalmatian coast went back to the Renaissance when Dubrovnik, known as Ragusa, was part of the Venetian Republic. While the Italians were willing, begrudgingly, to make certain concessions, ceding some territory to the Slavs while retaining possession of others, there was considerable opposition to the surrender of the big port city of Fiume

(Rijeka, in Serbo-Croatian). Although the city had a large Italian popu-
lation, it was completely surrounded by south Slavs and was considered
untenable by the Italians. Politicians of the stamp of the Prime Ministers
Nitti and Giolitti were willing to accept the loss of Fiume as inevitable; but
Italian nationalists and patriots saw the matter differently and made Italian
control of the city the hottest political issue of the day.

While the politicians wrangled back and forth over the Fiume question, D'Annunzio grasped the moment as ripe for the grand gesture. Now
admired as much for his exploits during the war as for his literary achievements, he swiftly took command of a disgruntled, restless band of veterans
and at dawn on September 12, 1919, set out from Venice to seize Fiume and
claim it for Italy in a bold move that presaged the march on Rome in 1922
of Mussolini and the Black Shirts.[5] Proceeding from Venice to Ronchi, near
Trieste, D'Annunzio and his "legionnaires"—as he called them, in memory of the ancient Roman soldiers—picked up more and more supporters
along the route. Overwhelmed by D'Annunzio's daring as well as by his
patriotic zeal and charm, the Allied military commander of Fiume, who
happened to be an Italian general, Pittaluga, virtually handed the city over
to the self-styled *comandante* and his hardy retinue.[6] Not only Italy, but
the Allied powers were dismayed. While arduous political maneuvering ensued, D'Annunzio went about the business of establishing his authority as
supreme commander of Fiume. Backed eventually by a force estimated at
three thousand men, D'Annunzio for the next sixteen months ruled Fiume
—generally referred to at the time as the Regency of Carnaro—as a benevolent dictator, or maybe better said, as an Italian Renaissance *condottiere*.

With correspondents and other observers from all over the globe attracted to the Adriatic city of about fifty thousand, D'Annunzio strutted
and postured, splendidly attired in a uniform of his own design and bedecked with medals. Again in a manner recalling Mussolini's later public
appearances in Rome, the *comandante* gave address upon address from the
balcony of the Government Palace of Fiume. Playing on the patriotism and
nationalism of the Italians, he vowed that Fiume would remain eternally
Italian and that he would resist any and all efforts to wrest the city from him
to the bitter end. No amount of persuasion on the part of Italian politicians,
who were willing to give up claim to the city under Allied pressure, had any
effect on him. Once he made his position clear, D'Annunzio went about
organizing the life of the city in accordance with his own political and social
outlook. Before long he devised a curious utopian and socialistic constitution for Fiume known as the Statute of the Carnaro, the provisions of which
he read to the townspeople from the balcony of the Government Palace.

D'Annunzio's "reign" over Fiume was destined, of course, to collapse. The situation was obviously intolerable to the Allies and the Italian authorities, who were being harder and harder pressed to take some action. The Treaty of Rapallo, which was concluded between Italy and the new Yugoslavia on November 12, 1920, followed President Wilson's idea of declaring Fiume a "free city." Although D'Annunzio denounced the treaty, his power to control the course of events had already begun to erode. However porous it may have been, a blockade of Fiume eventually took its toll and essential supplies, including food, became scarce. Daring modern-day pirate raids by the comandante's small navy rerouted money and some needed goods to the beleaguered city. But they also generated unfavorable publicity and hardened the resolve of the Italian government and the Allies. Discipline among the comandante's troops in Fiume had by now begun to break down and their arrogance and lawlessness bred resentment among the townspeople. Desertions, including that of the tiny Fiumian navy, began to increase, further destabilizing the situation. Sensing that the time was ripe for further action, the Italian prime minister, Giolitti, ordered a tightening of the blockade against Fiume. After a few skirmishes in which several men were killed, the Italian cruiser, Andrea Doria, was ordered to fire on the Government Palace. D'Annunzio narrowly escaped with his life. The Italian general in command of the operations against Fiume, Caviglia, threatened further punitive measures unless the terms of the Treaty of Rapallo were respected.

Well aware by now that his position was beyond hope, that the ranks of his loyal supporters had thinned dangerously, and that he had lost much of the enthusiasm and goodwill of the residents of Fiume themselves, D'Annunzio, ostensibly out of a desire to avoid a "massacre" of the townspeople, accepted what amounted to unconditional surrender. The comandante and his regency council resigned and a truce was called. D'Annunzio's last public act came on January 2, 1921, when he spoke at a graveside ceremony honoring the Italian soldiers and legionnaires—all thirty-two of them—who had fallen on the last day of Fiumian resistance. D'Annunzio lingered another sixteen days in the city, no one knows precisely why, and then went into political exile. The day of the poet-warrior had come and gone.

Soon after the Fiume episode, Italian—and worldwide—attention shifted dramatically from D'Annuzio and his exploits to the growing power of Mussolini and the Fascists. Although a professed admirer, and verbal supporter, of D'Annunzio, Mussolini was too cautious to alienate the Italian authorities and the Allied powers by making a public show of wholeheartedly embracing D'Annunzio's seizure of Fiume. By the time the poet retreated from politics, Mussolini had his own agenda to pursue and was much less concerned about ceremonial acknowledgments of D'Annunzio's greatness. But that these still counted for something was evident in the successful Fascist coup d'état of Milan on August 3, 1922. D'Annunzio, who happened to be in the city at the time, was carried by a band of jubilant Fascists like a prize trophy to the balcony of the city hall, where he made a barely audible speech to the assembled crowd generally praising the events that had just transpired. The subsequent Fascist march on Rome on October 29, 1922—which remotely owed something to the inspiration of D'Annunzio's march on Fiume—sealed Italy's fate until the end of World War II and ended any real relationship between the former comandante and the powerful new duce. Niceties, of course, were observed; it was still in Mussolini's best interests to have D'Annunzio in his camp. When the Fascist government formally annexed Fiume, on March 15, 1924, Mussolini proposed to the king that the poet be granted the title of prince of Monte-Nevoso, referring to the snowcapped mountain peak in the Carso range in commemoration of D'Annunzio's brief reign over Fiume. Ever vain, D'Annunzio accepted, despite his misgivings about Mussolini and the Fascists. Having in a sense discharged his last "obligation" with respect to a poet of faded reputation, Mussolini effectively distanced himself from what he regarded as a nuisance.

For his part, D'Annunzio felt progressively more estranged from the Fascists; when Mussolini fell into Hitler's embrace, D'Annunzio, who held the Nazi leader in utter contempt and mocked him on more than one occasion, could only retreat to his magnificently eccentric villa of Vittoriale on Lake Garda. There he lived out the rest of his life, surrounded by an incredible variety of objets d'art and mementos, including the airplane in which he flew over Vienna in 1918 and the bow of the cruiser Puglia, which had once illegally brought reinforcements to him in Fiume and which he got from the Italian navy after the ship had been taken out of service.

Filippo Tommaso Marinetti: The Futurist as Fascist

Although most of Marinetti's combat was waged on the field of art, he was no stranger to actual battle and extolled the virtues of war with far greater passion than had D'Annunzio. Beginning with the publication of his *Fondazione e Manifesto del Futurismo* (*The Founding and Manifesto of Futurism*) in the Parisian newspaper *Le Figaro* in February 1910, Marinetti conducted a relentless campaign to topple the old art within the framework of a demolition of the social status quo in general. Futurism, whose cause he was now advancing under the aegis of the new machine age, was meant to deliver a deathblow to the aestheticism and ethereality of symbolism, to the passivity of intellectual culture, and to the veneration of woman. Futurism was meant to be defiant, aggressive, revolutionary, physical, masculine. As Marinetti boldly stated in *The Manifesto of Futurism:*

> 1. We want to sing the love of danger, the habit of energy and fearlessness.
>
> 2. Courage, audacity, and revolt will be essential elements of our poetry.
>
> 3. Up to the present literature has exalted a pensive immobility, ecstasy, and sleep. We want to exalt aggressive action, a feverish insomnia, the racer's stride, the mortal leap, the punch and the slap.
>
> 4. We say that the world's magnificence has been enriched by a new beauty; the beauty of speed.[7]

As might be expected, the militancy of futurism would easily accommodate an advocacy of war:

> 9. We want to glorify war—the world's only hygiene—militarism, patriotism, the destructive gesture of libertarians, beautiful ideas worth dying for, and scorn for woman.
>
> 10. We want to destroy the museums, libraries, academies of every kind, and to fight moralism, feminism, every opportunistic or utilitarian cowardice. (10)

Marinetti's subsequent pronunciamentos, in the same bombastic, inflammatory rhetoric, further exhorted revolutionary dynamism, fearlessness, the strength to overcome the seductive power of woman, and the glorification of war. In *Uccidiamo il Chiaro di Luna!* (*Let's Murder the Moonshine!*, 1909), for example, we read: "For the moment we are content with blowing up all the traditions, like rotten bridges!—War? . . . Very well, yes: It's our only hope, our reason for living, our only desire" (14)! On July 8, 1910, true to the spirit of the new movement, a band of Futurists hurled down from the top of the Clock Tower in Venice countless thousands of leaflets proclaiming Marinetti's assault on the city as the embodiment of the old Italy that he despised. Titled *Contro Venezia passatista* (*Against Past-Loving Venice*), the new manifesto renounced past-loving Venice as "enfeebled and undone by worldly luxury . . . the Venice of foreigners, market for counterfeiting antiquarians, magnet for snobbery and universal imbecility, bed unsprung by caravans of lovers, jeweled bathtub for cosmopolitan courtesans, the great cesspit of passéism" (30). The new Venice that Marinetti and the Futurists wanted to create would be "an industrial and military Venice that can dominate the Adriatic Sea, that great Italian lake" (30).

Before World War I presented Marinetti and his followers the opportunity to see D'Annunzio in a new and different light, they denounced him in no uncertain terms—as, for example, in "Noi rinneghiamo i nostri maestri simbolisti ultimi amanti della luna" ("We Abjure Our Symbolist Masters, the Last Lovers of the Moon"), one of the pieces in the collection *Guerra sola igiene del mondo* (*War, the World's Only Hygiene*, 1911–15):

> Too long has Italy submitted to the enfeebling influence of Gabriele D'Annunzio, lesser brother of the great French Symbolists, nostalgic like them and like them hovering above the naked female body.
>
> One must at all costs combat Gabriele D'Annunzio, because with all his great skill he has distilled the four intellectual poisons that we want to abolish forever: 1) the sickly, nostalgic poetry of distance and memory; 2) romantic sentimentality drenched with moonshine that looks up adoringly to the ideal of Woman-Beauty; 3) obsession with lechery, with the adulterous triangle, the pepper of incest, and the spice of Christian sin; 4) the professorial passion for the past and the mania for antiquity and collecting. (261)

Marinetti's passion for war had the chance to move off the page and onto a real field of combat when in 1911, during the Italian-Turkish war provoked by the Italian conquest of Libya (which Mussolini in his early socialist period had condemned as imperialistic), he dashed off to witness the fighting for Tripoli. Inflamed by the Italian victories in North Africa, Marinetti declared his patriotism and visions of a new Italian empire in his "Tripoli italiana" ("Italian Tripoli," 1911): "Today Italy has for us the shape and power of a beautiful *dreadnought* with its squadron of torpedo-boat islands. Proud to feel that the warlike fervor that inspires the whole Country equals our own, we invite the Italian Government, which has finally become Futurist, to magnify all the nation's ambitions, despising the stupid accusations of piracy and proclaiming the birth of Panitalianism" (496).

An even stronger impression seems to have been made on him by the siege of Adrianople in 1912 during the first Balkan War, which Marinetti covered as a reporter for the Parisian paper *Gil Blas*. It was from these experiences that he got the inspiration for one of his most important (and longest) works, the 147-page *Zang Tumb Tumb: Adrianopoli Ottobre 1912* (1914). The "poem"—as the work is usually designated in Italian sources—will be discussed in the next chapter in the context of Marinetti's Futurist experiments with poetic language and typography and need not detain us much longer here. Virtually a compendium of its author's theories of *parole in libertà* (words in freedom), syntax, and sound in language, *Zang Tumb Tumb* was born of war and uses its arsenal of effects to capture the tempo and clamor of combat. As improbable as it may seem, Marinetti actually gave public recitals of passages from *Zang Tumb Tumb*. On his second visit

to England in the early summer of 1914, a dinner in his honor was organized in a London restaurant by the writer Wyndham Lewis and C. R. W.
Nevinson, a painter and the son of the journalist Henry Nevinson, whom
Marinetti had met at the front during the Balkan Wars. In his book *Paint
and Prejudice* (1937), Nevinson recalls Marinetti's performance at the dinner before an audience of about sixty guests:

> It was an extraordinary affair. Marinetti recited a poem about the siege of Adria-
> nople, with various kinds of onomatopoeic noises and crashes in free verse,
> while all the time the band downstairs played, 'You made me love you. I didn't
> want to do it.' It was grand if incoherent . . . . It certainly was a funny meal. Most
> people had come to laugh, but there were few who were not overwhelmed by
> the dynamic personality and declamatory gifts of the Italian propagandist.[8]

The outbreak of World War I found Italy in a quandary. Because of her
alliance with Germany and Austria-Hungary, she was obliged to enter the
war if either one of them had been attacked. But Italian claims on the city
of Trieste and the region of the South Tyrol made the Habsburg empire
more foe than friend. Thus, when Germany and Austria declared war on
England, France, and Russia, the Italians had a chance to withhold action
on their treaty obligations, at least temporarily. While waiting to see which
way the war would go, and which side would make the better offer in terms
of postwar territorial gains, Italy found itself in the midst of turmoil over the
matter of intervention. Thirsting for war, and anxious for Italy to acquire
as much land as possible from the conflict, the Futurists, with Marinetti in
the lead, were passionate supporters of the Allied cause. Taking advantage
of any and every opportunity to make their case, they held demonstrations
in major Italian cities in an effort to whip public opinion into a frenzy of
enthusiasm for intervention on the side of the Allies.

It was a convergence of interests that drew Marinetti and Mussolini
together. For Marinetti and the Futurists, equivocation was indefensible.
Their ideas about war, heroism, and sacrifice would at last be tested in the
field, and their hostility toward German culture, together with the widespread Italian dislike of Austria, placed them squarely in the camp of the
Allies. Still a member of the Socialist Party and editor of its newspaper,
Avanti!, Mussolini could not at first proceed with the reckless haste of the
Futurists. But he was as ambitious as he was headstrong, and soon caught
the pulse of public sentiment. In October 1914, Mussolini abandoned his
previous caution, threw his support to intervention, and accepted with few
regrets his expulsion from the Socialist Party the following month. Hardly
had he written his last article for *Avanti!*, when he surfaced as the editor of

a new paper, *Il Popolo d'Italia,* which served until 1921 as the mouthpiece of his own eclectic political views.

Natural allies, Marinetti and Mussolini easily made common cause. On March 31, 1915, they appeared together to promote intervention in the war. A subsequent rally in Rome (April 11) at which both men were scheduled to speak was broken up by the police and army. But Marinetti and Mussolini, together with a large crowd of their followers, succeeded in assembling in the Piazza di Trevi. Before Mussolini could speak, however, the police arrived on the scene and arrested Marinetti; Mussolini eluded capture but was taken into custody shortly thereafter when he tried again to hold the rally in the Piazza Barberini. The two leaders grew closer as a result of these brushes with the law, and Marinetti henceforth wavered little in his enthusiasm for and loyalty to Mussolini. Years after, in 1929, he published a memoir of sorts titled *Marinetti e il Futurismo* (*Marinetti and Futurism*), which he dedicated to the "great and dear Benito Mussolini." The work begins with a reminiscence of Mussolini that includes the following description:

> Square crushing jaws. Scornful jutting lips that spit with defiance and swagger on everything slow, pedantic, and finicking. Massive rocklike head, but the ultradynamic eyes dart with the speed of automobiles racing on the Lombard plains. To right and left flashes the gleaming cornea of a wolf.
>
> The round felt cap pulled down over the intense black of the eyes like the round black clouds that hover over the intense black of Apennine ravines. And when the cap is removed, the baldness of a Verlaine, a D'Annunzio, a Marinetti shines forth like an electric lamp. . . .
>
> His will cleaves the crowd like a swift torpedo boat, an exploding torpedo. Rash but sure, because his elastic good sense has judged the distance. . . .
>
> That is why we Futurists, prophets and preparers of the great Italy of today, are happy to salute in the forty-year-old President of the Council of Ministers, a marvelous Futurist temperament. (501–2)

Marinetti's faith in Mussolini and his leadership of the Italian people lasted well into World War II, up to the writer's death of a heart attack on December 2, 1944. A participant in the Ethiopian campaign, Marinetti commemorated the heroic exploits of his division as well as Il Duce's prowess as a military leader in *Il Poema africano della Divisione "28 Ottobre"* (*The African Poem of the "28th of October" Division,* 1935). One of his last works was the *Canto eroi e macchine della guerra mussoliniana* (*I Sing of the Heroes and Machines of Mussolini's War*), "a simultaneous aeropoem in words-in-freedom" dedicated to the glory of several Italian war heroes. Brimming with Marinetti's familiar high-altitude rhetoric, the work was published in 1942, the same year in which Marinetti visited Italian troops serving in Russia.

When Italy finally intervened in World War I on the side of the Allies, Marinetti was ecstatic. But the war effectively ended the integrity of futurism as a movement—some of its leading figures lost their lives in combat—and henceforth Marinetti would have to play second fiddle to Mussolini in the Italian political arena. Although he continued to promote various Futurist endeavors throughout the war years and afterward—most notably his program for a Futurist theater—Marinetti's consuming passion had now become war. After all the rhapsodizing on the theme of war, and having experienced combat only vicariously in the Italian-Turkish and Balkan campaigns of 1911–13, the Futurists were now face to face with the real thing. To his credit, Marinetti (as other Futurists) rose to the challenge and acquitted himself heroically. Hardly had Italy declared war on Austria-Hungary on May 24, 1915—formal declaration of war against Germany came only in 1916—when Marinetti joined the Alpini. He saw a fair amount of frontline action, was wounded in the battle of Kuk, was hospitalized for a while in Udine, and was decorated for gallantry. The official citation read: "In command of a machine gun squad, with exemplary courage, impetuous patriotism and inspiring enthusiasm, he was the first to enter Tolmezzo. He captured the town's entire command, overcame all attempts to counterattack and subsequently destroyed all the enemy's communication lines."[9]

Having survived the fires of war, thereby adding to his mystique, Marinetti, like Mussolini, plunged into political activism at war's end. Ardently espousing Italian irredentist claims against Austria-Hungary at the same time he championed the cause of veterans, Marinetti drew closer to Mussolini, whose nationalism and combativeness he shared. He became involved in the foundation of the Fasci Italiani di Combattimento, the nucleus of the Italian Fascist Party named after the interventionist groups of 1915 whose symbol was the ancient Roman emblem of authority, the *fasci* (bundle of rods). At the first national congress of Fascists, which took place in Milan in March 1919, Marinetti was elected a member of the central committee. The relationship between the writer-become-activist and the ambitious politician was truly symbiotic. Marinetti saw Mussolini as Italy's future and had no choice but to align himself with him and his Fascist movement. Mussolini, on the other hand, was well aware of the advantages to be gained from the support of a prominent writer and military hero, the head of a vigorous avant-garde movement that had attracted worldwide attention and a skilled orator and proven political agitator. In the bruising political year of 1919, when the Fascists lost to the Socialists in the national elections, Marinetti and Mussolini were upstaged by another writer-become-activist on the grand scale, Gabriele D'Annunzio. This was, after all, the year in which D'Annunzio and his volunteers marched on Fiume and claimed it for Italy. Although Marinetti had previously denounced D'Annunzio the poet as the embodiment of everything that was repugnant to the Futurists in the Symbolist movement, he swallowed his pride and rallied to his cause, even emulating D'Anunzio's famous leaflet-dropping flight over Vienna by taking to the air himself to drop leaflets over Rome urging support of D'Annunzio's seizure of Fiume.

With the political success of the Fascists in 1922 in the wake of their march on Rome, Mussolini's star brightened and Marinetti's dimmed. Mussolini no longer needed him and in the new political circumstances of the 1920s even found him something of an embarrassment, particularly when Marinetti refused to budge on his long-held anticlerical and antipapal views. Disgruntled over his lengthening distance from Mussolini and aware of differences in their outlook, Marinetti resigned from the Fascist Party at its second national congress in 1920, even accusing fascism, as he once had accused the city of Venice, of *passatismo*. However, he later rejoined the party and gave ample evidence of his renewed loyalty to the Fascists and to Mussolini personally.

Marinetti's career through the 1920s and 1930s to the outbreak of World War II was devoted to undiminished literary activity. Most of his writings in this period followed the pattern of previous collections of Futurist manifestos, political pronouncements, words-in-liberty, and memoirs. In the twenty-year period from 1920 to 1940, he published a words-in-liberty novel, *Gli Indomabili* (*The Untameables*, 1922), and six collections of nonfiction, much of it a restatement of familiar Futurist dogma: *Al de là del Communismo* (*Beyond Communism*, 1920), *Futurismo e Fascismo* (*Futurism and Fascism*, 1924), *Marinetti e il Futurismo* (*Marinetti and Futurism*, 1929), *Il paesaggio e l'estetica futurista della macchina* (*Landscape and the Futurist Aesthetic of the Machine*, 1931), *Spagna veloce e toro futurista* (*Speedy Spain and a Futurist Bull*, 1931), and *Il fascino dell'Egitto* (*The Fascination of Egypt*, 1933), a nostalgic recollection of Marinetti's birthplace. Perhaps the most interesting of his later works are his theoretical manifesto of aeropoetry, *Il manifesto dell'Aeropoesia* (*Manifesto of Aeropoetry*, 1931), and a volume of aeropoetry titled *L'Aeropoema del Golfo della Spezia* (*The Aeropoem of the Gulf of Spezia*, 1935). Closely related to the technique of words-in-liberty, the aeropoems are also exercises in *simultaneità* (simultaneity) under the title *Il Poema non umano dei tecnicismi* (*The Non-Human Poem of Technicalities*, 1940).

Nikolai Gumilyov:
The Acmeist as Cavalryman

Gumilyov's career as one of Russia's major poets was cut short by a Cheka firing squad in Petrograd in late August 1921.[10] He was thirty-five years old. The Cheka was the Bolshevik secret police, the progenitor of such organizations as the NKVD and KGB. Gumilyov was one of sixty-one people accused of being involved in an anti-Soviet plot known as the Tagantsev conspiracy, after its founder. It has never been definitively established what role, if any, he may actually have played in it.

Until his execution, Gumilyov was the personification of the man of letters as military hero and adventurer. Apart from the poetry and plays he wrote, Gumilyov was active as a literary organizer, founding the important literary-artistic journal *Apollon* in 1909, the Poets' Guild (Tsekh poetov) in 1911, and the so-called Acmeist school of poetry in 1912. In contrast to the Symbolists, with whom they broke ranks, the Acmeists cultivated a poetry free of symbolism's vagueness and preoccupation with the metaphysical and occult, and characterized by more objective, concrete imagery. Unlike poetry of the Symbolists, it seemed more down-to-earth, more in contact with "reality." Among the Acmeists were such outstanding twentieth-century Russian writers as Osip Mandelshtam and Anna Akhmatova, whom Gumilyov had married in 1910. But Gumilyov's formidable reputation as a ladies' man and his strong, independent personality, as well as his extensive foreign travel—the more exotic of which he undertook alone—severely strained the relationship. Although Akhmatova bore him a son, Lev, in 1911, the couple began living separate lives within three years after their marriage and divorced in 1918.

Gumilyov's penchant for adventure was fueled by his restlessness as much as by the keen attraction he felt for exotic places and peoples. In 1907 he made trips to Egypt and the Sudan; in 1909, 1910, and 1913, to Abyssinia and Somaliland. If his interest in Africa initially was of a then fashionable romantic-escapist nature (shared, for example, by F. T. Marinetti and Ernst Jünger), it deepened in time and even acquired a scholarly dimension. On his trip to Abyssinia in 1909 and 1910, he was actually part of an ethnographic expedition organized by the Russian academician V. V. Radlov. The material he gathered on Abyssinian folklore became the basis of his poetic cycle "Abissinskie pesni" ("Abyssinian Songs") and the lyric-epic poem *Mik: Afrikanskaya poema* (*Mik: An African Poem*, 1918). Gumilyov also enjoys the distinction of having been the first Russian translator of the ancient Babylonian epic, *Gilgamesh*. Apart from the poetry already mentioned,

African–Middle Eastern–Islamic settings and motifs appear in almost all of Gumilyov's major works. These include six volumes of poetry (*Romanticheskie tsvety* [*Romantic Flowers*, 1908], *Zhemchuga* [*Pearls*, 1910], *Chuzhoe nebo* [*Foreign Skies*, 1912], *Kolchan*, [*The Quiver*, 1916], *Kostyor* [*The Pyre*, 1918], *Shatyor* [*The Tent*, 1921], and *Ognenny stolp* [*Pillar of Fire*, 1921]); two plays (*Ditya Allakha* [*Child of Allah*, 1921] and *Otravlennaya tunika* [*The Poisoned Tunic*, written in Paris, 1918–18, and published posthumously, 1952]); and a collection of stories (*Ten' ot pal'my* [*Shade of the Palms*, 1922]).

Gumilyov's spirit of adventure and fearlessness — evidence of which can be found even in his early poetry — made his entry into military service in World War I a foregone conclusion. Unlike the overwhelming majority of the Russian artistic and intellectual elite of the time, he made no effort to avoid frontline duty. On August 24, 1914, he enlisted as a private in the Empress Alexandra's Guards Regiment of Uhlans. His first taste of combat came in Prussia against the Germans, and he fought later in Poland on the Austro-Hungarian front. Although Gumilyov had a weak constitution, which might have exempted him from any military service, he acquitted himself with bravery on the battlefield and as early as December 24, 1914, was awarded the distinguished St. George Cross, IVth Class. In recognition of further heroism under fire on January 15, 1915, he was made a noncommissioned officer, and on December 25 that same year was awarded a second St. George Cross, IIIrd Class. In March 1916 Gumilyov was again recognized for bravery and promoted to the rank of second lieutenant. He was also transferred to the Empress Alexandra's 5th Hussar regiment, where he remained until August 1916, when he was ordered to the Nikolaevsky Cavalry School in order to take an examination for the next higher rank. But he fell ill and failed to pass the examination. In the spring of 1917 Gumilyov was assigned to an expeditionary corps in the West and traveled to London through Finland, Sweden, and Norway. However, he remained in London only a few days, reappearing thereafter in Paris. Although he had hoped for an assignment with the Russian brigades in Salonika, the Provisional Government that had come to power in Russia in March 1917 had other plans for him. He was now attached to the Russian military commissariat in Paris, most probably in an intelligence capacity. He remained in Paris for six months, after which he returned to London, apparently intent on joining the British forces in Mesopotamia and Persia. By then, however, the Bolsheviks had swept the Provisional Government from office in the November Revolution of 1917, and Russia was no longer in the war.

From the time he returned to Petrograd via Scandinavia in April 1918 until his arrest and execution in August 1921, Gumilyov availed himself of whatever opportunities existed for writers to keep busy in extremely hard times. Most of his work was with Maxim Gorky's noble translating and publishing enterprise, Vsemirnaya Literatura (World Literature), with which Gorky sought both to raise the cultural level of ordinary Russians in the postrevolutionary period and to provide employment for writers and intellectuals who otherwise would have experienced far greater hardships. These were busy years for Gumilyov. He became engaged in a variety of literary activities, mostly under the umbrella of World Literature, and lectured widely on poetry and the craft of writing. In February 1921 he was chosen over the poet Aleksandr Blok as head of the Petrograd section of the All-Russian Union of Poets. Although independent and outspoken, a former imperial officer who was by conviction a monarchist, Gumilyov did not go out of his way to court Bolshevik disfavor. There is no evidence of any active opposition on his part to the new regime, no solid evidence of involvement in any antigovernment conspiracy. Although his arrest was loudly protested, the chain of events culminating in his execution had already been set in motion and could not be altered.

Gumilyov's great taste for adventure, so evident in his exotic travels, characterized his attitude to war. His enthusiasm for combat was palpable and, like Marinetti and Ernst Jünger, his feelings about the war were intensely nationalistic. He exulted in Russian victory as much as Marinetti extolled Italian military successes or Jünger celebrated the triumph of German arms. But like Jünger, he lacked Marinetti's flamboyance and self-dramatization.

Gumilyov's writings about the war are contained primarily in *Kolchan* (*The Quiver*, 1916), one of his best collections of poetry, and in his seventy-page prose memoir, *Zapiski kavalerista* (*Notes of a Cavalryman*), which originally appeared in the Petrograd newspaper *Birzhevye vedomosti* (*Stock-Exchange News*) from February 1915 to January 1916. Gumilyov exulted in war and he invested it with divine sanction in such typical poems from *The Quiver* as "Voyna" ("War") and "Nastuplenie" ("Attack"), English translations of which follow in prose format for the sake of space.[11]

WAR
Like a dog on a heavy chain,/ A machine-gun barks beyond the forest,/ And the shrapnel buzzes, like bees/ Collecting bright-red honey.
And the "hurrah" in the distance is like the song/ Of reapers, ending a hard day's labor./ You would say: This is a peaceful village/ On a most blissful evening.
And truly, the majestic business of war/ Is splendid and sacred./ Seraphims,

bright and winged,/ Are visible at the soldier's backs.

Bless now, oh Lord,/ The toilers slowly making their way/ Through fields soaked in blood,/ Sowing heroic deeds and reaping glory.

Like those who bend over the plow,/ Like those who pray and grieve,/ Their hearts burn before You,/ Burn as wax candles.

But grant, oh Lord, strength/ And the regal moment of victory to him/ Who will say to his defeated foe, "Dear Friend,/ Accept my fraternal kiss!"(213–14)

ATTACK

That country, which could be heaven,/ Became a den of fire./

We are on the offensive for the fourth day,/ And for four days haven't eaten a thing.

But on this terrible and splendid day,/ There's no need for earthly fare,/ Since the word of the Lord/ Nourishes us better than bread.

And the Sundays drenched in blood,/ Dazzling and light,/ Above me roars shrapnel,/ Blades take wing faster than birds.

I shout, and my voice is savage,/ Copper striking copper./ I, the bearer of a great thought,/ Cannot, cannot die.

Like hammers of thunder,/ Or the waters of raging seas,/ The golden heart of Russia,/ Beats rhythmically in my breast.

And how sweet to dress up Victory/ Like a girl, in pearls,/ Passing through the smoky trail/ Of the retreating enemy. (234–35)

Notes of a Cavalryman is a straightforward prose memoir of some of Gumilyov's combat experiences. The account is dispassionate, objective, free of the lyrical and romantic. Face to face with danger, Gumilyov is cool and fearless. When he and a fellow soldier were making their way stealthily through a village at night, on opposite sides of the street, he was reminded of a favorite childhood game; but reality quickly asserted itself:

It reminded me of "hide and seek," which I always played in summer in the country. There was the same suppressed breathing, the same pleasurable aware-ness of danger, the same instinctive skill at sneaking up on someone or of hiding. And you almost forgot that instead of the smiling eyes of a pretty girl or your companion in play, you could can run up against a sharp and cold bayonet aimed at you. I reached the end of the village. It was beginning to get lighter. Ahead of me I made out the dark, not large protuberances of trenches and I immediately remembered, indeed photographed in my memory, their length and direction. After all, that's why I came here. At just that moment I caught sight of a human figure. It stared at me and softly whistled a kind of special, obviously pre-arranged, whistle. It was the enemy; a clash was unavoidable.

I had only one thought, as living and powerful as passion, madness, ecstasy: I kill him or he kills me! He raised his rifle indecisively; I knew he couldn't fire at me because there were too many enemies nearby, so I rushed forward with lowered bayonet. In an instant, there was no one in front of me. Perhaps my foe dropped to the ground; perhaps he ran away. I stopped and began looking around. Something dark loomed up. I approached and touched it with my bayonet—nothing, a log. Something dark again appeared. Suddenly from one side an unusually loud shot resounded and a bullet whined awfully close to my face. I turned around; I had a few seconds before the enemy changed the cartridge in the rifle's magazine. But the opposing spewing out of shots from the trenches could already be heard—tra, tra, tra—and the bullets whistled, whined, and buzzed.

I ran back to my detachment. I felt no unusual fear; I knew that night firing was ineffective, and I just wanted to do everything to the best of my ability. Therefore, when the moon illuminated the field, I threw myself on the ground and this way crawled to the cover of houses. It was possible to make one's way there almost without danger.[12]

On opposite sides of the war, Ernst Jünger would have met a formidable opponent in Gumilyov, a man possessed of the same irrational passion for combat, the same appreciation of the killing instinct:

The firing had already died down when I joined the patrol. The commander was satisfied. He discovered the enemy without having lost a single soldier. In ten minutes our artillery would be at work. But I was frightfully upset that somebody was firing at me, thereby hurling a challenge at me, and that I did not accept it and laid low. Even the joy of being saved from danger did not soften that suddenly raging lust for battle and vengeance. I then understood why cavalrymen dream so of attacks. To swoop down on men who have hidden themselves in bushes and trenches and safely fire from the distance at visible riders, to force them to turn pale from the ever quickening clatter of hooves, the flashing of bared sabers and the terrifying sight of sloping lances, to easily overrun, indeed blow away, with one's swiftness an opponent three times as strong—that is the sole rationale of a cavalryman's entire life. (522)

Jünger would also have been able to relate to the profound sense of national pride Gumilyov experienced when the Russians seemed well on their way to early victory:

We were in Germany.

Since those days I have often thought about the great difference between the offensive and defensive periods in war. Of course, both of them are necessary if only in order to smash the enemy and win the right to a durable peace. But the mood of the individual combatant is affected not only by general considerations; every detail—the accidentally acquired glass of milk, the slanting ray of the sun that illuminates a group of trees, and his own successful shot—sometimes brings more joy than news about a battle won on another front. These highways running in different directions, these woods cleared like parks, these stone houses with their red tiled roofs filled my soul with the sweet desire to surge forward, and the dreams of Yermak, Perovsky, and other representatives of a conquering, triumphant Russia seemed so close to me. Wasn't this the road to Berlin, the proud city of a military culture, which one should enter not with a scholar's staff in hand but on horse and with a rifle across one shoulder? (520–21)

Ernst Jünger: The Man of Steel

Few contemporary literary figures exemplify better than Ernst Jünger the elitist exaltation in war as the ultimate self-realization of the man of action. Now 102 years old and acknowledged as one of the twentieth-century's most notable (and durable) writers, Jünger's intellectual and creative energies have remained astonishingly vital. Although for present purposes our attention will be focused mainly on his pre–World War II military and political writings, it would do Jünger's breadth and complexity a disservice to present him only as a glorifier of war and the German national spirit.[13] Yet for many he will always remain one of the more compelling writers on war and combat.

Born in 1895, Jünger's literary career began with the private publication in 1920 of his diary in novelistic form of frontline action on the Western front in World War I, *In Stahlgewittern* (*In Storms of Steel*), originally subtitled *Aus dem Tagebuch eines Stosstruppführers v. Ernst Jünger, Kriegsfreiwilliger, dann Leutnant und Kompagnieführer im Füs.-Regt. Prinz Albrecht von Preussen [Hannov. Nr. 73]* (*From the Diary of a Storm Troop Leader by Ernst Jünger, Volunteer, then Lieutenant and Company Commander in the Prince Albrecht of Prussia Regiment of Fusiliers [The Hannover 73rd]*).[14] Graphic in its detail, unsentimental, a celebration of the manly and heroic, the work could not find a publisher in a defeated, war-ravaged Germany rife with political and social unrest. A trade edition became possible only a year after its initial private printing. Revised several times—a matter we will return to—*In Storms of Steel* gradually attained renown and has since become Jünger's best known and most widely read work, despite the gruesomeness of descriptions such as the following (which Gumilyov, for example, generally avoided):

"Here, get up you! We're moving forward." I woke on grass wet with dew. As we were swept with machine-gun fire, we made haste back into our communication trench again and took possession of an abandoned French position on the outskirts of the forest. My attention was caught by a sickly smell and a bundle hanging on the wire. Jumping out of the trench in the early morning mist, I found myself in front of a huddled-up corpse, a Frenchman. The putrid flesh, like the flesh of fishes, gleamed greenish-white through the rents in the uniform. I turned away and then started back in horror: close to me a figure cowered beside a tree. It wore the shining straps and belt of the French, and high upon its back there was still the loaded pack, crowned with a round cooking utensil. Empty eye-sockets and the few wisps of hair on the black and weathered skull told me that this was no living man. Another sat with the upper part of the body clapped down over the legs as though broken through the middle. All round lay dozens of corpses, putrefied, calcified, mummified, fixed in a ghastly dance of death. The French must have carried on for months without burying their fallen comrades.[15]

Jünger mentions shortly after this description that he had made up his mind to omit all personal observations from *In Storms of Steel* on the grounds that the aim of the book was to deal with the experience of war purely and that he had attempted to deal with the psychology of war in another book (a reference to *Der Kamp als inneres Erlebnis* [*Combat as Inner Experience*]). Nonetheless he felt driven to say a few words about what he calls "this first glimpse of horrors." These words are worth quoting for what they reveal both of Jünger's own attitude toward the war before he was actually plunged into it as well as that of many of his generation:

The horror was undoubtedly a part of that irresistible attraction that drew us into the war. A long period of law and order, such as our generation had behind it, produces a real craving for the abnormal, a craving that literature stimulates. Among other questions that occupied us was this: what does it look like when there are dead lying about? And we never for a moment dreamt that in this war the dead would be left month after month to the mercy of wind and weather, as once the bodies of the gallows were. (22–23)

But whatever the horrors encountered in war, one got used to them, took them for granted, and went about one's business of soldiering, reminded that war was an exhilarating test of courage and fortitude. This was even truer of the officer who bore responsibilities of leadership. Taking issue with another officer who had allowed matters of importance to separate him from his men, Jünger writes: "All the same, an officer should never be parted from his men in the moment of danger on any account whatever. Danger is the supreme moment of his career, his chance to show his manhood at its best. Honor and gallantry make him the master of the hour. What is more sublime than to face death at the head of a hundred men?" (27).

As in Gumilyov, the manly willingness to confront death and the almost mystical exaltation in the blood sport of combat commingled with intense feelings of patriotic pride and nationalism. As Jünger recalls:

> Once again a German landscape flitted by me, tinged this time with the first dyes of autumn, and once again, as on that time at Heidelberg, I was gripped by the sad and proud feeling of being more closely bound to my country because of the blood shed for her greatness. Why should I conceal that tears smarted in my eyes when I thought of the end of the enterprise in which I had borne my share? I had set out to the war gaily enough, thinking we were to hold a festival on which all the pride of youth was lavished, and I had thought little, once I was in the thick of it, about the ideal that I had to stand for. Now I looked back . . . . And almost without any thought of mine, the idea of the Fatherland had been distilled from all these afflictions in a clearer and brighter essence. That was the final winnings in a game on which so often all had been staked: the nation was no longer for me an empty thought veiled in symbols; and how could it have been otherwise when I had seen so many die for its sake, and had been schooled myself to stake my life for its credit every minute, day and night, without a thought? (316)

The fervor of the soldier unafraid to shed his blood in the cause of country assumes in Jünger, as in Gumilyov, a religiomystical dimension. Jünger draws a comparison between the early Christian martyrs who embraced death in the arena for their beliefs and the soldier-patriots of his own time. Their courage, too, sprang from deep within the spirit and defied reason, which Jünger typically scorns. Without the faith that motivated the Christian martyrs and the men who laid down their lives for their country in the war, the fatherland, like the spirit, is doomed:

> When once it is no longer possible to understand how a man gives his life for his country—and the time will come—then all is over with that faith also, and the idea of the Fatherland is dead; and then, perhaps, we shall be envied, as we envy the saints their inward and irresistible strength. For all these great and solemn ideas bloom from a feeling that dwells in the blood and that cannot be forced. In the cold light of reason everything alike is a matter of expedience and sinks to the paltry and mean. It was our luck to live in the invisible rays of feeling that filled the heart, and of this inestimable treasure we can never be deprived. (317)

With the memory of combat and its impact on his psyche too powerful, too vivid to find release in just a single account, Jünger went on to make war the subject of several subsequent works. *Combat as Inner Experience*, essentially an essay, which followed *In Storms of Steel* in 1922, deals with the psychological and philosophical ramifications of war. In it Jünger lays stress on the naturalness of war in human society. The propensity for war, he argues, is fundamental to the human psyche. Man has a need to destroy and rebuild, to devastate and reconstruct, in order to experience a fullness of being. Hence war, as the means to achieving this experience, must be accepted and indeed glorified instead of being vilified:

> It is war that makes people and times what they are. . . . War, the father of all things, is ours as well; he hammered us, chiseled us, and tempered us into what we are. And always, so long as the revolving wheel of life still turns in us, this war will be the axle of those it spins. It trained us for battle, and we will remain fighters as long as we live. . . . [16]
>
> War is the most powerful encounter of peoples. . . . Whatever issues and ideas stirred the world, they were always settled in blood. If indeed all freedom, all greatness, and all culture were born in thought, in silence, only through war were they preserved, disseminated, or lost. . . .
>
> War is as much a part of the human being as the sexual drive; it is a law of nature. That is why we will never free ourselves from its spell. We must not deny it lest it devour us. (40)

Although *In Storms of Steel* hints at Jünger's capacity for intellectualizing his combat experiences, the primary concern in this first work is with the almost bald chronicling of battlefield events. In his revisions of it, Jünger obviously sought to expunge anything that detracted from the "purity" of the martial experience, relegating his reflections on and analysis of war and combat to separate pieces of writing such as *Combat as Inner Experience*.

In 1925 Jünger returned to recollections of combat in *Das Wäldchen 125: Eine Chronik aus den Grabenkämpfen 1918* (*Copse 125: A Chronicle of the Trench Warfare of 1918*), an elaboration of events previously described in *In Storms of Steel*.[17] It was followed the same year by *Feuer und Blut: Ein kleiner Ausschnitt aus einer grossen Schlacht* (*Fire and Blood: A Small Segment of a Great Battle*), another expansion of a chapter in *In Storms of Steel*, this time "Die grosse Schlacht" ("The Great Battle"). Apart from their continued analysis of the dialectics of war and peace, these works shed further light on Jünger's attitude toward writers whose liberal and pacifistic views differed from his own. The contempt voiced, for example, in *Copse 125* was not uncommon among literary activists who contrasted their own strength with the weakness and sickliness of those artists and intellectuals who abhorred war and repudiated nationalism. No less uncommon, as we can see in abundance in the writings of Marinetti, is the identification of such weakness with "femininity," hence the strong undercurrent of gender bias frequently found in the modernist cult of the physical. Moreover, the ease with which Jünger's views—as exemplified in the following passage from *Copse 125*—dovetailed with, and could be appropriated by, Nazi ideology in the 1920s and 1930s is self-evident:

> The evolution of war follows a line that is interrupted by longer or shorter intervals of peace. In any review of it, therefore, there are only broken lengths at our disposal and only deductions can be made. . . . Civilization is always on the march, and with it its possibilities of expression—among which, naturally, is to be reckoned the prevailing mode of war; always supposing that by civilization one does not mean the bloodless and anemic affair of which we are happy to leave the literary and pacific gentlemen in sole possession. If they had their way, we should find our great cities in the hands of Tartars and Cossacks the day after.[18]

Between the publication in 1925 of *Copse 125* and *Fire and Blood* and the outbreak of World War II in 1939, Jünger published six more works, one of which was a revised version of a collection of short pieces published nine years earlier. *Afrikanische Spiele (African Diversions)*, which appeared in 1936, is autobiographical in nature and recounts Jünger's youthful romantic fascination with Africa and especially the French Foreign Legion.[19] Unlike many young boys who spin out similar fantasies of adventure in far-flung places, Jünger acted on his, running away from home in late 1913 and joining the Foreign Legion in Verdun. But the discipline of the legion was too much like the discipline of family and school, so he attempted to desert from it as well. His two attempts at flight failed, and before long his father had secured his release from the Legion. *African Diversions* can, of course, be read as an account of youthful escapades in the North African desert. Perhaps its greater value lies in what it reveals of the future Prussian officer's love of adventure, his desire to live life to the fullest, and his contempt for the values of the bourgeois social order. Although expressed by different literary means, Jünger and Gumilyov had much in common in this respect.

Jünger's celebration of the life force animates *Das abentuerliche Herz: Figuren und Capriccios (The Adventurous Heart: Figures and Capriccios)*, a collection of some sixty short prose pieces that was published in 1929 and attracted little attention. It was reissued in 1938, after undergoing revisions that also expanded the number of pieces to seventy-one, and did significantly better. Revelatory of its author's propensity for the philosophical, indeed metaphysical, *The Adventurous Heart* also illuminates another side of the more mature Jünger—his serious study of the natural sciences, above all biology and entomology, from which images of plant and insect life are applied symbolically to reflections on life and man.

Jünger's last major piece of writing before the German invasion of Poland in September 1939 and his own return to military service was the short novel *Auf der Marmorklippen* (*On the Marble Cliffs*).[20] Outwardly a product of the imagination, set in a world of Jünger's fantasy, the disturbing, opaque novel seems rooted as well in the complex of Jünger's attitudes toward his own society: the Germany of the second half of the 1930s, with its triumphant Nazism, incendiary militarism, and repression. Whatever his previous elitist scorn of bourgeois liberalism and his zest for war, the realities of Hitlerian Germany struck Jünger as a prescription for disaster and he turned against it. No, there was no outward break with the Nazis, whose party Jünger had never wanted to join in any case; there was also no participation in any clandestine societies aimed at topping Hitler. And when called to service in World War II, Jünger went willingly, like the good German patriot and decorated former officer that he was, again serving on the Western front, albeit in quite different circumstances than the trench warfare and hand-to-hand combat of World War I. The break, if one can indeed call it that, with Hitlerian Germany was literary in nature and took the form of an antitotalitarian allegory. It would be difficult if not impossible to imagine that there were those incapable of reading between the lines, of seeing *On the Marble Cliffs* for what it was—an indictment of the Hitler regime as a demonic force destined to lead Germany to its utter destruction. But Jünger's reputation as the author of *In Storms of Steel* and of other novelistic and political writings of the 1920s and early 1930s easily reconciled with right-wing ideology made him virtually inviolable. This status was if anything enhanced when with the outbreak of the war he again donned the uniform of a German officer and went off to serve in France. In one of the ironies of his career, Jünger not only paid no penalty for *On the Marble Cliffs*, but saw his novel published in a special Wehrmacht edition of 20,000 copies as late as 1943.[21] The novel was, we understand, immensely popular with German soldiers during the war.

Jünger's works of the 1930s preceding *On the Marble Cliffs* gave no evidence that their author would ever turn from at least tacit support of the regime. After his war diaries of the 1920s, Jünger wrote a large number of essentially right-wing pieces, the most significant of which were "Die totale Mobilmachung" ("Total Mobilization"), which appeared originally in 1930 in his collection *Krieg und Krieger* (*War and Warriors*), and *Der Arbeiter: Herrschaft und Gestalt* (*The Worker: Rule and Gestalt*, 1932), an essay extending some 300 pages. Collectively, these works attempt to reconcile lessons learned in the war with the needs of postwar Germany. They maintain that the courage and commitment of the soldier willing to sacrifice himself for the fatherland, that sense of dedication, would be called on to overcome the inherent weaknesses of the liberal, pacifistic Weimar state, for which Jünger, as did the German Right in general, had nothing but contempt. But the fate of Germany in the war had other lessons to teach besides heroism and sacrifice. From Jünger's point of view, World War I was distinguishable from all preceding wars by the total mobilization by the state of its technological as well as social resources. Germany's failure to achieve total mobilization was one of the leading causes of its defeat. Hence in order to compete in the postwar era, Germany had to become part of what Jünger believed to be a worldwide process whereby human and technological resources were being mobilized with a kind of military discipline. His assessment of the situation, as in the following passage, leaves no doubt as to his belief in the inherent danger to Germany unless it made the leap to a fully industrialized, technologically advanced society able to dominate in peace as well as in war:

> The old chimes of the Kremlin have been reset to the melody of the Internationale. In Constantinople schoolchildren are learning to spell the Latin alphabet instead of the old arabesques of the *Koran*. In Naples and Palermo the Fascist police are arranging the pace of southern life according to the principles of modern traffic discipline. In the most distant and almost still fairy-tale lands of the world, parliament buildings are being dedicated. The abstractness, hence also the cruelty, of all human relations continuously increase. Patriotism is being replaced by a new nationalism strongly permeated with elements of awareness. In fascism, bolshevism, Americanism, Zionism, and in the movements of the colored peoples, progress is making previously unimagined advances. It turns cartwheels, so to speak, in order to continue its movement on a very simple level, following the compass of an artificial dialectic. It is beginning to place peoples in forms that differ little from those of an absolute regime, if one wishes to disregard the much narrower dimension of freedom and comfort. In many places the humanitarian mask is stripped away to make room for a half-grotesque, half-barbaric fetishism of the machine, a naive cult of technology. This happens especially in places where one does not possess a direct, productive relationship with the dynamic energies from whose destructive triumphant

advance the long-range artillery and the battle groups armed with bombs are only the martial expression.[22]

The state alone had the power and authority to bring about the requisite maximization of available national resources and skills. The infringement on individual freedom necessitated by such a broad overhauling of society was a small price to pay. In his analysis of the German defeat in the war in "Total Mobilization" and *The Worker*, Jünger recognized the importance of a cultural bias against industrialism and technology that had to be overcome once and for all if Germany was not only to survive in the postwar era but never again to suffer defeat in war. Jünger's sense of urgency about such a shift in values is understandable if seen in light both of his assessment of the postwar international situation and his belief in the inevitability, indeed naturalness, of future wars. Not only did Jünger advocate the total embrace of technology and industrialism on the part of the Germans, but he advanced the view that the Germans could set an example among industrial nations by demonstrating the compatibility of traditional values previously unsympathetic to industrialism and the cultivation of the most advanced technology. The achievement of such a symbiosis would be possible, of course, only in a right-wing authoritarian state that would command the requisite will and loyalty of its citizenry. The appeal of such views to the Nazi order that took power in Germany in 1933 was unmistakable, and even though Jünger never espoused Nazism or became a member of the Nazi Party, he was admired as a true patriot and visionary by the ideologues of the Third Reich.

Although no hard evidence links Jünger and the Italian Futurists, the militancy of their embrace of technology, including the worship of the airplane, has much in common. There is also a shared aesthetics of violence (nowhere more in evidence than in Jünger's writings about World War I), a rhapsodizing on the theme of the machine, and an exultation in the sense of danger as well as pleasure that accompanied such artifacts of the modern industrial age as the airplane, the tank, and the high-speed automobile. In the fast pace of the new postwar urbanized society, with its technological and industrial advances, it was possible to regain the terrifying exhilaration of wartime combat. And it was the experience of such powerful feelings, reaching deep into the soul of man, that gave meaning to life. If the bourgeois mentality was inhospitable to such an outlook, it mattered little since the soldier-worker of Jünger's totally mobilized future society would eradicate the middle class and its petty, obsolete concerns as surely as the Italian Futurists would destroy the bourgeois order by their own revolution.

A man of action who succeeded admirably in making language serve him efficiently and well, Jünger also wrote two fairly short essays on the properties of language: the thirty-page *Lob der Vokale* (*In Praise of Vowels*, 1934), on the expressive qualities of vowels, and the fifty-page *Sprache und Körperbau* (*Language and Body*, 1947), in which he addresses the issue of the interrelationship between speech and body. Generally overlooked by the now considerable literature on Jünger, the essays seem to have been intended as part of a larger study devoted to symbolism in language. "The subject has barely been touched," Jünger tells us in the conclusion to *Language and Body*. "A discipline of its own is being developed—not just a counterpart to logic, but indeed its very foundations. We do not think just because we *are*, but we also think *how* we are."[23] In *Language and Body*, the more interesting of the two essays, the focus is on how the different parts of the body generate figurative, or symbolic, forms of speech. Drawing on mythology, classical antiquity, folklore, religion, and philosophy (Plato, Vico, Kant), Jünger proceeds to explore the speech-body nexus under such rubrics as "The Hand" ("Right and Left"), "The Hand" ("Hand and Fist"); "Head and Foot" ("Above and Below"); and "The Five Senses" ("Touch," "Sight," "Hearing," "Taste and Smell"). A few examples from "The Hand" ("Right and Left") may demonstrate his line of reasoning. Above all other organs of the body, the hand, according to Jünger, is symbolic of the symmetry of the human organism. "Hand," as he points out, is an old synonym for "side," as in the English "on one hand," "on the other hand." Yet of all the symmetrical organs of the body (hands, eyes, ears, nostrils, feet, sexual organs, and so on), hands also show the greatest deviation. These differences, when compared to other paired organs, become the foundation of the symbolic status of speech. This is also a general law of the world of symbols, notes Jünger; the appearance of unity and equality conceals dichotomy. Although from the mathematical and logical point of view, both hands are equal, they are differently valorized. When we stand at a crossroads, Jünger explains, we have two directions before us, right and left. Language seems to make no qualitative distinction between them yet harbors a certain partiality, a preference for right as opposed to left. In German, for example, "direction" is *Richtung*, the root of which is *recht* (right). Hence *Richtung* in and of itself presupposes that the orientation to the right is the correct direction. Jünger says that this is even clearer in French where "right" (in the sense of direction) and "straight ahead" are identical—*droit* and *tout droit*. If, as Jünger argues, the right is the "queen," then the left is the "servant." That "left" is often associated with "yielding," "withdrawing," "evading," and so on, is evident in the common roots for both in certain languages. In French, for example, *gauchir*, from the same root as *gauche* (left), means "to give way" and *gauchissment* (something oblique) is the opposite of straight. By the same token, quoting Jünger,

> "left" is the symbol of the ungifted, the clumsy, and the ungainly. The person who is a burden to himself and others is *linkisch* [clumsy], *left-handed, laevus. . . .*
>
> Logically viewed, the right thing is on the right, and the wrong is on the left hand. The good result is *correct* (*richtig*); the bad one is wrong and hence in need of *rettificatione, rectification.*
>
> On the other hand, fate, providence, good fortune and bad fortune figure in the present context, in that for the most part light is assigned the right and darkness the left. Hence *sinister, sinistre* mean the same for left and unlucky, disastrous. *Le sinistré* [in French] is a person who is plagued by misfortune. (54–56)

Our principal interest in Jünger has been as a writer born of war who became a celebrant of the irrational energies unleashed by conflict. Never blind to the horrors of war, Jünger emphasized instead the exhilaration moments of intense danger are capable of summoning from within the depths of an individual's psyche. But the totality of Jünger's literary career embraces more than the World War I writings and the subsequent essentially right-wing analyses of the German situation in the postwar era, significant though these may be. Schooled in the natural sciences and philosophy, Jünger clearly found a certain gratification in pursuing these and related interests in the post–World War II period. He was regarded, then, with some suspicion, particularly in his own Germany, as a writer and thinker who had sung the praises of militarism and authoritarianism, thereby providing grist for the mills of Nazi propaganda, and had donned a Wehrmacht officer's uniform in World War II. Situating Jünger's World War I writings and the sociopolitical essays and books of the 1920s and 1930s in the broader context of the modernist cult of action provides us more of a rationale for his outlook toward war and the needs of the postwar German state. The tendency toward authoritarianism and right-wing (or left-wing) politics on the part of a number of modernist writer-activists, Jünger among them, was shaped by their extreme, and elitist, contempt for liberal bourgeois politics and the democratic social order. Theirs was a vision of a new Europe freed at last by war or revolution from the malaise of bourgeois intellectualism and inaction.

Having survived two world wars and the rise and fall of Hitler and the Nazi Party, Jünger eventually came to see a Germany vastly different than he had ever known or could have imagined—democratic, industrially powerful, integrated into a Western political and economic alliance. The old soldier could at last turn from an almost mystic exultation in conflict to the gentler contemplation of the workings of nature and language. As he puts it, with a certain poignancy, at the end of the conclusion to *Language and Body*: "This work was begun in the midst of the catastrophe of the year 1945 and completed. It was not undertaken so much to turn the mind and eyes away from the pictures of misery and destruction that surrounded us, but rather because after an accident, after a sudden fall, our first concern is for the body. We test it to see if we have remained intact. The same here" (99).

Ernest Hemingway: From War to Blood Sport

In his personal life as well as in his fiction, Hemingway splendidly lived the part of the writer as man of action. Although he was not above exaggerating his wartime exploits, Hemingway did volunteer for service as an ambulance driver during World War I and saw action in this capacity on the Italian front until he was wounded and sent home. These experiences formed the basis of his splendid novel *A Farewell to Arms* (1929), with its graphic account of the great Italian retreat at Caporetto in October 1917. Although he covered the Spanish civil war of 1936–38 as a reporter and did not actually serve with the International Brigades as did André Malraux, for example, he was close to the fighting on several occasions. The presence of danger is palpable in several of his war pieces and the civil war itself is powerfully reflected in his novel *For Whom the Bell Tolls* (1939).

After World War I Hemingway returned to Europe, settling in Paris as a member of the large American expatriate community that had formed there in the 1920s. It was in this period that he came to know Spain well and developed his great passion for bullfighting. Hemingway's reputation as a writer of fiction soared with the publication of *The Sun Also Rises* in 1926 and *A Farewell to Arms* three years later. Valued as a literary portrait of the aimless, self-indulgent life of the American expatriates in Paris at the time, *The Sun Also Rises* can serve as a paradigm of Hemingway's life-long fascination with blood sport. In *The Sun Also Rises* it is bullfighting in Spain, and it is in those sections of the book devoted to the annual running of the bulls in Pamplona and the subsequent fights that the novel acquires its greatest strength and even beauty.

Notwithstanding the presence of attractive and strong-willed women in his fiction, Hemingways's world is a masculine one, a world of masculine camaraderie, a world in which the taste for blood sport and the proximity to death define the male's masculinity and even virility. In *The Sun Also Rises* and in his classic work on bullfighting, *Death in the Afternoon* (1932), the intimacy with death in the ring intensified the sense of life; the physical interplay of the matador and the bull was a ballet of life and death. It was as if the human body reached its highest level of gracefulness in the movements of the matador—those of the young boy Romero, for example, in *The Sun Also Rises*. In Jake Barnes's conversations about bulls and bullfighting with the proprietor of the Montoya Hotel in Pamplona and the other aficionados, Hemingway is clearly projecting pride in his own knowledge and at the same time defining the exclusively masculine, and physical, nature of the initiates:

> We often talked about bulls and bullfighters. I had stopped at the Montoya for several years. We never talked for very long at a time. It was simply the pleasure of discovering what we each felt. Men would come in from distant towns and before they left Pamplona stop and talk for a few minutes with Montoya about bulls. These men were aficionados. Those who were aficionados could always get rooms even when the hotel was full. Montoya introduced me to some of them. They were always very polite at first, and it amused them very much that I should be an American. Somehow it was taken for granted that an American could not have aficion. He might simulate it or confuse it with excitement, but he could not really have it. When they saw that I had aficion, and there was no password, no set questions that could bring it out, rather it was a sort of oral spiritual examination with the questions always a little on the defensive and never apparent, there was this same embarrassed putting the hand on the shoulder, or a "Buen hombre." But nearly always there was the actual touching. It seemed as though they wanted to touch you to make it certain.[24]

Wounded during the war in his genitals to the extent that he cannot have sexual intercourse, which foredooms a normal relationship with Brett Ashley, whom he loves and who loves him, Barnes is at least partially redeemed as a man by the virility of his affection for the blood sport of bullfighting. Since Hemingway tells us little about Barnes's background—when, for example, his love and knowledge of bullfighting developed—the reader may conjecture that Barnes's *aficion* became a surrogate virility, psychologically compensating for his inability to have sex with a woman. And it is in this vicarious way that Barnes presents the breathtaking handsomeness and professional skill of the very young matador, Pedro Romero, through Brett's eyes on the second day of their attendance at the fights in Pamplona:

> I had her watch how Romero took the bull away from a fallen horse with his cape, and how he held him with the cape and turned him, smoothly and suavely, never wasting the bull. She saw how Romero avoided every brusque movement and saved his bulls for the last when he wanted them, not winded and discomposed but smoothly worn down. She saw how close Romero always worked to the bull, and I pointed out to her the tricks the other bullfighters used to make it look as though they were working closely. She saw why she liked Romero's cape-work and why she did not like the others.
>
> Romero never made any contortions, always it was straight and pure and natural in line. The others twisted themselves like corkscrews, their elbows raised, and leaned against the flanks of the bull after his horns had passed, to give a fake look of danger. Afterward, all that was faked turned bad and gave an unpleasant feeling. Romero's bullfighting gave real emotion, because he kept the absolute purity of line in his movements and always quietly and calmly let the horns pass him close each time. He did not have to emphasize their closeness. Brett saw how something that was beautiful done close to the bull was ridiculous if it were done a little way off. (168)

Romero's mastery creates a dance of death between himself and the bull:

> [The bull] turned and the group broke apart and Romero was taking him out with his cape. He took him out softly and smoothly, and then stopped and, standing squarely in front of the bull, offered him the cape. The bull's tail went up and he charged, and Romero moved his arms ahead of the bull, wheeling, his feet firmed. The dampened, mud-weighted cape swung open and full as a sail fills, and Romero pivoted with it just ahead of the bull. At the end of the pass they were facing each other again. Romero smiled. The bull wanted it again, and Romero's cape filled again, this time on the other side. Each time he let the bull pass so close that the man and the bull and the cape that filled and pivoted ahead of the bull were all one sharply etched mass. (217)

The sheer perfection of physical form, the symbiotic relationship now existing between man and animal, acquires an erotic power. When Brett succumbs to Romero, their brief, intense, wholly sexual relationship has an inevitability, sensed—and only weakly opposed—by Barnes from the moment Brett confesses her passion for the matador at first glance:

"Do you still love me, Jake?"

"Yes," I said.

"Because I'm a goner," Brett said.

"How?"

"I'm a goner. I'm mad about the Romero boy. I'm in love with him, I think."

"I wouldn't be if I were you."

"I can't help it. I'm a goner. It's tearing me all up inside." . . .

"Oh, darling, please stay by me. Please stay by me and see me through this."

"Sure."

"I don't say it's right. It is right though for me. God knows, I've never felt such a bitch."

"What do you want me to do?"

"Come on," Brett said. "Let's go and find him." (183–84)

By the early 1930s Hemingway's enthusiasm for big-game hunting rivaled his passion for the bullring and recalled that of Theodore Roosevelt. What he wrote about killing the great animals of the African plains contains the same nexus of emotionless blood sport and virility. Pursuing big game in Africa offered the personal danger, the highs and lows between fearlessness and fear, that bullfighting could offer the spectator in the stands only vicariously. Sensing fear in oneself on the hunt, even admitting it, did not compromise one's masculinity. But behaving in fear, in a cowardly way, once the target was in sight was unpardonable.

Courage in the face of the onrushing lion or buffalo becomes the measure of masculine virility in a story such as "The Short Happy Life of Francis Macomber." When Francis Macomber falters on a lion hunt, he humiliates himself in front of his "white hunter" guide, Robert Wilson, who by contrast is a "man's man": virile, steady in face of great danger, successful as a hunter of big game. Macomber also humiliates himself in front of his wife, Margot, who feels only contempt for her husband's display of weakness. In behaving as he does on the lion hunt, he loses his virility in her eyes. He becomes as ineffectual as a male as Jake Barnes is to Brett Ashley in *The Sun Also Rises*. And just as Brett is irresistibly drawn to the young matador, who embodies the principle of masculine virility and physicality, so is Margot Macomber drawn to Robert Wilson. Defiantly leaving the tent she shares with Macomber, she goes off to spend the night with Wilson. Since in *The Sun Also Rises* Jake can never overcome the physical obstacle barring fulfillment of the love he and Brett feel for each other, the relationship between them can never be resolved. Jake will continue to function as the pimp for Brett, as Robert Cohn accuses him of being at one point. In "The Short

Happy Life of Francis Macomber," however, Macomber's eventual ability to overcome fear, to realize himself as a man, to gain the respect of the white hunter, does not achieve a reconciliation between him and Margot. On the contrary; his weakness in the face of danger rationalizes her sense of superiority over him. When he overcomes his fear of death on the buffalo hunt, she senses a loss of power over him. A proud as well as handsome woman, used to having her own way, Margot Macomber cannot accept the prospect of living with a husband who has at last become a man no longer in need of proving himself to her and, more important, no longer afraid to leave her. Hemingway deliberately leaves vague the killing of Macomber near the end of the story. When a mortally wounded buffalo makes a frenzied last dash toward her husband, Margot picks up a high-powered rifle and fires at it, killing her husband. Although Margot is ostensibly grief stricken, Wilson treats her like a murderess who needs his help in covering up the crime. The ambiguity with which the story ends is tantalizing. Margot may well be acting out of fear for her husband's safety. But as the character has been drawn by Hemingway, she could not tolerate the evident loss of ability to dominate her husband now that he has at last become a man.

Despite the strength of some of his female characters and the poignant love story played out against the background of war in A Farewell to Arms, Hemingway's world is staunchly masculine. In portraying it in all its virility, Hemingway was well served by an appropriately virile idiom that has long been acknowledged for its contribution to twentieth-century prose style. But Hemingway was not wholly unique in this respect. Too rooted in the verbal self-indulgence of European symbolism, D'Annunzio stood little chance of creating a style befitting the poet-become-military hero of the Fiume episode. With Marinetti, it was a different matter. The founder of futurism despised symbolism and mocked D'Annunzio as much for his style as for his subjects—at least until the little poet became a swashbuckling adventurer in uniform. Apart from his bloodcurdling militarism, Marinetti was first and foremost a revolutionary in language. Trumpeting the virtues of male virility, sexism, anti-intellectualism, velocity, and urbanism, Marinetti strove to devise a literary language of revolutionary explosiveness and virile toughness calculated to overwhelm the effeteness, flabbiness, and "femininity" of traditional Italian. As we shall see in the next chapter, Marinetti's extreme avant-gardist innovations aimed at an overhaul of literary Italian that was far more provocative than the muscularity and leanness of Hemingway's writing. But Hemingway never pretended to be part of an avant-garde. His own temperament, and the world he created in his fiction, virtually dictated the style with which he has long been identified. For the man of action, excessive verbiage was out of character and unseemly, truly a sign of weakness. It was in much the same spirit that Gumilyov had spurned the verbal opulence of symbolism in favor of a concrete, down-to-earth way of writing that also went well with the mind-set of the adventurer, explorer, and war hero.

Henry de Montherlant: Tauromania French-Style

Among twentieth-century writers afflicted with the obsession with bullfighting, Hemingway's name probably stands out the most because of *The Sun Also Rises* and especially because of his treatise on bullfighting, *Death in the Afternoon*. But as a writer-aficionado, the Frenchman Henry de Montherlant more than compares favorably with the famous American tauromane.

The difference between Hemingway and Montherlant is that the Frenchman not only wrote about bulls, he fought them in the ring. He also discovered his fascination with bullfighting at an earlier age, in fact, when he was thirteen, by which time he had already been writing for a couple of years.[25] Expelled in 1912 from the Collège de Sainte-Croix at Neuilly for an innocent but ardent attachment to another boy, which was in those days regarded as unwholesome, the sixteen-year-old Montherlant was relieved to be freed from stuffy classrooms and the polite society for which he was being groomed (although he never entirely got over his expulsion and made it the subject of his play, *La Ville dont le prince est un enfant* [*The City Whose Prince Is an Infant*, 1951]). His real love was sports—soccer and cross-country racing, with bullfighting waiting in the wings. In this regard, Montherlant was very much in tune with the times. Sports had become immensely popular in early twentieth-century France (as, indeed, elsewhere in Europe) and were regarded as a means of regenerating the national body as well as the national spirit. In his study of cultural politics and the Parisian avant-garde, Mark Antliff mentions the emergence of sports as an important Cubist theme by 1913, citing as examples such paintings as André Dunoyer de Sefonzac's *The Boxers* (1911), Jean Metzinger's *The Cyclist* (1911), and Albert Gleize's *Football Players* (1912–13).[26] In his widely read *La morale des sports* (*The Morality of Sports*, 1907), Paul Adam extolled sports for their beneficial effects on man's courage and power.

When his father died in 1914, followed by his mother a year later, Montherlant (an only child) no longer faced any obstacles to joining the army in order to fight in World War I. Spurning a commission so that he could get to the front lines as soon as possible, he threw himself into combat with a gusto reminiscent of Gumilyov and Jünger. Montherlant craved action, excitement, personal participation. The faster the adrenaline flowed, the more alive he felt. The feelings he attributes to a character in his first novel, *Le Songe* (*The Dream*, 1922), could be applied equally to Montherlant himself:

> In love with the front . . .
>
> The idea intoxicated him. Without any military knowledge, ridiculously out of training, having lost the habit of walking, the madness of his action saved him. To this brilliant and irrational nature, anything justified itself by being extreme enough: the strong man finding rest in the extreme. The countless foreseeable sufferings became for him but variations on the beauty of living, opposed to happiness, but no less desirable than happiness. For the thousandth time, the strong man interchanged values, melted down the barriers, recomposed quite arbitrarily a world fitting and favorable to him. All was resolved in exultation. Not for an instant did he feel that he was doing his duty, for he did not feel unhappy.[27]

Badly wounded by a bursting shell, Montherlant nevertheless craved to return to the front when the conflict ended. His experiences in the war in part formed the subject of *The Dream*, which immediately established his reputation as one of the leading French writers of the day. Even more in the Jüngerian mode than *The Dream*, *Chant funèbre ou les morts de Verdun* (*Dirge for the Dead of Verdun*), which appeared in 1924, was an idealistic celebration of the brotherhood of those who shared the experience of war.

Although bullfighting became his reigning passion, Montherlant delighted in sports and physical culture in general, a fact reflected in his fiction and essays. Of particular interest in his writing about sports is Montherlant's support of female athletes. This is evident in *The Dream*, in which the great but ultimately unrequited love of the "hero" of the novel, Alban de Bricoule, is the beautiful runner, Dominique Soubrier. Through Dominique, Montherlant communicates his love of sport, his understanding of its mystique, and his delight in the physical perfection of the athlete that approaches the reverent. During a practice session for her "beloved thousand-meter race," Dominique muses on the battle of wits she is now engaged in with her leading rival:

> How she loved it, this intellectual aspect of sport, the mental excitement which mingles with the physical excitement in a matchless combination! Instinctively she had tended towards the branch of athletics which demands it most: the medium-distance race; sprints, jumping or throwing did not excite her in the same way, because they only call into play one's physical and technical abilities. At this moment she was conscious at the same time of her perspicacity, her technical knowledge, her bearing, her presence of mind, her vastly organized powers

of endurance; and then the freedom and the strength of her legs, the close grain of her cheeks which never shook as she ran, her ease of movement, all the potentialities in the muscled body, the deep reserves of strength and breath as yet unused in the heaving chest. Although she knew she was beautiful, she also knew that in a race she was transfigured; and the sense of this perfection was such that a sadness overcame her at the thought that it could not survive.(45)

In capturing the athlete's own delight in bodily perfection, in a lengthy scene in which Dominique surveys and explores her nude form in front of a mirror, Montherlant combines the lyricism of the poet with the knowledge of human anatomy of the medical student:

Her whole body was like delicately beaten metal. And suddenly, through this enrichment of the body—through the broadening of the neck, too—the face lost its importance, all its spirituality ran down into the torso which it illuminated; the knees themselves, so finely modeled, seemed to have acquired the intelligence of faces. The lateral grooves of the abdomen curved and rose, drawing away from each other, sliding beneath the breasts which they proffered, in a curve which was the curve of some flowering thing; and the three fascicles of the *serratus magnus* sprang out from beneath it, resplendent, like the rays of a hidden sun. The *antero-rectus* stood out on her thighs, a light, well-defined fascicle; and under the knee the tibial muscle, at the same angle, similarly shaped, seemed a smaller reflection of it. The lower extremities of the quadriceps bulged, breaking almost too abruptly the line of the thighs, as in the legs of dancers. (55)

And it is, paradoxically, Dominique's exquisite perfection of form that makes it impossible for Alban to make love to her, hence dooming their romantic relationship: "Faced with her body, now, the gestures of love no longer came to him. How could he lend himself to the transformation of the very prototype of purity into impurity!" (240).

Although Montherlant idealizes the confraternity of men on the playing field in *Les Olympiques* (*The Olympics*), a collection of prose pieces and verse in praise of sports published two years after *The Dream* in 1924, he also extols the contribution of women to athletics. However, in an introduction to "Mademoiselle de Plémeur: Championne du 'Trois Cents'" ("Mademoiselle de Plémeur; Champion of the Three Hundred Meters," 1923), written in 1938 and incorporated into later editions of *Les Olympiques*, he is careful to make the point that this contribution is not technical but aesthetic and moral. Anything but sexist in his approach to women— at least in his writing on sports—Montherlant takes men to task for their tyranny over women's fashion and the consequent unnatural constraints imposed on their bodies. Clearly an aesthete offended by what male standards of female dress have done to the feminine form, Montherlant is deadly serious, though the passage is not without its unintentional humor in its recollection of the writer's youthful attitudes:

Aesthetic. Here are women as they could be if the duplicity, viciousness, and bad taste of the male did not force them into ruinous actions: the distortion of the body by the corset, shoes that are too small, high heels, and of the figure by clothes, not to mention makeup. Morphologically, the only difference between a man and a woman is the chest and the pelvis, which are both more developed in the female for utilitarian reasons: the bearing and suckling of the child. If the female pelvis is too broad, it is ugly; it makes the figure heavy, squashes and shortens the legs, and makes them appear knock-kneed. The breasts, even if prominent, are beautiful, so long as they remain firm. The muscles, in a woman as in a man, are always beautiful provided they are not too pronounced: there is no beauty, nor even gracefulness, where there is no perception of inner strength, the "discrete strength" asked for by Aristotle (as the soul cannot have feeling that matters if unaccompanied by strength). . .

Up to the age of twenty-three, I was disconcerted by the paradox of nature that excites our passion for bodies that are ugly, and that we know are ugly. The female bodies depicted by the painters and sculptors of our time, the bodies of women I had seen undressed, although belonging to "pretty women," even professional models, were horrible, yet opinion was unanimous in proclaiming that these folds of fat, these hanging boobs and bulging bottoms, these saddle-backed, puffed-out, shapeless creatures, were the most sublime, and indeed the only, expression of Beauty with a capital B. Never having come across in life any of the female bodies of Greek statuary or of certain painters of another age, I concluded that they were idealized inventions. But in 1919 I saw young girls working out in stadiums, I saw others who had been trained according to the "natural method" of George Hébert, and I read Hébert's indispensable book, *L'Education physique féminine*. What a revelation! It was as if I had discovered another sex. I suddenly realized that the female body could be beautiful, if it were exercised. For six years or more, I was literally unable to take an interest in any girls other than athletes.[28]

Not unexpectedly, Montherlant also discovered the beauty of which the female form was capable among dancers. Hence this description of a group of young Isadora Duncan-like dancers that Dominique comes upon in *The Dream*:

Twelve girls were dancing soundlessly, and grace enfolded them utterly. A spirit of freedom danced also amid their steps. The young sun flowed over the young skins, and one might have thought the early hour had been chosen solely to produce this harmony. Rhythmically, with rapid feet, the young girls beat the ground. Their movements seemed to contain nothing beyond their beauty; yet each one of them was so composed as to vitalize this muscle, to liberate that organ, to throw this into relief, to make that articulation more supple, to bring to perfection a particular point in the economy of the human miracle; each movement, as it were, fulfilled creation. (51)

Once he discovered bullfighting, Montherlant became obsessed with it and viewed it as more than a sport. Steeped in its history and lore, he made it the subject of his second most famous novel, *Les Bestiaires* (translated into English as *The Matador*, or *The Bullfighters*). The tauromaniac of the work is the young Frenchman, Alban de Bricoule, whom Montherlant carried over from *The Dream*. Monomaniacal, or rather, tauromaniacal, Alban becomes passionately drawn to bullfighting from the time of his first corrida in Bayonne. He moves to Spain and insinuates himself into the world of the men who raise bulls and the men who fight them, learning everything he can about the blood sport, practicing wherever and whenever he has the chance, as in this scene:

The boys who worked in the slaughter house willingly allowed him to take over a few of the bulls earmarked for killing in exchange for a few douros. Fixing the muleta, he profiled himself before the bull four paces away and lunged with the sword, driving it in as close as possible to the spot generally known as the "cross," because it is there that the spine intersects the line extended from the shoulder blades. When the animal appeared to have received the death blow but did not fall, he tried the *descabello*: the blow between the horns pierces the spinal marrow and cannot fail to finish the bull off. This method, which is used in similar circumstances by quite a number of matadors, kept his hand in training for the day when he would have to deal with fighting bulls.

The truth was that he loved these animals too much to go very long without killing them. The cure for lust lies only in possession, and here possession meant the act of killing, which was only a variation of the other form of sacrifice.[29]

Alban admires ancient pagan Rome, which he sees as a masculine society, embodying the life principle in a way that Christianity does not—a Nietzschean attitude common among the modernist physical cultists and comparable to D. H. Lawrence's esteem of the ancient Etruscans. So he is gratified at being able to find a spiritual connection between himself, Rome, and the bull:

> Hercules was the founder of Seville and it was he who brought the cult of the Bull to Spain—and Hercules figured twice in the Bricoule coat of arms. From the first, Alban had felt an instinctive devotion for Julius Caesar—and it was Julius Caesar who had introduced the corrida in Rome. He had a singular liking for Scipio the African (his gentleness and kindness had such a strong appeal for him that at the age of eleven he compiled a short historical anthology in his honor)—and Italica, a suburb of Seville, not so very far from the ring, had been a colony of Scipio's. He admired the realism of the Borgia family—and a bull figured in the Borgia arms. He was fascinated by the Emperor Julian— and Julian was an ardent worshipper of Mithra, whose mysteries he celebrated in his palace at Constantinople. It was as though his whole life were bound to the two sacred beasts, the Bull and the She-Wolf, which are sculpted side by side above one of the entrances to the Nîmes arena. (149)

Alban's opportunity to engage a bull in the ring comes when a bull-breeding aristocrat of Seville, the Duke de la Cuesta, permits him to fight in his private arena. Before a large number of guests, Alban performs poorly, largely because of the odd behavior of the bull who prefers to run rather than fight. But he redeems his honor with a second bull who is a worthier opponent. As in Hemingway, the pairing of a superb bull and an adroit matador transforms the killing of the animal into a kind of ritualistic dance, a ceremony of transcendent power:

> Man and beast rose simultaneously, moving in harmony: the rhythm quickened, the rhythm slowed, now tightening, now slackening. Like the gods in the *Iliad*, time and space fought for them: a difference of two inches . . . a difference of half a second . . . . But with the divination that sprang from his love, Alban experienced everything the beast felt, at precisely the same moment, experienced all the more directly because, in hours of exaltation, he had identified himself with the bulls. And because he knew what this one would do next, he could master it, as he could not master the other bull, because he had no love for it; one only really conquers the people and things one loves, and victors are great lovers. . . .
>
> And now the nature of the struggle slowly changed, so that it was no longer harsh and dramatic. As in every other art, mastery finally gave rise to simplicity. the ritual passes became serene and majestic, and were seemingly accomplished as easily as actions in a dream, possessing the superhuman nobility and freedom of movements filmed in slow motion. To everyone watching the fight it

appeared that a sovereign power was being brought to bear in the center of the arena, a power which alone was capable of this detachment which had a touch of disdain about it: the sovereignty of the man was apparent to all. It was no longer a fight, it was a religious incantation performed by these pure gestures, more beautiful than the gestures of love. (200)

The novel ends shortly after Alban's triumph when the victorious matador comes across the carcass of the bull he has just slain being skinned and cut to pieces by butchers, in the kind of graphic detail for which Montherlant seemed to have a particular affinity. When he has had enough of blood and gore, Alban steps into a nearby church to thank God for "allowing him to live through this great day of his life close to someone he liked" (207).

Antoine de Saint- Exupéry:
The Post-Futurist Romance
of Winged Flight

The early twentieth-century fascination with the rapid progress of technology was nowhere more striking than in the romance with flight. The invention of the airplane fulfilled an age-old human desire to be able to soar like a bird and opened up a new world of limitless possibilities. The Italian Futurists were the first to appropriate the airplane in their art, composing scenarios for aerial ballets that were actually performed and extolling the use of the airplane as an instrument of war in the Italian campaign against Turkey in 1912. D'Annunzio had such a flair for the extravagantly dramatic and heroic, he might in all probability have been tempted to take up flying even without the example of the Futurists. But it would be difficult to imagine that his great enthusiasm for flight and his wartime aerial exploits were not inspired by the writings of Marinetti and other Futurists.

The airplane, and the romance of flight, found their greatest poet, however, in the Frenchman Antoine de Saint-Exupéry. Celebrated the world over for his children's tale, *Le Petit Prince* (*The Little Prince*, 1943), Saint-Exupéry discovered the airplane early and engaged in a love affair with it that dominated his life until his disappearance on July 31, 1944, after he had taken off in an American P38 from Bastia, Tunisia, on what was supposed to be a mapping mission east of Lyons.[30] Saint-Exupéry had been considered too old to fly and too inexperienced with new aircraft, but such was his intoxication with flying, and his patriotism, that he did everything humanly possible, pulled every string he could, to make sure that he would be used as a pilot in some way during the war. As clichéd—and callous—as it may sound, Saint-Exupéry parted with life in the one way that he would have wanted, in an airplane.

Apart from *The Little Prince*, Saint-Exupéry's up-and-down reputation as a writer rests on work fashioned out of his own experiences as a pilot. The undeniable appeal of these works, beginning with the novel *Courrier Sud* (*Southern Mail*, 1929), lies in the compelling accounts of adventures beyond the imagining of the ordinary person. Saint-Exupéry's enthusiasm for flight in the early years of aviation, when planes were technically primitive and flying, especially in the small aircraft used for the mails in the 1920s, was always dangerous, assumes an almost mystic quality. If the average reader cannot easily share Saint-Exupéry's obsession, he can be thrilled by Saint-Exupéry's exhilaration at flying in all weather conditions and the dangers in the air and on land. It took men—and again, with rare exceptions, this is a world of male adventure—of almost foolhardy courage and daring, steel nerves, and an unquenchable thirst for adventure to undertake the kind of flying described by Saint-Exupéry. The men of the air mails were a type of Nietzschean superman: defying the elements, willing to challenge nature and man, unafraid to confront their own souls. Unlike the multitude, these were men who had to love solitude since they generally flew by themselves; yet they were aware that they formed a unique breed, and they savored their own companionship whenever possible.

There was little place for women in this extraordinary fraternity. Although critics were enthusiastic about *Southern Mail* when it first appeared in 1929, there were misgivings about the intrusiveness of the novel's love story. An account of mail flying from Toulouse to Morocco and Senegal, *Southern Mail* breathed with the spirit of high adventure and manly challenge and accommodated romance only awkwardly. Stung by the criticism, Saint-Exupéry nevertheless learned from it and virtually eliminated women from his works about flying. The exception is the wife of the pilot Fabien in *Vol de nuit* (*Night Flight*, 1931). Her concern for her husband's safety when his plane fails to return from a night mail delivery to South America, besides introducing a poignant, human element into the tale, also functions as a foil used to set into bolder relief the steely, unemotional professionalism of the plane dispatcher Rivière, the true "hero" of the novel.

Night Flight would be Saint-Exupéry's greatest success besides *The Little Prince*. It won the prestigious Prix Femina award in France in 1931 and was soon translated into many languages. It was followed by the longer, more episodic, and patently autobiographical *récit*, *Terre des hommes* (*World of Man*, translated into English under the title *Wind, Sand and Stars*, 1939). Although not a novel, the work was awarded the coveted Grand Prix du Roman de l'Académie Française. Another well-received *récit*, *Pilote de guerre* (*War Pilot*, translated into English as *Flight to Arras*, 1942), is set against the collapse of France at the outset of World War II and describes the valiant but hopeless missions of French fliers against the German Luftwaffe.

Narrated in the first person, *Wind, Sand and Stars* is probably the best introduction to Saint-Exupéry and his world. It is a detailed autobiographical account of his early mail flights in the 1920s and 1930s with the Latécoère Company, the predecessor of Air France, from Toulouse, in southwestern France, to Dakar, Senegal, in what was at the time French West Africa. The principal ingredients of flight—men, machines, and elements—are given their due with knowledge, affection, and respect. Of almost equal importance are Saint-Exupéry's adventures on land, above all in the Sahara Desert, which he came to know intimately either from having to put down a disabled aircraft or because of pauses at small desert relay stations along the path of flight. Saint-Exupéry's propensity for philosophical commentary, which increased as time went on and is fortunately absent from a classic such as *Night Flight*, already manifests itself in *Wind, Sand and Stars*. Extrapolating from the Sahara to life itself, for example, he writes:

> Such is the desert. A Koran which is but a handbook of the rules of the game transforms its sands into an empire. Deep in the seemingly empty Sahara a secret drama is being played that stirs the passion of men. The true life of the desert is not made up of the marches of tribes in search of posture, but of the game that goes endlessly on. What a difference in substance between the sands of submission and the sands of unruliness! The dunes, the salines, change their nature according as the code changes by which they are governed.
>
> And is not all the world like this? Gazing at this transfigured desert I remember the games of my childhood—the dark and golden park we peopled with gods; the limitless kingdom we made of this square mile never thoroughly explored, never thoroughly charted. We created a secret civilization where footfalls had a meaning and things a savor known in no other world.
>
> And when we grow to be men and live under other laws, what remains of that park filled with the shadows of childhood, magical, freezing, burning? What do we learn when we return to it and stroll with a sort of despair along the outside of its little wall of gray stone, marveling that within a space so small we should have founded a kingdom that had seemed to us infinite—what do we learn except that in this infinity we shall never again set foot, and that it is into the game and not the park that we have lost the power to enter?[31]

After flying the mails from southern France across North Africa in the 1920s, Saint-Exupéry's next exploit was a long-distance flight in late

December 1935 from Paris to Saigon, the capital of French Indochina. As if his destiny at the time demanded that he come to earth unexpectedly in the desert, mechanical difficulties forced Saint-Exupéry and his copilot to abort the flight over Libya. The account of his survival in and eventual rescue from the desert forms one of the central episodes of *Wind, Sand and Stars*. Expecting to die, either from the elements or hostile Bedouins, Saint-Exupéry reflected on the meaning of his life. What he recalls of those thoughts in *Wind, Sand and Stars* illuminates as well the attitudes and impulses from which *Southern Mail, Night Flight,* and *Flight from Arras* also arose:

> Apart from your suffering [referring to his wife Consuelo, whom he later divorced], I have no regrets. All in all, it has been a good life. If I got free of this I should start right in again. A man cannot live a decent life in cities, and I need to feel myself live. I am not thinking of aviation. The airplane is a means, not an end. One doesn't risk one's life for a plane any more than a farmer ploughs for the sake of the plough. but the airplane is a means of getting away from towns and their bookkeeping and coming to grips with reality.
>
> I have nothing to complain of. For three days I have tramped the desert, have known the pangs of thirst, have followed false scents in the sand, have pinned my faith on the dew. I have struggled to rejoin my kind, whose very existence on earth I had forgotten. These are the cares of men alive in every fibre, and I cannot help thinking them more important than the fretful choosing of a nightclub in which to spend the evening. Compare the one life with the other, and all things considered this is luxury! (150)

Similar sentiments could have been expressed with equal conviction by any of the men of letters as men of action whom we have met in this chapter.

top:
Ernst Stern, Stage set
and costume designer. Courtesy
Ullstein (Berlin).

bottom:
The writer Carl Einstein.
Courtesy Ullstein (Berlin).

this page:
A gift carrier, American produc-
tion of *The Miracle* (1924).
Author's private collection.

opposite page:
The Century Theatre, New York,
transformed into a Gothic
cathedral for the American
production of *The Miracle* (1924).
Author's private collection.

this page:
Grete Wiesenthal as the dancer
in the Max Reinhardt production
of the pantomime *Sûmurûn*, 1914.
Courtesy Ullstein (Berlin).

opposite page:
Grete Wiesenthal in performance
at the Salzburg Festspiel, October
1928. Courtesy Ullstein (Berlin).

opposite page, top:
Mary Wigman in the first version
of *Witch Dance* (1914). Courtesy
Ullstein (Berlin).

opposite page, bottom:
Mary Wigman in *Dance of Death*
(1926). Courtesy Ullstein (Berlin).

this page:
Ernst Jünger as a World War I
officer. The photograph appears as
the frontispiece to the original
edition (1920) of *In Storms of Steel*.
Courtesy Klett-Cotta (Stuttgart).

this page:
The writer and philosopher
Fritz Mauthner. Courtesy Ullstein
(Berlin).

opposite page, top:
Jahn Turnfeier (Gymnastics
Festival) in Berlin. Boys' calisthen-
ics, Tempelhof Field, June 1911.
Courtesy Ullstein (Berlin).

opposite page, bottom:
Girl participants resting on
parallel bars during a pause in the
Jahn Turnfeier in Berlin, 1911.
Courtesy Ullstein (Berlin).

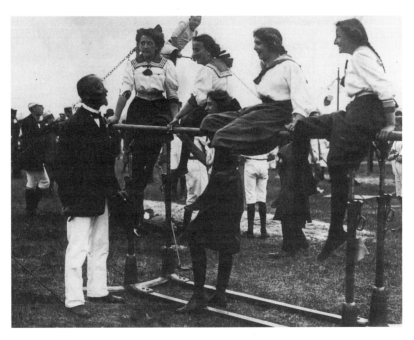

opposite page:
German Turnfest, Leipzig,
July 1913. Entrance march into the
festival square. Courtesy Ullstein
(Berlin).

this page:
Eugen Sandow (1903).
Photograpßer Napoleon Sarony,
New York. The David Chapman
Collection.

opposite page, top:
Rhythmic movement exercises.
Schule Hagemann, Hamburg,
1927. Courtesy Ullstein (Berlin).

opposite page, bottom:
Gymnastics. College of Physical
Education, 1926. Courtesy
Ullstein (Berlin).

this page:
Bund Deutscher Mädel (Union
of German Girls). Exercises with
Indian clubs, 1938. Courtesy
Ullstein (Berlin).

Hitler Youth, summer track and
field competition, Breslau,
September 1940. Courtesy Ullstein
(Berlin).

FIVE

Philosophy, Language,

and the Physical

Culture Movement

Have not names and tones been given to things that man might refresh himself on things? Speaking is a beautiful folly; with it, man dances over all things. How lovely is all talking, and all the lies of sounds! With sounds our love dances on many-colored rainbows.

FRIEDRICH NIETZSCHE, "The Convalescent,"
Thus Spoke Zarathustra

Beginning with Nietszche, certainly the most influential thinker before the spectacular impact of Bergson's *Creative Evolution* (1907), philosophical thought became increasingly more oriented toward spontaneity, intuition, and action. The role of rationality, of processes of intellectualization, was diminished in relation to the new authority of the spontaneous and intuitive. A key element in this development was the general repudiation of the long-held idea that knowledge of the world was contained in language. As we shall see, a new intense preoccupation—in many instances an obsession—with language among verbal artists developed alongside the new skepticism concerning language on the part of philosophers.

173

Nietzsche, Mauthner, Wittgenstein, and Language Skepticism

In the eleventh aphorism of *Menschliches, Allzumenschliches* (*Human, All-Too-Human*, 1878–79, first edition), Nietzsche voices with customary directness and clarity the central tenet of the language skepticism that was to become the overarching philosphical issue of the turn of the century, at least among philosophers in the formidable German tradition. In his opening statement, Nietzsche acknowledges the importance of language for culture: "In language, man juxtaposed to the one world another world of his own, a place which he thought so sturdy that from it he could move the rest of the world from its foundations and make himself lord over it."[1] Believing that in language he had knowledge of the world, man acquired "that pride by which he has raised himself above the animals" (19). But, Nietzsche suggests, man ultimately deluded himself into thinking that not only was he giving things labels, he was expressing the highest knowledge of things with words. Man lived for a long time with this self-delusion; however, in his own time, declares Nietzsche, "it is dawning on men that in their belief in language they have propagated a monstrous error." In view, though, of what man has achieved by means of his (erroneous) belief that through language he could gain mastery over the world, Nietzsche concludes by saying, almost in relief: "Fortunately, it is too late to be able to revoke the development of reason, which rests on that belief" (19). Although the eleventh aphorism in *Human, All Too Human* is perhaps Nietzsche's strongest statement on the epistemological value of language as man's grandest delusion, he deflated the language balloon in other works as well. In *Der Wille zur Macht* (*The Will to Power*; original posthumous edition, 1901), for example, he writes: "Now we read disharmonies and problems into things because we think *only* in the form of language—and thus believe in the 'eternal truth' of 'reason' (e.g., subject, attribute, etc.)" (522 [1886–87]). And "in comparison with music all communication by *words* is shameless. Words dilute and stultify; words depersonalize; words make the uncommon common" (810, [Spring–Fall 1887])."[2]

But the inherent contradictions in Nietzsche's attitude toward language became fair game themselves for the most prolific exponent of turn-of-the-century language skepticism, the Prague-born, German-language philosopher, Fritz Mauthner. Since he was a rather extraordinary character whom it was fashionable to shun for a long time in Austrian-German academic circles, a few introductory words are in order about Mauthner before considering his views on Nietzsche.

Although long neglected and made light of, Mauthner contributed importantly to the modernist literature on language.[3] A Jew from a Czech-speaking area of the Austro-Hungarian empire, Mauthner attributed his very early interest in language to the circumstances of his birth. As a Jew, he had a smattering of biblical Hebrew although the middle-class family into which he was born was secular. Like most Czech Jews, his first language was German. This was the language of the imperial administration, of business, culture, and learning, and Mauthner's father demanded that his children master High German. But like so many other Jews from the Czech lands of the empire, Mauthner also had a good knowledge of Czech, which most non-Czechs at the time regarded principally as a language of peasants and household servants, though it had once been the language of the proud kingdom of Bohemia.

Much of what we know about Mauthner personally is contained in the memoirs of his youth, originally published in 1918 under the title *Prager Jugendjahre* (*Growing Up in Prague*) as the first part of an autobiography that was never completed. The book was reprinted in 1969. Although he studied law at the university, Mauthner was strongly attracted to a literary career and in 1876 published (privately) his first work, a collection of sonnets. Nobody paid any attention to it, and Mauthner soon put the experience behind him. He had now moved to Berlin and was working for the *Berliner Tageblatt*. Besides editing the *Magazin für Literatur*, he advanced to the position as feuilleton editor of the paper in 1895. But, as Mauthner describes it in his memoirs, as early as 1873, that is, three years before he published his sonnets, he experienced "something of which at the time he had no idea if it was a tremendous project or an overwhelming feeling of resignation with respect to any literary activity."[4] What he experienced, in fact, was an irresistible attraction to questions of language, an attraction, followed by a sense of dedication, which he describes in his memoirs:

> The critical ideas concerning language that I published for the first time twenty-seven years later in three large volumes, and thrice more nine years after that, gripped me with a force that I was unable to resist. Without any preparatory work, the way one knocks off a lyrical poem, I sat myself down one day in order, in one wild spurt, to organize for myself the ideas that were troubling me so and to get to the bottom of what it was I was thinking about. For several weeks, I worked day and night on this first version of my critique of language, passionately and fully convinced that I was saying things that had never been heard before. (195)

Although his early progress was good, Mauthner was soon derailed by what he characterizes in *Growing Up in Prague* as his own intellectual inadequacies. He realized, for example, that he could not proceed without coming to grips with Kant. But not only did he have a minimal knowledge of Kant, he was unfamiliar with the ideas of other philosophers with the sole—and limited—exception of Schopenhauer. As for newer scholarship on language, he knew next to nothing. Mauthner is actually rather refreshing for the candor with which he confesses his lack of preparation for the great work on which he had embarked:

> I was an ignoramus in the field in which I believed I had revolutionary ideas. I was totally lacking the necessary school bag. Perhaps the great thinkers I did not know had worn out the soles of their shoes on what I regarded as my very own inspiration. The elation that had sent my thoughts soaring for weeks was followed by a mental anguish in which I vacillated between outright feelings of ecstasy and plans for suicide. I was helped in the latter by the persistent conviction I had had since the time of my sickness that I was a candidate for death. I threw the crude manuscript into the fire and took a solemn vow to give up any further thought of literary activity, to say nothing of the resumption of my legal studies. Instead, I planned to devote whatever time I had left me to the study of epistemology and linguistics so as to achieve some clarity concerning the revolutionary ideas with which I was then beset. (196)

Mauthner, in fact, did not abandon further literary activity despite his now all-consuming commitment to the study of language. A volume of parodies, *Nach berühmten Mustern (After Famous Models)*, appeared in 1878. Several novels followed soon afterward: *Von armen Franischko (Poor Franischko*, 1879), *Der neue Ahasver (The New Ahasuerus*, two volumes, 1882), *Berlin W (Berlin West*, three volumes, 1886–90), and *Die böhmische Handschrift (The Bohemian Manuscript*, 1897). Besides his duties at the *Berliner Tageblatt*, he also found time to become a founder of the Freie Bühne theater in Berlin.

Throughout all his steady literary output of the 1870s, 1880s, and 1890s, Mauthner continued plugging away at his book on language. When it was finished, it appeared in three large volumes in 1901 and 1902 (volumes one and two in 1901; volume three in 1902) under the general title *Beiträge zu einer Kritik der Sprache (Commentaries to a Critique of Language)*. Each volume was individually titled according to its subject. Thus, the first volume was called *Zur Sprache und zur Psychologie (On Language and Psychology)*; the second, *Zur Sprachwissenschaft (On Philology)*; and the third, *Zur Grammatik und Logik (On Grammar and Logic)*. Despite

the enormous time and energy that obviously went into the writing of the
Commentaries, Mauthner was apparently anything but exhausted by the
ordeal and moved ahead with further work on language and philosophy. In
1906 his small book, *Die Sprache* (*Language*), a refinement of his thoughts
on language, was published in Frankfurt. Another multivolume work, this
time a dictionary of philosophy under the title *Wörterbuch der Philosophie*
(*Dictionary of Philosophy*), originally appeared in two volumes in Munich
and Leipzig in 1910. A second edition, now consisting of three volumes, was
posthumously published in Leipzig in 1923–24. A third, enlarged edition of
the first volume of the *Commentaries, On Language and Psychology*, was
also published in Leipzig in 1923.

Now widely recognized as one of the groundbreaking philosophers of
language in the twentieth century, and the object of serious attention in the
English-speaking world, Mauthner gained recognition slowly and begrudgingly.[5] The reasons for the studied indifference to him seem threefold. To
begin with, he was as prolix as he was prolific, and the reader's interest and
patience can easily give way under the sheer weight of verbiage. Nevertheless, Mauthner is readable. Never pompous or stiffly academic in style, he
wrote in a German that often borders on the conversational. Style aside for
the moment, Mauthner was bound to displease the scholarly readers of the
time with both the boldness of his ideas, which are presented straightfor-
wardly—and unapologetically—and his repeated emphasis of newness and
importance. An example of this appears in the preface to the first volume
of the *Commentaries*, and it is not difficult to imagine the response of the
academic philosophers:

> My task. I had one. I am no specialist. A self-developed, great new task, the cri-
> tique of language. . . . I wanted to set forth, and allow to grow, my ideas that
> knowledge of the world is impossible through language, that there is no science
> of the world, that language is an unsuitable tool for knowledge. Since I wanted
> to expound my views exhaustively and convincingly, clearly and vividly, not
> logically nor in a word-playing manner, as a critic of language I had to come to
> know language in its depths and heights, I had to be able to look the folk in the
> mouth and to follow the researchers around their ring of scholarly concepts. . . .
>
> It does seem to me that this labor, which was my own—as was the task itself
> my own—has not been entirely fruitless, and that it has at least contributed to
> all the other disciplines in which I am not a specialist a new discipline, the cri-
> tique of language.[6]

Mauthner was also certain to provoke displeasure (to put it mildly) with
his remarks on Nietzsche in several pages on "Nietzsche und Sprachkritik"

("Nietzsche and the Critique of Language") in the fifth chapter ("Zufalls-sinne," "Chance Senses") of *On Language and Psychology*. Mauthner's reservations concerning Nietzsche are expressed early:

> Nietszche might have produced a more forceful critique of language . . . had he not concerned himself so one-sidedly with moral concepts, and had his own splendid power of speech not seduced him into wanting to be both thinker and verbal artist at one and the same time. His mistrust of language is boundless, but only insofar as it is not *his own* language. (366)
>
> Nietzsche would have been done with the language issue if he had distin-guished more clearly between language as artistic means and language as a tool of knowledge. In fact, he has given us no critique of language since he has allowed himself to be too much seduced by his own poetic language. (367)

While acknowledging Nietzsche's "hatred for language" ("*Hass gegen die Sprache*") and "even his disdain for himself as a wordmaker" (368), Mauthner consistently takes issue with Nietzsche over his presumed un-willingness to reject language as an epistemological tool, having limited himself, as Mauthner sees it, just to the repudiation of language as an instrument for the expression of mood (*Stimmung*). Agreeing with Nietz-sche that language is splendid material for verbal art, Mauthner establishes the irreconcilable difference between himself and Nietzsche by rejecting language as "a miserable tool for knowledge" ("*ein elendes Werkzeug der Erkenntnis*," 369).

With Nietzsche thus effectively neutralized, Mauthner set forth his own unequivocal views on language. Those that are pertinent to this study can be summarized as follows. Language (or speech, since Mauthner uses *Sprache* to denote both) cannot convey the content of thought. To verbalize destroys the uniqueness of that which is thought. Experience also cannot be translated into words. Reality can only be lived; it cannot be embalmed in words. Only through action can the world of reality be understood. Lan-guage is a wholly unsuitable instrument either for acquiring knowledge or expressing it. Language itself is a metaphor for reality, and it is the task of the poet to create just such metaphors. Espousing an empiricist point of view, Mauthner held that nothing is knowledge in human thought that was not first in the senses: "And thus we have already discovered that language or thought can comprise only a chance picture of the world of reality since all we know of the world of reality is what our seven chance senses [*Zufalls-sinne*] can transmit."[7]

At the end of his monumental *Commentaries*, Mauthner reiterated the theme of his entire critique of language—the disparity between the human desire to know the world and the inadequacy of language, of words, as the means of achieving that knowledge:

> Thus stands mankind, with its unquenchable longing for knowledge of the world, armed just with language. The words of this language are ill suited to communication since words are memories and no two people ever have the same memories. The words of language are ill suited to knowledge since each individual word is wrapped up in the neighboring tones [*Nebentöne*] of its history. The words of language are, in the final analysis, unsuited to penetrating the essence of reality since words are memory markers for the discoveries of our senses and since these senses are chance senses, which in truth learn nothing more of reality than a spider does of the palace in whose bay window plant it has spun its nest. (III, 650)

Mankind must, therefore, reconcile itself to never knowing reality. It must, in Mauthner's closing words, "calmly despair of it." In a final put-down of pre-Mauthnerian philosophy, he again dismisses "all philosophizing as the shuttling to and fro between wild despair and the happiness of calm illusion" (*"das Auf un Ab zwischen wilder Verzweiflung und dem Glücke der ruhigen Illusion"*). If mankind is ever to overcome its epistemological despair, it can do so, according to Mauthner, only through what he calls "calm despair" (*"die ruhige Verzweiflung"*): "Calm despair—not without smiling at itself in the process—alone can hazard the final attempt to make modestly clear to itself the relationship of humans to the world. It must do so by renouncing self-deception, by acknowledging that the word does not help, and by a critique of language and its history" (III, 650).

How Mauthner's ideas on language fed into the modernist cult of physicality is easily appreciated. Since the world cannot be known through language and no thought exists that is not first in the senses, which of their nature are chance or contingent, then there is no adequate substitute for direct experience. To repeat Mauthner's own dictum: "Only through action do we understand the world of reality."

If less dismissive of the epistemological value of language, Mauthner's fellow Austrian, Ludwig Wittgenstein, surpassed Mauthner in deflating language.[8] Now regarded as one of the most important, and difficult, thinkers of the twentieth century, Wittgenstein went farther than any other philosopher of his time in attempting to achieve the purification of language he deemed absolutely essential to meaningful philosophical discourse. Since an enormous literature of sophisticated analysis has arisen around Wittgenstein and his contributions to philosophical thought, I will not presume to add to it here. What I would like to do is suggest, by reference to his first and singly most important work (and the only one published in his lifetime), the *Tractatus logicus-philosophicus: Logisch-philosophische Abhandlung* (*Logical-Philosophical Treatise*), that the great compression of the treatise and its deceptive simplicity of style issued from the same sense of crisis and skepticism that nurtured so much of the modernist Austrian and German preoccupation with language.[9]

Wittgenstein began writing the *Tractatus* before World War I.[10] His military service for a time interrupted work on it, but he returned to it and actually completed it before the war ended in 1918. From the viewpoint of chronology, the treatise can be set squarely in the time frame of the modernist literary confrontation with matters of language. Composed between 1911 and 1918, it appeared for the first time in 1921 in the German periodical *Annalen der Naturphilosophie* (*Annals of Nature Philosophy*), edited by Heinrich Ostwald. It was published as a separate, bilingual (German and English) volume in London in 1922. The translation was the work of Frank Ramsey, Wittgenstein's closest friend at Cambridge University in England, where Wittgenstein received his Doctor of Philosophy degree and eventually became a professor of philosophy. The English edition was prefaced with a detailed introduction by the philosopher Bertrand Russell, a great admirer of Wittgenstein's, who helped his career at Cambridge despite their intellectual and temperamental differences.

In his short preface to the *Tractatus*, Wittgenstein sets forth the aim of his little book in deceptively modest terms: "This book deals with the problems of philosophy, and shows, I believe, that the reason why these problems are posed is that the logic of our language is misunderstood. The whole sense of the book might be summed up in the following words: what can be said at all can be said clearly, and what we cannot talk about we must pass over in silence."[11]

The *Tractatus*, which runs well under a hundred pages in the German original, is composed of a series of propositions presented with extraordinary compression and precision. The very style and structure of the *Tractatus* reflect Wittgenstein's training as an engineer and, in those passages where propositions are proven by symbolic logic, the mathematician's predilection for formulae and equations. But Wittgenstein brought to the composition of arguably his most difficult work not only the love of precision of the engineer and mathematician, but also an undeniable awareness of the immense popularity of the aphorism in turn-of-the-century Vienna. Among its leading practitioners was the eminent satirist Karl Kraus, who, while not a philosopher, shared Wittgenstein's concern with precision in language. A relentless crusader for truth and honesty in all areas of society,

Kraus made language, or rather the abuse of language, his principal battle-field and championed the cause of a vigorous, uncompromising renovation of contemporary Viennese linguistic culture. Wittgenstein not only knew Kraus's work but held him in high esteem, not the least for the ethical dimension of Kraus's approach to language. Just as Kraus campaigned for a "cleansing" of language in order to rid it of distortions, above all, those of the Viennese journalistic establishment, so did Wittgenstein hope to eliminate the obfuscations of traditional philosophy through a rigorous analysis of the logic of language. As he states toward the end of the *Tractatus*, as if by way of summation:

> The correct method in philosophy would really be the following: to say nothing except what can be said, i.e. propositions of natural science—i.e. something that has nothing to do with philosophy—and then, whenever someone else wanted to say something metaphysical, to demonstrate to him that he had failed to give a meaning to certain signs of his propositions. Although it would not be satisfying to the other person—he would not have the feeling that we were teaching him philosophy—*this* method would be the only strictly correct one. (6.53)

Wittgenstein then brings the *Tractatus* full circle by repeating at the very end what he advances in his preface as, indeed, the sense of the work as a whole: "What we cannot speak about we must pass over in silence" (7). In other words, unless the limits of language as the expressions of thoughts are understood, philosophy will continue to pose problems it should have no need to pose.

Apart from the logic of the *Tractatus* itself, nothing in the small work better exemplifies Wittgenstein's obsession with clarity and precision than the decimal system he used to number each of his propositions. However, in addition to the underlying division of the *Tractatus* into key propositions, numbered one through seven, Wittgenstein allowed for further refinement of the basic propositions as well as their interconnection by introducing as many as five digits after the decimal point. This was intended to indicate not only the relative weight of the individual proposition in the *Tractatus*, but also to provide for commentaries on them. Hence, the propositions numbered 1.1, 1.2, and so on, are commentaries on proposition 1, whereas 1.11, 1.12, and 1.13 are commentaries on proposition 1.1. But the system is worked out to such a degree of refinement that the reader of the treatise has to contend with arcane subdivisions on the order of 5.5262 and 5.5301. While at the other end of the spectrum of philosophical style from Mauthner, whose work, of course, he knew and alludes to once (negatively) in the *Tractatus*, Wittgenstein's compression and rigorous logic create impedimenta for all but the most well-trained students of philosophy no less than the sometimes tedious prolixity of Mauthner. Also in common with Mauthner, Wittgenstein believed in the absolute rightness of his views. That Wittgenstein was convinced that he held in his hand the solution to the problems of philosophy is evident in such propositions in the *Tractatus* as the following:

> Philosophy aims at the logical clarification of thoughts. . . . Without philosophy thoughts are, as it were, cloudy and indistinct: its task is to make them clear and to give them sharp boundaries. (4.112)
>
> [Philosophy] will signify what cannot be said, by presenting clearly what can be said. (4.115)
>
> Everything that can be thought at all can be thought clearly. Everything that can be put into words can be put clearly. (4.116)

As if setting aside metaphysics so that philosophy may be free to achieve its proper goal, Wittgenstein declares in 2.04, 2.05, and 2.06, respectively, that: "The totality of existing states of affairs is the world"; "The totality of existing states of affairs also determines which states of affairs do not exist"; and that "The existence and non-existence of states of affairs is reality (We also call the existence of states of affairs a positive fact, and their non-existence a negative fact)." This then culminates in the axiomatic: "The sum-total of reality is the world" (2.063). Wittgenstein further refines his attitude toward the metaphysical later in the *Tractatus*. After denying the existence of "the subject that thinks or entertains ideas" (5.631), he asks the question: "Where *in* the world is a metaphysical subject to be found?" and answers the question by referring to the case of the eye and the visual field: "You will say that this is exactly like the case of the eye and the visual field. But really you do *not* see the eye. And nothing *in the visual field* allows you to infer that it is seen by the eye" (5.633). From these propositions, Wittgenstein argues the true nature of the "metaphysical subject":

> Thus there really is a sense in which philosophy can talk about the self in a non-psychological way.
>
> What brings the self into philosophy is the fact that "the world is my world."
>
> The philosophical self is not the human being, not the human body, or the human soul, with which psychology deals, but rather the metaphysical subject, the limit of the world—not a part of it. (5.641)

Near the end of the *Tractatus*, Wittgenstein addresses the meaning of life and death in similar spirit. Just as the "metaphysical subject" is not a part of the world but demarcates the limit of it, so, too, is the solution to the riddle of life in space and time outside space and time. As Wittgenstein puts it:

> Not only is there no guarantee of the temporal immortality of the human soul, that is to say of its eternal survival after death; but, in any case, this assumption completely fails to accomplish the purpose for which it has always been intended. Or is some riddle solved by my surviving forever? Is not this eternal life as much a riddle as our present life? The solution of the riddle of life in space and time lies *outside* space and time. (6.4312)

Consonant with the logic of the *Tractatus* as a whole, the inability to verbalize the answer signifies the inability to verbalize the question. This being the case, the riddle does not exist. "If," as Wittgenstein argues, "a question can be framed at all, it is also *possible* to answer it." But even when "all *possible* scientific questions" have been answered, the problems of life have not at all been touched. Since language in terms of logic cannot provide the answers to the "meaning" of life, or death, any attempt at verbalization would be futile. "The solution of the problem of life," declares Wittgenstein, "is seen in the vanishing of the problem." And, he questions rhetorically, alluding doubtless to his own experiences: "Is not this the reason why those who have found after a long period of doubt that the sense of life became clear to them have then been unable to say what constituted that sense" (6.521)? Reiterating that there are indeed things that are inexpressible, that defy expression in words (the compression of the German here, "*Es gibt allerdings Unaussprechliches*," itself almost defies translation), Wittgenstein concludes that the inexpressible will, however, make itself shown ("Dies *zeigt* sich") and that "that is the *mystical*" (6.522).

The composition of the *Tractatus*—its austerity and obsessive sense of order—becomes the more intelligible if seen against the background of Wittgenstein's personal life. Although born into an extraordinarily wealthy and gifted family, he renounced his wealth and strove for a life that skirted the edge of privation. This was certainly facilitated by his reclusiveness. Like the well-known Viennese architect Adolf Loos, whom he knew personally and much admired, Wittgenstein abhorred the decorative and ornamental and aimed at stark simplicity. In order to achieve his own kind of Tolstoyan self-abnegation (and the influence of Tolstoy was hardly negligible), he stripped his life of everything he regarded as superfluous. Renouncing his share of his family's wealth was an act of liberation for Wittgenstein, one that took great inner strength and courage. Unencumbered by the responsibilities, and expectations, of considerable wealth, Wittgenstein was free to devote himself to a logic of language as cleansed of the unessential as was his personal way of life. Single-minded in his commitment to the task he set himself, capable of sacrifice and privation, Wittgenstein in his own way was truly a man of action. When the time came to serve in war, he neither shirked duty nor sought safety, but instead acquitted himself with great courage. The standards he set himself and the standards to which he wanted to hold philosophy accountable set Wittgenstein, I believe, squarely in the mainstream of the modernist repudiation of traditionalism, intellectual passivity, and self-congratulatory verbiage.

Except for a small circle of academic enthusiasts in England, and even fewer followers in the German-speaking world, Wittgenstein was not in a position to have any real influence on the modernist movement. However much modernism itself bore on the development of his own thought, his ability to shape modernism was severely limited by circumstances. Wittgenstein's *Tractatus*, the only philosophical work by him to be published in his lifetime, appeared in its most accessible form—the bilingual edition by Routledge and Kegan Paul—only in 1922. The original publication of the treatise the year before in Ostwald's *Annalen der Naturphilosophie* passed almost without notice. While highly regarded by his devoted band of Cambridge University admirers—Bertrand Russell, John Maynard Keyes, Frank Ramsey, G. E. Moore—Wittgenstein began to have contact with Moritz Schlick and other members of the future Vienna Circle of logical positivists only in the late 1920s. Even then, despite Schlick's genuine admiration for him, significant philosophical as well as personal incompatibilities limited Wittgenstein's role in the group. At the present time, however, with virtually all of Wittgenstein's writings in published form and widely translated, the austere, difficult thinker has become the focus of extraordinary interest worldwide and the subject of a huge body of literature. What better proof of the extent to which he has captured the popular imagination than the publication in 1996 of an intellectually respectable but comic-book style "introduction" to Wittgenstein.[12]

Bergson and Vitalism

The fame Wittgenstein has come to enjoy beginning in the late 1970s, long after the waning of modernism, came to the French philosopher Henri Bergson in his own lifetime. However, unlike that of Wittgenstein, Bergson's fame radiated far beyond academic and literary circles. He was truly a household name. And like that other contemporary worldwide celebrity of Francophone culture, the Belgian playwright and philosopher Maurice

Maeterlinck, Bergson has until recently been little remembered and little read.[13]

What brought Bergson the great fame he enjoyed in his day was the broad appeal of his views to the developing modernist outlook. Apart from Nietzsche, Bergson was truly the philosopher par excellence of modernism. That reputation hinged largely on a single book, *L'Evolution créatrice* (*Creative Evolution*, 1907). It was not, to be sure, Bergson's only work and not his most brilliant. He began his career as a thinker in 1889 with the publication of *Essai sur les donnés immédiates de la conscience* (translated under the title *Time and Free Will: An Essay on the Immediate Data of Consciousness*). Other books followed in rapid succession: *Matière et mémoire: essai sur la relation du corps à l'esprit* (translated into English as *Matter and Memory*, 1896), *Le rire* (*Laughter*, 1901), "Introduction à la métaphysique" ("Introduction to Metaphysics," 1903), and in 1907, *Creative Evolution*. After a long hiatus, during which Bergson was awarded the Nobel Prize for Literature in 1927, he published two more books, *Les Deux Sources de la morale et de la religion* (*Two Sources of Morality and Religion*, 1932) and *La Pensée et le mouvant: essais et conférences* (known in English under the title *The Creative Mind*, 1934).

But by the time these two last books appeared, Bergson was in eclipse. World War I and the emergence of fascism and Nazism in Europe in the 1920s and 1930s severely compromised the essential optimism of Bergsonian vitalism and demonstrated that it could as well provide the philosophical underpinnings for extremism on both ends of the political spectrum. The relentless attacks on Bergson from conservative, traditionalist elements within the Roman Catholic Church, which were upset over the theological implications of *Creative Evolution*, also eventually took their toll on his reputation. So, too, did the barrage of criticism leveled against his philosophy over the span of many years by Julien Benda, a Parisian man of letters, critic, and aesthetician deeply offended by what he perceived to be Bergson's calculated assault on reason and rationalism.[14]

Notwithstanding Bergson's extensive output and the considerable interest in him into the 1920s, no work of his enjoyed the reception of *Creative Evolution*. A fine stylist and logician (in terms of his ability to present convincing arguments for his own views), Bergson remains eminently readable. This is true of most of his writing. But it was the combination of what he had to say as well as the way he said it that assured the phenomenal popularity of *Creative Evolution*.

At a time in European society and culture marked by profound restlessness with the status quo and a real hunger for change in virtually every area of life, Bergson arrived with a philosophy that immediately found an enthusiastic reception among many. Exposing the limits of the scientific explanation of natural phenomena and mechanistic determinism, he argued for spontaneity in nature and the human will. Intellect, he proposed, is skillful in dealing with the inert, with matter. But when it comes to life, it is inept. "The intellect," he wrote in *Creative Evolution*, "is characterized by a natural inability to comprehend life." [15] Life, however, transcends intellect in that it is in a constant state of flux, constantly evolving, ever recreating itself. Since it lives in real time, life cannot be apprehended by intellect, which operates effectively as a cognitive instrument only on that which is static. Intellect, to Bergson, "dislikes what is fluid, and solidifies everything it touches. We do not *think* real time. But we *live* it" (52–53). If not by means of the intellect, how then was man to comprehend life? Through instinct, through intuition, unconsciously. As Bergson put it: "In short, while instinct and intelligence both involve knowledge, this knowledge is rather *acted* and unconscious in the case of instinct, *thought* and conscious in the case of intelligence" (161). Although Bergson insisted on the complementarity of intelligence and instinct, he made a strong case for the differences between them. A product of the evolutionary force to which reality owes its mobility, intelligence nevertheless lacks the ability to grasp the dynamic process that produced it and of which it yet remains a part. That rather is the function of instinct, which through the faculty of intuition acts spontaneously, unconsciously. But the instinctive is inaccessible to intelligence: "That which is instinctive in instinct," Bergson wrote, "cannot be expressed in terms of intelligence, nor, consequently, can it be analyzed" (185). Instinct and intuition relate closely in Bergson's thought to his concept of time. Time, he argued, was real—hence his term *durée réelle* (real duration)—and could never be grasped by the methods of science. Only intuition—meaning, in essence, experience as memory—perceives time.

At the core of *Creative Evolution* lies the idea that the universe must have begun as a spontaneous creative impulse. This *élan vital*, as Bergson termed it, did not end with the creation of the universe but exists as an ongoing process. However, it is constantly being opposed, or thwarted, by matter, which resists change. As Bergson declared: "The impetus of life . . . consists in a need of creation. It cannot create absolutely, because it is confronted with matter, that is to say with the movement that is the inverse of its own. But it seizes upon this matter, which is necessity itself, and strives to introduce into it the largest possible amount of indetermination and liberty" (274). The intellect and intelligence are identified with matter in that they must of necessity immobilize and solidify things so that they may be studied, codified, and taught. This activity inhibits and constrains the creative evolutionary impulse which responds to its own imperative. Hence the tension and conflict between the dynamic and inert, between intelligence and intuition, between matter and spirit.

The great appeal of the ideas expressed in *Creative Evolution* lay primarily in their challenge to the authority of natural science and determinism. This was a solid blow leveled against the long-held belief that everything in life was consciously knowable. By shifting the emphasis from the intellect to instinct, from intelligence to intuition, from the conscious to the unconscious, Bergson was validating the cognitive status of the nonrational. Raising high the standard of spontaneity was a clarion call to all those chafing beneath the yoke of tradition and convention. The *élan vital*, insofar as it was understood, was perceived as an embrace of creativity, of creative freedom, of liberation from fixity. Not seeing the end of the creative process was no longer a hindrance; indeed it was part of the process itself.

So sympathetic did Bergson's views seem to artists at odds with traditionalism, materialism, and mechanism, that his influence on modernism was extraordinary and greater than that of any contemporary philosopher with the exception of Nietzsche. As the newer research on Bergson has shown, it embraced the Cubists, the French writers Charles Péguy, Marcel Proust, and Paul Valéry, and such diverse writers in English as T. S. Eliot, James Joyce, Ezra Pound, and Virginia Woolf.[16]

The Revolution in Literary Language

Paralleling the break with tradition in philosphical thought was the modernist revolution in literary language. Encouraged by the new emphasis on the spontaneous and unconscious, as well as by the primitivist inclinations of modernism, literary artists launched a wide-ranging assault on established patterns of language use in creative writing. This campaign to revitalize literary language, to sweep away the lifeless forms of the past, to restore what was felt to be a lost primordial vigor, and to move into new, uncharted territory was one of the most extraordinary facets of the entire modernist movement. Beginning at least with Mallarmé, the literary artist began to take a fresh look at every facet of language, from the sound patterns of words to "buried" meanings, to grammatical and syntactic structures, to typography and the physical layout of the poem on the page, and even to the semantic potential of empty space. From the point of view of boldness, nothing at the time equaled Mallarmé's "Un Coup de Dés jamais n'abolira le hasard" ("A Throw of the Dice Will Never Abolish Chance"). The poem, usually referred to just as "Un Coup de Dés," appeared for the first time in the international journal *Cosmopolis* in May 1897; it was published separately only in 1914. Because of its unconventional physical layout, Mallarmé had originally intended for the poem to appear in double-page format. But when it was not printed that way by *Cosmopolis*, he decided to write a preface for it explaining its innovations while assuring his readers that he had, in fact, not broken radically with traditional lyric poetry.[17] The most obvious departure from convention in the poem is its layout and typography: lines of varying length distributed unevenly across the page in different print sizes and styles. The impression created is that of disconnected fragments of verse adrift in a sea of blank space. Knowing its importance in the overall design of the poem and its strangeness to the reader, Mallarmé addressed the matter of the empty space on the page almost at the beginning of his preface:

> The "blanks," in effect, assume importance and are immediately striking; versification demands them as a surrounding silence, so that a lyric poem, or one with few feet, generally occupies, situated in the middle, about a third of the leaf. I do not transgress this measure, I merely disperse it. The paper intervenes each time an image, on its own, ceases or withdraws, accepting the succession of others. Since it is not a question, as it always is, of regular sound patterns or verses, but rather of prismatic subdivisions of the Idea, the instant they appear, and however long their conjuncture in some exact mental setting, the text imposes itself, in variable places, near or far from the latent conducting wire, for the sake of verisimilitude. The literary advantage, if I may say so, of this copied distance that mentally separates groups of words or words from one another, is that it seems to speed up or slow down the movement, of scanning it, and even of intimating it in accordance with a simultaneous vision of the Page: the latter is taken as the unit in the way that elsewhere the Verse or the perfect line is.[18]

The physical layout of "A Throw of the Dice," which calls attention to the surrounding emptiness in a way that recalls the use of unpainted space in classical Japanese painting—which had already come to fascinate European viewers in the 1890s—is by no means the only innovation in the poem. As Mallarmé points out in his preface, the basic unit of the poem is now the page and no longer the line of verse. Moreover, since the poem is meant to be printed on double pages, and has been since the original *Cosmopolis* edition of 1897, each double page has its own character. The typography of the printed poem was also bound to attract attention in that the natural tendency of the reader would be to mentally pronounce the words in large or bold print louder than those in smaller print (and some of the print is very small) or in italics. Mallarmé comments on this in his preface: "The difference in the printed letters between the dominant motif, a secondary and adjacent ones, dictates their importance for oral expression, and the range, in the middle, at the top, or at the bottom of the page, indicates a rising or falling of the intonation" (455).

Marinetti, the leader of the Italian Futurist movement, would use typography in a similar way in the printing of his own works. As Henry Weinfield points out in his fine edition of Mallarmé's collected poems: "What is most innovative about the poem, from a formal point of view, is the way in which the conception has been *materialized*—in a manner that makes the physical layout, the spacing, and the typography not merely a representation of the poem but an integral aspect of the poem itself." [19]

Apart from the disposition of the words on the page and the typography, "A Throw of the Dice" looks ahead to Marinetti and the Futurists in its complete abandonment of punctuation and in its disrupted syntax. In some instances—for example, the section beginning (in capital letters) "LE MAÎTRE"—the reading is further complicated because of the verso and recto (left-hand side and right-hand side) lines that require the reader to read both from top to bottom on a page and also from left to right across the double page of text. The rhythm of the passages on the double page are meant to suggest the turbulent waves of the sea in a storm or the listing to one side and then another of a sunken ship. Hence, to a very great extent, the alignment of the words on the page and the different typefaces used were intended to capture the ebb and flow of a poem about the predoomed human effort to seek out order in a world of chaos.

The boldness of the physical layout of Mallarmé's "A Throw of the Dice" was not lost on other writers. His German disciple, the poet Stefan George, who had been close to Mallarmé and his circle in Paris in the late 1880s and early 1890s, was as fastidious about the appearance of his verse as he was about its structure. Besides introducing his own reforms in punctuation and capitalization, he also addressed the matters of orthography and typography. In the long-standing dispute over the continued use in German printing of the old Gothic typeface, or *Fraktur*, as opposed to a Roman print (as used, for example, in English), George favored the latter for its simplicity, legibility, and compatibility with much of the rest of Europe. Consonant with this preference, George called for an end to the old German pattern of capitalizing every noun. In his own practice, capitals were to be used only at the beginning of sentences, for proper names, and for emphasis. He also designed a typeface resembling his own handwriting. Like Mallarmé's innovations, those of George—executed for the first editions of several of his books of poetry by the artist Melchior Lechter—preceded and doubtless to some extent influenced the yet more drastic experiments with page layout and typography of the Italian and Russian Futurists from Marinetti to Mayakovsky.

The Russian painter Wassily Kandinsky, who lived in Munich in the period of the ascendancy of George and his circle of initiates, known as the George Circle, was close to members of the group (especially Karl Wolfskehl) and shared many of their views. Intent, like the Symbolists, on integrating the verbal, visual, and auditory, Kandinsky in 1904 published a set of visual poems under the title *Gedichte ohne Worte* (*Verses Without Words*, also known as *Poems Without Words*). These were, in fact, woodcuts of a lyrical nature characterized by an abstraction and compression of form similar to the musical and transcendent qualities the Symbolists sought to achieve in their poetry. That Kandinsky also related the woodcut to music is evident both in the musical subjects of a few of the woodcuts as well as in the way their composition and color produce the effect of musical chords. Kandinsky used the German word *Klang* (musical chord) to characterize the effect by which the successful work of art communicates its inner meaning. In order to strike a responsive chord in the soul of the viewer, the work of art had to resonate (Kandinsky here uses the German verb *klingen*, "to resonate"). The concept has enormous significance in Kandinsky's creative work, both visual and literary, and informs his writing on art as well. In 1909 Kandinsky followed his first collection of woodcuts with a second portfolio, to which he gave the title *Xylographies*; the name derives from an uncommon word for woodcut ("xylography," in English) and at the same time refers to the musical instrument, the xylophone. Four years later, in 1912, Kandinsky published his graphic masterpiece *Klänge* (*Sounds*, or *Resonances*), a collection of thirty-eight poems in prose, twelve color woodcuts, and forty-four black-and-white woodcuts.[20]

The woodcuts accompanying the poems in *Sounds* for the most part have no semantic relation to the poems; they do not, in other words, "illustrate" the poems. For the original Russian edition of seventeen poems, which was to have been published in 1911, Kandinsky had intended for the woodcuts to be the visual corollaries of the poems, but this edition never materialized. The prose poems themselves are extremely short, lexically and syntactically simple, and feature considerable repetition. Their "meanings" are elusive. Indeed, "meaning" in the denotative sense seems not to have been Kandinsky's intention. As keenly interested in a transformation of poetic language as the Futurists and Dadaists, Kandinsky pursued change in a different way. In light of his ideas on "Klang," or "inner resonance," his aim was not the "liberation" of words through syntactic disruption, or the unearthing of the primordial nexus between sound and sense, but rather the estrangement of representational language. Just as the woodcuts in *Sounds* hint at the enigmatic and abstract, so, too, do the poems in their strange, elusive character signal a shift from representation to abstraction. By unsettling the reader's assumptions or suppositions concerning the phenomenal world, Kandinsky hints at other levels of "reality" inaccessible by and large to the rational mind. Perception is almost constantly jostled, shaken off balance, to the point where certitude is called into question and challenged. Fortunately, the poems are short enough to permit a few examples. In "Weisser Schaum" ("White Foam") a rider mercilessly beats a horse, presumably to get it to go faster. But the animal cannot go faster, and as the beating continues, the horse's natural black color gradually gives way to the whiteness of the foam covering it:

> I'd like to know why it's like this and not that. It could be different, very, very different.
> On a ravenblack horse a woman rides through flat green fields.
> I can't see the end of these fields. The woman is dressed in red, her face is hidden by a canaryyellow veil. The woman beats the horse without mercy. It just can't go any faster. Anyway it's already foaming and is growing whiter and whiter from the white hot foam. The woman sits upright without swaying and beats the black horse.
> Don't you think it would be better if the black horse could die?
> It's turning all white from the white hot foam!
> But it can't die. Oh no! That it can't do.
> How different it could be, how very different.[21]

The poem approaches the surreal—the enigmatic action, the interplay of colors (green fields, the woman rider dressed in red, the canaryyellow veil over her face, the ravenblack horse turning white with foam). The unhyphenated color compounds appear this way in the original German virtually throughout *Sounds*. A pattern of repetition intensifies the strangeness of the poem: the first line reappears at the end, and the whiteness of the foam overpowering the animal's black color and its inability to die are also repeated. But why can't the horse die, and why cannot it (whatever "it" refers to here—life?) be different? What occult power has determined that things must be as they are? Must nature suffer forever at the hands of man?

A similar apparent determinism is conveyed in "Glocke" ("Bell"), which is structured out of disconnected simultaneity:

Once in Weisskirchen a man said: "I never, never do that."

At the exact same time in Mühlhausen a woman said: "Beef with horseradish."

Both of them said what they said, because there was no other way.

I hold a pen in my hand and write with it. I wouldn't be able to write with it if it were out of ink.

The great big beast that took such joy in chewing its cud was knocked senseless by quick, repeated, hollow-sounding blows to the skull. It sank down. An opening in its body let the blood run its course. Much thick, sticky, smelly blood ran for an interminable time.

With what wonderful skill they tore off the thick, warm, velvety hide covered with beautiful ornamental patterns of brownwhite hair. Skinned hide and red steaming odorful meat.

Very flat land, disappearing flat into all horizons.

Far to the left, a little birch grove. Still very young, soft white trunks and bare branches. Nothing but brown fields, carefully plowed in straight rows. In the middle of this giant circle a little village, just a few graywhite houses. Right in the middle a church steeple. The little bell is pulled by a rope and goes: ding, ding, ding, ding, ding . . . (38)

Again, as in "White Foam," things are as they are because they cannot be otherwise. The world of *Sounds* is narrowly circumscribed. The disconnectedness of the imagery hints at surreal alogicality. So, too, does the naturalistic picture of the slaughterhouse butchering of a cow. Arranging his word pictures as a painter, Kandinsky shapes the images into discrete miniatures. Repetition, a structural principle of *Sounds*, has more than a single function. On one level, it creates an incantatory effect that enhances the poem's strangeness. On another level, it tends to focus perception on the individual word or phrase, somewhat in the manner of Marinetti's words in liberty.

There is also a playing with words and images in Kandinsky's *Sounds* that recalls the deliberate childlike stylization of the *Galgenlieder* (*Gallows Songs*, 1905) by the German poet Christian Morgenstern. Dedicated to "dem Kinde im Manne" ("the child in man") and inspired by Nietzsche's dictum "Im echten Manne ist ein Kind versteckt: das will spielen" ("There is a child in every real man that wants to play"), the *Gallows Songs* employs whimsicality, naïveté, and the child's sense of language to suggest the idea that through humor and a lack of seriousness, in the spirit of childish play, the world can be better understood. Take, for example, the poem "Galgenberg" ("Gallows Hill"):

Blödem Volke unverständlich
treiben wir des Lebens Spiel.

Gerade das, was unabwendlich,
fruchtete unserm Spott als Ziel.

Magst es Kinder-Rache nennen
An des Daseins tiefem Ernst;
wirst das Leben besser kennen,
wenn du uns verstehen lasst.

Beyond the stupid people's grasp,
we pursue the game of life.
Indeed that which gave
purpose to our joke.

You can call it children's revenge
on the deep seriousness of existence.
But you'll come to know life better
if you understand us.[22]

A decade before the Dadaist *Lautgedichte* (sound poems) of Hugo Ball at the Cabaret Voltaire in 1916, Morgenstern, in the poem "Das grosse Lalula" ("Big Lalula") had already given an example of his own ridicule of conventional language through a similar concoction of "words" made up of arbitrary combinations of vowels and consonants:

Kroklokwafzi? Sememi!
Seiokrontro—prafriplo:
Bifzi, bafzi; hulalemi:
quasti basti bo . . .
Lalu lalu lalu lalu la!

Hontraruru miromente
zasku zes rü rü?
Entepente, leiolente
klekwapufzi lü?
Lalu lalu lalu lalu la!

Simarar kos malzipempu
silzuzankunkrei (;)!
Marjomar dos: Quempu Lempu
SIRI SURI SEI [] !
Lalu lalu lalu lalu la! (40)

The Italian Futurists, with Marinetti pointing the way, were the logical successors of the Symbolists in the effort to revitalize literary language, notwithstanding their repudiation of Symbolist aesthetics and metaphysicality. Much of Marinetti's energy went into his self-declared war on syntax. In order to uncover the "authentic" meanings of words, they first had to be released from the yoke of syntax, which, in Marinetti's view, had a corollary in the artificial restraints of bourgeois social conventions. The campaign to revitalize language by liberating words from the tyranny of syntax—hence the slogan *parole in libertá* (words in freedom)—paralleled the Futurists' commitment to lift society from under the heavy burden of bourgeois attitudes and institutions.

Marinetti's opening salvo against the traditional literary language was his "Manifesto tecnico della letteratura futurista" ("Technical Manifesto of Futurist Literature") of May 11, 1912. Inspired, as usual, by the innovations of the modern technological age, Marinetti mentions at the outset of his manifesto that awareness of the "ridiculous inanity of the old syntax inherited from Homer" came to him while seated above the fuel tank of an aeroplane flying "two hundred meters above the mighty chimneys of Milan."[23] He then resolves that there was a "desperate need to liberate words, to free them from the prison of the Latin period" (40). To achieve this liberation, he advocates several bold syntactic steps. These include abolishing adjectives, adverbs, punctuation, and conjunctives and using verbs only in the infinitive form. Adjectives have to go, according to the leader of the Futurist movement, because "the naked noun preserves its essential color." Since it suggests a pause, a meditation, the adjective is incompatible with the Futurists' "dynamic vision." Marinetti's brief against the adverb was based on his belief that it is an "old buckle" tying one word to another, thereby preserving a "tiresome unity of tone." In place of conjunctives, Marinetti recommends, for greater forcefulness, that a noun be followed by another noun to which it is connected by analogy. One of the examples he gives of this reflects Marinetti's passion for war and the new military hardware of the time: *uomo-torpediniera* (man-torpedo-boat). Having done away with adjectives, adverbs, and conjunctives, punctuation, with its "absurd" commas and periods indicating stops, is no longer necessary. Instead, mathematical signs ($+ - \times \div = < >$) and musical signs can be used to accentuate certain movements and indicate their directions.

He also advocates doing away with all forms of a verb except the infinitive. This would eliminate the authorial "I," by which he meant psychology. A little later in his manifesto, Marinetti explains that this is necessary since the man "who has been utterly ruined by libraries and museums, and is subordinate to a frightening logic and wisdom, has absolutely nothing more interesting to offer" (44). The place of the "I" in literature would then be taken by matter whose essence would have to be grasped "by blows of intuition, something physicists and chemists are no longer able to do." Marinetti cautions against informing matter with human feelings; instead, he advises, "guess your different direct impulses, their powers of compression, of expansion, of cohesion, of disintegration, their throngs of molecules in mass or their whirls of electrons." Another reason for using a verb only in the infinitive would be to better give the sense of the "continuity of life and the elasticity of the intuition that perceives it."

Marinetti further refined his views on syntax in his treatise "Distruzione della sintassi Immaginazione senza fili Parole in libertà" ("Destruction of Syntax Imagination without Wires Words in Liberty, May 11, 1913). Lest the term "imagination without wires" not be understood, Marinetti offered this explanation: "By imagination without wires, I have in mind the absolute liberty of images or analogies, expressed with unbound words and without conducting syntactic wires and without any punctuation." (63)

Marinetti began writing *parole in libertà* as early as 1912. His first work in the new style was "Battaglia Peso + Odore" ("Battle Gravity + Smell"), dating from August 1912 and inspired by the fighting in Libya during the Italian-Turkish war of 1911–12. It is just under three pages long and actually forms a part of his "Technical Manifesto of Futurist Literature." In Marinetti's parlance, "weight" (*peso*) is to be understood as the power of objects to fly (*facoltà di volo degli oggetti*) and "smell" (*odore*), the power of objects to scatter (*facoltà di sparpagliamento degli oggetti*).[24] "Battle Gravity + Smell" was followed by *Zang Tumb Tumb* (dated October 1912), which was a response to the battle of Adrianople against the Turks in October 1912. *Dune* (1914), a seven-page pyrotechnical display of Futurist typography, came next, followed by 8 *Anime in una bomba: Romanzo esplosivo* (8 *Souls in One Bomb: Explosive Novel,* 1919), in which the recollection of random episodes from the war serve as the pretext for Marinetti's dissection of his own personality and his division of it into eight parts, each of which forms a separate "chapter" of the work. Actions and events related to the war alternate with erotic passages characteristic of Marinetti's coupling of male aggressive behavior as manifest in war and the subjugation of the female. Even at his most erotic and suggestive, Marinetti is not without humor; the "Second Soul," which takes the form of "A letter from Bianca, Plump Virgin and Teacher of botany, to a Futurist," begins: "My love, you are sweet, divine! I love you, I hate you. I want you, I don't want you. I am afraid of your brutal love. I fight it the way one should fight the Phytomyza Flavicornis that devours the roots of savoy cabbages."[25]

Marinetti's last major work in the *parole in libertà* style was *Gli indoma-*

bili (*The Untameables*, 1922), a bleak allegorical tale of a chaotic, failed attempt to improve the lot of oppressed workers in an industrial society. Although Marinetti himself describes *The Untameables* as *un libro paroli-bero* (a words-in-liberty book), the work actually marks a departure (as does *8 Souls in One Bomb*) from this technique in favor of more conventional narrative. There are almost no typographical eccentricities and traditional rules of syntax are largely observed. *Parole in libertà*, it seems, was not destined to become a permanent feature of Italian literary style despite the aggressiveness with which it was proclaimed and practiced at the height of the Futurist revolution.

The Russian Futurians, Futurists, and Cubo-Futurists shared with Marinetti and company the same enthusiasm for breaking with tradition, but with much less of their Italian counterparts' militancy and obsession with violence. As elsewhere in the European avant-garde of the early twentieth century, such leading Russian linguistic innovators as Velimir Khlebnikov and Aleksei Kruchonykh sought above all to revitalize poetic language through sound. What this meant in effect was that the recovery of the meanings behind primordial sound patterns would result in a kind of semantic "purification"; derived meanings would yield to the newly discovered "authentic" meanings. In this sense, of course, the quest for primordial authenticity situates the Russian experiments with sound, like those of Hugo Ball and Jean (Hans) Arp in the heyday of the dada movement, within the mainstream of modernist primitivism in the arts. In Russia this trend was represented primarily by the artist Mikhail Larionov. Khlebnikov's essay "The Warrior and the Kingdom" (1913) begins, in fact, with the credo of the warrior who both embodies and seeks the primitive past:

> The warrior of the kingdom of the future hereby demands respect and a serious consideration of his beliefs.
> 1. He is armed like a hunter of wild beasts, with a net to trap ideas and a harpoon to defend them. He is naked and powerful.
> Who are we? . . .
> We are the mouthpiece of fate. We have come from the bowels of the Russian sea. We are warriors, and in our persons we initiate a new estate in the social order. . . .
> We maintain that an understanding of tribal life is revealed in numerals, and that it is thus possible to reconstruct the contours of primitive life.[26]

A well-trained and inventive mathematician as well as poet, Khlebnikov occasionally introduced mathematical concepts, mainly those of geometry, and numerology, into his theoretical writing.[27] On the whole, however, much of his energy as a language innovator went into demonstrating the correspondences between the sounds and meanings of words. Although his examples are always drawn from the Russian language, Khlebnikov believed that his ideas were universally applicable. Here, for example, from his essay "Izberyom dva slova" ("Let Us Consider Two Words," 1912), is how he analyzes words beginning with the same consonant whose meaning is altered by changes in vowels and how he shows that the very shape of a letter can be semantically relevant. His aim, of course, is to refute the argument that the relation between sign and object is purely arbitrary:

> Let us consider two words: *lysina* [bald spot] and *lesina* [tree trunk]. Mountains lacking *les* [forest] are called *lysyi* [bald]; the exact area deprived of *les* is called *lysina* [bald spot]; an individual tree, a part of *les*, can be referred to as *lesina*. Should we not attribute an opposition in meaning to these two words distinguished only by a change of vowel, *y* to *e*? Can we consider that *l* and *s* contain a constant element of identity, while *y* and *e* are markers of disparity? . . . (266)
>
> This *l* in the sense of a striving upward begins two words: *les* [forest] and *lysyi*, *lysina* [bald, bald spot]. Signifying in part of their meanings either the existence or nonexistence of one and the same element, the two words are distinguished by the alternation of *e* and *y*. *E* marks the presence of longing toward height that defines the nature of a forest; *y*, the absence of that longing. If we understand *e* as the smallest phonetic carrier of the meaning *existence*, we can easily explain these two words if we interpret *ly* and *le* as markers for the genitive and dative cases respectively (by analogy with *ryby* [of a fish] and *rybe* [to a fish]: the action of the genitive case signifies the diminution or subtraction of that which is given—the dative case—by means of syllabic composition. Put that which is substantive together with a striving toward height, and you get a forest [*les*]; subtract it from a striving toward height, and the result is baldness [*lysina*]. (269)

And in this excerpt from "Razgovor dvukh osob" ("A Conversation Between Two Individuals," 1913), Khlebnikov demonstrates how, in his opinion, numbers reveal the ancient features of mankind:

> These seven stages of the moon's ascent to Earth recall the seven heavens, and many other "sevens" as well. But in the names of numbers we recognize the ancient features of mankind. Isn't the number *sem* [seven] simply a truncated version of the word *sem'ia* [family]? In the names of numbers we can find traces of certain activities characteristic of the tribal life of primitive man suitable to a group with that particular number of members.
>
> A group of five young savages and two full-grown men out hunting was de-

nominated by the number seven [*sem*]; the number eight [*vosem*], formed by adding the prefix *vo* [into], indicated that a new entity had joined the group.

Primitive man needed no help from others while eating [*eda*], and the number one [*edinitsa*] correctly signifies precisely that activity. The teeth of that word crunch the shinbones of game, and the bones crack. This tells us that primitive man experienced hunger. (290)

The poetry Khlebnikov wrote based on such beliefs—and which he dubbed *zaum* (trans-sense, or transrational)—at times consisted entirely of speech sounds; in this respect, it anticipated the experiments of the Dadaists at the Cabaret Voltaire in 1916. Given his feeling for language and his obsession with roots and the relation between the shapes of letters, sounds, and meaning, it hardly comes as a surprise that Khlebnikov delighted in creating his own words (neologisms) and peppering his poetry with them. Equally characteristic of his poetic writing was his fondness for stripping away the patinas of accrued meanings—he believed they were represented in the primary and even secondary definitions offered in dictionaries—and retrieving the words' original meanings. In this sense, he drew close to Marinetti's idea of words in liberty. Without doubt the best example of Khlebnikov's "etymological" poetry, and his most famous work, is the poem "Zaklyatie smekhom" ("Incantation by Laughter," 1910), which has been described as a "poetic exploration of the possibilities of morphological derivations inherent in the Russian language."[28] Khlebnikov's poem, "Byly napolneny zvukami truschchoby" ("The Thickets Were Filled with Sounds"), which was published in the same literary miscellany as "Incantation by Laughter," is a fine specimen of a poem constructed wholly out of speech sounds.

Aleksei Kruchonykh, with whom Khlebnikov's name is invariably linked in the writing of transrational poetry, was a vigorous exponent and theorist of Russian cubo-futurism.[29] More extreme in some respects than Khlebnikov, his goal as a poet was to rid Russian poetry of the weighty baggage of the past: meaning, psychology, and philosophy. So as not to repeat the errors of their predecessors, he claims that he and his fellow "primitivists" rejected ancient masters and "antique principles." By the same token, they also rejected previous primitives who pretended to be "semi-literates." With these obstacles out of the way, "there arose before us in all its majesty the grandiose task of creating form *from nothing*."[30] His best-known poem in the *zaum* style was "Dyr bul shchyl" (title, of course, untranslatable), which Kruchonykh, with all the flamboyance of the dedicated literary revolutionary and iconoclast, was fond of characterizing as more Russian than all of Pushkin's poetry. The poem is short enough to quote in full:

Dyr bul schchyl
ubeshchur
skum
vy   so   bu
r   l   e   e

In common with the Italian Futurists, Kruchonykh also sought to convey through his poetry the chaos and cacophonies of modern life. Besides
dispensing with punctuation and using typographical means to emphasize
words and sounds, like the Italians, Kruchonykh engaged in a kind of one-
upmanship among the literary rebels by deliberately flaunting grammatical
errors and assigning textures to various sounds. He also became well-known
for his creation of neologisms, which he fully expected would become part
of the language. Kruchonykh went avant-gardist typography one better not
only by publishing himself almost all his own works, but by publishing his
handwritten texts of poems.[31]

The deliberate verbal mayhem of such artists as Jean Arp and Hugo Ball
at the Cabaret Voltaire, where dada was born, represents the extreme of
the modernist revolt against traditional language and the social order with
which it was identified. It was, in a sense, the end station of the journey that
had begun with Mallarmé and Morgenstern and had made its way through
Kandinsky, the Italian Futurists, and the Russian *zaum* poets. Indeed, it
would be difficult to imagine surpassing the experiments of the Dadaists
without lapsing into silence or utter madness. When Hugo Ball collapsed
in nervous exhaustion after the magic-like recitation of his "Lautgedichte"
or "Sound Poems" on June 23, 1916, it was as if an entire movement came
crashing to the podium with him.

Dada was an expression of frenzied revolt against the European order
that had plunged the world into the nightmare of global conflict in 1914. It
was its own declaration of war against a society whose madness was manifest
in the enthusiasm with which it greeted the outbreak of the "Great War."
Huddled together in the safe haven of Zurich, where they were spared
the mindless savagery of the battlefields, the exiles who had established
the Cabaret Voltaire—the Germans Hugo Ball, his wife Emmy Hennings,
Richard Huelsenbeck, Leonhard Frank, and Klabund; the Romanian artists Tristan Tzara and Marcel Janco; and the Alsatian poet Jean (Hans)
Arp—turned it into a riotous outburst against the world they had left behind. The insanity and irrationality of war fueled the experiments with
rhythm and sound for which dada became renowned.

Much of what we know of the Cabaret Voltaire and the rise of dada come from the diary Hugo Ball kept from November 1914 to September 29, 1921, and to which he gave the title *Die Flucht aus der Zeit* (*Flight Out of Time*). It was originally published in 1927, the year of Ball's death. In his entry for July 9, 1915, after he had already relocated to Zurich and some six months before the Cabaret Voltaire came into existence, Ball noted that Marinetti had sent him specimens of words in liberty. Apparently the shared enthusiasm for literary experimentation overrode their diametrically opposed attitudes toward the war. Ball wrote:

> Marinetti sends me *parole in libertà* by himself, Cangiullo, Buzzi, and Go-voni. They are the purest letter posters; you can unfurl a poem like this like a map. Syntax has been thrown out of joint. Letters have been shattered and re-assembled in only a makeshift way. There is no language anymore, proclaim the literary astrologers and spiritual chief shepherds. It must be discovered all over again. Resolution as far as the innermost creative process.[32]

Kandinsky was another artist who in Ball's opinion spoke directly to their own age. With Kandinsky in mind, Ball wrote in his diary on March 5, 1916:

> The image of the human form is more and more disappearing from the paint-ing of these times, and all things appear only in a state of decomposition. This is one more proof of how ugly and worn the human countenance has become, and of how every single object of our environment has become detestable. The decision of poetry to do away with language for similar reasons is near at hand. These are things that have probably never happened before. (84)

With so jaundiced a view of the time in which he lived and of West-ern civilization he now regarded as grotesquely ugly, Ball was ready for his own demolition of prevailing values. The arrival of the yet more radically inclined Richard Huelsenbeck in Zurich on February 11, 1916, provided the impetus. In his entry in *Flight Out of Time* for February 11, 1916, im-mediately after reporting Huelsenbeck's arrival, Ball noted that Huelsen-beck began pleading that the "rhythm (the Negro rhythm) [of the cabaret] be strengthened. He'd like nothing better than to drum literature into the ground" (80). Huelsenbeck had recited "Negro poems" (*Negerlieder*) of his own concoction during an Expressionist evening in Berlin and was now anxious to transplant this "genre" of primitivism in the ripe soil of the Cabaret Voltaire. To artists such as Huelsenbeck, who spurned Western civilization and sought inspiration in a fashionable primitivism, "primitive" and "African" were equatable. What they admired in what they understood to be black African songs and dances was their wild, frenzied rhythms, their animal-like physicality, and their unabashed eroticism. The sounds of native African languages entranced them; they seemed to come out of the heart of the jungle, primordial, harking back to the dawn of human civilization. Because of Huelsenbeck's enthusiasm for them, "African poems" became a staple of Cabaret Voltaire evenings and were usually accompanied by the loud banging of a large kettle drum.

Ball's first serious act of literary demolition occurred when he, Huelsenbeck, Tzara, and Janco participated in a recitation of a *poème simultan* (simultaneous poem). In his entry for March 30, 1916, in *Flight Out of Time*, he defined this as

> a contrapuntal recitative in which three or more voices speak, sing, whistle, or whatever, at the same time in such a way that these combinations make up the elegiac, humorous, or bizarre content of the piece. The willfullness of an organon is forcefully expressed in such a simultaneous poem, and so is its limitation by the accompaniment. Noises (a "rrrrr" drawn out for minutes, or crashes, sirens, and so on) are superior to the human voice in energy.
>
> The *poème simultan* concerns the value of the voice. The human organ represents the soul, the individuality in its odyssey with its demonic companions. The noises represent the background: the inarticulate, the disastrous, the decisive. The poem seeks to elucidate the swallowing up of man in the mechanistic process. In a typically compressed way it shows the conflict of the *vox humana* (human voice) with a world that threatens, ensnares, and destroys it, a world whose rhythm and noise are ineluctable. (87)

Although Ball never experimented further with the simultaneous poem, other Dadaists did. Tristan Tzara composed a *poème simultan* called "Lumière Froide" ("Cold Light") that was recited by seven voices at the Third Dada Soirée on April 28, 1917, and Arp, Tzara, and Walter Serner, another participant in Cabaret Voltaire programs, wrote a cycle of simultaneous poems under the title *Die Hyperbel vom Krokodilcoiffeur und dem Spazierstock* (*The Hyperbole of the Crocodile's Hairdresser and the Walkingstick*).

Ball's most original contribution to the Cabaret Voltaire and dada were his so-called sound poems (*Lautgedichte*, in German). These were series of sounds marked off as words and organized in the form of verse. They were pure invention, experiments in the evocative power of sounds lacking any semantic significance, hence their appeal. Although they contain almost no recognizable European lexical elements, they are vaguely African sounding and in this sense relate to the "African" poems recited at the Cabaret Voltaire by Huelsenbeck and others. Ball was by no means the creator of this type of poetry. We have already met "Das grosse Lalula" ("The Big Lalula") in Christian Morgenstern's *Gallows Songs* collection of 1905. The German poet Paul Scheerbart had included the "sound poem" "Kikakoku" in his collection *Ich liebe Dich!* (*I Love You*), which was published in Berlin 1897.

The early practitioners of sound poetry cultivated it as a kind of nonsense verse compatible with the world of the child from which the avant-garde drew much of its inspiration. Besides embodying the spirit of play, the sound poem in its nonsensicality also seemed to undermine the exaltedness of poetic composition. A certain shift of emphasis occurs, however, with Ball and other Dadaist writers of sound poems. Although still intended to shock and provoke, the sound poem now related more readily to the primitivist agenda of modernism.

Altogether Ball composed six sound poems, all of which were recited at the Cabaret Voltaire on June 23, 1916. At first glance they seem to be little more than arbitrary groupings of sounds intended to evoke certain associations. But if examined more closely (as I have done elsewhere[33]), they reveal repetitive patterns and arrangements of sounds that hint at grammatical structure. These features, as well as the "African" tonal pattern of the poem (in which at least the word "rhinoceros" is intelligible), are easily seen in what well may the best known of Ball's sound poems, "Gadji beri bimba." What follows is the first stanza of the three-stanza work:

> Gadji beri bimba
> gadji beri bimba glandridi laula lonni cadori
> gadjama gramma berida bimbala glandri galassassa laulitalomini
> gadji beri bin blassa glassala laula lonni cadorsu sassala bim
> gadjama tuffm i zimzalla binban gligla wowolimai bin beri ban
> o katalominai rhinozerossola hopsamen
> bluku terullala blaulala loooo . . .[34]

While the contemporary reader may sense a playfulness, even clownishness, in the piece, Ball himself was utterly serious about the experimental nature of his sound poems and approached their composition and recitation with a kind of missionary zeal. In a sense, the poems can be regarded as the incantations of a verbal magician. Ball liked to think of himself that way and was attired appropriately for his performance on June 13, 1916. A photograph of him at the time shows him sheathed in a cylindrical "Cubist" costume with a high conical hat (a shaman's, as he described it) and a huge collar that came well down over his shoulders and gave the impression of wings when he raised his arms.

Ball was so exhausted by his recitation, physically and psychically, that he never repeated the performance. It was also his last appearance at the Cabaret Voltaire, which closed shortly thereafter. After drifting away from the avant-garde experiments of the Zurich period, Ball became involved in politics, and after "reconverting" to Roman Catholicism, turned to asceticism and the history of Christianity. These later interests resulted in two of his last books, *Byzantinisches Christentum* (*Byzantine Christianity*, published in 1923) and *Die Folgen der Reformation* (*The Consequences of the Reformation*, published in 1924), essentially a repudiation of German Protestantism. Ball also completed a sympathetic biography of the German novelist Herman Hesse (this was published the year of Ball's death), which was written from the viewpoint of the orthodox Catholic convinced of the imminence of Hesse's break with Protestantism.[35]

Even before his tumultuous final appearance at the Cabaret Voltaire on June 23, 1916, Ball had already become convinced of the success of the language revolution spearheaded by himself and his fellow Dadaists. As he wrote in *Flight Out of Time* for June 18, 1916:

> We have now driven the plasticity of the word to the point where it can hardly be outdone. We achieved this result at the expense of the logically constructed, rational sentence, and also by abandoning documentary work (which is possible only by means of a time-consuming grouping of sentences in a logically ordered syntax). Of great help to us in our efforts were first of all the special circumstances of these times, which do not allow genuine talent either to rest or mature and thus put its capabilities to the test. Then there was the emphatic drive of our group, whose members were always trying to surpass one another by intensifying demands and stresses. You can laugh if you want; language will one day reward our zeal, even if no directly visible results are granted it. We have loaded the word with strengths and energies that helped us to rediscover the evangelical concept of the "word" (*logos*) as a magical complex image. (101–2)

Even more noteworthy than this statement of accomplishment was Ball's declaration in the last paragraph of the same entry that he and his colleagues at the Cabaret Voltaire had, in fact, surpassed the efforts of Marinetti and the Futurists, suggesting thereby that there was nothing further to be done; the language revolution had come to an end:

> With the abandonment of the sentence for the sake of the word, the group around Marinetti began "parole in libertà" in earnest. They removed the word from the thoughtless and automatically distributed sentence structure (the world picture), nurtured the impoverished big-city word with light and air, and again gave it warmth, movement, and its original carefree freedom. But we took one step farther. We sought to endow the isolated word with the richness of an invocation and the luminosity of a constellation. And strangely, the magi-

cally filled word conjured up and gave birth to a *new* sentence that was not in the least tied to or dependent on conventional sense. Referring to a hundred thoughts at the same time, without naming them, this sentence allowed the originally playful, but sunken, irrational being of the auditor to resound. It awakened and strengthened the lowest strata of memory. Our efforts touched upon areas of life and philosophy of which our oh-so-levelheaded, precocious surroundings never let themselves even dream. (102)

The Physical Culture Movement

The modern physical culture movement began to develop in the nineteenth century before the advent of modernism itself. Nevertheless, no previous period in European history embraced physical culture, including sports, with the intensity and seriousness of purpose as the modernist. Behind this embrace lay the new awareness of the body, the campaign among artists and men of science for a greater openness with respect to the issue of human sexuality, growing nationalism, the militancy and primitivism of the avant-garde, and the spreading antipathy toward intellectual culture.

The spectacular enthusiasm for physical culture at the turn of the century derived from several sources, three of which stand out with particular clarity: the emergence and high visibility of the physical culture showman and entrepreneur; the new passion for sports, culminating in the first modern Olympics in 1896; and the development of mass physical culture movements. If they did not develop in tandem, they certainly did not develop in isolation.

Perhaps a symptom of the rise of popular interest in the care and nurturing of the body and in physical prowess was the phenomenal appeal during the late nineteenth and early twentieth centuries of such physical culture gurus as Bernarr Macfadden and Eugen Sandow. Were it not for recent biographies—Robert Ernst's of Macfadden and David L. Chapman's of Sandow—it would not be an exaggeration to say that neither man would be much remembered today.[36] In their time, however, they were celebrities and enjoyed a wide following. Although eventually overcome by tabloid sensationalism, Macfadden was as much the physical culture entrepreneur as he was the model of how a regimen of regular exercise and a healthy diet could maintain fitness well into older age. Nor did Macfadden neglect sexual health. Outwardly a moralist who preached family virtues, Macfadden believed in an active (but not profligate) sex life free of prudish attitudes and, if his wives are to be believed, practiced what he preached with gusto. In time, his liberated views on sex, nude posing, inventions such as the "peniscope" for penis enlargement, and well-publicized marital

toward improving the physical status of the British soldier. Like his well-known magazine, *Sandow's Magazine of Physical Culture and British Sport* (1898–1907), Sandow's books were all originally published in England. An American version of the magazine, issued in conjunction with the opening on January 1, 1903, of Sandow's College of Physical Culture in Boston, proved unsuccessful and ceased publication after only four monthly issues had appeared.[39] The College of Physical Culture, with its fine gym, was conceived as an American version of the luxurious, and successful, Sandow's Institute of Physical Culture in London's Piccadilly Circus. Sandow was equally adept at marketing body-enhancing products, among them a grip dumbbell that enjoyed wide use, a liniment for athlete's muscles known as Sandow's Embrocation, and a "Symmetrion," a wide, adjustable band with attachable elastic cords, pulleys, and handles designed primarily to enable women to achieve greater symmetry of form. For a time, Sandow and his entrepreneurial brother-in-law, Warwick Brookes, Jr., also marketed a fat-free cocoa drink under the brand name Sandow's Health and Strength Cocoa.

The poor performance of the British army in the Boer War of 1899–1902 caused much anguish in England and led to the establishment of a royal investigative commission. A major contributing factor, it was felt, was the low fitness standards of the average soldier. Far too many recruits were in poor health, weak, and constitutionally incapable of coping with the rigors of soldiering. Not only was there no national physical training movement comparable to the German Turnverein or the Czech-Slavic Sokol, state schools, from which the majority of the middle- and lower-class recruits came, lacked regular programs of gymnastics. It was this concern that underlay Lord Robert Baden-Powell's founding of the Boy Scout movement, as we shall soon see. But before the Boy Scouts came into existence, Sandow the strongman hoped to lead the way in developing an English national fitness program. Despite the esteem in which he was held, however, he lost out on this occasion to the proponents of the Swedish Lingian system of exercises. These were devised by the Swede Per Henrik Ling and were introduced into England on a small scale as early as the late 1840s by a Hungarian immigrant, Dr. Matthias Roth.[40] Roth was a tireless campaigner on behalf of the rigorous Swedish program of calisthenics for boys and girls and had won prominent adherents to his side before Sandow became involved in the issue. When officers of the royal army and navy began to be sent to Stockholm to study, there was no doubt that the Lingian system would prevail. But Sandow was undaunted and continued to devote much of his energy to raising the level of physical education in Great Britain. When World War I came, he believed that not much progress had been achieved since the Boer War in improving the health and physique of the average British recruit and toward that end wrote *Life Is Movement*. Sandow left behind him a legacy of physical self-perfection and manly virility that kept his name alive long after his death and far outstripped that of his admiring follower, Bernarr Macfadden.

Boy Scouts, Turnverein, and Sokol

However popular the examples of such body perfectionist gurus as Bernarr Macfadden and Eugen Sandow, it was the emphasis on the collective that came to characterize the modernist approach to body training. The political element is also inescapable. Physical culture as a mass movement came to be looked upon not only as a source of national pride, but perhaps even more important, as a source of national strength. A case in point is the Boy Scout movement founded in England in 1908 by Lord Robert Baden-Powell.[41] Despite the emphasis on the bonding of boys from different social classes, appreciation of nature, self-reliance, and a sound, disciplined physique, the movement was also a training camp for young men who might some day be called upon to maintain the integrity of the far-flung, almighty British Empire. Wyndham Lewis surely perceived this when he wrote in *The Art of Being Ruled* (1926), with his usual causticity:

> The sporting training of the Englishman and American makes him into a fighting machine. Even his military training is disguised as sport. This Robot is manipulated by the press. By his education he has been made into an ingeniously free-looking, easy-moving, "civilized," gentlemanly Robot. . . .
>
> When the vast populations of Asia have been similarly organized, athleticized, introduced to "sport," trained as boy-scouts and Asiatic "guides," the same will apply to them: the Japanese being for Asia what I have said Russia and Italy are for us.[42]

A hero of the Boer War, Baden-Powell conceived the idea of the Boy Scouts, based in part on his experiences and observations during the war, as early as 1904. But the actual origin of the movement is generally dated from the publication of Baden-Powell's text, *Scouting for Boys*, first in serial form beginning on January 15, 1908, then as a separate publication on May 1 of the same year. Although committed in principle to a mix of social classes, the behavioral model for the scouts was the elitist English public (but really private) school system. And although in principle open to boys of whatever ethnic background and religious persuasion, those of color and non-Christians, Jews especially, were not encouraged to join. Like similar movements on the Continent—the German gymnastic and Wandervögel organizations in particular—the Boy Scouts were also antiurban. Not only was the immersion in nature regarded as essential to the physical and mental-fitness goals of the movements, but the contemporary urban environment was viewed with suspicion because of its increasingly alien character. In central Europe as well as in England, greater immigration (from eastern Europe in particular) had begun to produce a racist backlash. The idea took hold that an authentic indigenous culture could be found only away from the city, in provincial and rural areas where the suspect foreigners and foreign values had not yet extended their tentacles and where resistance in any case would be greater.

Although staunchly professing antimilitarism so as not to be thought of as a training ground for future officers, the uniformed scouts were, in fact, part of a paramilitary organization, subject to a strict code of discipline and well trained in fitness and survival routines that had much in common with a military regimen. And however much Baden-Powell and his associates sought to play down the patriotic and paramilitary nature of the Boy Scouts, emphasizing instead good citizenship, good acts, and self-reliance, there is no getting away from the fact that just as the name of the scouts harked back to a military tradition ("scouts," "guides"), the organization itself was envisaged as a future bulwark of British imperial values and policies. Indeed much the same can be said for other national European physical culture movements and for the extraordinary enthusiasm for sports at the turn of the century. In virtually all cases, the experience of war—or better said, defeat in war: the Germans in the time of Napoleon, the French after the disastrous Franco-Prussian war of 1871, the British after the Boer War—raised the level of consciousness about a need for improved physical standards. Suppressed national ambitions among subject peoples, especially the Slavs of the Habsburg empire, acted as similar stimuli.

Older than the English Boy Scouts, the German gymnastic organization known as Turnverein and the Czech (and Slavic) Sokol movement were profoundly nationalistic and easily capable of assuming a political as well as paramilitary character. Both the German and Czech organizations not only developed rapidly into fully national movements, operating in small towns as well as the largest cities, they also traveled to the United States with the many immigrants from central and eastern Europe in the nineteenth and early twentieth centuries and set down deep roots in this country.

The German Turnverein movement was initiated by Friedrich Ludwig Jahn when he opened his *Turnplatz* (athletic grounds) in Berlin on June 19,

1811. From its inception, the Turnverein was intended to be a movement of broad national and popular character. Indeed, Jahn had already made a reputation for himself as the author of *Deutsches Volkstum* (*German Nationality*, 1810), a work of unequivocal patriotic and nationalistic character motivated by Napoleon's defeat of the Germans between 1801 and 1807 and especially by the humiliation of Prussia under the terms of the Treaty of Tilsit of 1807. In essence an appeal to German national consciousness and for German national unity, *German Nationality* set the stage for Jahn's organization of a national physical culture movement, which saw the light of day the following year, 1811. As if prophetically anticipating the German "wars of liberation" against the French of 1813–15, culminating in Napoleon's downfall, Jahn established a movement of national physical and spiritual regeneration clearly intended to boost not only German morale but German combat readiness. At the heart of his program lay the same call for German self-sufficiency that the philosopher Johann Gottfried Fichte made the cornerstone of his famous *Reden an die deutsche Nation* (*Addresses to the German People*, 1808). Jahn's ideas are set forth vigorously in the book he wrote with his former pupil, Ernst Eiselen, *Die Deutsche Turnkunst zur Einrichtung der Turnplätze* (*The Art of German Gymnastics and the Establishment of Athletic Grounds*, 1816). Besides the more conventional forms of gymnastics incorporated by Jahn into his training program, much emphasis was placed on fencing and military exercises (*Kriegsübungen*). Of the latter, Jahn and Eiselen write: "Military exercises, even without weapons, shape a manly bearing, awaken and invigorate the sense of order, accustom one to obedience and to attentiveness, and teach individuals to regard themselves as members of a great whole. A well-trained troop of soldiers is a spectacle of the greatest unity of power and will. Each and every gymnast (*Turner*) is expected to mature into a combatant without being drilled."[43]

The insistent nationalism permeating *The Art of German Gymnastics* is evident even in the area of language. Consideration of the appropriate idiom for the new national program of gymnastics he was advocating provided Jahn the pretext for a vigorous—and lengthy—condemnation of foreign linguistic borrowings in German, and inordinate praise for the inexhaustible richness of his mother tongue:

> It is an undisputed right to refer to something German in the German language, to give a German work a German word. Why should we go begging to foreign tongues and with cup in hand to foreign lands for that which we possess abundantly and better in our own country? No well-grounded student of languages, no true German *man of the people* (*Volksmann*), has ever stuck up for word mix-

ing. . . . All word mixing, in general, comes from ignorance, linguistic laziness, and showing off. Unfortunately, all the complaints and speeches in the world are of no help against this so long as German children are deliberately cheated out of their mother tongue in childhood, and so long as children are robbed of their speech-mothers, and speech–wet nurses are forced on them. (LVI–LVII)

As an example of the flexibility and richness of German, Jahn demonstrates the lexical tree of verbs, nouns, and adjectives that can be grown from the root *Turn*. What follows is about half the original text: "Turnen, mitturnen, vorturnen, einturnen, wetturnern; *Turner, Mitturner, Vorturner, turnerisch*; *turnlustig, turnfertig, turnmüde, turnfaul, turnreif, turnstark*; *Turnkunst, Turnkünstler, turnkünstlerish*; *Turnkunde, Turnlehre, Turngeschichte*; *Turnanstalt, Turngesellschaft, Turngemeinde, Turngemeinschaft*; *Turnplatz, Turnfeld, Turnplan, Turnhof, Turnstelle, Turnbahn*" (LX). Indeed, so much of Jahn's preface to *The Art of German Gymnastics* is devoted to language that one might easily imagine it an introduction to a treatise on linguistics.

The nationalism of Jahn's philosophy of physical training sank deep roots in German culture. It was to resurface in a far more sinister way in the Nazi era, when military defeat—in World War I—was again advanced as the rationale for a vigorous new program of physical as well as moral national regeneration. But even success in war, such as the defeat of the French in 1870–71, did not eliminate the nationalistic and racial dimension of the German approach to physical culture. We can see this represented, I believe, in Professor Fritz Winther's *Körperbildung als Kunst und Pflicht* (*Physical Education as Art and Duty*), which appears to have been published in 1919—the book is undated—but must have been written either before World War I or in the early years of the war.

Although implicit in Jahn's *Art of German Gymnastics*, racial hygiene stands at the forefront of Winther's treatise. Whereas Jahn and, more than a century later, the architects of the Nazi physical culture and sports programs were similarly motivated by German defeat in war, Winther's point of departure is the toll that the German victory in the Franco-Prussian war and subsequent newfound wealth have taken on the national well-being, both physical and moral. *Physical Education as Art and Duty* begins, in fact, with the dire assessment: "Victory and wealth weaken the strict discipline of our fathers. The great ideas of fatherland, tradition, and community are losing their gravity; unbridled egos pursue paths of lawlessness; dissipation, both sensual and otherwise, is becoming the order of the day, and weakness and depravity follow."[44] The Germans, in other words, have become spoiled by success, to such an extent that Professor Winther expresses grave concerns about their racial health.

Apart from their success in war in 1870–71, the Germans also turned soft as a result of their postwar economic prosperity. The most dangerous thing for the parvenu, according to Winther, is "so-called riches" ("*sogenannten Glücksgüter*"), insofar as he does not know how to handle his good fortune, unlike someone "from an old family that has become hardened over time against ostentation." In matters of finance (though, to be sure, not in intellectual matters, Winther hastens to assure his readers), the Germans are a "parvenu people" ("*Parvenuvolk*"), a people from whom the "rudest compulsion" was removed by a "fortunate war, the upswing in trade, and by industry." Yet, "degeneration threatens" (7). So bleak is the picture, especially in terms of the "poor oversight" of the health and strength of the young and the "neglect" of military preparedness, that Winther speaks of "racial suicide" ("*Rassenselbstmord*"). In order to combat it, the good professor's research has led him to conclude that three steps are necessary: physical culture, a campaign against alcoholism, and morality in sexual life and racial hygiene. The importance Winther attaches to physical education as the foundation of a sound culture of the body can be gleaned from his assertion that it is a "dictate of our time—the well-being of the individual demands it no less energetically than the future of the race" (8).

Although Winther's preoccupation with racial hygiene owes much to the nationalism of Friedrich Ludwig Jahn and anticipates—though in demonstrably milder form—the racial madness of Nazi ideology, *Physical Education as Art and Duty* also reflects the cultural climate of the late nineteenth and early twentieth centuries. Winther is no less concerned with the physical education of the female as he is with that of the male; his ideas on women's dress, for example, follow the liberal thought of his day. Most important, he accords dance an exceptionally prominent role in physical education and training and exhibits throughout his book a more than passing knowledge of leading contemporary dancers (Isadora Duncan, Ruth St. Denis, Else Wiesenthal, Sent Mahesa, Ellen Tels, Clotilde von Derp, Rita Sacchetto, Gertrud Leistikow, Anna Pavlova, Aleksandr Sakharov), as well as the theories and programs of such figures as Dalcroze and Laban. Indeed, the lion's share of *Physical Education as Art and Duty* is devoted to the importance of dance and rhythmic training in physical education. "Through gymnastics and dance," writes Winther," all creative capabilities are aroused, not suppressed" (34).

Winther's emphasis on dance further reflects the strong national bias with which his book is informed. Comparing German and Anglo-American physical culture movements, for example, he notes:

> In Germany rhythm and love of nature have modulated, to the advantage of health, the power approach of Anglo-American sports in accordance with the lyrical and musical talents of our people. On one hand, rhythmic expressive gymnastics are spreading above all in Germany; on the other hand, in consequence of the fusion of bodily exercise and love of nature the sport of hiking is blossoming tremendously, as the Wandervögel (Ramblers' Association) and, in part, the scouts movement attest. However, a strong current of Anglo-American competition has, to our disadvantage, not filtered through to us (19).

Ardent nationalism—minus the racial dimension of German physical culture theory—was also characteristic of the Czech Sokol ("Falcon") movement, which came into existence in 1862 and eventually spread throughout virtually the entire Slavic world, including Russia. While they disavowed any military objectives, like the Boy Scouts, the Sokols could be regarded as paramilitary. They were established with the clear purpose of bolstering Czech ethnic pride at a time when the fissures in the solid, stolid facade of the Habsburg monarchy offered some promise that Czech national aspirations—greater autonomy, eventually national independence —were no longer an impossible dream. Subjected for centuries to relentless Germanization under Habsburg rule, the Czechs struggled mightily throughout the nineteenth century to establish a modern vernacular literary language and to instill in the Czech people a sense of ethnic pride. The Sokol organization proved a splendid—and successful—instrument with which to achieve such goals. A mass movement ostensibly dedicated to physical culture and reaching into every corner of Czech society, the Sokol was in a superb position to foster the national culture, with its emphasis on the cultivation of the Czech language and the ultimate national goal of an independent Czech state.

The founder of the Sokol was Miroslav Tyrš (of German ethnic origin and originally named Friedrich Tirsch), a sometime liberal member of the Young Czech political party, who eventually became a professor of art history in the Czech part of the Charles University in Prague.[45] A close collaborator of Tyrš, and the first elected president of the movement, was Jindřich (Heinrich) Fügner, a German businessman from Prague who made common cause with Czech national aspirations. Tyrš was familiar with Friedrich Ludwig Jahn's writings and work and saw the German Turnverein as an appropriate model for a Czech gymnastic organization that would play a similar role in the national revival movement. Like the organization established by Jahn, the Czech Sokol had a strong petty-bourgeois and working-class demographic bias. T. G. Masaryk, the first president of an independent Czechoslovak state, commented in his book *The Czech Question* (1908) on the inherent contradiction of the Sokol's indebtedness to a German model—Jahn's Turnverein—and its intensely Czech national character, which strongly opposed German influences in Czech society and culture and sought the reversal of centuries of Germanization. But the contradiction need not be taken seriously. The founder of the Sokol, Tyrš, was of German origin, like many Czechs, but he wholly identified with the Czech national movement, as did his close associate, Heinrich Fügner, also an ethnic German with a weak knowledge of the Czech language. As natural as it may have been for Tyrš to turn to Jahn's well-known Turnverein as a model for a similar Czech organization, his profound commitment to Czech nationalism guaranteed that the German-influenced Sokol would not be a conduit for yet further German influence among the Czechs.

The Sokol spread rapidly in the Czech lands, and by 1912, fifty years after its founding, could boast of 100 clubs with a membership in excess of 150,000. Gymnastic exercises, of course, were the basis of the movement but were often combined with national celebrations that integrated physical training and a heightened sense of national identity. The uniforms in which the Sokol members marched were a combination of foreign and indigenous elements: the characteristic red shirt was a borrowing from the legions of the Italian nationalist leader Garibaldi; the jacket was patterned after that of Polish revolutionaries and was noteworthy for its South Slavic-style embroidered button closures; the appropriate falcon feather that adorned the hats they wore. In common with the Boy Scouts and the turn-of-the-century German Wandervögel youth organization, the Sokols emphasized the revitalizing benefits of contact with nature and went on regular outings into the countryside in full regalia. Little wonder that the Sokol was sometimes referred to as "the Czech national army."[46]

In 1882, two years before his death, Tyrš presided over the first All-Sokol *slet*, a mass gymnastic festival that brought clubs from throughout the Czech lands to Prague in celebration of the twentieth anniversary of the capital's own Sokol. Although the organization continued to grow, this first *slet* seemed to symbolize a coming of age for the Sokol and the apogee of the movement.

However paramilitary the Sokol movement may have been, it would not be fair to regard it as protofascist. Nevertheless, its intense nationalistic character, by definition anti-German, fueled antagonism against the Jews once Czechoslovakia became an independent state in 1918. With relatively few exceptions, the large and very old Jewish community of Prague identified far more with German culture than with Czech. This is hardly surprising. Until the establishment of an independent Czechoslovak state after World War I, Czech culture and the Czech language tended to be regarded as parochial, even by many Czechs. German culture, however, was a world culture. In light, then, of the strong German cultural presence in the Czech lands, the Jews of Prague gravitated more toward German than Czech, preferring to identify and be identified with a prestigious, internationally celebrated culture. Some of the most famous members of Prague's early twentieth-century German literary community were Jews, such as Max Brod, Franz Kafka, Egon Erwin Kisch, and Franz Werfel. We have already met the philosopher Fritz Mauthner, a Prague Jew who wrote exclusively in German. Independence if anything stoked the fires of Czech nationalism even more, and Jews who had opted for German rather than Czech became targets of resentment. Anti-Semitic sloganeering and anti-Semitic acts increased and caught many Jews in the awful predicament of redefining themselves or face the increasing isolation of their otherness.

Whatever the antecedent history of the various European physical culture movements examined here so far, they reached their peak in the modernist period, in no small measure because of the modernist concern with the body. Much the same can be said for the passion with which sports came to be cultivated in the late nineteenth and early twentieth centuries. From the popular pursuit of bicycle riding and racing to the literary celebration of track and field, such as we find in Henry de Montherlant, sports enjoyed a level of interest and cultivation unparalleled since ancient times.

The role of antiquity in the shaping of the modernist outlook toward the body is not without importance. With the intensification of German nationalism and racism in the Hitler period, the classical Greek athlete was regarded not only as the model for but also the forebear of the Teutonic male. Nietzsche's enthusiasm for Greek antiquity and paganity, and the generally high level of the German attraction for classical Greek civilization at the turn of the century, set the stage for subsequent developments in the 1920s and 1930s. The ancient Romans and Etruscans also had their admirers, and for similar associations with manly virtues and an idealized pre-Christian paganism. Montherlant's ability to identify with the Romans was paralleled by D. H. Lawrence's admiration for the ancient Etruscans.

The Rebirth of the Olympics

The twin modernist enthusiasms of antiquity and physicality combined to revive the ancient Olympic games. While a few previous minor attempts had been made, none succeeded like the campaign of Baron Pierre de Coubertin, who rightly deserves the title of "father of the modern Olympics."[47] Coubertin's interest in sports and physical culture was kindled, not unexpectedly, by the Prussians' defeat of the French in 1871 and their subsequent annexation of Alsace and Lorraine. Overcome by a deep sense of national shame, Coubertin dreamed of French revenge on the Prussians. But the matter of the physical inferiority of French youth, to which Coubertin in large measure attributed the French defeat, had to be addressed. A man with a mission, Coubertin devoted his energies to raising the level of French physical education and of transplanting to France the love of sports he found among the English and Americans. A great admirer of *le sport anglais* and the emphasis on athletics in British secondary schools, which he wrote about in his book *L'Education en Angleterre: Collèges et universités* (*Education in England: Colleges and Universities*, 1888), Coubertin also respected the sports programs of American institutions of higher learning. He wrote about these in his book *Universitaires Transatlantiques* (1890), which was based on his travels in the United States in 1889. The following year, Coubertin and his friend Georges St. Clair founded the most important French sports association in its time, the Union de Sociétés Françaises de Sports Athletiques (USFSA). The new association absorbed the track organization known as Unions de Sociétés Françaises de Courses à pied, which had been founded in 1887.

By now less consumed with the passion to avenge the French defeat and more inclined to peaceful internationalism as a superior form of conflict resolution, Coubertin began giving serious thought in 1892 to the revival of the ancient Olympic games. Although it took no small persuasion on the baron's part to convince people that the project was both desirable and feasible, he decided that he would make a great public pitch for the support of the games in 1892. The occasion was to be the anniversary of the establishment of USFSA, but since this organization had been founded only two years before, Coubertin reckoned the founding from 1887, when the Unions de Sociétés Françaises de Courses à pied first came into existence, to have a more impressive five years. Be that as it may, in conjunction with the "fifth" anniversary of USFSA, Coubertin staged an elaborate affair on November 25, 1892, to which French and foreign dignitaries were invited. It was then that he announced his plan to revive the Olympic games. Skepticism and even incredulity could not deter him; in search of more international backing for his plan, Coubertin attended the World's Columbian Exposition in Chicago in 1893 as an official representative of the French Ministry of Education. He used a return visit to the United States to push for support for his project in other American cities, speaking before representatives of various American athletic organizations. But there was little enthusiasm for the idea of a modern Olympics, and Coubertin, still refusing to be discouraged, traveled next to England, where his reception was more gratifying.

In the end, Coubertin's doggedness and tenacity paid off. He went ahead with his plans to hold an international conference on the projected revival of the Olympics at the Sorbonne on June 16, 1894. The congress was headed by Coubertin himself, as representative of France and continental Europe; C. Herbert, secretary of the Amateur Athletic Association of Great Britain; and Coubertin's leading American supporter, Professor W. M. Sloane of Princeton University.[48] After a week of deliberations amid a great deal of pomp and ceremony, much of it (none too subtlely) oriented along ancient Greek lines, a majority of the delegates—among them prominent educators and public figures—approved Coubertin's project. He was also given the authority to create an international committee (later known as the *Comité Internationale Olympique*, the International Olympics Committee) to oversee the organization of the first Olympic games in modern times.

As Coubertin recalls in *Olympic Memoirs*, he originally planned to hold the first modern Olympic games in Paris and in the first year of the new century. However, he was persuaded by Demetrios Bikelas (or Vikelas), the Greek delegate to the 1894 congress and later first president of the International Olympics Committee, that the first games should be held, appropriately, in Greece, and in 1896.[49] Once the site and the date were agreed on, Coubertin, Bikelas, and others got together to hammer out the details governing the first and all subsequent Olympics. These included such matters as the equality of all sports, whether "major" or "minor," and the convening of the games in a different country every four years so as to reduce the financial burden on any single one.

Although it would seem a foregone conclusion that Greece would welcome the proposal to serve as host for the resurrected Olympic games of antiquity, there was significant opposition to it in government circles. Greece had won its independence from the Ottoman Empire only in 1832, and there were those who believed that the new state was hardly in a position to bear the high cost of the games. Coubertin and Bikelas used their apparently formidable powers of persuasion to make a strong case among

Greek politicians, sports figures, and men of wealth for the Greek venue for the games; the personal intervention of Crown Prince Constantine and his brothers assured the final victory.

But Coubertin still had hurdles to jump before the games became a reality. He had to fight an uphill battle to overcome opposition both in France and Germany. Aloofness and petty squabbling among certain French gymnastics and sports associations threatened to prevent a French team from being formed. The premier German gymnastics association, the Deutsche Turnerschaft, withheld its cooperation, nettled by the fact that the idea for the revival of the games had originated with a Frenchman. Tireless, upbeat, deeply committed, Coubertin took one hurdle at a time until he reached his goal. With appropriate fanfare, the participation of 295 male athletes (women began to participate in the Olympics only in 1900), mostly from Greece, and before some 40,000 spectators, most of whom were Greek, the first Olympic games since ancient times at last took place. Teams were small, international representation limited, and technical difficulties unavoidable at this early stage in modern Olympics history. But once inaugurated, the games acquired a momentum of their own and there was no turning back. Except for the world wars of 1914–18 and 1939–45, the Olympics have been held every four years and have grown spectacularly in size and appeal.

Impressed with the relative success of the first games, the public response to them, and the performance of their own athletes — especially the win in the first marathon of a peasant named Spiridon Louys — the Greeks made a shameless effort to monopolize the games and deny Coubertin virtually any role in their revival.[50] Although offended by these manifestations of an understandable but highly inappropriate Greek nationalism, Coubertin swallowed his pride for the sake of the future of the Olympics and publicly had nothing but praise for the support of the Greek royal family and the prowess of Greek athletes. Indeed in writing in *Olympic Memoirs* about the behavior of the Greeks in the aftermath of the games of 1896, Coubertin displayed remarkable understanding:

> But try and make a nation gone wild with excitement see reason, a whole people suddenly confronted with a living vision of its most glorious past. The whole Greek world had thrilled in unison at the spectacle. A sort of moral mobilization took place. Even the monks on Mount Athos, at that time separated from the mother country by an unwelcome frontier, sent donations for the celebration of the Games. And while, to the rest of the world, the revival of the Olympiads was still no more than a brilliant, picturesque item of news, on Greek minds it was having the effect of the most potent elixir.[51]

SIX

Religion, Race,

Gender, Politics, and the

New Physicality

Our age is not only the most Jewish, but also the most feminine of all ages.

OTTO WEININGER, *Sex and Character*

The physical cultism of the late nineteenth and early twentieth centuries was accompanied by a repudiation of organized religion. In retrospect, this would seem to have been inevitable. The institution of the house of worship, of the church and synagogue, came to be viewed as repugnant because of its identification with bourgeois society and the support of the status quo and established order attributed to it. The more widespread the assault on the pillars of that society, the more the church was regarded as another such pillar to be torn down. This animosity expressed itself in different ways. For those individuals unwilling to abandon a belief in the need for faith, alternative spiritualities were sought. These led for the most part to Hinduism and Buddhism, in light of the contemporary fascination with the East. The organizational structure of these religious systems was too little known to represent a problem and in any case could not easily be related to Western bourgeois society. Hinduism and Buddhism were also perceived to be more mystical and less worldly than either Christianity or Judaism and so accorded comfortably both with the metaphysical aspirations of the Symbolists and the antimaterialist posture of the modernists in general.

Among those uncomfortable with the church as they knew it—we are speaking primarily of Christianity since, in its principal forms, that has been the dominant religion of Europe—yet unwilling to abandon Christianity for Judaism, Hinduism, Buddhism, or Islam (to which some were also drawn), the only solution was to press for a renovation of the church. The cleaning out, the purification, if you will, of contemporary bourgeois society being widely advocated had to be applied as well to the church. This expressed itself, above all, as a desire to return the Christian faith to the principles identified with Jesus Christ. By relearning and reaffirming the essence of Christianity as embodied in the life and teachings of Jesus, the layers of institutionalization that had, especially in the nineteenth century, turned the Christian church into a bourgeois structure would somehow miraculously crumble and the purity of the true faith would animate a new church body.

The desire to identify once more with the original teachings of Christ resulted in a fresh focus on the figure of Jesus himself and on early Christianity. The scholarly movement to uncover as much information as possible about Jesus the man, which assumed new vigor in the closing decades of the nineteenth century, began most importantly with the French historian Ernst Renan's massive *La vie de Jésus* (*The Life of Jesus*, 1866). This pioneering work of reconstructive scholarship initiated a branch of research now known as Christology and promoted as much emulation as controversy. Inevitably, the new preoccupation with the historical Jesus and with the early Christians was reflected in the arts. Literary works with early Christian settings, such as *Quo Vadis?* (1905) by the Polish novelist Henryk Sienkiewicz, Poland's first Nobel laureate for literature, was typical. The novel was eventually brought to the screen and became a great success. *Ben Hur* was another popular film based on a similar novel.

Once the modernist cult of the physical responded to the new interest in Jesus and the early Christian community, a curious process of revision ensued. Spurning the image of the frail (and to them embarrassing) figure of Jesus on the cross, modernist writers transformed the pale, limp Jesus into a robust, manly activist. Judas also became a favorite target of modernist biblical revisionism. From the cowardly and greedy betrayer of the New Testament, he was reinvented as a dynamic revolutionary whose mission was to keep Jesus from faltering in the campaign to liberate the Jewish people from Roman oppression. This revisionist literature comprises a respectably significant body of work in different languages—among them the Russian Leonid Andreev's novella "Judas Iscariot" (1907), the Spaniard

Jacinto Grau's play *La redención de Judas* (*The Redemption of Judas*, 1903), and the American Robinson Jeffers's poetic play *Dear Judas* (1928)—but for reasons of space, they cannot be dealt with here except in the broadest terms. It may worth noting additionally that modernist biblical revisionism proved remarkably durable well into the second half of the twentieth century—consider, for example, such works as the Greek Nikos Kazantsakis's controversial novel, *The Last Temptation of Christ* (1957), which was made into an even more controversial movie; the American Taylor Caldwell's popular novel *I, Judas* (1977); and such historical studies in English as Hyam Maccoby's *Judas Iscariot and the Myth of Jewish Evil* (1992) and Michael Dickinson's *The Lost Testament of Judas Iscariot* (1994).

Nietzsche and Modernist
Anti-Christianism

Modernist biblical revisionism and anti-Christianism owed much to Nietszche. Although widely regarded as a major stimulus to the pandemic of late nineteenth- and early twentieth-century anti-Jewish sentiment, Nietzsche was even more influential in the dissemination of anti-Christian attitudes wholly in line with the new modernist cult of the physical.

There is hardly a major work by Nietzsche that does not bear some indictment of Christianity, either directly or indirectly. His most concentrated attack comes in *Der Antichrist* (originally written in 1888, published in 1895), the first essay of his projected four-part *Revaluation of All Values* (which was, in the end, the only essay completed). Although usually translated into English as *The Anti-Christ*, Walter Kaufmann points out in the preface to his translation of it that *Der Antichrist* can also mean "The Anti-Christian," a reading by all means more in the spirit and sense of the work.[1]

The basis of Nietzsche's indictment against Christianity is established almost at the beginning of *The Anti-Christ*. In response to the question he poses as to what is good, Nietzsche replies: "Everything that heightens the feeling of power in man, the will to power, power itself";[2] by contrast, what is bad: "Everything that is born of weakness" (570). Contemptuous of the weak and "failures," Nietzsche asks the question: "What is more harmful than any vice?" and answers his own question by pointing an accusing finger directly at Christianity: "Active pity for all the failures and the weak: Christianity" (570).

Nietzsche's brief against Christianity was predicated on his belief that Christianity—Christian teaching and Christian morality—waged constant war against the superior individual, the man of strength defined as strength of will and purpose. Christianity aligned itself with the weak, with the lowest strata of human society, with the herd (whose morality Nietzsche denounces additionally in book two of the posthumously published *Will to Power*):

> Christianity . . . has waged deadly war against this higher type of man; it has placed all the basic instincts of this type under the ban; and out of these instincts it has distilled evil and the Evil One: the strong man as the typically reprehensible man, the "reprobate." Christianity has sided with all that is weak and base, with all failures; it has made an ideal of whatever *contradicts* the instinct of the strong life to preserve itself; it has corrupted the reason even of those strongest in spirit by teaching men to consider the supreme values of the spirit as something sinful, as something that leads into error — as temptations. The most pitiful example: the corruption of Pascal, who believed in the corruption of his reason through original sin when it had in fact been corrupted only by his Christianity. (571–72)

The Christian conception of God is scorned with particular vehemence for its life-denying character:

> The Christian conception of God — God as god of the sick, God as a spider, God as spirit — is one of the most corrupt conceptions of the divine ever attained on earth. It may even represent the low-water mark in the descending development of divine types. God degenerated into the *contradiction* of life, instead of being its transfiguration and eternal Yes! God as the declaration of war against life, against nature, against the will to live! God — the formula for every slander against "this world," for every lie about the "beyond"! God — the deification of nothingness, the will to nothingness pronounced holy! (585–86)

Nietzsche's disdain for Christianity, and Judaism, was not paralleled in his treatment of other religions, notably Buddhism. This was entirely compatible with the contemporary quest for alternative belief systems on the part of those for whom Christianity appeared corrupted by its incorporation into the bourgeois system of values. Although it would be tempting to attribute the turn-of-the-century enthusiasm for Eastern religions, above all Buddhism, to Nietzsche's favorable comments on it in a work such as *The Anti-Christ*, this would be difficult to substantiate. As antibourgeois sentiment and a concomitant anti-Christianism spread, particularly among artists and intellectuals, non-Christian religions were among the alternatives sought out to replace the discredited Christian system. Buddhism was one of these alternatives; its repudiation of worldly acquisition, its cultural remoteness from European bourgeois experience, and its Eastern origins lent it a cache with which hardly any other belief system could compete.

Nietzsche's enthusiasm for it, once *The Anti-Christ* became known, might certainly have encouraged interest in it, but the popularity of Buddhism in turn-of-the-century Europe acquired its own momentum and might well have attracted Nietzsche to it rather than the other way around.

Although he classifies both Buddhism and Christianity as "nihilistic religions" and religions of "decadence," Nietzsche draws important distinctions between them, to the obvious advantage of Buddhism:

> Buddhism is a hundred times more realistic than Christianity; posing problems objectively and cooly is part of its inheritance, for Buddhism comes after a philosophic movement which spanned centuries. The concept of "God" had long been disposed of when it arrived. Buddhism is the only genuinely positivistic religion in history. This applies even to its theory of knowledge (a strict phenomenalism): it no longer says "struggle against *sin*" but, duly respectful of reality, "struggle against *suffering*." Buddhism is profoundly distinguished from Christianity by the fact that self-deception of the moral concepts lies far behind it. In my terms, it stands *beyond* good and evil. (586–87)

In light of the importance of the body and bodily hygiene in Nietzsche's thought, his emphasis on the physiological dimension of Buddhism is understandable. According to Nietzsche, the excessive sensitivity, which manifests itself in a "refined susceptibility to pain," and overspiritualization that he finds in Buddhism led to a depression that the Buddha sought to overcome by means of hygienic measures:

> Against it he recommends life in the open air, the wandering life; moderation in eating and a careful selection of foods; wariness of all intoxicants; wariness also of all emotions that activate the gall bladder or heat the blood; no *worry* either for oneself or for others. He prescribes ideas which are either soothing or cheering, and he invents means for weaning oneself from all the others. He understands goodness and graciousness as health-promoting. (587)

Nietzsche and the Jews

Nietzsche's dismissal of Christianity as a religion for the herd and as a system of morality for the weak led inevitably to a denunciation of Judaism as the source from which Christianity flowed. To Nietzsche's way of thinking, Judaism was the ultimate rejection of nature, of natural values, and to the extent that Christianity appropriated that rejection it, too, deserved condemnation. As he writes in *The Anti-Christ:*

> The Jews are the strangest people in world history because, confronted with the question whether to be or not to be, they chose, with a perfectly uncanny delib-

erateness, to be *at any price*: this price was the radical *falsification* of all nature, all naturalness, all reality, of the whole inner world as well as the outer. They defined themselves sharply *against* all the conditions under which a people had hitherto been able to live, been *allowed* to live; out of themselves they created a counter-concept to *natural* conditions; they turned religion, cult, morality, history, psychology, one after the other, into an incurable *contradiction to their natural values*. We encounter this same phenomenon once again and in immeasurably enlarged proportions, yet merely as a copy: the Christian church cannot make the slightest claim to originality when compared with the "holy people." That precisely is why the Jews are the most *catastrophic* people of world history: by their aftereffect they have made mankind so thoroughly false that even today the Christian can feel anti-Jewish without realizing that he himself is *the ultimate Jewish consequence*. (592–93)

Although statements like these have at times been appropriated by those intent on making the case for Nietzsche's anti-Jewishness, it is important to realize that Nietzsche held no particular bias against Jews and tended to regard with disfavor the mounting racial and political anti-Semitism of late nineteenth-century Germany. Nietzsche's principal brief was against Christianity, as he chose to view it, and Judaism was condemned insofar as it had spawned Christianity and shaped its moral-ethical system.[3]

The Belphégor Polarity

Before following the trajectory from Nietzschean thought to the English writers D. H. Lawrence and Wyndham Lewis, two of the most controversial modernist literary figures of the century, let us pause at this point to consider the argument against the Jews put forth by the French writer on culture and aesthetics, Julien Benda, whom we previously encountered as an arch foe of Bergsonian philosophy. It would probably be fair to assume that were it not for the publication in 1996 of Anthony Julius's book, *T. S. Eliot, Anti-Semitism, and Literary Form*, and the subsequent review of it by Louis Menand in the *New York Review of Books*,[4] few people would remember Benda, if indeed they ever heard of him in the first place. In analyzing the nature and sources of T. S. Eliot's negative attitudes toward Jews, Julius discusses the probable contribution of ideas expressed in Benda's book, *Belphégor: Essai sur l'esthéthique de la société française dans la première moitié du XXe siècle (Belphegor: An Essay on the Aesthetics of French Society in the First Half of the Twentieth Century)*. The book was published originally in 1918 and reissued, curiously perhaps, in 1947.[5] It was translated into English by S. J. I. Lawson and published in New York by Payson and Clarke in 1929.

A Jew himself—the son of a tradesman who had emigrated from Belgium—Benda was far less virulent in his treatment of the Jews than such notorious architects of turn-of-the-century French anti-Semitism as Edouard Drumont, the author of the inflammatory *La France Juive* (*Jewish France*, 1886), and Charles Marras, the head of the ultranationalistic, anti-Semitic organization Action Française and author of *Trois idées politiques* (*Three Political Ideas*, 1898), in which the Jews are blamed for the poison of individualism and even Protestantism. Nevertheless, *Belphegor* carries a sweeping condemnation of a certain kind of Jew that Julius believes resonated in the England of Eliot's time.

Belphegor is a wide-ranging, in some ways eccentric attack on the aesthetics of contemporary French culture for its surrender to the indistinct; the shapeless; the impressionistic; the emotionally affective; the lyrical, mystical, and musical; and the feminine. It is, in other words, a denunciation of those qualities identified with symbolism and impressionism. A rationalist in a classical mode, Benda was troubled most by what he regarded as the contemporary "hatred of intelligence," much of it fostered, of course, by the teachings of Nietzsche and Bergson:

> We have drawn attention elsewhere to the various forms in which this hatred appears: persistent refusal to discriminate between intelligence and dry, unimaginative reasoning, in order to bring the former into disrepute; the attempt to make us believe that great discoveries are made by means of a faculty (intuition) which "transcends" the intelligence, in mental chaos, in defiance of all logic, and with a snap of the fingers at intellectualism; the pleasure rather than regret they find in setting forth the limitations, the failures of science; and their insistence that intelligence is connected with our practical, utilitarian, physical and baser needs and belongs to—indeed is identified with—the world of matter, the dregs of the universe, etc.[6]

In seeking to find the answer to the question he poses later in *Belphegor*—"Whence arises this frantic effort of present French society to force intellectual work into the realm of emotion?"—Benda offers a refinement of what he presents as the view of "some people" (*certaines personnes*) that there is one and only one explanation: the presence of the Jews (*la présence des Juifs*):

> A tempting theory, undoubtedly. If we may draw a distinction—perhaps too subtle for men who write for the people—we would point out that there are two kinds of Jews: the severe, moralistic Jew, and the Jew who is always greedy for sensation—speaking symbolically, the Hebrew and the Carthaginian, Jeho-

vah and Belphegor, Spinoza and Bergson. We cannot deny the Carthaginians' passion for literature creative of emotion, their cult of the theater and of the comedian, their thirst (Alexandrian) for the indistinct, for the nondefined, for the mysterious, for the confusion of subject and object; nor can we help noticing the coincidence of the present French aesthetic, as we just portrayed it, with the enormous part the Jews have had in its development during the past few years. Certain races seem to have an inherent rage for sensation which in other races develops only in the course of years, just as certain species of animals have by nature a virus which others have to acquire. (113)

Sensing where the line of his argument may be leading, Benda backs somewhat away from it:

This explanation, however, seems to us highly unsatisfactory. First, because there is nothing to show that groups of society unfrequented by Jews are less inclined to the spasmodic aesthetic we are discussing, or to prove that, for instance, "anti-Semitic" or even "non-Semitic" groups are less in love with mystery and infinitude, less enthusiastic about the comedian, about the drama of love or of [Maurice Maeterlinck's] Mélisandes. And even more, because this, like all explanations that attempt to account for the diseased state of an organism by pointing out the presence of an external force, loses sight of the fundamental cause: the *receptivity* of the organism, the degenerate condition into which it must have lapsed before the external force could do its work. I am willing to admit that present-day French society may have been precipitated into Alexandrianism by the influence of the Jews, like the contemporaries of Philetas of Cos, and those of Juvenal. But society was already Alexandrian. The same cause would not have produced the same effect two centuries earlier. A crystal will not precipitate a fluid mass unless that mass is of the same nature as itself. The influence of the Jews in the twentieth century leads us straight back to the question: why was society susceptible to this influence? Why was it Alexandrian? (113–14)

While sharing Nietzsche's proclivities toward the classical, Benda was drawn to the Apollonian rather than Dionysian; and except for his willingness to acknowledge the Jews' role in the corruption of modern aesthetic culture, at least in his native France, he did not share Nietzsche's views on Christianity or Judaism or the German philosopher's adulation of strength. However, his deprecation of the role of women in culture was compatible with Nietzsche's strong sense of masculinity and anticipates attitudes to be met shortly in D. H. Lawrence and Wyndham Lewis. One of the crucial reasons, Benda argues, for the "present French society's aesthetic" is the fact that "it is entirely created by women." He continues:

Many an author will tell you that he writes only for women, that only women read any more. You can prove this for yourself: suppose you discuss art, literary doctrines or aesthetics in the drawing-room after dinner. With the exception of a few youngsters and the professionals, not a man will take part in the conversation. . . . One may say that today, since men are killing themselves with work and have neither time nor taste for leisured activities, the leadership in things mental and spiritual is in good society monopolized entirely by women. (123)

Acknowledging the prominence of women in the French salons of the past, Benda nevertheless argues that the situation in his own time is different:

The difference is that the women of that time had a respect for the masculine type of mind, and valued their own in proportion as they approached it, whereas today (and this is a turning-point in the history of culture) they openly despise the mental structure of man and have set up a violent cult of the feminine soul. The former exalted their sex because they maintained it as capable of reasoning as the other; the latter, because it is free from reasoning, and is simply passion, instinct, intuition. (124)

Benda's *Belphegor* was published in 1918. It is by no means inconceivable that in the formulation of his views on women, as well as on the cultural role of the Jews in France in his own time, Benda was, to some extent, echoing ideas previously put forth by Otto Weininger in *Geschlecht und Charakter* (*Sex and Character*, 1903). One of the most compellingly misogynistic works of all time, *Sex and Character* was a learned, ponderous, and decidedly idiosyncratic analysis of human sexuality and character reflective of the more tolerant turn-of-the century climate for such discourse. Weininger, a Viennese Jew who later converted to Protestantism, was a mere twenty-three years old when *Sex and Character* was published. As if the contents of the book were not enough to attract attention, Weininger added immeasurably to its mystique, and his own, by committing suicide—in the house where Beethoven died—four months after its publication.

By no means the easiest reading and long (599 pages in the twenty-fourth German edition [1922] that I possess), *Sex and Character* proved immensely provocative, earning its young author as many detractors as admirers. The work went through two editions in 1903, four in 1904, seven more from 1905 to 1911, and over a dozen since. It has been translated into a number of languages, including English (1906), Japanese, and Yiddish. To some Weininger was a genius, to others he was deranged, and the "Weininger controversy" has continued to the present.[7]

Sex and Character was a product of its age in several respects. Without the greater permissiveness of the turn of the century, without the new interest in human sexuality and the ability to conduct discourse on it with fewer restraints than previously, and without Freud, *Sex and Character* would doubtless not have appeared when it did, or perhaps never have been written at all. The feminism of the period and the misogyny, which developed partly as a reaction to it and partly as an outgrowth of the nearly exclusively male-oriented cult of physicality, were clearly the initial stimuli to its writing. The morbidly obsessive preoccupation with the Jew and the anti-Semitism engendered by the extremist racist thinking rampant in Europe in the late nineteenth and early twentieth centuries also contributed to the shaping of Weininger's views.

In simplest terms (which undeniably do Weininger a certain injustice), *Sex and Character* attempts to explore sexual differentiation across a broad typological spectrum by arguing that masculinity and femininity are relative values determined by the number of cells of the opposite sex in the individual body. The more female cells a male has, the more feminine he is, and vice versa. The ideal male is one with the fewest number of female cells; the ideal female is one with the fewest number of male cells. Ideal types, however, are just that, ideal, and hence exceptionally rare. Bisexuality and homosexuality are also to be understood with reference to the same theory of gender cell orientation.

Although my description of the contents of *Sex and Character* to this point might suggest that Weininger's study is a piece of objective scholarship, it is anything but that. Despite its scholarly character and the undeniably serious moral issues posed by it, the book is a sustained, irrational deprecation of the female, which when all is said and done, denies her any social, intellectual, moral, or spiritual value whatsoever.[8] The female of the species is even repugnant physically, better artistically represented unclad than seen that way in the flesh: "It is well known that the female is not prettiest in her nakedness. For the most part in reproduction through the work of art, as a statue or painting, the unclothed woman can be pretty. But the live naked woman essentially cannot be found to be attractive by anyone since the sexual drive renders impossible that modest reflection which remains a necessary prerequisite for establishing the beauty of anything."[9]

In a swipe at the feminist movement of the time, Weininger even includes the female genitalia in his indictment of woman:

> But one cannot remain silent concerning certain repulsive noisemakers of recent years who through the insistence of their publicity on behalf of the female

genitalia prove that just agitation is necessary to make people believe them and to reveal the insincerity of those claims of whose contents they purport to be convinced. Apart from such people, one can declare that no man finds female genitalia especially pretty, and indeed every one of them finds them ugly (313).

Moreover, "the completely naked woman creates the impression of something incomplete, still striving for something outside herself, and this is incompatible with beauty" (313). That something that the female strives for is, of course, the male member; lacking this, woman is anatomically doomed to inferior status. Even the ideal female type is inferior to the ideal male type since she can never transcend womanness. As Weininger declares: "The superior female forever remains far beneath the most inferior male" (400). Woman exists only as sexuality, and because she is denied an ego, a consciousness, she cannot even understand that she is mere object.

If Weininger's views on woman were not enough to stir controversy (though the widespread misogyny of the turn of the century guaranteed him no small number of male sympathizers), his views on the Jews were certain to. For these views as well he had ample supporters. *Sex and Character* devotes only a single chapter to Jews (*Das Judentum*), but it is memorable. Having reduced the female to a subspecies, albeit a dangerous one, Weininger then proceeds to repudiate Jewishness because of its femininity, meaning that Jewishness, like womanness, lacks any positive attributes and for essentially the same reasons. The equation of Jewishness and femininity was one made often throughout the turn of the century, as we have already seen in Benda; it was to acquire a more chilling dimension with Nazism, which owed much to Weininger for development of its ideology. Weininger claimed for the most part to differentiate "Jewishness" as a state of being from racial properties and to suggest that Aryans could also be guilty of "Jewishness," as well as responsible, to some degree, for the phenomenon of "Jewishness" itself. But his indictment of Jewishness usually embraces the Jew (*der Jude*) as a racial type despite a disclaimer such as the following, which is still anything but flattering: "I am not dealing with a race or a people, still less, to be sure, with a legally recognized denomination. Jewishness [*Judentum*] should be regarded only as a mind set [*Geistes-richtung*], as a psychic constitution that represents a possibility for all of humanity and in historical Jewry has found merely its most grandiose realization" (402).

Weininger's indictment of the Jews for the most part reiterates his claims against the female of the species and produces such gems of wisdom as the following:

The Jew, like woman, has no ego and hence no intrinsic value. (408)

Men who pimp always have Jewishness in them, and this is the point where the strongest correspondence between womanness and Jewishness is reached. (413)

From this lack of depth it is also clear why the Jews are unable to produce any great men, and why Jewry, like woman, is denied the highest ingenuity. The most prominent Jew of the last nineteen centuries, whose pure Semitic origin is beyond doubt . . . was the philosopher Spinoza. However, the usual enormous overrating of him has less to do with any immersion in his works or any study of them than with the chance circumstance that he was the only thinker Goethe had ever read closely. (420)

Whatever their absurdities and inconsistencies, Weininger's views were soaked up by the Nazis and other enemies of the Jews for whom *Sex and Character* was further grist for the mills of hatred, the more effective because of its scientific-scholarly character. Attempts to "rehabilitate" *Sex and Character*, at least in part by directing attention to the philosophical and scientific questions Weininger seeks to resolve in it, founder on the shoals of the book's monstrosities.

The Nietzschean Network:
D. H. Lawrence

Greatly shaped by Nietzschean and Bergsonian thought, Lawrence's ideas are virtually the opposite of those of Julien Benda. Whereas Benda repudiated the pagan and primitive as well as the romantic admiration of both, Lawrence worshipped at the altar of paganity, as amply attested in several of his nonfictional works, most notably *Apocalypse* (1931) and *Etruscan Places* (1932), the last of his Italian travel books, which also include *Twilight in Italy* (1916) and *Sea and Sardinia* (1921).

Disgusted with Western industrial civilization after World War I, Lawrence began what he called his "savage pilgrimage" in search of a more fulfilling life. This quest carried him to Sicily (and to writing the first of his Italian books), to Ceylon, Australia, and finally to the American Southwest. Lawrence and his wife returned to Europe in 1925. His last novel, and his most famous, *Lady Chatterly's Lover*, was banned in 1928. Lawrence was the subject of much controversy because of the sexual content of his fiction, and the virtual ostracism he was made to endure adversely affected his finances—in order to satisfy his creditors, his paintings were confiscated the year after the ban was imposed on *Lady Chatterly's Lover*. Lawrence again left England, this time settling in Vence, France, where he died in 1930 at the age of forty-four.

Posthumously published a year after his untimely death, *Apocalypse* can be read as a distillation of Lawrence's long-held views on contemporary society, paganity, Christianity, and the inadequacies of intellect. In sharp contrast to Benda, Lawrence greatly esteemed Bergson. Following Bergson, and Freud, another source of influence, Lawrence regarded strong feelings and sensations—passion, in other words—as superior to intellect. He also greatly admired that intense "physical" life, which he juxtaposed to the intellectual and which he believed the world had all but lost. Idealizing paganity as the repository of those virtues in man he despaired of finding in his own time, Lawrence became a worshipper of the remote past and a serious student of the cultures of such ancient peoples as the Etruscans and the ancestors of the Indians of the American Southwest. The obvious incompatibility of this embrace of paganity and a Christianity that repudiated paganity motivates the Nietzschean deprecation of Christianity characteristic of *Apocalypse*, as we can see from the following excerpts:

> The instinctive policy of Christianity towards all true pagan evidence has been and is still—supress it, destroy it, deny it. This dishonesty has vitiated Christian thought from the start. . . . We accept the Greeks and Romans as the initiators of our intellectual and political civilization, the Jews as the fathers of our moral-religious civilization. So these are "our sort." All the rest are mere nothing, almost idiots. All that can be attributed to the "barbarian" beyond the Greek pale: that is, to Minoans, Etruscans, Egyptians, Chaldeans, Persians, and Hindus, is, in the famous phrase of a famous German professor: *Urdummheit*. Urdummheit, or primal stupidity, is the state of all mankind before precious Homer, and of all races, all except Greek, Jew, Roman, and—ourselves![10]

Since the Jews parented Christianity, the repudiation of Christian thought running throughout *Apocalypse* carries with it a concomitant repudiation of the Jews, not in racial terms—as insinuated though disclaimed by Otto Weininger in *Sex and Character*—but because of their exclusion of the pagan:

> The Jews always spoilt the beauty of a plan by forcing some ethical or tribal meaning in. The Jews have a moral instinct against design. Design, lovely plan, is pagan and immoral. So that we are not surprised, after the experience of Ezekiel and Daniel, to find the *mise en scène* of the vision muddled up, Jewish temple furniture shoved in, and twenty-four elders or presbyters who no longer

know quite what they are, but are trying to be as Jewish as possible, and so on. . . . Everything Jewish is *interior*. Even the stars of heaven and the waters of the fresh firmament have to be put inside the curtains of that stuffy tabernacle or temple. (55)

But the Jewish mind hates the moral and terrestrial divinity of man: the Christian mind the same. Man is only postponedly divine: when he is dead and gone to glory. He *must not* achieve divinity in the flesh. So the Jewish and Christian apocalyptists abolish the mystery of the individual adventure into Hades and substitute a lot of martyred souls crying under the altar for vengeance—vengeance was a sacred duty with the Jews. (65)

Elitist in outlook, Lawrence also excoriated Christianity for its enablement of the humble, and in this respect especially reflects Nietzsche's influence:

The longer one lives, the more one realizes that there are two kinds of Christianity, the one focused on Jesus and the Command: Love one another!—and the other focused, not on Paul or Peter or John the Beloved, but on the Apocalypse. There is the Christianity of tenderness. But as far as I can see, it is utterly pushed aside by the Christianity of self-glorification: the self-glorification of the humble. . . . (11)

The weak and pseudo-humble are going to wipe all worldly power, glory, and riches off the face of the earth, and then they, the truly weak, are going to reign. It will be a millennium of pseudo-humble saints, and gruesome to contemplate. But it is what religion stands for today: down with all strong, free life, let the weak triumph, let the pseudo-humble reign. The religion of the self-glorification of the weak, the reign of the pseudo-humble. This is the spirit of society today, religious and political. (12)

Lawrence's loathing of Christianity-Judaism and his elitism had an obvious parallel in his worship of physical beauty and strength. This comes through clearly in most of his fiction. Expectedly, the male of the species is the most emphasized, and these figures are usually—though not always—drawn from the lower classes. Their distance from so-called polite society, which Lawrence abhorred with a passion, spares them any dilution of their "primitiveness," their animality, as it were. Lawrence makes much of the sexual appeal of such men, and the women most strongly attracted to them are generally strong willed and strong spirited, women able to rise to the challenge of the virile male. It was only such women that Lawrence was capable of admiring.

Although not as well known as *Sons and Lovers* and *Lady Chatterly's Lover*, *St. Mawr* (1925), the first of Lawrence's novels to be partially set in America (on an Arizona ranch), is virtually paradigmatic of his treatment of male and female strength. The novel derives its name from that of a magnificent stallion who embodies the beauty and strength of form Lawrence adulated. As the novel progresses, the stallion stands at the center of the parallels in the lives of a mother and daughter that form the basic structure of the work. The daughter is Louise (Lou) Witt, a young American from Louisiana living in England who marries Rico, the son of a government official from Melbourne, Australia. However, the relationship between them proves unsatisfying.

Lou's mother is the type of strong woman Lawrence regarded highly. When we meet her she is accompanied by her groom, Geronimo Trujillo (Phoenix), the son of a Mexican father and a Navajo mother, from Arizona. When Lou buys St. Mawr for Rico so that they both may strike handsome figures when riding in the park in London, she hires a groom named Lewis, a Welsh equivalent of Phoenix. A parallel soon develops between her mother and Lou in their relations with their respective grooms.

Both Lewis and Phoenix are "natural" men, uneducated, unsophisticated, "primitive" in Lawrence's positive sense of lacking the pretensions and hypocrisies of the gentlemen of "polite society." They are further defined as "natural" men by their proximity to powerful animals, in this case, horses. The more time she spends around St. Mawr, the more Lou herself becomes fascinated with the animal. Not only does he radiate a vitality she had not previously encountered in men, including her own husband, but also a kind of supernatural presence. When he is injured in a riding accident, Rico threatens to sell St. Mawr with the understanding that he will be made into a gelding or destroyed. In order to save the horse, Lou decides to take St. Mawr to America with her, leaving her husband behind and bringing along Phoenix to look after it. In the meantime, Mrs. Witt, Lou's mother, falls in love with the taciturn Welsh groom, Lewis, and proposes marriage to him; however, he declines since he fears being dominated by a woman. In the case of both Lewis and Phoenix, their appeal to the women is animal, which, metonymically, is centered on their thick, abundant, mane-like hair. As Lou and her mother share their thoughts on men prompted by Mrs. Witt's growing fascination with Lewis, Lou echoes Lawrence's yearning for the wonder of pure animal existence and his disdain for the fruits of the intellect. Trying to voice what it is she finds different about Lewis, Mrs. Witt declares:

"Like an animal! But what a strange look he has in his eyes!, a strange sort of intelligence! and a confidence in himself. Isn't that curious, Louise, in a man with as little mind as he has? Do you know, I should say he could see through a woman pretty well."

"Why, mother!" said Lou impatiently. "I think one gets so tired of your men with mind, as you call it. There are so many of that sort of clever men. And there are lots of men who aren't very clever, but are rather nice: and lots are stupid. It seems to me there's something else besides mind and cleverness, or niceness or cleanness. Perhaps it is the animal. Just think of St. Mawr! We call him an animal, but we never know what it means. He seems a far greater mystery to me than a clever man. He's a horse. Why can't one say in the same way, of a man: *He's a man?* There seems no mystery in being a man. But there's a terrible mystery in St. Mawr." (48)

A nexus also exists for Lawrence between speech and the kind of primitive man represented by Phoenix and Lewis. At one point, he describes Phoenix's reaction to Lou's admonishment that he not do anything further to aggravate Rico's tender nerves: "Phoenix was watching her closely, to take it in. He still was not good at understanding continuous, logical statement. Logical connexion in speech seemed to stupefy him, make him stupid. He understood in disconnected assertions of fact (42).

When they finally reach America, Lou buys a small ranch in New Mexico, where she hopes to find the peace that has until then eluded her. Although Phoenix will stay on to look after horses, no romance will develop between them. Attracted to his sensuality and primitiveness, the half-breed's underlying *machismo* repels her and she understands that he can never be more than a servant. In the novel's closing moments, she confides to her mother that, where men are concerned, mere sensations can no longer satisfy her. "No, mother," she declares, "of this I am convinced: either my taking a man shall have a meaning and a mystery that penetrates my very soul, or I will keep to myself." When her mother replies that in all probability she will spend her life keeping to herself, Lou is in no way intimidated and instead speaks rapturously of the elemental wildness of the southwestern landscape to which she now feels an almost mystical attachment, similar to her earlier feelings toward St. Mawr.

Lawrence poured into the figure of Lou much of his own contempt for the weakness and ordinariness of his society, a society in which greatness—as he understood it—was a truly rare commodity. Wherever he looked, Lawrence saw the puniness of the men around him and damned them all the more effectively by viewing them through the eyes of a young woman who eventually gains the inner strength to walk away from them. The stallion, St. Mawr, excites in Lou the first stirrings of the vitalistic for which her spirit craves. Immersing herself in the rugged landscape of the American Southwest at the end of the novel, Lou is at peace with herself, having finally found the true outlet for her passion.

The vitalism Lawrence embraces in *St. Mawr* became the basis of his admiration for the ancient Etruscans, as expressed in the best of his Italian writings, *Etruscan Places* (1932). Belief in the vitality of the universe, toward which man has a natural and instinctive longing, was at the core of Etruscan belief. How completely Lawrence identified with it is evident in a passage such as the following:

> To the Etruscan all was alive; the whole universe lived; and the business of man was himself to live amid it all. He had to draw life into himself, out of the wandering huge vitalities of the world. The cosmos was alive, like a vast creature. . . .
>
> The old idea of the vitality of the universe was evolved long before history begins, and elaborated into a vast religion before we get a glimpse of it. When history does begin, in China or in India, Egypt, Babylonia, even in the Pacific and in aboriginal America, we see evidence of one underlying religious idea: the conception of the vitality of the cosmos, the myriad vitalities in wild confusion, which still is held in some sort of array: and man, amid all the glowing welter, adventuring, struggling, striving for one thing, life, vitality, more vitality: to get into himself more and more of the gleaming vitality of the cosmos.[11]

With the coming of the Greeks and the Romans, however, the Etruscan celebration of nature was supplanted by the desire to tame nature, to bend it to the will of man, to dominate it. And this hostile approach to nature contained the seeds of the future Christian fear of it:

> The old religion of the profound attempt of man to harmonise himself with nature, and hold his own and come to flower in the great seething of life, changed with the Greeks and Romans into a desire to resist nature, to produce a mental cunning and a mechanical force that would outwit Nature and chain her down completely, completely, till at last there should be nothing free in nature at all, all should be controlled, domesticated, put to man's meaner uses. Curiously enough, with the idea of the triumph over nature arose the idea of a gloomy Hades, a hell and a purgatory. To the peoples of the great natural religions the after-life was a continuing of the wonder-journey of life. (75–76)

Wyndham Lewis: In Praise of Strong Men but Damn the Moderns

Outrageous and fascinating, shocking and entertaining, repudiated by many and admired by some, Wyndham Lewis is now recognized as one of the most extraordinary writers in English in the twentieth century.[12] Separating his often outlandishly expressed if not uniquely held views on contemporary society and politics from his fiction is neither easy nor helpful, and in any case not my interest here. Lewis developed an elitist attitude toward society, both as an artist and intellectual. This turned him against democracy and the liberal bourgeois tradition and made him an admirer of authoritarianism as represented by the Bolshevik leaders (though he eventually scorned Soviet-style communism), Mussolini, and Hitler (whom public outrage forced him to repudiate, at least in part). Geared to the masses and hence by nature suspicious and even intolerant of the artist and intellectual, bourgeois liberal democracy—in Lewis's view—had to be swept aside. This could be accomplished only by the radical means of revolution. The *fascismo* (as he usually refers to it) of Mussolini was as revolutionary a movement to Lewis as was bolshevism in Russia. Both toppled the old order and supplanted it with authoritarian rule. While Lewis had no hope for artists and intellectuals actually wielding power, the next best thing, as he saw it, would be an elitist authoritarian society presided over by a tolerant leader who would acknowledge the special status and needs of the gifted and would rule accordingly. A mass-oriented, mechanistic society such as that in a Western democracy only marginalized artists and intellectuals, unappreciative of the first, thereby wasting their talents, and apprehensive about the latter, thereby impeding their contributions to social betterment and change.

Well-versed in the art of satire, Lewis was particularly adept at putting down such modern artistic trends as mysticism, the deprecation of language, the idealization of the child, and anti-intellectualism, and of such a contemporary social movement as feminism. Although known for his romantic affairs, Lewis warned against a "war" for female domination masquerading as a campaign for "equal rights" (to which he was not opposed).

The single most important collection of Lewis's thoughts on society and politics is his book of essays, *The Art of Being Ruled* (1926). Well read in history, literature, and philosophy, Lewis was also comfortable with social and political thought. Ideas of Proudhon, Marx, Rousseau, Sorel, Fouillée, and Bertrand Russell are discussed at length, and the book abounds in references to Bergson, Brunetière, Fourier, Hobbes, Péguy, Santayana, Goethe,

Macchiavelli, Nietzsche, Bernard Shaw, and Zola. Lewis expounded his views further in such works as *The Lion and the Fox* (1927), *Time and Western Man* (1927), *The Wild Body* (1927), *The Apes of God* (1930), *Hitler* (1931), *Left Wings Over Europe* (1936), *Count Your Dead—They Are Alive* (1937), *The Jews: Are They Human?* (1938), and *The Hitler Cult and How It Will End* (1939). Idiosyncratic in style as well as thought, Lewis is always best taken in terms of his own expression, which the following excerpts (preserving Lewis's original lack of capitalization) from *The Art of Being Ruled* demonstrate. On the need for revolution to end the hegemony of "liberalist democracy," Lewis expressed his admiration for the Bolshevik coup d'etat in Russia and Mussolini's assumption of power in Italy in these words:

> Russian society for fifty years before the revolution was painfully confused, dragged this way and that by its liberalism and mysticism, as the great Russian writers witness. The sovietic power has put an end to all that painful confusion as though by magic. The means were terrible ones: the Bolsheviks did not believe in "gradualness" and biologic growth, perhaps, enough. Many of the means taken to create the new state are no doubt susceptible of infinite improvement. And the most difficult task of any *real*—that is, powerful and severe—form of government is to reconcile the requirements of authority with the personal initiative that is impatient of rules, and yet must not be crushed unless you wish to rule machines, not men. Nothing on earth to-day can overthrow such powers as the sovietic or fascismo. The sovietic or the fascist chiefs, like other people, have to do the best they can with the material to their hand: and they are not perfect themselves. What they have done in a short time in the way of organization must be the admiration of the world.[13]

If we are to understand Lewis's political thought, we have to realize that notwithstanding his elitist uplifting of the status of the artist and intellectual he passionately opposed individual freedom in the Western democratic sense. Lewis envisioned a great human community of equals under the rule of some central authority. That it was the exaggerated sense of individual liberty, the actual illusion of personal freedom, that weakened democratic Europe Lewis had no doubt whatsoever. He elaborated his position by recalling Goethe's division of people into two species, puppets and natures:

> He said the majority of people were machines, playing a part. When he wished to express admiration for a man, he would say about him, "He is a *nature*." This division into *natural* men and *mechanical* men (which Goethe's idiom amounts to) answers to the solution advocated in this essay. And to-day there is an absurd war between the "puppets" and the "natures," the machines and

the men. And owing to the development of machinery, the pressure on the "natures" increases. We are all slipping back into machinery, because we *all* have tried to be free. And what is absurd about this situation is that so few people even desire to be free in reality. (139–40)

Lewis's remarks about freedom echo Dostoevsky, whose works—as well as those of other Russian writers—he knew well. But the contradiction in his reasoning shows up in the authoritarianism he advocates as the antidote to the perversion of freedom that has so debilitated the Western democracies, and yet the privileged place in the "new order" he reserves for the new elite of artists and intellectuals. Since, as Lewis sees it, artists and intellectuals are debased, exploited, and trivialized in the liberal bourgeois democracy, that system of democracy must be overturned and replaced with an authoritarian regime in which the artistically and intellectually gifted will flourish.

Lewis's elitism is not, however, class-conscious. To the contrary. "The western democratic principle," he declares, "has always been too anarchic to be sensible. It sees things in pieces. It even sees life in pieces: its personality is unstable and easy to isolate. Such are some of the capital causes for the rapid eclipse of European power. Its character of 'independence,' its pretended franchises, its 'nationalisms,' make it unable to organize as *one* white race; and politically, organization is everything: talent, martial qualities, nothing" (72). The underlying sham nature of democracy, according to Lewis, is exposed by the *frankness* of authoritarianism. Western parliamentary democracy is no more nor less than a grand ruse by the few to exercise control over the many while convincing them through control of the media especially that they enjoy more freedom than anyone else on earth.

Lewis wrote a series of newspaper articles based on his impressions of Berlin after the first Nazi Party electoral victories in the Reichstag in September 1930. The articles were gathered into a book and published in 1931 under the title *Hitler*. Lewis presents himself in the work as an interpreter of National Socialism and Hitler to the British public, but he makes the point that he is neither a critic nor advocate of the movement or its principal figure: "It is as an exponent—not as critic nor yet as advocate—of German National-socialism or Hitlerism, that I come forward."[14] This disclaimer notwithstanding, Lewis admired Hitler and sought to show him and the movement he stood for in the most favorable light. His enthusiasm grew from several sources: his extreme distaste for Marxism, his contempt for capitalism, his opposition to the status quo (read here bourgeois society), and his ideas on race.

In *Hitler*, Lewis contrasts the German *Blutsgefühl* (blood feeling), to which he attributes an important physical dimension, with fashionable (and to him loathsome) turn-of-the-century exoticism. Of the blood feeling, he writes:

> What the doctrine of the *Blutsgefühl* aims at . . . is this. It desires a *closer and closer* drawing together of the people of one race and culture, by means of bodily attraction. It must be a true bodily solidarity. Identical rhythms in the arteries and muscles, and in the effective neural instrument—that should provide us with a passionate *exclusiveness*, with a homogeneous social framework, within the brotherly bounds of which we could live secure from alien interference, and so proceed with our work and with our pleasures, whatever they may be. (107)

But where *Blutsgefühl* is physical and manly, "exoticism," of which Lewis felt the English were suffering a "perfect frenzy," is "a drug, with the stupid intoxication of its perfume, that has at last thoroughly enervated our minds" (111). It was, in a sense, the essential nonmasculinity of the exotic that damned it in Lewis's eyes: "No very active man could experience it—he would be too absorbed with the satisfactions of his own personal activity to wish to transfer his attentions so far away from his vital and effective centre—his own creative principle of life. Essentially it is non-creative: it possesses the characteristics of the traditional feminine surrender, rather than of the male insurgence and egoism" (116).

Lewis's repudiation of Marxism was rooted in his individualistic, elitist belief that it was a dehumanizing assault on "the person" for whom it would substitute the thing, just as it substituted quantity for quality. Hitler and Nazism would, by comparison, retain respect for the personality, albeit in the case of Hitler, admittedly to excess. Lewis's abiding hatred for the Communist system would vent itself later in fictional form in his novel *The Revenge for Love* (1937).

In expressing his dislike for "the present Capitalist system" in *Hitler*, Lewis condemns "Big Business" for promoting a "Sex-war," an "Age-war," and a "Colour-line-war" for the purpose of cheapening labor and enslaving men more and more. Lewis also saw Hitler and National Socialism as a defense of European civilization against the "sentimentalizing" by its intellectuals "with regard to the Non-White world." He declared:

> How about giving your White Consciousness a try for a little—it is really not so dull as you may suppose! A "White Australia"—that may be impracticable. But at least there is nothing impracticable about a "White Europe." And today Europe is not so big as it was. It is "a little peninsula at the Western extremity of Asia." It is quite small. Why not all of us draw together, and put our White

Civilization in a state of defense? And let us start by mutually cancelling all these monstrous debts that are crushing the life out us economically.(121)

Lewis's general approbation of Nazi racist policy required qualification in the specific case of the Jews. Doubtless fearing that this aspect of Hitlerite thought would alienate many of the people he was trying to win over to his views, Lewis explained away Nazi anti-Jewishness as primarily a German national characteristic that could not everywhere be exported with the same intensity. In assuming the position that attitudes toward the Jews may after all vary from country to country, he even has a few words of caution for the Germans themselves:

> The Hitlerite must understand that, when he is talking to an Englishman or an American about the "Jew" (as he is prone to do), he is apt to be talking about that gentleman's *wife!* Or anyhow *Chacun son Jew!* is a good old English saying. So if the Hitlerite desires to win the ear of England he must lower his voice and coo (rather than shout) *Juda verrecke!* [Die, Jew] if he *must* give expression to such a fiery intolerant notion. Therefore—a pinch of malice certainly, but no 'antisemitism' for the love of Mike!(42)

But even the virulence of Hitler's campaign against the Jews could not undermine Lewis's essentially benevolent view of the Führer:

> Hitler is *not* a straightforward, simple, fire-eating, true-blue, sabre-rattling, moustachioed puppet at all. I do not think that if Hitler had his way he would bring the fire and the sword across otherwise peaceful frontiers. He would, I am positive, remain peacefully at home, fully occupied with the internal problems of the *Dritte Reich.* And as regards, again, the vexed question of the 'antisemitic' policy of his party, in that also I believe Hitler himself—once he had obtained power—would show increasing moderation and tolerance. In the *Dritte Reich,* as conceived by Hitler, that great jewish (sic) man of science, Einstein, would, I think, be honoured as he deserves. (48)

Never one with terribly fixed views nor particularly discomforted in modifying or even reversing his views, Lewis eventually wrote two books intended to clarify, soften, or repudiate ideas expressed in *Hitler* and in his other, in some ways more outrageous, books praising the Nazi leader, *Left Wings Over Europe* (1936) and *Count Your Dead—They Are Alive* (1937). In 1938 he published a small book with the unfortunate, and misleading, title *The Jews: Are They Human?* The purpose of it was to counter the impression that his previous utterances on Jews had been essentially negative in inspiration. But Lewis's attempt to recover lost ground, as it were, comes across as a backhand slap as the attitudes toward Jews expressed in *The Jews: Are They Human?* still carry the stigmatizing baggage of the past. By continuing to speak of the "Jewish Problem" Lewis keeps alive the idea that the Jews are somehow a problem. But the Jews are now let off the hook by the shifting of the blame for the existence of the "Jewish Problem" from the Jews to the Christians. The problem, it seems, lies in the character of the Christian nations and in their attitude toward the Jews. It is the Christian nations who have taught the Jews bad habits and not the other way around. Moreover, the fault lies ultimately with religion:

> The Jew did not like the Christian "heresy," as they considered it. They insisted, with consummate lack of tact, upon their own religion. They were an opposition shop. Our priests reacted violently. Also the part the ancestors of the Jews were described as playing at the time of the drama of our profoundly sensational cult, gave our forefathers a horror of them. As objects of dislike, and even of *horror*, they became at once cowed and sullen. This reacted unfavorably upon their disposition, as it would have done upon ours.[15]

In sum, the Christians are to blame for making the Jews what they became in time and, as such, the objects of contempt. It is now up to the Christians, therefore, to undo the damage. Lewis calls on them to "give all people of Jewish race a new deal among us" and to make an end finally "of this silly nightmare once and for all."

Noble sentiments, perhaps sincerely held. But even while attempting to redress a centuries-old wrong, Lewis reinforces the notion of the existence of a "Jewish Problem" and continues to impute to Jews contemptible traits for which, he now claims, they themselves are ultimately not responsible. However, even Lewis was entitled to a change of mind, and on the eve of World War II, he wrote a condemnation of the Nazis, *The Hitler Cult and How It Will End* (1939). For many, it was long overdue.

SEVEN

Denouement:

Nazi Ideology,

Jews, and the Cult

of the Body

The transition from such writers as Benda, Weininger, Lawrence, and Lewis to Nazi ideologues and Adolf Hitler himself is regrettably easy. Whether condemning the Jew for fathering a Christianity against which they had various briefs to file or for being the cause of social, political, and artistic trends they disapproved of, or for embodying femininity in a period of aggressive masculinity, these writers contributed to the pandemic of late nineteenth- and early twentieth-century anti-Semitism. In doing so they helped shape the dehumanization of the Jew, a process that was completed in Germany in the Hitler era and carried to its logical extreme in World War II. One may ask at this point what this has to do with the modernist cult of the physical.

The relentless drumbeat of anti-Semitic writing at the turn of the century, from which few countries in Europe were exempt and to which France, Austria, and Germany contributed the most, set up the Jew for what befell him in the Holocaust. By the time Hitler wrote *Mein Kampf* (*My Struggle*) in 1925, the Jew had already been defined as a pariah and held responsible in one or another way for most of the ills of the day. But the feminization of the Jew was particularly pernicious in light of the inherent antifeminism of a distinctly masculine-oriented physicality. As a body, the Jew became as distanced from a cohering cult of the physical as he was becoming distanced from society as a whole. Moreover, the identification of the Jew with rational and intellectual culture at a time when the irrational and unconscious were in the ascendancy further widened the gap. The celebration of the pagan and primitive came at the expense usually of the Judaeo-Christian moral tradition, as we have seen with Nietzsche and Lawrence. Turn-of-the-century racist theory completed the process of irreversible alienation. The new ideal of the masculine body left the Jew beyond the pale. Among the Germans, Jewish degeneracy—physical as well as moral—was juxtaposed to classical, Nordic supremacy. Attributing to the Jew an awareness of his own inferiority facilitated imputing to him strategies of subterfuge to destroy Nordic ideals out of envy and fear. The fate of the Jew was sealed. Demoted to the level of a subhuman species and portrayed as corporeally degenerate, the Jew was effectively locked out of the modernist cult of the physical except in universally negative terms. Racial and social alienation now assumed a deadly physical aspect.

Although Hitler's ideas on the Jews as expressed in *Mein Kampf* served as the blueprint for the campaign to exterminate the Jews during World War II, they were shaped to a great extent by the prevailing climate of European anti-Semitism and the sizable body of anti-Jewish writings from a variety of sources. Of contemporary German anti-Semitic propagandists, none had as decisive an impact on the development of Hitler's thought as Alfred Rosenberg, who was executed as a war criminal at Nuremberg in 1946. Known best for his book *Der Mythos des 20. Jahrhunderts* (*The Myth of the Twentieth Century*, 1930), Rosenberg went on to become the leading Nazi ideologist in the Hitler period.

Rosenberg's anti-Semitic writings in the form of short essays began to appear in the *Völkischer Beobachter* as early as 1921, a few years before the publication of *Mein Kampf*. These were collected in an edition published in 1938 under the title *Kampf um die Macht: Aufsätze von 1921–1932* (*The Battle for Power: Essays from 1921–1932*).[1]

The principal Nazi claims against the Jews are adumbrated in Rosenberg's essays and for the most part follow the lines of anti-Semitic literature in other languages from the late nineteenth and early twentieth centuries. These fall into certain familiar (and predictable) categories: Jewish greed and shady financial practices have undermined the world financial system ("Gegen die jüdische Bankenpest" ["Against the Jewish Banking Plague"], "Die Börsenrevolte des Judentums" ["The Stock Exchange Revolt of the Jews"]); the Jews aim at world domination and toward that end advance the cause of bolshevism, which is a Jewish concoction ("Jüd-ische Weltpolitik" ["Jewish World Politics"], "Der jüdische Bolschewismus" ["Jewish Bolshevism"], "Sowjet—Judäa" ["Soviet—Jewry"]); the Jews scoff at Christianity and belittle the figure of Christ ("Die Verhöhning Christi durch die Juden" ["The Jewish Mockery of Christ"], "Der ewige Juden-hass gegen Christus" ["Eternal Jewish Hatred of Christ"]); the Jews seek to demoralize Christian society and hence exercise a monopoly over inter-national prostitution ("Der internationale Mädchenhandel und sein jüd-isches Monopol" ["The Jewish Monopoly of Prostitution"]); the Talmud, one of the pillars of Judaism, is a muddled, bizarre document that pro-motes anti-Christian hatred ("Gegen den Talmud" ["Against the Talmud"], "Talmudperlen" ["Pearls of the Talmud"]); Zionism is a Jewish political conspiracy ("Zionistischer Bankrott" ["Zionist Bankruptcy"], "Die zionis-tische Selbstentlarvung" ["The Zionists Unmask Themselves"], "Bismarck, das Deutsche Reich und die Juden" ["Bismarck, the German Empire, and the Jews"]).

As prolific as he was venomous, Rosenberg complemented his essays against Jews with a series of books, to mention just a few: *Die Spur des Juden im Wandel der Zeiten* (*The Trail of the Jews in Changing Times*, 1920), his most comprehensive and detailed attack on Judaism; *Pest in Russland* (*Plague in Russia*, 1922), an analysis of the role of Jews and the "Jewish conspiracy" in the Bolshevik revolution; *Judentum, Jesuitismus, Deutsches Christentum* (*Jewry, Jesuitism, German Christianity*, 1932), in which he contrasts the perfidious Judaic tradition and that of the Jesuits with the true Germanic Christianity; and *Unmoral im Talmud* (*Immorality in the Talmud*, 1943), a World War II publication "de-masking" the morally cor-ruptive teachings of the Talmud. In 1927 Rosenberg published an attack on Zionism under the title *Der Weltverschwörer Kongress zu Basel* (*The World Conspiratorial Congress in Basel*, 1927) in which Zionism is linked with the notorious *Protocols of the Elders of Zion*. Four years earlier, in 1923, Rosenberg had edited a German translation of *The Protocols of the Elders of Zion* (*Die Protokollen der Weisen von Zion*). He also translated into German Roger Gougenot des Mousseaux's inflammatory *Le Juif: le judaisme et la judaisation des peuples chrétiens* (*The Jew: Judaism and the Judaization of the Christian Peoples*, 1869) under the title *Der Jude, das Judentum, und die Verjudung der christlichen Völker*, 1921). Mousseaux was a notorious French racist of the nineteenth century, second in importance only to Count Arthur de Gobineau. In a similar vein, Rosenberg edited and introduced selected works of Dietrich Eckart (Munich, 1928), a somewhat bohemian poet and virulent anti-Semite who, until his death in 1923, exerted considerable influence on Hitler as well as Rosenberg.

Adolf Hitler deals forthrightly, and chillingly, with the genesis and character of his hatred toward Jews in *Mein Kampf*. Much of his animus is directed against what he identifies as the parasitism and moral corruption of the Jew. Rejecting the idea that Jews are Jews by virtue of their religion, Hitler argues instead for the consideration of Jews as a race. As such, they are then dehumanized by being likened to parasites that invade a foreign body until they eventually destroy it:

> [The Jew] . . . was never a nomad, but only and always a *parasite* in the body of other peoples. That he sometimes left his previous living space has nothing to do with his own purpose, but results from the fact that from time to time he was thrown out by the host nations he had misused. His spreading is a typical phenomenon for all parasites; he always seeks a new feeding ground for his race. . . . He is and remains the typical parasite, a sponger who like a noxious bacillus keeps spreading as soon as a favorable medium invites him. And the effect of his existence is also like that of spongers: wherever he appears, the host people dies out after a shorter or longer period.[2]

Extolling the superiority of the Aryan race, more specifically the superiority of the Germans, Hitler then presents the Jew as the very antithesis of the Aryan. Since the Germans are a "racially pure people, which is conscious of its blood," they can never be enslaved by the Jew. "In this world," he continues, "[the Jew] will forever be master over bastards and bastards alone" (325). The Jew nevertheless will seek to gain mastery over the Aryan Germans by trying systematically to "lower the racial level" by a "continuous poisoning of individuals" (325). The pattern of portraying the Jew as a parasite or bacillus, already evident in *Mein Kampf*, became a constant of German anti-Jewish writing up to and during World War II.

Now how does the Jew, a racially inferior species, go about attempting to "lower the racial level" of the Germans? By attacking the German body. Lacking the morality of the Christian Aryans, the Jews support every form of immorality, promote prostitution, engage in the "white slave" trade, and bear responsibility for the increase in the rise of syphilis, to which Hitler devotes several pages in *Mein Kampf*. The greatest danger, of course, lies in German-Jewish intermarriage and, in fact, in any sexual relationship between Jews and Germans from which children may issue. The inroads of the Jew into Aryan society, permitting him to carry out his agenda of racial contamination, are the result of liberal social and political attitudes and financial cynicism. The alarming spread of syphilis is a direct consequence of what Hitler regards as moral laxity. And it is this moral laxity, or indifference, especially on the part of the leadership of the state and nation, that ultimately threatens the breakdown of German society by making it possible for the Jew to sow the seeds of degeneration. If Hitler does not directly accuse the Jews of spreading syphilis—the issue was too complex even for the simplifications of *Mein Kampf*—his words make it clear that it is indeed the Jews who must be regarded as the greatest contaminant in German society: "This Jewification of our spiritual life and mammonization of our mating instinct will sooner or later destroy our entire offspring, for the powerful children of a natural emotion will be replaced by the miserable creatures of financial expediency which is becoming more and more the basis and sole prerequisite of our marriages" (247).

Hitler equated racial purity with national greatness. As he wrote in *Mein Kampf*: "All great cultures of the past perished only because the originally creative race died out from blood poisoning" (289). Hence for the Germans to regain their greatness as a people and recover from the ravages of World War I, they must strive to maintain the purity of their Aryan race by all means possible. Of greatest immediate concern were the twin dangers of prostitution and venereal disease. These could be effectively combated only if changes in social conditions were undertaken. This meant, in turn, new thinking on education and physical training. *Mein Kampf* advances the view that many of the social evils from which contemporary German society was suffering were attributable to the imbalance in the educational system between mental instruction and physical culture. Hitler denounced the *gymnasium*, or secondary school, as a "mockery of the Greek model." He regarded the intelligentsia as spineless and incapable of offering resistance to the "Jewish disease" of bolshevism, which had made serious inroads in more impoverished regions of postwar Germany. The intelligentsia was weak because it was "degenerate physically," the result not of poverty but of education. Referring to the unsettled conditions and militancy of the 1920s, Hitler declared: "In times when not the mind but the fist decides, the purely intellectual emphasis of our education in the upper classes makes them incapable of defending themselves, let alone enforcing their will. Not infrequently the first weakness for personal cowardice lies in physical weakness" (253).

It was also, in Hitler's view, this same excessive emphasis on purely intellectual instruction and the accompanying neglect of physical training that encouraged the emergence of sexual ideas at too early an age: "The youth who achieves the hardness of iron by sports and gymnastics succumbs to the need of sexual satisfaction less than the stay-at-home fed exclusively on intellectual fare. And a sensible system of education must bear this in mind" (253).

In order, therefore, for German society to revitalize itself in the aftermath of the war and recover its compromised racial superiority, Hitler insisted that the whole educational system be organized so as "to use the boy's free time for the useful training of his body" (254). Although girls' physical training was eventually incorporated into the overall German gymnastics program, Hitler's emphasis on the male was typical both for Nazi ideology and modernist physicality in general. The subsequent concentration in Germany on the cultivation of the body through organized programs of physical education and sports was already adumbrated, as we can see, in *Mein Kampf*. No less programmatic was the coupling of physical training and the struggle against the poisoning of the soul. By the latter, Hitler understood rampant prostitution, syphilis, and other "big-city" vices that in his mind were the offshoots of a morally debased culture. Hence along with the emphasis on the cultivation of the body, Hitler emphasized a thorough "cleansing" of contemporary culture:

> Theater, art, literature, cinema, press, posters, and window displays must be cleansed of all manifestations of our rotting world and placed in the service of a moral, political, and cultural idea. Public life must be freed from the stifling perfume of our modern eroticism, just as it must be freed from all unmanly, prudish hypocrisy. In all these things the goal and the road must be determined by concern for the preservation of the health of our people in body and soul. The right of personal freedom recedes before the duty to preserve the race. (255)

The same year that Hitler became chancellor of Germany and the Nazis came to power with him, a broad national agenda for physical culture and sports was developed in line with the precepts enunciated in *Mein Kampf*. On April 29, 1933, SA-Gruppenführer (Group Leader) Hans von Tschammer und Osten was named Reischsportkommissar (Reich Sports Leader) and placed in charge of the program.[3] A new body governing German sports, the Reichsführerring, was founded on May 24 that same year, followed a month later by a new organization of German tournament, sports, and gymnastics teachers known as the Reichsverband Deutscher Turn-, Sport- und Gymnastiklehrer. On July 19, von Tschammer und Osten was appointed the head of that organization as well. The Fifteenth German Gymnastics Festival, or *Turnfest*—the first in the Nazi period—was held in Stuttgart from July 25 to July 30, 1933. Hitler spoke at the opening ceremonies and used the opportunity to award von Tschammer und Osten another portfolio, that of leader of the German Gymnastic Federation (*Deutsche Turnerschaft*).

To all intents and purposes, von Tschammer und Osten was now the leader of the entire German physical education and sports program under the Nazis. So prominent was he in the German sports world under Hitler that he eventually became the president of the International Olympic Institute.

In the reorganization of German physical education and sports after Hitler's ascension to the chancellorship, it was understood that the basic guidelines for the new program had already been laid down in *Mein Kampf*. All that was needed was their practical implementation, a task entrusted to von Tschammer und Osten who as Reich sports leader proved an able and dedicated leader.[4] This meant, first of all, indoctrination in Hitler's racial doctrines. The natural superiority of the Nordic peoples was to be stressed and "Nordic" and "heroic" (*heldisch*) were to be equated. Delineating Occidental-Nordic man as the prototype of the hero, Walther Jaensch, a docent at the Deutsche Hochschule für Leibesübungen (German College of Physical Training), wrote in the book *Körperformung, Rasse, Seele und Leibesübungen* (*Body Building, Race, Soul, and Physical Training*, 1936):

> Coming out of a small, uninhabitable corner of the world, he [Nordic man] conquered this world despite his quantitative inferiority.
>
> This spirit of Occidental man appears again to have arisen now in Germany. We are breaking out of defeat, and we recall the strength of our fathers who extended the Reich as far as Asia. Our new youth, who have advanced into every corner of life with undreamt of force, again has the profile of that Viking-like race of conquerors who once upon a time pushed off from the shores of the Northland in order to make the world subservient to them.[5]

And Walther Schlüter, in a book on physical education, declared: "The Germanic people is a manly people! This resounds loudly from the songs and sagas of our forebears. There is nothing here that recalls softness, neither in body or spirit. The watchword of Germanness is battle: battle against nature, battle against men."[6]

The attributes of the Nordic-Germanic type were bolstered by claims of racial kinship with the ancient Greeks. As Hans Glauning, director of the press section of the Reich Ministry of Education, explained: "Today we understand why ancient Hellas time and again has attracted the great spirits of the German people. It is the *racial kinship*, through which the spirit of Greek culture is intelligible to us . . . It is for that reason alone that the German people can grasp the world of antiquity with such particular empathy, since this ancient culture, just like the German, arose from a Nordic genotype."[7]

The year of the Berlin Olympics, 1936, SS-Oberführer Karl Motz drew the now obligatory parallels between the ancient sports heroes and their Germanic successors: "The ancient Greeks, who came together to compete at Olympia, were blonde and blue-eyed, brothers and sisters of our own forebears. The old as well as the new Olympiad originated with Germanic man, from the same blood-related affirmation of the body. It is un-German to deviate from this attitude toward physical exercises and contradicts the idea of the proud master race."[8]

Since the physical training of the young in the Hitler era was also viewed as a form of preparedness for combat, Nazi ideologues glorified the idea that battle (Kampf) had been a principle of life among the ancient Greeks, hence a further link between Greece and the Germanic peoples. Johannes Dannheuser, a senior official at the Reich Academy for Physical Education in Berlin, wrote in 1939, the year World War II broke out: "In Greece, as in the Germanic North, battle was the principle of life. Just as the Germanic boys and men willingly vied against each other for their lives, so did people of related blood in southern regions compete out of the same primordial joy in battle and for the sake of military preparedness."[9]

But there were occasionally rare deviations from the norm. In a curious departure from the general pattern of equating the ideal Germanic type with the classical Greek hero, Bruno Malitz, a leading ideologist of Nazi physical culture, took exception to the practice of "German scholars and German school teachers (in many cases Jewish)" of holding up the Greek Heracles as the model of strength. For German youth the model had to be Siegfried, one of the heroes of German folklore whom Wagner brought to the stage so triumphantly in his *Ring* cycle. With Siegfried as their model, German youth should be "big and powerful, with muscles of steel and firm body, and not Jewishly effeminate, all powdered and made up."[10] Notice again, as in Weininger three decades earlier, the equation of Jewishness and femininity.

The negative contrast of Jew and German within the context of Nazi physical culture became mandatory after the German Gymnastics Federation finally accepted the notorious "Aryan paragraphs" designed to stifle Jewish life in Germany. Besides the systematic elimination of Jews from all German sports organizations, vicious anti-Semitism became integrated into the ideology and teaching of German physical culture. In other words, as the values of "a sound mind in a sound body" were inculcated into German youth, so, too, were the views that the Jew was the most dangerous enemy of the German people, that the Jew sought mastery over the German race, that the Jew was out to undermine the strength of the German people since he recognized that it was the main obstacle confronting him on his path to world domination, that the Jew preached pacifism, and that the Jew was effeminate and misshapen. Bruno Malitz, who was quoted above, wrote:

> Jewish teaching undermined the power of the people. Manliness is a thorn in its eye since it fears it, for it alone stands in the way of the Jewish destruction of the world. *But National Socialism embraces the struggle against feminine, subversive Jewry and hurls itself against it.* No longer will lecherous Jewboys be able to shame our girls and women, and greedy Jewgirls turn German men into errand-boys of their Asiatic service. It is a pity for the strength of the German people to be dissipated in Jewish arms. . . .
>
> The battle will be carried out in Germany and *German men* will have to wage it mercilessly and decisively. Jewry seeks to weaken man internationally through pacifism. That is why, in the clever Jewish way, it makes use of sport, hence combat, but eliminates "politics" from it and promotes it internationally, explaining that peaceful struggle must replace the warlike, that sport unites peoples and makes them capable of peaceful achievements. Nothing however, is said about the fact that this is supposed to happen under Jewish leadership.[11]

Writing in *Der Dietwart* in 1939, Wilhelm Schneemann had this to say about the Jewish build and Jewish physical characteristics:

> Generally speaking, the Jew is relatively weakly built physically. The frequently observed excessive corpulence does not alter the fact. Günther speaks of rather "calfless" legs to be found among Jews and mentions additionally that crooked, rather misshapen legs (by our standards) are often to be seen among them. . . . Also conspicuous is the distinct thinness of the thighs. A high incidence of flat-footedness is common. The "Jewish" gait has something creeping and sluggish about it. According to Schleich, the gait is "groping, dragging, shuffling." Anyone in a position to observe can for the most part recognize the person walking in front of him as a Jew from his gait.
>
> The "round back" that is often to be found among Jews is also peculiar. Günther believes that it is less a genetic predisposition than an acquired characteristic.
>
> A slim circumference of the shallow-looking rib cage is just as common among Jews as unusually short arms. However, a minority of Jews have arms that are disproportionately long and thin, that "hang over the knee" . . .
>
> When you observe Jews in their movements you have the impression that their limbs are set in their joints differently than among Germans. Legs and arms dangle; their movements seems to lack control as if they were partly inde-

pendent of the will of their owner. One might imagine that the limbs are only loosely attached to their joints by means of slack ligaments.[12]

There is no need for further examples. Demonized, reduced to a sub-human species, transformed into the very antithesis of the now-revered classical Greek athlete or the Teutonic equivalent, Siegfried, the Jew became targeted for extinction in a rationalization many found easy to accept. The modernist obsession with the physical had now run its full course. Where a culture of the body had supplanted a culture of the mind, the genocide of a people resented for putative intellectual superiority and scorned as physically inferior came to lose much of its moral stigma. The road traveled from the ascendancy of pantomime in the late nineteenth and early twentieth centuries to the extremist cultivation of the body as a symbol of racial superiority was frighteningly short.

Notes

Chapter 2 Modernist Pantomime and the Retreat
from Speech in the Drama

1. Particularly helpful in understanding the development of pantomime in the nineteenth century, primarily in the French context, are John A. Hendersen, *The First Avant-Garde 1887–1894: Sources of the Modern French Theatre* (London: George G. Harrap & Co., 1971), 120–22, John McCormick, *Popular Theatres of Nineteenth-Century France* (London: Routledge, 1993), 134–47, and Robert Storey, *Pierrots on the Stage of Desire: Nineteenth-Century French Literary Artists and the Comic Pantomime* (Princeton, N.J.: Princeton University Press, 1985).

2. From Reinhardt's *Regie-Buch* (production manuscript), in Oliver Sayler, ed., *Max Reinhardt and His Theatre* (New York: Brentano's, 1924), 322. The complete text of the Regie-Buch, in English translation, appears as Appendix I, 249–322.

3. J. L. Styan, *Max Reinhardt* (Cambridge: Cambridge University Press, 1982), 96.

4. Norman Bel Geddes, *Miracle in the Evening: An Autobiography*, ed. William Kelley (New York, 1960), 275.

5. Ernst Stern, *My Life, My Stage* (London, 1951), 96.

6. Gusti Adler, *Max Reinhardt . . . aber vergessen Sie nicht die chinesischen Nachtigallen* (Munich: Deutscher Taschenbuch Verlag, 1983), 71. The pantomime was also made into an American film in 1959, with Carroll Baker as the nun.

7. Adler, *Max Reinhardt*, 146–49.

8. George Jean Nathan, *American Mercury* 1, no.1 (1924), 369.

9. Stern had a special fondness for dancers. Four of his drawings of dancers, in costumes he designed, appear in Paul Nikolaus, *Tänzerinnen* (Munich: Delphin Verlag, 1919). A brief appreciation of Stern's dance costume designs appears on 85–87.

10. For an account of the 1911 London production of *Sumurûn*, see Huntly

Carter, *The Theatre of Max Reinhardt* (New York: Benjamin Bloom, 1914; reissued 1964), 197–209.

11. *Times* (London), February 20, 1911, 10.

12. Marsen Hartley, "The Reinhardt Machine," in Sayler, ed., *Max Reinhardt and His Theatre*, 89.

13. For the texts of Wedekind's writings on the circus and music hall, see "Zirkusgedanken" (153–62), "Im Zirkus" (163–69), and "Middlesex Musikhall: Ein Fragment aus meinem Londoner Tagebuch" (188–90) in Frank Wedekind, *Prosa: Erzählungen, Aufsätze, Selbstzeugnisse, Briefe*, ed. Manfred Hahn (Berlin: Aufbau-Verlag, 1969). "Zirkusgedanken," about performances of the Circus Herzog, was first published in the *Neue Zürcher Zeitung* on June 29 and 30, 1887. "In the Circus" also deals with performances of the Circus Herzog that Wedekind took in while in Zurich. The piece was first published, in two parts, also in the *Neue Zürcher Zeitung* on August 2, 1888, and August 5, 1888. The music-hall piece was first published just under the title "Fragment aus meinem Londoner Tagebuch" on November 28, 1896, in Julius Schaumberger's journal, *Mephisto* (vol. I, no. 10).

14. Frank Wedekind, *Drama 2 Gedichte*, ed. Manfred Hahn (Berlin: Aufbau-Verlag, 1969), 763.

15. For the best edition of the work in German, see *Die Kaiserin von Neufundland: Grosse Pantomime in drei Bildern*, in Wedekind, *Drama 2 Gedichte*, 343–78. The pantomime has been translated into English: Frank Wedekind, "The Empress of Newfoundland: A Spectacular Mime Play in Three Acts," trans. Anthony Vivis, intro. Julian Hilton, *Comparative Criticism: A Yearbook*, ed. E. S. Shaffer, vol. 4 (Cambridge: Cambridge University Press, 1982), 233–67.

16. Wedekind, *Drama 2 Gedichte*, 353.

17. On the "Grosse Liebe" project, see especially Thomas Medicus, *"Die grosse Liebe": Ökonomie und Konstruktion der Körper im Werk von Frank Wedekind* (Marburg/Lahn: Guttlandin & Hoppe, 1982).

18. The German text of this appears in Wedekind, *Prosa*, 652–53.

19. Ibid., 90–91.

20. Elizabeth Boa, *The Sexual Circus: Wedekind's Theatre of Subversion* (Oxford: Basil Blackwell, 1987), 192–96.

21. Joseph A. von Bradish, "Der Briefwechsel Hofmannsthal-Wildgans," *Publications of the Modern Language Association* 19 (1934), 947.

22. Hugo von Hofmannsthal, *Gesammelte Werke in Einzelausgaben: Prosa II* (Frankfurt am Main: S. Fischer Verlag, 1951), 12–13.

23. Hugo von Hofmannsthal, "Eine Monographie," *Gesammelte Werke in Einzelausgaben: Prosa I* (Frankfurt am Main: S. Fischer Verlag, 1950), 265.

24. *Die neue Körpersprache: Grete Wiesenthal und ihr Tanz* (Vienna: Eigenverlag der Museen der Stadt Wien, 1986), 38. This volume is the catalogue of an exhibition of the same name held at the Historisches Museum der Stadt Wien from May 18, 1985, to February 23, 1986.

25. For an interesting analysis of the work, see Gisela Bärbel Schmid, "Das

unheimliche Erlebnis eines jungen Elegants in einer merkwürdigen visionären Nacht": Zu Hofmannsthals Pantomime 'Das fremde Mädchen,'" *Hofmannsthal Blätter* 31/32 (1985), 46–57.

26. Grete Wiesenthal, "Tanz und Pantomime," *Hofmannsthal Blätter* 34 (1986), 37.

27. Grete Wiesenthal, "Pantomime," *Hofmannsthal Blätter* 34 (1986), 44.

28. Hofmannsthal, *Gesammelte Werke: Dramen VI*, 696.

29. Ernst Stern and Heinz Herald, eds., *Reinhardt und seine Bühne: Bilder von der Arbeit des Deutschen Theaters* (Berlin: Dr. Eysler & Co., 1920), 119.

30. Stern and Herald, *Reinhardt und seine Bühne*, 113.

31. Hofmannsthal, *Gesammelte Werke: Dramen VI*, 698.

32. Michael Hamberger, introduction to Hugo von Hofmannsthal, *Selected Plays and Libretti* (New York: Pantheon Books, 1963), xxvii–xxviii.

33. Hugo von Hofmannsthal, *Gessamelte Werke* 8 [*Reden und Aufsätze I 1891–1913*] (Frankfurt am Main: Fischer Taschenbuch Verlag, 1979), 502.

34. For a complete English translation of the pantomime, see Arthur Schnitzler, *Paracelsus and Other Plays*, trans. G. J. Weinberger (Riverside, Calif.: Ariadne Press, 1995), 185–205.

35. Meyerhold's production of *Columbine's Scarf* is discussed in the context of his other experiments with commedia dell'arte in Edward Braun, trans., ed., *Meyerhold on Theatre* (New York: Hill & Wang, 1969), 113–15.

36. For more information on Evreinov and *The Chief Thing*, see Spencer Golub, *Evreinov: The Theatre of Paradox and Transformation* (Ann Arbor, Mich.: UMI Research Press, 1984); Sharon Carnicke, *The Theatrical Instinct: Nikolai Evreinov and the Russian Theatre of the Early Twentieth Century* (New York: P. Lang, 1989); and Harold B. Segel, *Twentieth-Century Russian Drama from Gorky to the Present: Updated Edition* (Baltimore: Johns Hopkins University Press, 1993), 127–36.

37. My information on Carl Einstein's life and career comes from the chronicle appended to Carl Einstein, *Werke Band 1: 1908–1918*, ed. Rolf-Peter Baacke, with Jens Kwasny (Berlin: Medusa, 1980), 512–13.

38. Brooks Atkinson, *Broadway*, 2d ed. (New York: Macmillan, 1974), 120.

39. Einstein, *Werke Band 1*, 57.

40. Gabriele Brandstetter, "Körper im Raum—Raum in Körper: Zu Carl Einsteins Pantomime 'Nuronihar,'" Klaus H. Kiefer, ed., *Carl-Einstein-Kolloquium 1986* (Frankfurt am Main: Verlag Peter Lang, 1988), 123. Brandstetter's short article develops the idea that space and time (afternoon, evening, night) are created by dance, which in *Nuronihar* is the same as pantomime. Neither the dancer nor the landscape of the dance are positioned in stage space but are instead "qualities" (*Eigenschaften*) of the dance itself.

41. Mikhail Kuzmin, *Dnevniki pisateley* 3–4 (1914), 12–15.

42. M. Kuzmin, *Teatr I–III*, ed. A. Timofeev (Oakland, Calif.: Berkeley Slavic Specialties, 1994), 260.

43. Quoted by Timofeev, M. Kuzmin, *Teatr IV*, ed. A Timofeev (Oakland, Calif.: Berkeley Slavic Specialties, 1994), 398.

44. On the reception of *All Souls' Day in Toledo*, see Kuzmin, *Teatr IV*, 398–400.

45. Doubtless because of its subject matter, the play was staged only once, on February 23, 1914, on the private stage located in the home of Evfimiya and Vasily Nosov, two wealthy St. Petersburg patrons of the arts.

46. Kandinsky, *Essays über Kunst und Künstler*, ed. Max Bill (Stuttgart: Verlag Gerd Hatje, 1955), 51.

47. A good English translation of the entire text appears in Kandinsky, *Complete Writings on Art*, ed. Kenneth C. Lindsay and Peter Vergo (New York: Da Capo Press, 1982), 267–83. My quotations from the work are drawn from this translation.

48. See Harold B. Segel, *Pinocchio's Progeny: Puppets, Marionettes, Automatons, and Robots in Modernist and Avant-Garde Drama* (Baltimore: Johns Hopkins University Press, 1995), 49–54.

49. Maurice Maeterlinck, *Théâtre*, vol. I (Brussels: P. Lacomblez; Paris: Per Lamm, 1903), 245.

50. A. P. Chekhov, *Dramaticheskie proizvedeniya v 2-kh tomakh 2: 1889–1904* (Leningrad: "Iskusstvo," 1985), 312. My translations from *The Cherry Orchard* are based on this edition.

51. Hugo von Hofmannsthal, *Der Schwierige: Lustspiel in drei Akten* (Frankfurt am Main: Fischer Tachenbuch Verlag, 1992), 48.

52. Lev Lunts, *Vne zakona: p'esy, rasskazy, stat'i* (St. Petersburg: "Kompozitor," 1994), 205. All quotes from Lunts's works are from this edition.

53. The Russian word for this is *byt*, which is rather difficult to translate into English. It generally denotes a faithfully portrayed segment of life.

54. For a chronological list of Stein productions, from 1934 to 1981, see Betsy Alayne Ryan, *Gertrude Stein's Theatre of the Absolute* (Ann Arbor, Mich.: UMI Research Press, 1984), 165–86.

55. Gertrude Stein, *Geography and Plays* (Madison: University of Wisconsin Press, 1993), 279.

Chapter 3 The Dance Phenomenon

1. On Loïe Fuller's life and career, see her autobiographical *Fifteen Years of a Dancer's Life* (London: Herbert Jenkins, 1913) and, especially, Richard Nelson Current and Marcia Ewing Current, *Loie Fuller: Goddess of Light* (Boston: Northeastern University Press, 1997).Of particular interest in the Currents' book is the section of color plates (between pages 144 and 145) of painting, posters, sculptures, and other art works inspired by Fuller. The appendix to the book (343–51) contains a list of artists and their representations of Fuller.

2. On Isadora Duncan's life and career, see her autobiography, *My Life* (Garden City, N.Y.: Garden City Publishing Co., 1927). The account ends with Duncan's 1921 invitation to come to the Soviet Union to open a school of dance.

3. For Greek influence on Duncan, see Ann Daly, *Done Into Dance: Isadora Duncan in America* (Bloomington: Indiana University Press, 1995), 14–15, 100–104, 106–14.

4. Daly, *Done Into Dance*, is a good study of Duncan in America; her performances in *Iphigenia in Aulis* and other works by Gluck are discussed in 145–48.

5. The best book on Ruth St. Denis is Suzanne Shelton, *Divine Dancer: A Biography of Ruth St. Denis* (Garden City, N.Y.: Doubleday, 1981). Until the appearance of the Shelton biography, the standard account of St. Denis's career was Walter Terry, *Miss Ruth: The "More Living Life" of Ruth St. Denis* (New York: Dodd, Mead & Co., 1969).

6. Susan Au, *Ballet & Modern Dance* (London: Thames & Hudson, 1988), 92.

7. For an excellent study of Mary Wigman in English, see Susan Manning, *Ecstasy and the Demon: Feminism and Nationalism in the Dances of Mary Wigman* (Berkeley: University of California Press, 1993). For a good collection of Mary Wigman's own writings on dance, see Walter Sorell, ed., trans., *The Mary Wigman Book: Her Writings Edited and Translated* (Middletown, Conn.: Wesleyan University Press, 1975.

8. For further information on Dalcroze and his work at Hellerau, see Isa Partsch-Bergsohn, *Modern Dance in Germany and the United States: Crosscurrents and Influences* (London: Harwood Academic Publishers, 1994), 6–9.

9. Samuel Thornton, *Laban's Theory of Movement: A New Perspective* (Boston: Plays, Inc., 1971), is a good introduction to Laban's contributions to the development of modern dance.

10. For a good account of Monte Verità and the art colony that flourished in Ascona in the first two decades of the twentieth century, see Martin Green, *Mountain of Truth: The Counterculture Begins. Ascona, 1900–1920* (Hannover, N.H.: University Press of New England, 1986).

11. Joos is dealt with fairly extensively in Partsch-Bergsohn, *Modern Dance in Germany and the United States.*

12. The collaboration also resulted in a book. See Rudolf Laban and F. C. Lawrence, *Effort: Economy in Body Movement* (London: Macdonald & Evans, 1947; 2d ed., Boston: Plays, Inc. 1974).

13. Walter Sorell, ed., trans., *The Mary Wigman Book* (Middletown, Conn.: Wesleyan University Press, 1975), 34–35.

14. For a good collection of photographs of Wigman in *Hexentanz I*, see Kurt Linder, *Die Verwandlungen der Mary Wigman* (Freiburg im Breisgau: Urban-Verlag, 1929), 47–49 (the eight pages of photographs are unnumbered).

15. Manning, *Ecstasy and the Demon*, 97.

16. Ibid., 107.

17. Sorell, *The Mary Wigman Book*, 124.

18. For a detailed and balanced account of Wigman's career under the Nazis, see the chapter "Body Politic," in Manning, *Ecstasy and the Demon*, 167–220.

19. Henrik Ibsen, *Four Major Plays I*, trans. Rolf Fjelde (New York: New American Library, 1965), 93.

20. August Strindberg, *Strindberg: Five Plays*, trans. Harry G. Carlson (New York: New American Library, 1984), 62.

21. Fyodor Sologub, *Pyat' dram* (St. Petersburg: Izdatel'stvo "Sirin," 1913), 254. This is the eighth volume of Sologub's collected works in the "Sirin" edition.

22. Hugo von Hofmannsthal, *Selected Plays and Libretti*, ed. Michael Hamburger (New York: Pantheon, 1963), 12. The translation of *Electra* in this edition is by Alfred Schwarz.

23. Oscar Wilde, *Plays* (New York: Penguin, 1982), 328. For an interesting interpretation of the figure of Salome in the play, see Amy Koritz, *Gendering Bodies/Performing Art: Dance and Literature in Early Twentieth-Century British Culture* (Ann Arbor: University of Michigan Press, 1985), 75–85.

24. *The Collected Plays of W. B. Yeats* (London: Macmillan, 1966), 214. For additional views of the dance element in Yeats's words, see Koritz, *Gendering Bodies/Performing Art*, 85–100, and, especially, Terri A. Mester, *Movement and Modernism: Yeats, Eliot, Lawrence, Williams, and Early Twentieth-Century Dance* (Fayetteville: University of Arkansas Press, 1997), 27–65.

25. For a biography of Ninette de Valois, see Kathrine Sorley Walker, *Ninette de Valois: Idealist without Illusions* (London: Hamish Hamilton, 1987).

26. Ninette de Valois, *Come Dance with Me: A Memoir 1898–1956* (Cleveland: World Publishing Company, 1957), 105.

27. Gerhart Hauptmann, *Und Pippa tanzt!: Ein Glashüttenmärchen* (Frankfurt am Main: Ullstein, 1996), 22–23. For a somewhat antiquarian translation of the play into English, see Ludwig Lewisohn, ed., *The Dramatic Works of Gerhart Hauptmann*, vol. 5 (New York: B. W. Huebsch, 1915), 131–248

28. For a brief discussion of this in English, and on *Und Pippa tanzt!* in general, see Warren R. Maurer, *Understanding Gerhart Hauptmann* (Columbia: University of South Carolina Press, 1992), 207–8. The discussion of *Und Pippa tanzt!* can be found on pages 104–14.

29. Maurer remarks on this in *Understanding Gerhart Hauptmann*, 113–14.

30. Ibid., 110.

31. Georg Kaiser, "Europa: Spiel und Tanz in fünf Aufzügen," *Werke. Erster Band: Stücke 1895–1917*, ed. Walther Huder (Frankfurt am Main: Propyläen Verlag, 1971), 586.

32. For more detailed studies of Mallarmé's views on dance and the performing arts, see Deirdre Priddin, *The Art of the Dance in French Literature: From Théophile Gautier to Paul Valéry* (London: Adam & Charles Black, 1952), 54–81; and, especially, Mary Lewis Shaw, *Performance in the Texts of Mallarmé: The Passage from Art to Ritual* (University Park: Pennsylvania State University Press, 1993).

33. Stéphane Mallarmé, "Ballets," *Crayonné au théâtre, Oeuvres complètes*, ed. Henri Mondor and G. Jean-Aubry (Paris: Gallimard, 1945), 304. Additional quotations from this essay are numbered in the text.

34. Shaw, *Performance in the Texts of Mallarmé*, 53.

35. Stéphane Mallarmé, "Autre étude de danse: Les fonds dans le ballet," *Crayonné au théâtre, Oeuvres complètes*, 308. Additional quotations from this essay are numbered in the text.

36. On Margueritte and his pantomimes, see especially Robert F. Storey, *Pierrot: A Critical History of a Mask* (Princeton, N.J.: Princeton University Press, 1978), 116–20, 123–25, 127–35.

37. The letter appears in Paul Valéry, "*Lettres à quelques-uns,*" *Oeuvres*, vol. 2, ed. Jean Hytier (Paris: Gallimard, 1960), 62–63.

38. The excerpts from *L'Ame et la danse* are from Paul Valéry, *Ouevres*, vol. 2, ed. Jean Hytier (Paris: Gallimard, 1960). For an English translation of the work, see Paul Valéry, *An Anthology*, ed. James R. Lawler (Princeton, N.J.: Princeton University Press, 1977), 291–326. The anthology is taken from the collected works of Valéry in the Bollingen Series of Princeton University Press.

39. Valéry, *An Anthology*, 306.

40. Frank Kermode, "Poet and Dancer before Diaghilev," *Puzzles and Epiphanies: Essays and Reviews 1958–1961* (London: Routledge & Kegan Paul, 1962), 26.

41. Valéry, *Oeuvres*, vol. 2, 1406–7. The original letter appears in Valéry, *Lettres à quelques-uns*, 189–91.

42. Alfred Döblin, "Die Tänzerin und der Leib," *Die Ermordung einer Butterblume und andere Erzählungen*, 6th ed. (Munich: Deutscher Taschenbuch Verlag, 1986), 16.

43. Hilde Burger, ed., *Hugo von Hofmannsthal—Harry Graf Kesler: Briefwechsel 1898–1929* (Frankfurt am Main: Insel Verlag, 1968), 130.

44. Shelton, *Divine Dancer*, 67–68.

45. Hugo von Hofmannsthal, *Gesammelte Werke in Zehn Einzelbänden: Reden und Aufsätze I 1891–1913* (Frankfurt am Main: Fischer Taschenbuch Verlag, 1979), 497. An English version of the essay, under the title "Her Extraordinary Immediacy," was published in *Dance Magazine*, September 1968, 37–38.

46. Burger, ed., *Hugo von Hofmannsthal—Harry Graf Kessler*, 135–36.

47. Hugo von Hofmannsthal, *Gesammelte Werke in Einzelausgaben: Prosa II* (Frankfurt am Main: S. Fischer Verlag, 1951), 362–63.

48. For a good source of information on Grete Wiesenthal, see Reingard Witzmann, ed., *Die neue Körpersprache: Grete Wiesenthal und ihr Tanz* (Vienna: Eigenverlag der Museen der Stadt Wien, 1986). This is the catalogue of an exhibition held at the Museum of the City of Vienna from May 18, 1985, through February 23, 1986. For a short introduction to Wiesenthal and her dance in English, see Michaela Strebl, "Vanguard of the Liberated Waltz," *Austria Kultur*, vol. 5, no. 6 (Nov./Dec.) (New York: Austrian Cultural Institute, 1995), 16–17. In 1919 (the year in which she opened her own dance school in Vienna), Grete Wiesenthal published her autobiography, *Der Aufstieg: Aus dem Leben einer Tänzerin* (Berlin). The book was reprinted by Rowohlt Verlag in 1947 under the new title, *Die ersten Schritte*. On Grete Wiesenthal's contribution to dance, see Ingeborg Prenner, "Grete Wiesenthal: Die Begründerin eines neuen Tanzstils," Ph.D. diss., University of Vienna (1950).

49. On the Cabaret Fledermaus, see Harold B. Segel, *Turn-of-the-Century Cabaret: Paris, Barcelona, Berlin, Munich, Vienna, Cracow, Moscow, St. Petersburg, Zurich* (New York: Columbia University Press, 1987).

50. Grete Wisenthal, "Amoretten, die um Säulen schweben," in Helmut A. Fiechtner, ed., *Hugo von Hofmannsthal: Der Dichter im Spiegel der Freunde* (Bern: A. Francke AG Verlag, 1963), 187. This is an expanded edition of the original volume published in Vienna in 1949 by Humboldt-Verlag. Wiesenthal's contribution appeared in the original edition and was reprinted in the second edition.

Chapter 4 The Man of Action as Man of Letters

1. For a good, and handsomely illustrated, book on Roosevelt as a naturalist and hunter, with particular attention to weaponry, see R. L. Wilson, *Theodore Roosevelt: Outdoorsman* (New York: Winchester Press, 1971).

2. William Henry Harbaugh, *Power and Responsibility: The Life and Times of Theodore Roosevelt* (New York: Farrar, Straus & Cudahy, 1961), 56.

3. Wilson, *Theodore Roosevelt*, 177.

4. Of the English biographies of D'Annunzio, the most readable are Anthony Rhodes, *D'Annunzio: The Poet as Superman* (New York: McDowell, Obolensky, 1959), and Philippe Jullian, *D'Annunzio*, trans. Stephen Hardman (New York: Viking Press, 1973). For a concise summary of D'Annunzio's career, see also Charles Klopp, "Gabriele D'Annunzio," *European Writers: The Twentieth Century*, vol. 8 (New York: Charles Scribner's Sons, 1989), 175–203. Klopp is also the author of a small monograph on D'Annunzio under the title *Gabriele D'Annunzio* (Boston: Twayne World Publishers, 1988).

5. In *Mussolini: A Biography* (New York: Vintage Books, 1983), 37–38, Denis Mack Smith mentions that D'Annunzio claimed credit for the idea of the march on Rome and that it had been first considered in Fiume in 1919. Mussolini, however, had no desire to share the stage with the popular poet and carefully hedged his bets before and after the Fiume affair. Secretly, Mussolini schemed to capture various Italian cities and to win a certain legitimacy for the Fascist regime by naming D'Annunzio as the honorary president of a new Italian republic.

6. For an account in English of D'Annunzio's takeover of Fiume, see Michael A. Ledeen, *The First Duce: D'Annunzio at Fiume* (Baltimore: Johns Hopkins University Press, 1977).

7. F. T. Marinetti, *Teoria e invenzione futurista* (Verona: Arnoldo Mondadore Editore, 1968), 9–10. For a good collection of Marinetti's writings in English translation, see especially F. T. Marinetti, *Let's Murder the Moonshine: Selected Writings*, trans. R. W. Flint and Arthur A. Coppotelli (Los Angeles: Sun & Moon Classics, 1991; originally published in a different version by Farrar, Straus & Giroux, 1972).

8. C. R. W. Nevinson, *Paint and Prejudice* (New York: Harcourt, Brace & Co., 1938), 77–78.

9. Rosa Trillo Clough, *Looking Back on Futurism* (New York: Cocce Press, 1942), 35.

10. The best introduction to Gumilyov's career and poetry can be found in Nikolai Gumilev, *Stikhotvoreniya i poemy* (Leningrad: Sovetsky Pisatel', 1988), 5–

78. My translations of Gumilyov's two poems are based on this edition; appropriate page numbers are given in the text. For an English study of Gumilyov, see Earl D. Sampson, *Nikolay Gumilev* (Boston: Twayne Publishers, 1979). The book, however, is not always factually reliable.

11. On the treatment of Gumilyov's war poems in Russian literary criticism, see Ben Hellman, "An Aggressive Imperialist? The Controversy over Nikolaj Gumilev's War Poetry," *Nikolaj Gumilev 1886–1986: Papers from The Gumilev Centenary Symposium Held at Ross Priory University of Strathclyde 1986*, ed. Sheelagh Duffin Graham (Oakland, Calif.: Berkeley Slavic Specialties, 1987), 133–48.

12. Nikolay Gumilev, *"Kogda ya byl vlyublen . . .": Stikhotvoreniya, Poemy, P'esy v stikhakh, Perevody, Rasskazy* (Moscow: Shkola Press, 1994), 535–36.

13. For a convincing study of the need to resist oversimplification in assessing Jünger's ideas and attitudes, see Thomas Nevin, *Ernst Jünger and Germany: Into the Abyss, 1914–1945* (Durham: Duke University Press, 1996). For a study principally of Jünger's thought, with some interesting insights into his literary language, see also Marcus Paul Bullock, *The Violent Eye: Ernst Jünger's Visions and Revisions on the European Right* (Detroit: Wayne State University Press, 1992

14. The novel was first translated into English in 1929. It was published by Chatto & Windus of London under the title *The Storm of Steel: From the Diary of a German Storm-Troop Officer on the Western Front*. The translation was reprinted in 1975 by Howard Fertig, New York.

15. Ernst Jünger, *The Storm of Steel: From the Diary of a German Storm-Troop Officer on the Western Front*, trans. Basil Creighton (New York: Howard Fertig, 1975; translation originally published by Chatto & Windus, London, in 1929), 22.

16. All translations from the work are based on the edition that appears in Ernst Jünger, *Sämmtliche Werke: Essays I. Betrachtungen zur Zeit* (Stuttgart: Klett-Cotta, 1980).

17. An English translation, under the title *Copse 125: A Chronicle from the Trench Warfare of 1918*, was also published by Chatto & Windus of London, in 1925. The work was reprinted by Howard Fertig in 1993.

18. Ernst Jünger, *Copse 125: A Chronicle from the Trench Warfare of 1918*, trans. Basil Creighton (New York: Howard Fertig, 1988; original ed., London: Chatto & Windus, 1930), 128.

19. The work was published by Lehmann (London) under the title *African Diversions* in 1954.

20. The novel was published in English by Lehmann of London for the first time in 1947; an American edition was published that same year by New Directions (New York). Penguin Books brought out a new edition of the work in 1970.

21. Gerhard Loose, *Ernst Jünger* (New York: Twayne Publishers, 1974), 62.

22. Jünger, *Sämmtliche Werke: Essays I*, 140–41.

23. Ernst Jünger, "Sprache und Körperbau," *Sämmtliche Werke: Essays VI. Fassungen I* (Stuttgart: Klett-Cotta, 1979), 99.

24. Ernest Hemingway, *The Sun Also Rises* (New York: Macmillan [Scribner/Classic Collier Edition], 1986), 132. The page numbers of other quotations from the novel appear in the text.

25. On Montherlant, see John Cruickshank, *Montherlant* (Edinburgh: Oliver & Boyd, 1964); John Batchelor, *Existence and Imagination: The Theatre of Henry de Montherlant* (St. Lucia, Brisbane: University of Queensland Press, 1967); Robert B. Johnson, *Henry de Montherlant* (New York: Twayne Publishers, 1968); Lucille F. Becker, *Henry de Montherlant: A Critical Biography* (Carbondale, Southern Illinois University Press, 1970).

26. Mark Antliff, *Inventing Bergson: Cultural Politics and the Parisian Avant-Garde* (Princeton, N.J.: Princeton University Press, 1993), 94–99.

27. Henry de Montherlant, *The Dream*, trans. Terence Kilmartin (New York: Macmillan Company, 1922), 37.

28. Henry de Montherlant, *Les Olympiques* (Paris: Éditions Bernard Grasset, 1938), 108–10.

29. Henry de Montherlant, *The Matador*, trans. Peter Wiles (London: Elek Books, 1957), 56.

30. For a good, well-illustrated biography of Saint-Exupéry in English, see Stacy Schiff, *Saint-Exupéry: A Biography* (New York: Alfred A. Knopf, 1994).

31. Antoine de Saint-Exupéry, *Airman's Odyssey: Wind, Sand and Stars, Night Flight, Flight to Arras* (San Diego: Harcourt Brace Jovanovich, 1984), 107–8. The translation of *Wind, Sand and Stars* is by Lewis Galantière .

Chapter 5 Philosophy, Language, and the
Physical Culture Movement

1. Friedrich Nietzsche, *Human, All Too Human: Menschliches, Allzumenschliches*, trans. Marion Faber, with Stephen Lehmann (Lincoln: University of Nebraska Press, 1996), 18–19.

2. My translations from *The Will to Power* are based on the edition Friedrich Nietzsche, *Der Wille zur Macht: Versuch einer Umwertung aller Werte*, ed. Peter Gast (Stuttgart: Alfred Körner Verlag, 1964). This is volume 9 in *Sämtliche Werke in zwolf Bänden*. The numbers in the text are those of the original notes and their dates of composition.

3. For critical assessments of Mauthner's critique of language, see especially Gershon Weiler, *Mauthner's Critique of Language* (Cambridge: Cambridge University Press, 1970); Katherine Arens, *Functionalism and Fin de Siècle: Fritz Mauthner's Critique of Language* (New York: Peter Lang, 1984); Elizabeth Bredeck, *Metaphors of Knowledge: Language and Thought in Mauthner's Critique* (Detroit: Wayne State University Press, 1992); and Martin Kurzreiter, *Sprachkritik als Ideologiekritik bei Fritz Mauthner* (Frankfurt am Main: Peter Lang, 1993). There is also interesting material in Linda Ben-Zvi, "Samuel Beckett, Fritz Mauthner, and the Limits of Language," *PMLA* 95, no. 2 (1980), 183–200. For a brief survey of the language issue in turn-of-the-century Austrian philosophical thought, see William M.

Johnston, *The Austrian Mind: An Intellectual and Social History 1848–1938* (Berkeley: University of California Press, 1983), 176–99.

4. Fritz Mauthner, *Prager Jugendjahre* (Frankfurt am Main: S. Fischer Verlag, 1969), 195.

5. As an example of the newer German scholarship on Mauthner, see e.g. Martin Kurzreiter, *Sprachkritik als Ideologiekritik bei Fritz Mauthner* (Frankfurt am Main: Peter Lang, 1993). The best studies of Mauthner in English to date are Gershon Weiler, *Mauthner's Critique of Language* (Cambridge: Cambridge University Press, 1970), and Katherine Arens, *Functionalism and Fin de siècle: Fritz Mauthner's Critique of Language* (New York: Peter Lang, 1984; Berlin: Institute for Germanic Studies, Stanford University, 1984).

6. Fritz Mauthner, *Beiträge zu einer Kritik der Sprache*, vol. I, *Zur Sprache und zur Psychologie*, 2d ed. (Stuttgart: J. G. Cotta, 1906), XI. All quotes from the first volume of Mauthner's *Beiträge* are from this edition.

7. Fritz Mauthner, *Beiträge zu einer Kritik der Sprache*, vol. III, *Zur Grammatik und Logik* (Stuttgart: J. G. Cotta, 1902), 579.

8. The best biography of Wittgenstein in English remains Ray Monk, *Ludwig Wittgenstein: The Duty of Genius* (New York: Penguin Books, 1990). On Wittgenstein in the context of contemporary Vienna, see Allan Janik and Stephen Toulmin, *Wittgenstein's Vienna* (New York: Simon & Schuster, 1973). Although superseded by a great deal of newer scholarship on Wittgenstein, this is still a readable and useful study.

9. For a very well-known study of Wittgenstein and the *Tractatus* in the context of contemporary Viennese society and culture, see Allan Janik and Stephen Toulmin, *Wittgenstein's Vienna* (New York: Simon & Schuster, 1973).

10. For the best biography of Wittgenstein in English, see Ray Monk, *Ludwig Wittgenstein: The Duty of Genius* (New York: Penguin Books, 1990; original ed., New York: Free Press, 1990).

11. I am following the new translation of the *Tractatus* by Pears and McGuiness. See Ludwig Wittgenstein, *Tractatus Logico-Philosophicus*, trans. D. F. Pears and B. F. McGuiness (London: Routledge & Kegan Paul, 1961, 1974), 3. I have also compared the translation with the original in Ludwig Wittgenstein, *Tractatus logico-philosophicus: Logisch-philosophische Abhandlung* (Frankfurt am Main: Suhrkamp Verlag, 1963), 7. Further quotations from the Pears and McGuiness translation are identified in the text either by page or proposition number.

12. John Heaton and Judy Groves, *Introducing Wittgenstein* (New York: Totem Books, 1996).

13. As evidence of the new interest in Bergson and vitalism, see, especially, Frederick Burwick and Paul Douglass, eds., *The Crisis in Modernism: Bergson and the Vitalist Controversy* (Cambridge: Cambridge University Press, 1992), and Mark Antlff, *Inventing Bergson: Cultural Politics and the Parisian Avant-Garde* (Princeton, N.J.: Princeton University Press, 1993).

14. For a study of Benda and Benda's campaign against Bergson, see Ray Nich-

ols, *Treason, Tradition, and the Intellectual: Julien Benda and Political Discourse* (Lawrence: Regents Press of Kansas, 1978). Benda's principal attacks on Bergson came in the books *Bergsonisme* (1912) and *Une Philosophie pathétique* (1913).

15. Henri Bergson, *Creative Evolution*, trans. Arthur Mitchell (Westport, Conn.: Greenwood Press, 1975; original ed., New York: Random House, 1944), 182.

16. On Bergson's influence on French literature, see especially A. E. Pilkington, *Bergson and His Influence: A Reassessment* (Cambridge: Cambridge University Press, 1976). The following studies deal with Bergson's influence on English and American writers: Shiv K. Kumar, *Bergson and the Stream of Consciousness Novel* (New York: New York University Press, 1963); Sanford Schwarz, *The Matrix of Modernism: Pound, Eliot and Early 20th-Century Thought* (Princeton, N.J.: Princeton University Press, 1985); Paul Douglass, *Bergson, Eliot and American Literature* (Lexington: University of Kentucky Press, 1986); Tom Quirk, *Bergson and American Culture: The Worlds of Willa Cather and Wallace Stevens* (Chapel Hill: University of North Carolina Press, 1990).

17. Stéphane Mallarmé, *Collected Poems*, trans. and ed. Henry Weinfield (Berkeley: University of California Press, 1994), 264.

18. Stéphane Mallarmé, *Oeuvres complètes* (Paris: Gallimard, 1945), 255.

19. Mallarmé, *Collected Poems*, 265.

20. For a complete English translation of Kandinsky's *Klänge*, see Wassily Kandinsky, *Sounds*, trans. Elizabeth R. Napier (New Haven: Yale University Press, 1981). The German originals are also given at the end of the book (121–29).

21. Kandinsky, *Sounds*, 86–87; German text, 126. Kandinsky's German is so simple, at times almost childlike, that it translates easily. Hence there was no reason to try versions of my own that would vary much at all from those of Elizabeth R. Napier.

22. Christian Morgenstern, *Alle Galgenlieder* (Kehl: Swan, 1993), 36.

23. F. T. Marinetti, *Teoria e invenzione futurista: Manifesti, Scritti politici, Romanzi, Parole in libertá*, ed. Luciano De Maria (Verona: Arnoldo Editore, 1968), 40–41. Unless otherwise indicated, all quotations from Marinetti's works are based on the texts as they appear in this edition.

24. Marinetti, "Manifesto tecnico della letteratura futurista," *Teoria e invenzione futurista*, 45.

25. Marinetti, "8 anime in una bomba," *Teoria e invenzione futurista*, 727.

26. Velimir Khlebnikov, *Letters and Theoretical Writings*, trans. Paul Schmidt, ed. Charlotte Douglas (Cambridge, Mass.: Harvard University Press, 1987), 292, 295. All remaining quotations from Khlebnikov's essays are from this edition. For additional studies of Khlebnikov's life and career in English, see, especially, Nils Åke Nilsson, ed., *Velimir Chlebnikov: A Stockholm Symposium April 24 1983* (Stockholm: Almqvist & Wiksell International, 1985); W. G. Weststeijn, *Velimir Chlebnikov and the Development of Poetical Language in Russian Symbolism and Futurism* (Amsterdam: Rodopi, 1983); and Raymond Cooke, *Velimir Khlebnikov: A Critical Study* (Cambridge: Cambridge University Press, 1987).

27. See, for example, his 1912 essay "Teacher and Student: A Conversation (on Words, Cities, and Nations)," in Khlebnikov, *Letters and Theoretical Writings*, 277–87.

28. Vladimir Markov, *Russian Futurism: A History* (Berkeley: University of California Press, 1968), 7. See also Markov's *The Longer Poems of Velimir Khlebnikov* (Berkeley: University of California Press, 1962).

29. For a good study of Russian cubo-futurism, see Vahan D. Barooshian, *Russian Cubo-Futurism 1910–1930* (The Hague: Mouton, 1974).

30. A. E. Kruchenykh, "Primitivy XX-go veka," *Izbrannoe*, ed. Vladimir Markov (Munich: Wilhelm Fink Verlag, 1973), 191.

31. There are examples of these, as well as the illustrations accompanying them, in Kruchenykh, *Izbrannoe*, 13–79, 197–224, 260–66, 271–77, 443–59. Specimens of the typography and page layout of a number of Kruchenykh's works appear throughout the volume.

32. Hugo Ball, *Die Flucht aus der Zeit* (Zurich: Limmat Verlag, 1992), 41–42.

33. Segel, *Turn-of-the-Century Cabaret*, 337–42.

34. Hans Arp et al., *Dada Gedichte: Dichtungen der Gründer* (Zurich: Verlag die Arche, 1957), 28–29.

35. Ball's later career is well covered in Philip Mann, *Hugo Ball: An Intellectual Biography* (London: Institute of Germanic Studies, University of London, 1987), 109–82.

36. See Robert Ernst, *Weakness Is a Crime: The Life of Bernarr Macfadden* (Syracuse: Syracuse University Press, 1991); and David L. Chapman, *Sandow the Magnificent: Eugen Sandow and the Beginnings of Bodybuilding* (Urbana: University of Illinois Press, 1994).

37. On the matter of Sandow's unmarked grave and the possible reasons behind it, see Chapman, *Sandow the Magnificent*, 184–88.

38. Ibid., 33, 34.

39. Ibid., 148–49.

40. On the Lingian system in England, see Ibid., 127–28.

41. On Baden-Powell and the Boy Scouts, see Michael Rosenthal, *The Character Factory: Baden-Powell and the Origins of the Boy Scout Movement* (New York: Pantheon Books, 1986). The best biography of Baden-Powell, which also deals with the founding of the Boy Scouts, is Tim Jeal, *Baden-Powell* (London: Hutchinson, 1989).

42. Wyndham Lewis, *The Art of Being Ruled* (New York: Harper & Brothers, 1926), 115–16.

43. Friedrich Ludwig Jahn and Ernst Eiselen, *Die deutsche Turnkunst* (Berlin: Sportverlag, 1960), LV. This is a facsimile edition of Jahn and Eiselen's original *Die deutsche Turnkunst zur Einrichtung der Turnplätze*, which was published at the authors' expense in Berlin in 1816.

44. Fritz Winther, *Körperbildung als Kunst und Pflicht* (Munich: Delphin-Verlag, 1908), 7.

45. For a good introduction to the Sokol, see Claire Nolte, " 'Our Task, Direction and Goal': The Development of the Sokol National Program to World War I," in *Die slawische Sokolbewegung: Beiträge zur Geschichte von Sport und Nationalismus in Osteurope*, ed. Diethelm Blecking (Dortmund: Forschungsstelle Ostmitteleuropa, 1991), 37–52. In the same volume, see also Marie Provazníková, "Das war der Sokol: Unter dem Protektorat," 53–84, which deals with the Sokol in German-occupied Czechoslovakia in World War II; and Gerald A. Carr, "The Spartakiad: Its Approach and Modification from the Mass Displays of the Sokol," 85–103, on sport and physical culture in post–World War II Czechoslovakia. Other essays in the volume deal with the Sokol movement in Slovakia, Poland, Bulgaria, Yugoslavia, and among the Slavic Sorbs of Germany.

46. Nolte, quoted 40.

47. On Coubertin and the Olympics, see Allen Guttman, *The Olympics: A History of the Modern Games* (Urbana: University of Illinois Press, 1992), 7–35. See also the chapter "Pierre de Coubertin and the Introduction of Organized Sport" in Eugen Weber, *My France: Politics, Culture, Myth* (Cambridge, Mass.: Harvard University Press, 1991), 207–25. Additional studies of Coubertin and the birth of the modern Olympics include Kurt E. Zentner, *Pierre de Coubertin: Ein Beitrag zur Entwicklung des modernen Sports* (Borna-Leipzig: R. Noske, 1935); John A. Lucas (John Apostal), *Baron Pierre de Coubertin and the Formative Years of the Modern International Olympic Movement, 1883–1896* (Microform Publication, School of Health, Physical Education and Recreation, University of Oregon, c. 1964); John J. MacAloon, *The Great Symbol: Pierre de Coubertin and the Origins of the Modern Olympic Games* (Chicago: University of Chicago Press, 1981); Thomas Alkemeyer, *Körper, Kult und Politik: Von der "Muskelreligion" Pierre de Coubertins zur Inszenierung von Macht in den Olympischen Spielen von 1936* (Frankfurt am Main: Campus, 1996). For biographies of Coubertin, see especially André Senay and Robert Hervet, *Monsieur de Coubertin* (Paris: Points & Contrepoints, 1960), and Louis Callebat, *Pierre de Coubertin* (Paris: Fayard, 1988).

48. For more information on the congress, see Coubertin's own memoirs, Pierre de Coubertin, *Mémoires Olympiques* (*Olympic Memoirs*) (Lausanne: Bureau International de Pedagogie Sportive, 1931). An English translation under the title *Olympic Memoirs* was reprinted by the International Olympic Committee in 1989.

49. On the negotiations in France and Greece that immediately preceded the first modern Olympic games in 1896, see Coubertin, *Olympic Memoirs*, 11–18.

50. Guttman, *The Olympics*, 19–20.

51. Coubertin, *Olympic Memoirs*, 24.

Chapter 6 Religion, Race, Gender, Politics,
and the New Physicality

1. Walter Kaufmann, ed., trans., *The Portable Nietzsche* (New York: Viking Press, 1968), 565.

2. Kaufmann, *The Portable Nietzsche*, 570. All further references to *The Anti-*

Christ are drawn from the translation in this edition and are indicated by page number in my text.

3. For a good, fairly concise interpretation of Nietzsche's complex and not always consistent attitudes toward Jews, anti-Jewishness, and anti-Semitism (as a political movement in Germany and Austria at the time), see Robert C. Holub, "Nietzsche and the Jewish Question," *New German Critique* 66 (1995), 94–121.

4. *New York Review of Books*, June 6, 1996, 34–41.

5. The later edition of the book is the one most commonly found in libraries. See Julien Benda, *Belphégor: Essai sur l'esthéthique de la société française dans la première moitié du XXe siècle* (Paris: Emile-Paul Frères, 1947).

6. Benda, *Belphegor*, trans. S. J. I. Lawson (New York: Payson & Clarke, 1929), 14–15.

7. On the posthumous interest in Weininger, see especially the last chapter ("Postérité d'Otto Weininger") in Jacques Le Rider, *Le cas Otto Weininger: Racines de l'antiféminisme et de l'antisémitisme* (Paris: Presses Universitaires de France, 1982), 218–39. Le Rider's book is probably the best introduction to Weininger and *Sex and Character*. For a critique of Le Rider's book, which takes issue with attempts to reduce *Sex and Character* to an antifeminine and anti-Jewish treatise, see Allan Janik, "Writing about Weininger," in *Essays on Wittgenstein and Weininger* (Amsterdam: Rodopi, 1985), 96–115.

8. For an interesting analysis of *Sex and Character* as a product of male hysteria and a castration complex, see Misha Kavka, "The 'Alluring Abyss of Nothingness': Misogyny and (Male) Hysteria in Otto Weininger," *New German Critique* 66 (1995): 123–45.

9. Otto Weininger, *Geschlecht und Charakter* (Vienna: Wilhelm Braumüller Universitäts-Verlagsbuchhandlung, 1922), 24th ed., 312. I am excluding from my translations the italicized lines of the original.

10. D. H. Lawrence, *Apocalypse* (New York: Penguin Books, 1976), 42.

11. D. H. Lawrence, *D. H. Lawrence and Italy: Twilight in Italy; Sea and Sardinia; Etruscan Places* (New York: Penguin, 1985), 49–50.

12. There is now a solid body of literature in English on Lewis as a painter, a writer, and a political thinker. For the best biography of him, see Jeffrey Meyers, *The Enemy: A Biography of Wyndham Lewis* (London: Routledge & Kegan Paul, 1980). Meyers also edited *Wyndham Lewis: A Revaluation. New Essays* (Montreal: McGill-Queens University Press, 1980), a collection of eighteen essays. Timothy Materer, *Wyndham Lewis: The Novelist* (Detroit: Wayne State University Press, 1976) is devoted wholly to the study of his fiction. For more general studies of his art, see Hugh Kenner, *Wyndham Lewis* (Norfolk, Conn.: New Directions Books, 1954), and William H. Pritchard, *Wyndham Lewis* (New York: Twayne Publishers, 1968). For a pioneering early book on Lewis, see Hugh Gordon Porteus, *Wyndham Lewis: A Discursive Exposition* (London: D. Harmsworth, 1932). On Lewis's political views, the best studies are D. G. Bridson, *The Filibuster: A Study of the Political Ideas of Wyndham Lewis* (London: Cassell, 1972), and Fredric Jameson, *Fables of Aggression: The*

Modernist as Fascist (Berkeley: University of California Press, 1979). For a useful collection of selections from Lewis's major works, see Julian Symons, ed., *The Essential Wyndham Lewis: An Introduction to His Work* (London: André Deutsch, 1989).

13. Wyndham Lewis, *The Art of Being Ruled* (New York: Harper & Brothers, 1926), 79.

14. Wyndham Lewis, *Hitler* (New York: Gordon Press, 1972; originally published by Chatto & Windus, London, 1931), 4.

15. Wyndham Lewis, *The Jews: Are They Human?* (London: George Allen & Unwin, 1939), 109–10.

Chapter 7   Denoument

1. Alfred Rosenberg, *Kampf um die Macht: Aufsätze vom 1921–1932* (Munich: Zentralverlag der NSDAP, 1938).

2. Adolf Hitler, *Mein Kampf*, trans. Ralph Mannheim (Boston: Houghton Mifflin Co., 1971), 304–5. All further quotes from *Mein Kampf* are from this edition.

3. My information on physical education and sports under Hitler is based on the materials in Hajo Bernett, *Nationalsozialistische Leibeserziehung: Eine Dokumentation ihrer Theorie und Organisation* (Stuttgart: Karl Hofmann, 1966).

4. Von Tschammer und Osten describes the reorganization and the goals of German physical training and sports under Hitler in an article included in a propaganda volume on the "new Germany," published in English in London in 1938. See Hans von Tschammer und Osten, "German Sport," *Germany Speaks by 21 Leading Members of Party and State*, with a preface by Joachim von Ribbentrop (London: Thornton Butterworth, 1938), 219–28.

5. Walther Jaensch et al., *Körperformung, Rasse, Seele und Leibesübungen. Zwei Teile in einem Band*, vol. II (Berlin: A. Matzner, 1936), 75. Quoted in Bernett, *Nationalsozialistische Leibeserziehung*, 28–29.

6. Walther Schlüter, *Leibesübungen und körperliche Erziehung*, no. 16 (1935), 315. Quoted in Bernett, 30.

7. Quoted in Bernett, 32.

8. Karl Motz, *Rhythmus* (1936), 31. Quoted in Bernett, 33.

9. Johannes Dannheuser, *Politische Leibeserziehung*, no. 6 (1939), 77. Quoted in Bernett, 33.

10. Bruno Malitz, "Die Leibesübungen in der nationalsozialistischen Idee," *Nationalsozialistische Bibliothek*, no. 46, 2d ed. (Munich: Eher, 1934), 34. Quoted in Bernett, 30.

11. Malitz, "Die Leibesübungen," *Nationalsozialistische Bibliothek*, 43, 45. Quoted in Bernett, 37.

12. Wilhelm Schneemann, *Der Dietwart*, series 17, (1938), 442 ff. Quoted in Bernett, 38–39.

Bibliography

Abrahamsen, David. *The Mind and Death of a Genius.* New York: Columbia University Press, 1940.

Alkemeyer, Thomas. *Körper, Kult und Politik: Von der "Muskelreligion" Pierre de Coubertins zur Inszenierung von Macht in den Olympischen Spielen von 1936.* Frankfurt am Main: Campus, 1996.

Antliff, Mark. *Inventing Bergson: Cultural Politics and the Parisian Avant-Garde.* Princeton, N.J.: Princeton University Press, 1993.

Arens, Katherine. *Functionalism and Fin de Siècle: Fritz Mauthner's Critique of Language.* New York: Peter Lang, 1984.

Ball, Hugo. *Die Flucht aus der Zeit.* Zurich: Limmat Verlag, 1992.

Baltz-Balzberg, Regina. *Primitivität der Moderne, 1895–1925: Der Verfall des Deutschen Theaters 1895–1925.* Königstein: Hain, 1983.

Barooshian, Vahan D. *Russian Cubo-Futurism 1910–1930.* The Hague, 1974.

Bennett, Bruce L., and Deobold B. Van Dalen. *A World History of Physical Education: Cultural, Philosophical, Comparative.* 2d ed. Englewood Cliffs, N.J.: Prentice Hall, 1971.

Bernett, Hajo. *Nationalsozialistische Leibeserziehung: Eine Dokumentation ihrer Theorie und Organisation.* Stuttgart: Karl Hofmann, 1966.

Blecking, Diethelm. *Die Geschichte der nationalpolnischen Turnorganisation "Sokół im Deutschen Reich 1884–1939.* Münster: Lit, 1987.

———, ed. *Die slawische Sokolbewegung: Beiträge zur Geschichte von Sport und Nationalismus in Osteuropa.* Dortmund: Forschungsstelle Ostmitteleuropa, 1991.

Blum, Cinzia Sartini. *The Other Modernism: F. T. Marinetti's Futurist Fiction of Power.* Berkeley: University of California Press, 1996.

Bredeck, Elizabeth. *Metaphors of Knowledge: Language and Thought in Mauthner's Critique.* Detroit: Wayne State University Press, 1992.

Brenneke, Reinhard. *Militanter Modernismus: Vergleichende Studien zum Frühwerk Ernst Jüngers*. Stuttgart: M & P, Verlag für Wissenschaft und Forschung, 1992.

Bullock, Marcus Paul. *The Violent Eye: Ernst Jünger's Revisions on the European Right*. Detroit: Wayne State University Press, 1992.

Burwick, Frederick, and Paul Douglass, eds. *The Crisis in Modernism: Bergson and the Vitalist Controversy*. Cambridge: Cambridge University Press, 1992.

Callebat, Louis. *Pierre de Coubertin*. Paris: Fayard, 1988.

Chapman, David L. *Sandow the Magnificent*. Urbana: University of Illinois Press, 1994.

Cooke, Raymond. *Velimir Khlebnikov: A Critical Study*. Cambridge: Cambridge University Press, 1987.

Cruickshank, John. *Montherlant*. Edinburgh: Oliver & Boyd, 1964.

Current, Richard Nelson, and Marcia Ewing Current, *Loie Fuller: Goddess of Light*. Boston: Northeastern University Press, 1997.

Daly, Ann. *Done Into Dance: Isadora Duncan in America*. Bloomington: Indiana University Press, 1995.

Ernst, Robert. *Weakness Is a Crime: The Life of Bernarr Macfadden*. Syracuse: Syracuse University Press, 1991.

Green, Harvey. *Fit for America: Health, Fitness, Sport, and American Society*. New York: Pantheon, 1986.

Green, Martin. *Mountain of Truth: The Counterculture Begins. Ascona, 1900–1920*. Hannover, N.H.: University Press of New England, 1986.

Grover, Kathryn, ed. *Fitness in American Culture: Images of Health, Sport, and the Body, 1830–1940*. Amherst: University of Massachusetts Press; Rochester, N.Y.: Margaret Woodbury Strong Museum, 1989.

Gumpert, Gregor. *Die Rede vom Tanz: Körperästhetik in der Literatur der Jahrhundertwende*. Munich: Wilhelm Fink Verlag, 1994.

Guttmann, Allen. *The Olympics: A History of the Modern Games*. Urbana: University of Illinois Press, 1992.

Hall, G. Stanley. *Educational Problems*. Vol. 1. New York: D. Appleton & Co., 1911.

Henderson, John A. *The First Avant-Garde 1887–1894: Sources of the Modern French Theatre*. London: George G. Harrap & Co., 1971.

Herf, Jeffrey. *Reactionary Modernism: Technology, Culture, and Politics in Weimar and the Third Reich*. Cambridge: Cambridge University Press, 1984.

Hesse, Eva. *Die Achse Avantgarde-Faschismus: Reflexionen über Filippo Tommaso Marinetti und Ezra Pound*. Zurich: Verlags AG Die Arche, 1991.

Hitler, Adolf. *Mein Kampf*. Trans. Ralph Mannheim. Boston: Houghton Mifflin Company, 1971.

Hofmannsthal, Hugo von. *Gesammelte Werke in Einzelausgaben: Prosa I*. Frankfurt am Main: S. Fischer Verlag, 1950.

———. *Gesammelte Werken. Dramen VI: Ballette, Pantomimen, Bearbeitungen, Übersetzungen*. Frankfurt am Main: Fischer Taschenbuch Verlag, 1979.

Holub, Robert C. "Nietzsche and the Jewish Question." *New German Critique* 66 (Fall 1995), 94–121.

Huber-Wiesenthal, Rudolf. *Die Schwestern Wisenthal: Ein Buch eigenen Erlebens.* Vienna: Saturn-Verlag, 1934.

Huyssen, Andreas. "Fortifying the Heart—Totally: Ernst Jünger's Armored Text." *New German Critique* 59 (Spring/Summer 1993), 3–23.

Jahn, Friedrich Ludwig, and Ernst Eiselen. *Die deutsche Turnkunst.* Berlin: Sportverlag, 1960.

Jameson, Frederic. *Fables of Aggression: Wyndham Lewis, the Modernist as Fascist.* Berkeley: University of California Press, 1979.

Janik, Allan, and Stephen Toulmin. *Wittgenstein's Vienna.* New York: Simon & Schuster, 1973.

Jeal, Tim. *Baden-Powell.* London: Hutchinson, 1989.

Johnston, William M. *The Austrian Mind: An Intellectual and Social History 1848–1938.* Berkeley: University of California Press, 1971; 1st paperback ed., 1983.

Khlebnikov, Velimir. *Letters and Theoretical Writings.* Trans. Paul Schmidt, ed. Charlotte Douglas. Cambridge, Mass.: Harvard University Press, 1987.

Kolakowski, Leszek. *Bergson.* Oxford: Oxford University Press, 1985.

Koritz, Amy. *Gendering Bodies/Performing Art: Dance and Literature in Early Twentieth-Century British Culture.* Ann Arbor: University of Michigan Press, 1995.

Kruchonykh, A. E. *Izbrannoe.* Ed. Vladimir Markov. Munich: Wilhelm Fink Verlag, 1973.

Kurzreiter, Martin. *Sprachkritik als Ideologiekritik bei Fritz Mauthner.* Frankfurt am Main: Peter Lang, 1993.

Lawrence, D. H. *St. Mawr & The Man Who Died.* New York: Random House, 1953.

———. *Psychoanalysis and the Unconscious and Fantasia of the Unconscious.* New York: Viking Press, 1960.

———. *Apocalypse.* New York: Penguin Books, 1976.

———. *D. H. Lawrence and Italy: Twilight in Italy; Sea and Sardinia; Etruscan Places.* New York: Penguin, 1985.

Lewis, Wyndam. *The Art of Being Ruled.* New York: Harper & Brothers, 1926.

———. *Hitler.* New York: Gordon Press, 1972.

———. *The Hitler Cult.* New York: Gordon Press, 1972.

———. *The Jews: Are They Human?* London: George Allen & Unwin, 1939.

Linder, Kurt. *Die Verwandlungen der Mary Wigman.* Freiburg im Breisgau: Urban-Verlag, 1929.

MacAloon, John J. *The Great Symbol: Pierre de Coubertin and the Origins of the Modern Olympic Games.* Chicago: University of Chicago Press, 1981.

MacDonald, Robert H. *Sons of the Empire: The Frontier and the Boy Scout Movement, 1890–1918.* Toronto: University of Toronto Press, 1993.

Mallarmé, Stéphane. *Collected Poems.* Trans. Henry Weinfield. Berkeley: University of California Press, 1994.

———. *Oeuvres complètes.* Paris: Gallimard, 1945.

Mann, Philipp. *Hugo Ball: An Intellectual Biography.* London: Institute of Germanic Studies, University of London, 1987.

Manning, Susan A. *Ecstasy and the Demon: Feminism and Nationalism in the Dances of Mary Wigman.* Berkeley: University of California Press, 1993.

Marinetti, F. T. *Canto eroi e macchine della guerra Mussoliniana.* Verona: A. Mondadori, 1942.

———. *Let's Murder the Moonshine: Selected Writings.* Ed. R. W. Flint, trans. R. W. Flint and Arthur A. Coppoptelli. Los Angeles: Sun & Moon Classics, 1991.

Markov, Vladimir. *Russian Futurism: A History.* Berkeley, Calif.: University of California Press, 1968.

Mauthner, Fritz. *Beiträge zu einer Kritik der Sprache.* Vol. I, *Zur Sprache und zur Psychologie,* 2d ed. Stuttgart: J. G. Cotta, 1906. Vol. II, *Zur Sprachwissenschaft.* Stuttgart: J. G. Cotta, 1901. Vol. III, *Zur Grammatik und Logik.* Stuttgart: J. G. Cotta, 1902.

McCormick, John. *Popular Theatres of Nineteenth-Century France.* London: Routledge, 1993.

Mester, Terri A. *Movement and Modernism: Yeats, Eliot, Lawrence, Williams, and Early Twentieth-Century Dance.* Fayetteville: University of Arkansas Press, 1997.

Montherlant, Henry de. *Les Olympiques.* Paris: Éditions Bernard Grasset, 1938.

Nevin, Thomas. *Ernst Jünger and Germany: Into the Abyss, 1914–1945.* Durham: Duke University Press, 1996.

Nevinson, C. R. W. *Paint and Prejudice.* New York: Harcourt, Brace & Co., 1938.

Nietzsche, Friedrich. *Der Wille sur Macht: Versuch einer Umwertung aller Werte.* Ed. Peter Gast. Stuttgart: Alfred Körner Verlag, 1964.

———. *The Will to Power.* Trans. Walter Kaufman and R. J. Holingdale. New York: Vintage Books, 1968.

———. *Human, All Too Human: Menschliches, Allzumenschliches.* Trans. Marion Faber, with Stephen Lehmann. Lincoln: University of Nebraska Press, 1996.

Nilsson, Nils Åke, ed. *Velimir Chlebnikov: A Stockholm Symposium, April 24 1983.* Stockholm: Almqvist & Wiksell International, 1985.

Paglia, Luigi. *Invito alla lettura di Marinetti.* Milan: Mursia, 1977.

Pioi, Richard J. *Stung by Salt and Water: Creative Texts of the Italian Avant-Gardist F. T. Marinetti.* New York: Peter Lang, 1987.

Prenner, Ingeborg. "Grete Wiesenthal: Die Begründerin eines neuen Tanzstils." Ph.D. diss., University of Vienna, 1950.

Priddin, Deirdre. *The Art of the Dance in French Literature: From Théophile Gautier to Paul Valéry.* London: Adam and Charles Black, 1952.

Riordan, James. *Sport in Soviet Society: Development of Sport and Physical Education in Russia and the USSR.* Cambridge: Cambridge University Press, 1977.

Rosenberg, Alfred. *Kampf um die Macht: Aufsätze vom 1921–1932.* Munich: Zentralverlag der NSDAP, 1938.

Rosenthal, Michael. *The Character Factory: Baden-Powell and the Origins of the Boy Scout Movement.* New York: Pantheon Books, 1986.

Saint-Exupery, Antoine. *Airman's Odyssey*. San Diego: Harcourt Brace Jovanovich, 1984.

Sayler, Oliver M., ed. *Max Reinhardt and His Theatre*. New York: Brentano's, 1924.

Schiff, Stacy. *Saint-Exupéry: A Biography*. New York: Alfred A. Knopf, 1994.

Schulte, Joachim. *Wittgenstein: Eine Einführung*. Stuttgart: Reclam, 1989.

Schwartz, Sanford. *The Matrix of Modernism: Pound, Eliot, and Early Twentieth-Century Thought*. Princeton, N.J.: Princeton University Press, 1985.

Seltzer, Mark. *Bodies and Machines*. New York: Routledge, 1992.

Senay, André, and Robert Hervet. *Monsieur de Coubertin*. Paris: Points & Contrepoints, 1960.

Shaw, Mary Lewis. *Performance in the Texts of Mallarmé: The Passage from Art to Ritual*. University Park: Pennsylvania State University Press, 1993.

Shelton. Suzanne. *Divine Dancer: A Biography of Ruth St. Denis*. Garden City, N.Y.: Doubleday & Co., 1981.

Showalter, Elaine. *Sexual Anarchy: Gender and Culture at the Fin de Siècle*. New York: Penguin, 1991.

Sorell, Walter, ed. and trans. *The Mary Wigman Book*. Middletown, Conn.: Wesleyan University Press, 1975.

Storey, Robert F. *Pierrot: A Critical History of a Mask*. Princeton, N.J.: Princeton University Press, 1978.

———. *Pierrots on the Stage of Desire: Nineteenth-Century French Literary Artists and the Comic Pantomime*. Princeton, N.J.: Princeton University Press, 1985.

Tisdall, Caroline, and Angelo Bozzolla. *Futurism*. New York: Oxford University Press, 1978.

Valéry, Paul. *Oeuvres II*. Ed. Jean Hytier. Paris: Éditions Gallimard, 1960.

Weber, Eugen. *My France: Politics, Culture, Myth*. Cambridge, Mass.: Harvard University Press, 1991.

Wedemeyer, Bernd. *Starke Männer, starke Frauen: Eine Kulturgeschichte des Bodybuildings*. Munich: Verlag C. H. Beck, 1996.

Weiler, Gershon. *Mauthner's Critique of Language*. Cambridge: Cambridge University Press, 1970.

Weststeijn, W. G. *Velimir Chlebnikov and the Development of Poetical Language in Russian Symbolism and Futurism*. Amsterdam: Rodopi, 1983.

Wiesenthal, Grete. *Der Aufstieg: aus dem Leben einer Tänzerin*. Berlin: Ernst Rowohlt Verlag, 1919.

Wittgenstein, Ludwig. *Tractatus logico-philosophicus: Logisch-philosophische Abhandlung*. Frankfurt am Main: Suhrkamp Verlag, 1963.

———. *Tractatus Logico-Philosophicus*. Trans. D. F. Pears and B. F. Mcguiness. London: Routledge & Kegan Paul, 1961; 1st paperback ed., 1974.

Zentner, Kurt E. *Pierre de Coubertin: Ein Beitrag zur Entwicklung der modernen Sports*. Borna-Leipzig: R. Noske, 1935.

Index

For reasons of space, foreign titles appear only in translation.

Library of Congress Cataloging-in-Publication Data

Segel, Harold B., 1930–
    Body ascendant : modernism and the physical imperative /
Harold B. Segel.
        p.   cm. — (PAJ books)
    ISBN 0-8018-5821-6 (alk. paper)
    1. Drama.   2. Performing arts.   3. Fascism and art.   4. National
socialism and art.   5. Body, Human (Philosophy)   6. Body, Human,
in literature.   I. Series.
PN1655.S45   1998
809.2′04—dc21   97-44815 CIP